Fictions of Labor considers William Faulkner's representation of the structural paradoxes of labor dependency in the southern economy from the antebellum period through the New Deal. Linking the occlusive stylistics of Faulkner's writing to a generative social trauma that constitutes its formal core, Richard Godden argues that this trauma is a *labor* trauma, centered on the debilitating discovery by the southern owning class of its own production by those it subordinates. By way of close textual analysis and careful historical contextualization, *Fictions of Labor* produces a persuasive account of the ways in which Faulkner's work rests on deeply submerged anxieties about the legacy of violently coercive labor relations in the American South.

CAMBRIDGE STUDIES IN AMERICAN LITERATURE AND CULTURE

Fictions of Labor

Continued following p. 288

FICTIONS OF LABOR
William Faulkner and the South's Long Revolution

RICHARD GODDEN

University of Keele

CAMBRIDGE
UNIVERSITY PRESS

PUBLISHED BY THE PRESS SYNDICATE OF THE UNIVERSITY OF CAMBRIDGE
The Pitt Building, Trumpington Street, Cambridge CB2 1RP, United Kingdom

CAMBRIDGE UNIVERSITY PRESS
The Edinburgh Building, Cambridge CB2 2RU, United Kingdom
40 West 20th Street, New York, NY 10011–4211, USA
10 Stamford Road, Oakleigh, Melbourne 3166, Australia

First published 1997

Printed in the United States of America

Typeset in Baskerville

Library of Congress Cataloging-in-Publication Data
Godden, Richard, 1946–
Fictions of labor : William Faulkner and the South's long
revolution / Richard Godden.
p. cm. – (Cambridge studies in American literature and
culture ; 108)
ISBN 0-521-56142-6
1. Faulkner, William, 1897–1962 – Political and social views.
2. Literature and society – Southern States – History – 20th century.
3. Industrial relations – Southern States – Historiography.
4. Working class – Southern States – Historiography.   5. Labor supply –
Southern States – Historiography.   6. Southern States – In
literature.   7. Afro-Americans in literature.   8. Race relations in
literature.   I. Title.   II. Series.
PS3511.A86Z7834   1997
813'.52 – dc20   96-25581
CIP

A *catalogue record for this book is available from*
the British Library.

ISBN 0 521 56142 6 hardback

To Charles Swann and to the memory of John Goode

CONTENTS

vii

ACKNOWLEDGMENTS

John Goode once remarked that he was tired of cultural materialism, of which there was too much; he added that what we need is more historical materialism – in pursuit of which I have needed historians. Martin Crawford, Mary Ellison, Bill Riches, and Colin Richmond have been long suffering in the face of my questions, and in their advice they have gracefully intimated how little I am a historian, how crucial is that failing, and how I might make up for it. I thank them for their tact and patience. Similar diplomacy has marked Peter Nicholls' reading of my work; his comments persuaded me that despite a declared wish to have no unconscious myself, I had best move toward an account, if not of the unconscious, then of the unthinkable, in order to begin to handle the announced opacities of my subject. Extended immersion in Faulkner's writing may bear out the force of Adorno's aphoristic observation that the best sentences do not understand themselves, while doing little either for the prose style or for the mental clarity of the reader. Various people struggled to monitor my engagement with Faulkner: Keith Carabine insisted on asking, "Yes, but what does it mean?" Noel Polk edited with grace and good sense. Anne Goodwyn Jones and Peter Nicolaisen exhibited different styles of curiosity. Jack Matthews summed up what I was doing, better than I understood. Charles Swann, despite monumental doubts about Faulkner, read what I wrote, asked the hard questions, and supplied reading lists. Others have worked to correct my inclination to the oblique. Over a number of years Jonathan Dancy, Andrew Dobson, John Goode, and I read a range of materials together; between them they exemplified the labor of making it plain. Rhian Hughes, by way of her generous directness, has long insisted that, whatever the doings of the superstructure, we have a duty to touch base, and to recognize the pervasiveness of its masked presence.

ix

Bits and pieces of what follows were critically read or usefully re-marked on by John Bowen, Richard Gray, Richard King, Douglas Tallack, and Shamoon Zamir. The last chapter would not have been possible without an earlier and jointly written essay: for permission to use some of that material toward related but different ends, and indeed for the reticent astringency of her work more generally on Faulkner, I thank Pamela Knights (née Rhodes). All the above men-tioned are in some degree responsible for what follows; I hope that the book does not shame their responsibility.

Chapters or parts of chapters have appeared in different forms in *New Essays on The Sound and the Fury*, edited by Noel Polk; *Intertextuality in Faulkner*, edited by Michel Gresset and Noel Polk; and in *Essays in Poetics, ELH, The Faulkner Journal*, and *The Irish Journal of American Studies*. I thank those editors and the journals for permission to re-print that work here.

INTRODUCTION

―――――

"It must relate to property; because nothing else survives in this world. Love grows cold and dies; hatred is pacified by annihilation."

Nathaniel Hawthorne, *The American Claimant*[1]

"History is what hurts."

Fredric Jameson[2]

At the risk of being defensive, I shall start by ghosting three objections that could reasonably result from a cursory drift down the index and across the pages of *Fictions of Labor*. Why so much about so little? Why still more on someone of whom so much has been written? Why so much that stays so close? Mine is a study of just three novels, spanning a decade and linked by the death, revival, partial demise, and semi-resurrection of one character. Quentin Compson has his ups and downs, which are focal because they reflect and are reflections upon the formation, resilience, and failure of a southern owning class. The years from *The Sound and the Fury* (1929) to *If I Forget Thee, Jerusalem* (1939) contain the New Deal–induced labor revolution that southern planters had been deferring since Radical Reconstruction (1867–77). Consequently, they contain the dramatic transformation of those planters from lords of bound labor to payers of a wage. But they also contain *As I Lay Dying* (1930), *Sanctuary* (1931), and *Light in August* (1932), arguably major fictions about which I appear to have nothing to say. My silence reflects the narrowness of my chosen focus, which focus stems in turn from a conviction that, in the last instance, the long decade of Faulkner's greatest work is best understood through a generative social trauma constituting its formal core. That trauma is a labor trauma, centered on a primal scene of recognition during which white passes into black and black passes into white along perceptual tracks necessitated by a singular and pervasively coercive system of production.

1

The Bundrens are, among other things, a unit of family labor, but although Anse coerces work from almost everyone, he coerces no tenants, and therefore he and his family lack historical typicality. Likewise, for all that Joe Christmas takes to the road in a working man's flat hat, and through his selective use of the epithet "nigger" iconoclastically challenges Jefferson's capacity to tell black from white, the linchpin of his cultural vandalism is his sexuality and the uses to which he puts it. Bobbie Allen's and Joanna Burden's beds and not the planer shed are the sites where Joe handles the forbidden areas around which punitive social categories cluster. Sexual pathology may and should be understood in its articulated relation to economic questions – I try as much in my consideration of the cult of southern virginity as it determines the desires of the Compson brothers – but in *Light in August* sex is viewed through the optic of race to the diminishment of issues of labor, whereas in *Sanctuary* attentiveness to the sexual gives the novel both its narrowed power and its rhetorical inflexibility.

Although it is possible to read almost any of Faulkner's writing during the 1930s in terms of founding and ramifying anxieties about the legacy of violently maintained labor relations, the novel that addresses the South's peculiar regime of accumulation head on is *Absalom, Absalom!* – hence its centrality to what follows. Not only is Sutpen's story compulsively retold over time, but the manner of its telling charts a social history of the various manifestations of a ruling class dependent upon bound black workers (bound first as chattels and then, in the words of the economic historian Jay Mandle, as a tenancy "not slave, not free"[3]). The poor boy, Sutpen, knocks on a plantation door in west Virginia, circa 1827: he tells of it, and of its consequences in 1835. His audience, General Compson, is a planter; but at this time of telling Sutpen is maintaining the shell of his great house as little more than a hunting lodge and has yet to marry the daughter of merchant capital and thereby to affirm his membership of the plantocracy. In 1864, having become the largest planter in the region, but with the Confederacy close to defeat, he tells it again to the same listener; the story changes because Sutpen's commitments to embattled planter property are greater. That class property, or at least the sale of land derived from it, sends the General's grandson to Harvard and therefore grounds Quentin's comprehensive retelling of the story of Sutpen's Hundred. Faulkner gathers these narratives between 1934 and 1936. His perspective on what I would, derivatively, call the land that labor masters made runs, therefore, from 1827 to 1936, embracing antebellum, postbellum, and New Deal Souths. Quentin Compson's voice holds it all together, hence my framing of Chapters 2, 3, and 4 (the *Absalom, Absalom!* materials) between studies of *The Sound and the Fury* and *If I Forget Thee, Jerusalem.*

It is not, I think, the function of an introduction to give the game away. Suffice to say that Quentin's first (extended) and last (diminished) appearances serve to introduce and conclude my reading of *Absalom, Absalom!* On June 10, 1910, he learns that the degree to which his family history depends upon sexually and racially mistaken images of the black is the degree to which he has no useable past. The knowledge, which temporarily kills him, prepares him to act as a labor historian whose subject will be the genealogy of the class to which his family has apprenticed him. Such an apprenticeship is by 1939 archaic. With sharecropping (the postchattel manifestation of bound labor) declining toward untypicality, and with a federally induced transition to wage labor under way, Quentin can return only as a ghost, haunting Faulkner's dystopic analysis of the kinds of subjects formed by autonomy and wage in a "free" market. Harry Wilbourne encrypts Quentin as an inference, one whose presence momentarily provokes a utopian revision of the binding master and the bound laborer, themselves figures who, by 1939, are being translated toward different social typicalities.

With luck, enough of the game stands revealed to indicate why I discuss only these three novels and their interrelations. But it remains the case that Faulkner commands too much of the wrong kind of attention. A quick flick through various critical indexes indicates that he has long since been industrialized, and, moreover, that *Absalom, Absalom!* outcanons all but the most canonical texts. My defense for adding to the exegetic pile is that, although I get to where I go thanks to the work of others, I find my own and my subject's constellation of difficulty in the place of labor – a place to which Faulknerians have not often been. Labor, here, is southern and is understood as historically changing through forms of bondage to waged "freedom." This transition effects a movement from a cultural dominant rooted in "dependency" to one based on "autonomy," with the First Agricultural Adjustment Act (1933) providing pivotal momentum for change. Yet my concern is not with agricultural history per se, nor with an alternative thematics (tracing the incidence of sharecroppers in Faulkner's work as it reflects tenant displacement in the mid-1930s); rather, I am preoccupied with how a revolution at the center of the southern economy releases from the forms of life that have made that economy typifying contradictions whose resolution takes shape as narrative options and stylistic habits that are, quite literally, forced out of a historically determined and pervasive structure of feeling. That felt structure, turning on the interdependency of owner and owned, materializes as specific racial and sexual pathologies, but these inflections (lived and stylistic) remain, in the last instance, causally connected to what I shall be calling the primal scene of bound southern labor – that unthinkable and productive episode during which the master both recognizes and represses the fact that since his mastery is slave-made, he and his are blacks in whiteface.

The game is afoot. But to hark back to my third objection, why do I proceed almost exclusively by rehearsing Faulkner's textual strategies? Many are the close readings of Faulkner, generally conducted under some version of a celebratory modernist rubric, whereby "difficult" is translated as "rich," "dense," or "complex." Such parlance implies that after work, pleasure may come. But Faulkner's "difficult" writing is not pleasurable, and reading him is often an intolerable labor. Impressionistically, the experience can resemble running on the spot, only to find that you are descending, and have been button-holed in a pit. "Rich" is an inappropriate epithet where close reading yields not some new account that the text may be made to bear, nor even an expression of interpretive freedom born in a spirit of ludic dialogue between author and recipient. Rather, Faulkner's "difficulty," at least in the novels considered here, is driven by his penurious habit of secretion – a habit which demands that the reader attend closely in order to recover, from Faulkner's choked, subverted, underarticulated, and yet imperious prose, inferences of a tale that is not being told.

"Secretion" is as close as I can get to my sense of the primary activity of this writing. The pun is intended to indicate how Faulkner's language most habitually "conceals and makes secret" while at the same time "producing by means of secretion," discharging, from its virtually invisible secrets, matter in the form of a "sub" or "anti" semantics, essential to the functioning of the linguistic body. So, for example, Sutpen calls his son "Bon," a name that conceals the patronym "Sutpen." But as a secret it secretes because Sutpen, according to General Compson, "named them all – the Charles Goods and the Clytemnestras."[4] "Bon" means both "good" and, by extension, "goods" and therefore contains, on its surface, Sutpen's sense that what comes from his body is black goods: a tacit recognition that, unless policed, may reverse itself, leading to the disabling insight that a white master's body is little more than a receptacle for appropriated black property. How properly improper that the name of the master should be displaced by what that name contains.

I stress that all this lies on or close to the surface, and that its cause – a labor trauma particular to a southern system of production

– is neither an absent source nor a deferred center; rather, it saturates these texts at the level of their preoccupations and of their intonations.

"Intonation" is the key term here, because I hope, by way of it, to explain why I feel obliged closely to read works already closely read and reread. The Russian linguist Valentin Vološinov, concerned to explore how the nonverbal situation of any utterance materializes within the sign, tells a story about a brief intonation:

> A couple are sitting in a room. They are silent. One says, "Well!" The other says nothing in reply. For us who are not present in the room at the time of the exchange, this "conversation" is completely inexplicable. Taken in isolation the utterance "well" is void and quite meaningless. Nevertheless the couple's peculiar exchange, consisting of only one word, though one to be sure which is expressively inflected, is full of meaning and significance and quite complete.[5]

How are we to understand "well" when its various verbal parts – phonetic, morphological, and semantic – fiddled with add up to so much fiddle? Even the addition of intonation – perhaps indignant, perhaps humorous – reveals little until it is recognized that tone is the route to the nonverbal context. At the moment of utterance, both individuals look up and out of a single window to see snow falling:

> *Both knew* that it was already May and long since time for spring, and finally that they both were sick of the protracted winter. *Both were waiting* for spring and *were annoyed* by the late snowfall. The utterance depends directly on all this.[6]

Given its implicitly shared purview, "well" does rather more than reflect the nonverbal situation; it resolves or sums up the value of that situation. Perhaps, because spring has been a long time in coming, planting will be delayed and food scarce. Snow, date, labor, laborer . . . each stays in its allotted place, beyond the window, on the calendar, out in the empty fields or idle in the room – but all meet and materialize within the intonation "well!", from which they go indexically forth to rematerialize the very materials from which they came . . . window, calendar, field, labor. . . . His parable allows Vološinov to elaborate on intonation, speaking of it as "tending towards personification,"[7] as if it were reaching not for a referent but "beyond objects and things to the living participants and instigators of life."[8] Consequently, his speaker, becalmed by snow, appears to reproach "winter" as a stubborn and animate force or "actual culprit."[9] Given that "well" takes so much from and gives so much back to its context of use, Vološinov concludes his parable with a moral (of which I am so persuaded that I shall quote it at length):

> The following must always be borne in mind . . . *intonation and gesture are active and objective in intention.* They express not only the passive mental state of the speaker, but besides there is always stored in them a living, dynamic relationship with the outside world and the social environment – friends, enemies, allies. By using intonation . . . a person takes up an active social position with regard to certain values, and this position is conditioned by the very bases of his social existence. It is precisely this objectively sociological aspect of intonation . . . and not [its] subjectively psychological side which should interest theoreticians of the arts, since in it reside also the aesthetic-creative forces of [these] phenomena which create and organize artistic form.[10]

But let us suppose that what is seen out of the window is more secretive than snow. On which note, I shall shift windows. For Vološinov's Russian winter, substitute Rosa Coldfield's view from her "office" of the "dead September afternoon," into which "peaceful" scene, care of her intonation ("the voice not ceasing"), a "man-horse-demon" will "abrupt," with "behind him his band of niggers."[11] Or, perhaps, consider Quentin Compson's glimpse from a Boston tram – which, thanks to an internal dispute over idiom between the phrase "colored people" and the epithet "nigger," gives way to a rail-car window, somewhere between Massachusetts and Mississippi – beyond which "was a nigger on a mule."[12]

To look through such windows, glossed by Vološinov, is to see neither referents nor objects and persons, but social and semantic processes (masked as objects and persons) being given material shape (as objects and persons) by intonational energies which realize, and are realized by, that from which they take their indexical point. In both cases these windows give onto southern scenes that are made meaningful by the destabilized coexistence of black and white populations. What I am about to claim will take a book to prove, but, in skeletal form, my case is that during the 1930s Faulkner's essentially socially indexical language addresses a traumatic secret, everywhere evident in the objects and persons of a white-owned world made by black work, but everywhere occluded – since the acknowledgment that white depends on black (rather than vice versa) would turn the world the white owners didn't make upside down. However, during the 1930s, the secret seeps because the very patterns of labor that cast the white master as the person black people made (while requiring that both parties keep the secret) were themselves being recast.

But what has this to do with "intonation" or close reading? I shall return to Vološinov's linguistic points by way of an allusion to trauma theory. Nicolas Abraham and Maria Torok argue that a traumatic or unthinkable event produces distorting silences, whose distortions (realized most fully in language) are the primary route to the founding distress. Their translator, Nicholas Rand, offers a useful summation:

> [S]ilence is an independent clinical and theoretical entity. Whether it characterizes individuals, families, social groups, or entire nations, silence and its varied forms – the untold or unsayable secret, the feeling unfelt, the pain denied, the unspeakable and concealed shame of families, the cover-up of political crimes, the collective disregard for painful historical realities – may disrupt our lives. Abraham and Torok's work studies the personal and interpersonal consequences of silence. According to them, silence represents that which cannot be assimilated into the continuity of psychic life.[13]

(For "psychic life" one might substitute "social life.") A route if not out of then around the traumatic silence is the "cryptonomy" or "verbarium," which is "a verbal procedure leading to the creation of a text,"[14] whose sole purpose is to hide words that are hypothesized as having to remain beyond reach. Such texts do not in any simple way repress the traumatic situation; instead, they generate the very situation that must be avoided, creating in words the catastrophe that those words displace.

Enabled, in part, by the social and psychic indexicality of a linguistic model drawn together from the work of Vološinov and of Abraham and Torok, I shall argue that, during the 1930s, Faulkner returns obsessively to the intonation of social trauma. My critical practice will seek to show that the best place to discover the trauma and its nature is in the words themselves, and in the way their distortion indexically addresses material conditions of labor, most typically by pointing away from that about which they speak. All of which is sadly gnomic, but should serve to put a few ground rules in place.

QUENTIN COMPSON

TYRRHENIAN VASE OR CRUCIBLE OF RACE?

I

Faulkner's post-publication statements about *The Sound and the Fury* swaddle the book in maidenheads: having shut his door on publishers, he "began to write about a little girl" and to "manufacture [a] sister."[1] In a further analogy for writing he cites the old Roman

> who kept at his bedside a Tyrrhenian vase which he loved and the rim of which he wore slowly away with kissing it. I had made myself a vase, but I suppose I knew all the time that I could not live forever inside of it. . . .[2]

The vase is a crackable euphemism; in *Flags in the Dust* (1927), the manuscript whose apparent rejection caused Faulkner to close his door, Horace Benbow makes a similar vessel. Having learned to blow glass in Venice, he manufactures "a small chaste shape . . . not four inches high, fragile as a silver lily and incomplete." He calls the vase Narcissa, for his sister, and is anatomically concise about the source of his skills. Of Venetian glass workers, he notes:

> They work in caves . . . down flights of stairs underground. You feel water seeping under your foot while you are reaching for the next step, and when you put your hand out to steady yourself against the wall, it's wet when you take it away. It feels just like blood.[3]

Venice and vagina elide, even as vase and hymen cross.

The pervasiveness of the hymen is reaffirmed by Faulkner's accounts of the novel's source, which places the sexuality of small girls at the first as at the last. On several occasions he insisted that the novel "began with a mental picture"[4] of Caddy's soiled undergarment up a tree; under the tree two brothers watch the stained drawers ascend. The day of the "muddy...drawers" is structurally central to Faulkner; his comments suggest that the four sections "grew" from a repeated attempt to explicate that "symbolical... picture."[5] In which case, Sartre's question retains its relevance, "Why is the first window that opens out on this fictional world the consciousness of an idiot?"[6]

It may be sufficient to say that any novel is the sum of its parts and that by April 8, 1928, much will be revealed, most of it to do with the decay of the Compson household. Traditionally, the novel's underlying inclination has been read as a movement toward clarification: from silence to articulation, from idiocy to omniscience, from discontinuous to continuous time, from Old to New South, even from id to super-ego. The interpretations proliferate, but the consensus used to have it that formally *The Sound and the Fury* reveals itself. In which case, why make exposition so difficult by starting with an idiot?

More recently, critical emphasis has shifted from presence to absence; Barthean notions of suspended meaning, and Derrida's claim for language as the infinite deferral of meaning, have been revealingly appealed to, so that generous "openness" and incompleteness as prolongation replace explication as the novel's keynote. Yet the new order, while it may privilege Benjy as a site of experimental textuality, tends to turn him into a linguistic fact rather than to address him as a fact of consciousness. The move transposes Caddy – Benjy's chief preoccupation – from sister to discourse feature. To place brother and sister in "the space of writing"[7] is to dissolve them as conscious subjects. By subjecting them to the play of language, whether as "empty signifier[s]" or Derridean "supplements,"[8] critics of a structuralist and poststructuralist persuasion have made it almost impossible to perceive them as historical subjects (language, after all, is slow to respond to historical change and fast to regress into the infinitely textual).

I make no excuse for attributing an active consciousness to Benjy. Too many readers continue to listen to the dismissals of Faulkner's Appendix (1946) and of his *Paris Review* interview (1956), or to allow an initial uncertainty to be shaped by critical accounts falling into one of two camps. The first sentimentalizes Benjy as a moral touchstone, a vessel of the heart uncontaminated by intellect. To the second he is a machine – a camera with a tape recorder attached. Mystic hearts and machines are alike, indifferent to time. "Timelessness"[9] is a fine preservative, so Faulkner credits Benjy with it and adds for good measure that he is "an animal."[10] Whatever his creator may say, Benjy is not "impervious to the future," nor as a language user

can he "be the past."[11] It might be objected that to extend Benjy's
sense of time on the grounds that he thinks in narrative sentences
merely points up a formal limitation. The argument goes: Novelists
have to use words, and Faulkner seems to have used the simplest
available. Why then, if his interests were exclusively pre-linguistic,
didn't he adopt an external viewpoint? The shambling idiot who
walks into Dilsey's kitchen (in section four) is a far more convincing
linguistic blank than the first section's approximation to imbecilic
consciousness. I cannot accept that Benjy is a literary device whose
linguistic habits, where they exhibit any degree of complication, are
simply expressing technical limitations.

Benjy balances on the brink of silence, but he uses words which,
as our only access to his imagination, are the first clue to the small
girl hidden there. Once again evidence is limited. Benjy for the most
part lacks most linguistic things – syntactical variants, tense changes,
synonyms, negatives, exclamation and question marks are just a few
of them. At his disposal he has the scaffolding of thought – ambu-
latory verbs, a few nouns, the simple past tense, "and," the occasional adverb, full stops. . . . Poverty or passivity are not the only
conclusion that can be drawn from the list. Irena Kaluza concludes
from her study of Benjy's sentence structure that he is "monolithic"
and capable only of "mechanical identification."[12] What she misses
is that Benjy is as rich in small sisters as he is poor in linguistic
resources. Having no question or exclamation mark, he sets Caddy
beyond inquiry and outrage. A basic sentence format denies complication. He has few negatives with which to exclude his sister, no
causal words to explain her, and limited adjectives with which to
modify her.

The degree to which Benjy's language is tailor-made to preserve
a singular sister may be traced through his use of tenses. He sets two
tenses aside to work exclusively in the past. More accurately, his goal
is an original time almost outside time, with Caddy. My point is that
this is not a passive "timelessness" but a contrivance for which he
labors. Caddy alone at the branch with Benjy is an artifact that has
to be invented. Benjamin is the mechanic, Faulkner the designer.
Most critics fail to see the artifice under the plainness; they speak of
"an objective view of the past"[13] or "a capacity for the raw intensities
of pleasure and pain."[14] The greatest factor behind this assumption
is passivity:

> Benjy is incapable of association of ideas; therefore his memory
> is stimulated by physical sensation – a sound, or a motion, or

the sight of an object in the present, or in a scene being re-
lived.[15]

I chose Edmond Volpe simply because, unfortunately, he continues
to be representative. More recent criticism echoes him, having Benjy
"slip from one moment of loss to another,"[16] without "faculties for
controlling"[17] that slippage, because "as an idiot he simply does not
know"[18] what makes him moan or stop:

> [W]hatever he experiences flashes in and out of existence, be-
> cause he is totally devoid of the consciousness that is the pre-
> requisite for an overall field of perception which would
> guarantee a pattern for these experiences.[19]

And, as a result, "surrounded by words he cannot use, he is used by
words,"[20] recording speech "verbatim, like a tape recorder, whether
or not he understands its meaning";[21] the resultant transcript resembles "a Barthean *écriture degree zero*. . . writing free of social orientation."[22] To André Bleikasten shall go the summation:

> There is no central *I* through whose agency the speech might
> be ordered and made meaningful. . . . Hence the startling *ec-
> centricity* of all his experiences: sensations, perceptions and
> emotions are accorded exactly the same status as objects and
> occurrences in the outer world . . . and Benjy is at least the pas-
> sive and incomprehensive watcher of what is happening to
> him.[23]

Note "passive" and "patternless"; such phrasing does not suggest
how actively Benjy mixes memories. A time shift is an act of analogy
that brings one time into conjunction with another; the result could
be expressed as a simile in which Benjy prefers the original to the
secondary term. In any comparison he will incline toward the earlier
aspect; therefore, of the some 106 pieces that make up April 7, 1928,
the majority occur before 1910. Preference for particular times suggests design and a capacity to draw temporal distinctions. A notional
plot, even if termed "deep structure," disposes of Wolfgang Iser's
idea that everything that Benjy sees is patternless and equally present.

Paul Ricoeur's account of pre-plotting may be useful here. He
suggests in *Time and Narrative* that to experience is to be always and
already emplotted. As cultural entities, he argues, we move among
interwoven signs, rules, and norms that translate any of our actions
into "a quasi-text"; these signs make up a cultural texture immanent

with potential text, what he calls "(as yet) untold stories." So – our background entangles us in the prehistory of our culture's told stories:

> This "prehistory" of the story is what binds it to a larger whole and gives it a "background." This background is made up of the "living imbrication" of every lived story with every other such story. Told stories have to "emerge" from this background. With this emergence also emerges the implicit subject. We may thus say, "the story stands for the person" . . . [it follows that] narrating is a secondary process, that of "the story's becoming known." Telling, following, understanding stories is simply the "continuation" of these untold stories.[24]

Since, for Ricoeur, "untold stories" form the subtext from and through which subjects "emerge," acts of consciousness based upon them are perhaps best spoken of as "semi-conscious," or "partially articulated," intentions. I specifically avoid the terms "unconscious" and "subconscious" because, all too often, they are associated with an absence of intention.[25] But just how "imbricated" or "intentional" can a mute with an adult body and a mental age of perhaps three be?

In answer, take the reiterated phrase "Caddy smelled like trees." It is clear from "the mental picture" which began it all that a tree dominates the "(as yet) untold stories" which make up the novel. The tree is particularly monumental in Benjy's experience because it describes the line between the told and the untold. Benjy was born in April 1895; his grandmother Damuddy died three years later, in 1898. The date of her death is conspicuously signaled by Caddy's subversive tree climbing. It would seem that Benjy stopped when he saw his sister's muddy drawers – that is to say, he refuses to grow mentally beyond the point at which the signs for sexuality and death enter his life. The boundary is symbolically marked by a stain over the hymen; Benjy labors to erase the mark. No word in the section antedates 1898. In 1897 he *was* the blank toward which for thirty years he has been trying to carry his sister. The tree and the stain are therefore Benjy's earliest encounter with signs. Other signs cluster near the tree: a snake slips under the house, the father's prohibition is mentioned, the name "Satan" is called by a black woman – my point is not to rehearse Faulkner's rehearsal of *Genesis* but to suggest that these "sensations" are best understood as signs imminent with rules and norms, forming a "prenarrative" whose texture Benjy appreciates. Further, because up to this moment Benjy was without words, tree climbing here marks the fall into not only a potential or "inchoate story" about sex and death but also into language. "Caddy smelled like trees" involves Benjy in much more than a favorite odor. The phrase is urgent with temporal distinctions that he must negotiate. According to the "(as yet) untold story" within whose texture Benjy's consciousness was quite literally born, the tree and the woman combine as an unsettling dryad. This tree is central to linked stories – Eden and The Fall. Its word points two ways. Its odors are sweet and stale. "Caddy smelled like trees" is not a mechanical catch phrase; it is a difficult exclusion involving harsh editing.

When one word projects diametrically opposed plots and implies two temporal layers, it is not surprising that Faulkner's attempts to mark the time shifts occurring during April 7 fail. A distinction between roman and italic script cannot signal the awkward niceties of Benjy's time scale. It is doubtful whether a range of colored inks would have done much more than help the reader to an earlier sense of the major episodes. The idea was discussed by Faulkner and his editors and dropped when printing techniques and cost proved prohibitive.[26] But had the method been adopted, would Faulkner have printed "trees" in two colors and if so, where would the division have occurred? The absurdity of the question emphasizes the limitation of any typographical answer.

For several years I read the different print faces as encoding different times. Only gradually did it dawn on me that where the italics are brief (of no more than one or two lines), they signal a transference; this having been done, the new time reverts to roman type. As I grew more familiar with the text, certain anomalies stood out – unmarked shifts in continuous roman passages, typographic change without temporal change. Initially these seemed to be errors, certainly careless and probably willful. My annoyance diminished with a growing sense that Benjy's idiocy was more interesting than the techniques that expressed it. By crediting the idiot with imagination, I found that anomaly became subtlety beyond the register of typeface. Edmond Volpe has listed five unmarked shifts of scene[27]; there are more, although given that their number is not legion it is not important. Faulkner employs print surfaces only as a guideline. Having introduced the problem, he leaves the reader to discover for him- or herself the ramifications of shifting time:

Frony said. "Is they started the funeral yet."
"What's a funeral." Jason said.

"Didn't mammy tell you not to tell them." Versh said.

"Where they moans." Frony said. "They moaned two days on Sis Beulah Clay."

They moaned at Dilsey's house. Dilsey was moaning. When Dilsey moaned Luster said, Hush, and we hushed, and then I began to cry and Blue howled under the kitchen steps. Then Dilsey stopped and we stopped.

"Oh." Caddy said. "That's niggers. White folks dont have funerals."

"Mammy said us not to tell them, Frony." Versh said.

"Tell them what." Caddy said.

Dilsey moaned, and when it got to the place I began to cry and Blue howled under the steps. Luster, Frony said in the window. Take them down to the barn. I cant get no cooking done with all that racket. That hound too. Get them outen here.

I aint going down there, Luster said. I might meet pappy down there. I seen him last night, waving his arms in the barn.

"I like to know why not." Frony said. "White folks dies too. Your grandmammy dead as any nigger can get, I reckon."

"Dogs ared dead." Caddy said. "And when Nancy fell in the ditch and Roskus shot her and the buzzards came and undressed her."

The bones rounded out of the ditch, where the dark vines were in the black ditch, into the moonlight, like some of the shapes had stopped. Then they all stopped and it was dark, and when I stopped to start again I could hear Mother, and feet walking fast away, and I could smell it. Then the room came, but my eyes went shut. I didn't stop. I could smell it. T.P. unpinned the bedclothes.

"Hush." he said. [p. 21]

Frony is the first clue, by way of her relation to her brothers, the older Versh and the younger T.P. It should be noted that Faulkner uses the sequence of Benjy's attendants – first Versh, then T.P., and finally Luster – as a temporal index. At the outset, the passage is about Damuddy's death (1898); with Versh in attendance, the Compson children have been sent from their house to Dilsey's cabin, in front of which they play. The first set of italics marks a time jump, care of "moaned," whereby African American grief in 1898 shifts its object to a time as yet untraceable. The shift is brief, and the children's conversation (from 1898) continues, only to be interrupted by a further outbreak of Dilsey's moaning. Again Damuddy cannot be its object, as Frony has grown up, graduating from "playing in the dirt by the door" (p. 20) to cookery; however, cooking proves impossible, surrounded by distress, so Frony packs Benjy off to the barn, accompanied by Luster. But Benjy, jumping time again, takes her with him (and so out of the italics), as a child. While the children, including Frony, walk, they talk about Damuddy and death in general, directing Benjy's attention to the ditch that contains Nancy's bones. Clearly, between "stopped" and "start" yet another temporal shift occurs, but without a typographical signal, posing a problem over how Benjy gets from the outbuildings to his own bedroom. Prior to mention of the ditch (and outside italics), Benjy is in 1898 with Versh. After "starting again," it is T.P. who unpins and dresses him. It follows that he has been asleep ("stopped") and has woken in another time, which a subsequent and rare negative, "It wasn't father" (p. 38), identifies as 1912 – the date of Mr. Compson's death. Fourteen years pass unregistered because Benjy goes to sleep in one panic and wakes in another. Since his first encounter with an association between Damuddy and "funeral," he has been trying to quit 1898. The result has been a sequence of deaths. Five jumps have yielded four bodies in the space of less than one page; "undressed" is the point of greatest confusion – the word is a clue pointing several ways, to the "bright, smooth shapes" that come when the child Benjy has been undressed and put to bed with Caddy, to the stained drawers that Dilsey strips from the small girl, to the increasingly fancy clothes of his sister's adolescence. Unable to orientate himself and use the clue advantageously, Benjy jumps. He travels fourteen years to discover another death. Not surprisingly, with the bones of Damuddy, Roskus, Nancy, and Mr. Compson rising from every available ditch, it is not clear to Benjy that he has moved at all.

My reading stipulates that for the most part Benjy is actively aware of the two sides of any temporal comparison; his aim is that the peaceful side cancel the less peaceful, peace for the most part being synonymous with events before 1910, the year of Caddy's marriage and subsequent departure. Often the hope is unrealized. Nonetheless, each interpolated memory is an attempt at the perfect simile that will render all time synonymous with ur-time. The perfect simile is a metaphor whose two terms have forged a unity such as "chair" and "leg" can only hint at, a unity in which the word and that for which it stands are one. The only way for the temporal simile to imply prelapsarian unanimity is for it to incline to the past. Occasionally perfection occurs. Studying the fire or near to "the smooth bright shapes" of sleep, Benjy will forget time and fail to register the words and events that happen around him. When this occurs, momentarily he is with Caddy in the garden. Because his ur-time is beyond comparison, it disposes of all linguistic analogy. Necessarily it makes no mark on the text and results in an invisible gap, or the perfect uninscribed simile. I will mark the gap (/):

> She led me to the fire and I looked at the bright, smooth shapes. I could hear the fire and the roof./
> Father took me up. He smelled like rain.
> "Well, Benjy." he said. "Have you been a good boy today."
> Caddy and Jason were fighting in the mirror. [1900: p. 40]

or

> Quentin and Luster were playing in the dirt in front of T.P.'s house. There was a fire in the house, rising and falling, with Roskus sitting black against it./
> "That's three, thank the Lawd." Roskus said. "I told you two years ago. They ain't no luck on this place."
> "Whyn't you get out, then." Dilsey said. She was undressing me. [1912: p. 19]

Benjy does not notice Mr. Compson enter the library or hear the fight. In Dilsey's cabin the fire absorbs whatever occurs between the idiot's entry and his preparation for bed. The intervals involved are probably considerable. By marking two gaps in the text (/), I have contravened Benjy's imagination. The discovery of a gap requires that a case be made for how Benjy was able to quit time. An unrecorded transference, once found, raises a question as to why Benjy thought two discontinuous events, one event. Faced with this issue, the editorial task very rapidly becomes historical. To see differences in undifferentiated details is to see cause and to suppose a history that is both personal and cultural. All of which is the exact opposite of what Benjy works for. By giving the reader so much to do, Faulkner absolves himself from the strain of taking away Benjy's innocence. The degrees to which any reader invents Benjy's consciousness is the degree to which the reader is stained with the fall that cognition implies.

I have overstated the case for Benjy's imagination to counter what I take to be a wrongheaded mechanistic consensus. Therefore, before going further, I shall attempt a less polemic account of his consciousness. April 7, 1928, like any day in Benjy's life, is full of cues, some of which enable him to switch back toward a time virtually prior to time. Others, because they might carry him forward to a more recent past or to the present, necessitate evasive action, action that he frequently fails to take or that proves unsuccessful, leaving him stranded in April 7. The alternative explanation is that every day Benjy suffers a stream of mechanical blackouts, over which he has no control and thanks to which he finds himself randomly anywhere from 1898 to 1928. My reading is located between the two. Benjy's control over time *is* spasmodic; yet it is consistent enough to be spoken of as *his* control. How else, for example, to explain the curious congruity of Caddy's loss of virginity and Versh's story about secondhand impregnation among bluegums?

> Caddy came to the door and stood there. . . . I went toward her, crying, and she shrank against the wall and I saw her eyes and I cried louder and pulled at her dress. She put her hands out but I pulled at her dress. Her eyes ran.
>
> *Versh said, Your name Benjamin now. You know how come your name Benjamin now. They making a bluegum out of you. Mammy say in old time your granpaw changed nigger's name, and he turn preacher, and when they look at him, he bluegum too. Didn't use to be bluegum, neither. And when family woman look him in the eye in the full of the moon, child born bluegum. And one evening, when they was about a dozen them bluegum chillen running around the place, he never come home. Possum hunters found him in the woods, et clean. And you know who et him. Them bluegum chillen did.* [pp. 42–3]

Late in the summer of 1909, Caddy lost her virginity. Benjy recognizes the loss – an insight that need not involve mysterious intuition. He does not stare at eyes because he has insight but because, like fire and glass, the eye moves and reflects light, and at this moment Caddy's eyes are probably moving far too fast. In any case, the important point is that, upon his discovery of her loss of virginity, Benjy goes back almost nine years to November 1900, when his name was changed. The shift appears to have no mechanical trigger, yet there is evidence of a narrow imagination producing at least partially conscious comparisons. Caddy's sexual change is associated with Benjy's name change, in an essentially cultural analogy involving two impurities, so that loss of virginity is likened to loss of a first or maiden name. Since Benjy has been named Maury after his mother's brother, it seems that his sister's sexual activity has forced him to recognize linguistic duplicity. In effect, then, Benjy counters his disturbing insight by recalling a particular story about multiple names. A Mississippi bluegum is a black conjuror with a fatal bite. Versh's bluegum has the additional gift of magic eyes, a gift that seems to have resulted directly from a name change. Simply by looking at his congregation, the bluegum preacher can make them all, even unborn children, bluegum too. As a bluegum, then, Benjy can claim paternity over any child that his sister may have conceived in 1909. If he is bluegum, too, and can look into Caddy's shifty eyes, he will re-impregnate her in an innocent incest that involves no penetration. According to the story, Benjy is the father of Caddy's child.

The complexity of the analogy realizes a childishly simplistic purpose: Benjy wants his small sister for himself, and to that end he has engaged in "plotting"; he has invented a temporal comparison allowing him to move from an unpleasant event in 1909 to an earlier but less troubling loss. The shift works for him because, as a bluegum, Benjy can control his sister's sexuality. My attribution of an act of consciousness to Benjy – a character most typically described as "unmapped . . . [and] without the hint of a project"[28] – stems from a conviction that even those with severe learning difficulties are liable to whatever subterranean stories characterize the culture within which they pass their long childhoods.

That Benjy should play bluegum at this precise moment suggests that even a person with a mental age of perhaps three, albeit one in a thirty-three-year-old body, knows the pre-plots of his time. By means of a black mask, Benjy, at some level, intends to get his sister back, but the end of his redemptive anecdote is problematic; "oldtime" refers to slavery, during which regime a master might manifest his will by canceling a slave's name, thereby consigning the slave to thing-status by severing his or her genealogical ties at the stroke of a pen. Historians refer to this as the imposition of "natal death."[29] In effect, Mrs. Compson, by removing her brother's name from her son (at the moment when his retardation is apparent), blackens her child, making him a slave to her willful preoccupation with the purity of Bascomb blood. The blackness sticks, so much so that Benjy can imagine innocent incest only from within a bluegum's black skin. It follows that sexual congress, even where only ocular, results in a guilt whose form interweaves white and black potency and ties both to death (*"Possum hunters found him in the woods, et clean"*). The manner of that death may yet give Benjy satisfaction, because playing bluegum involves a muted revolt against the master's or mother's will. Because Versh's story is an anecdote from slavery times, its hero can be read only as "uppity"; the preacher takes revenge on his owner by means of a look whose very existence implies untraceable sexual assaults on black, and perhaps white, women. Such a gaze is dangerous inside an institution so peculiar that no slave may look directly into a white eye for fear of punishment. The bluegum, after a successful career featuring "*about a dozen . . . chillen*," is necessarily punished. Dilsey is the story's source (at least for Versh), and perhaps her lesson is that the bluegum dies because he is just too re-

bellious for a domestic servant whose life has been dedicated to
sustaining a white household; but she may hand the story down because she knows that servants cannot endure masters without sustenance from a quietly subversive anecdotal tradition. Either way, the
story emerges from a dense cultural web within which white and
black purposes clash and cross. Furthermore, Benjy's use of the apparently simple tale is packed with "(as yet) untold stories" about
seemingly necessary relationships between virginity and incest, and
incest and miscegenation. I do not mean to suggest that the network
is available to Benjy, but clearly his initial time jump from 1909 to
1900 *is* motivated; he achieves an act of corrective incest by means
of the cultural pre-plots to which he has been apprenticed.

Benjy's chief purpose on April 7, 1928, is to confound his sister's
growth with earlier memories. One particular cluster of episodes resists all his attempts at re-plotting: Damuddy's death (1898) and Caddy's wedding (1910) are inseparably associated. At a deeply cultural
level the equation between fatality, sex, and the black constitutes a
collective representation strong enough to stamp the impaired mind
of an adult child. To say that Benjy has no temporal principle is to
ignore his efforts to erase this particular cultural imprint. The Fall,
like time and racial fear, is part of the prehistory of Faulkner's culture, and Benjy is not exempt from it. When Frony whispers to the
tree-climbing Caddy in 1898, "What you seeing," Benjy answers "a
wedding"; that is to say, he remembers Caddy's wedding in 1910:

> "What you seeing." Frony whispered.
> *I saw them. Then I saw Caddy, with flowers in her hair, and a long
> veil like shining wind. Caddy Caddy.* [p. 24]

Benjy's imbrication in "(as yet) untold stories" ties funerals to weddings and associates both with a tree. The association triggers an
atypical sensitivity to speech; Benjy is aware not only that Frony *has*
a voice, but also that she has done something to it by whispering. A
time switch from death (1898) to matrimony (1910) confirms the
co-presence of language and blacks within a rapidly thickening symbolic web. As he stands on a box, staring through the parlor window
at his sister's reception, Benjy grows self-conscious about the noises
that come from his mouth; "my throat made a sound . . . my throat
keep on making a sound" (p. 25). For a man who is unaware that
he has been castrated unless he looks at himself, this is a moment
of unusual perception. Funerals give way to weddings. Weddings induce words, and words about a ceremony involving sexual exchange
inevitably discover a subversive black; Benjy recalls T.P.'s drunken
attempts to "hush" him – the very notion of a black physically mas-

tering a white in a basement is subversive enough, without the rec-
ollection that T.P. mocks the household patriarch, calling Mr.
Compson "a sassprilluh dog, too" (p. 25). The tangled inversion of
master and servant is eventually corrected when the master's eldest
son puts the black down, and the daughter leaves the reception to
reembrace her brother:

> Quentin kicked T.P. and Caddy put her arms around me, and
> her shining veil, and I couldn't smell trees any more and I
> began to cry.
>   *Benjy, Caddy said, Benjy. She put her arms around me again, but I
> went away.* "What is it, Benjy" she said. "Is it this hat." [p. 25]

Working backward through the associative logic within which Benjy
struggles to recover Caddy (circa 1898), we see that blacks, language,
sexuality, and The Fall are linked. Benjy resists their linkage. As soon
as he encounters the wedding cues – a "shining veil" and the scent
of 1910 flowers – he strives to convert them into a hat and some
perfume worn by Caddy in 1906, when, according to Jason, she only
thought she was grown up (p. 25). At fourteen Caddy could still wash
most of her knowledge away and restore the smell of trees, a smell
that even as it comforts her idiot brother has in it, for him, a potential for temporal and narrative duplicity.

To summarize: in Benjy's consciousness, each instance of memory
is an opportunity to render that moment synonymous with an initial
memory. Put tersely, Benjy's mental habits center on an original
image that he seeks to pre-originate – a narrative principle that
Faulkner seems to espouse in his post-publication statements. Just as
Benjy's thought desires to transgress its own origin, so the founding
"mental picture" of the stained drawers tends to fold back into still
more original images. In "An Introduction" (1933), which he did
not see published, Faulkner speaks of the "unmarred sheet[s]"[30] of
the manuscript or the interior of a vase. The vase has already been
described as a displaced form of the sister's hymen; its male owner
attempts to live inside it (Benjy pre-1898) but finds that the very act
of preservation by kissing (incest) leads to erasure (Benjy post-1898).
Vase, paper, and child act in very similar ways; attempting to characterize the "ecstasy," "nebulous" yet "physical,"[31] that writing the
Benjy section gave him, Faulkner likens the manuscript to "unmarred sheet[s] beneath my hand inviolate and unfailing"[32] – a
complex innuendo forms, in which paper turns into the white space
of a bed (Benjy's blank), while language (so black) "mars" that
original purity by "marrying" it. Since, in an earlier analogy, Faulkner likened the book to a sister, writing becomes synonymous with

a curiously untraceable act of incestuous miscegenation (Benjy as "bluegum") – without trace because the paper appears to absorb the black marks of the script.[33] Unpicking puns in a single strained simile may try credibility, but it is necessary in order to establish a submerged affinity between Benjy and Faulkner's associative and temporal habits – an affinity turning on the virginity of a sister.

II

All of which begs the question: Why should a sister's hymen matter quite so much? From a first reading of *The Sound and the Fury*, it will be clear that each of the brothers has difficulties getting over his sister; her "honour" and its loss are central to them all. I have space only to outline the case: Benjy frequently shares Caddy's bed, at least until he is thirteen, and bellows at her departure or at the departure of objects associated with her (slipper, mirror-box, fire). Quentin spends a fair part of his Cambridge day trying to restore an immigrant girl to her parental house; he calls her "sister" and in memory circles back to events surrounding Caddy's protracted loss of "honour." He appears to believe that incest might serve if not to heal the hymen at least to involve the incestuous pair in a shame so great as to "isolate" them from "the loud world." His preferred medium of isolation is fire, borrowed, in effect, from Horace Benbow's Venetian cellars. Quentin does rhetorically what Horace did in actuality, he blows a glass maidenhead, in which "purged and purified . . . soapbubble"[34] he seeks to cleanse his sister; as brother and sister "merge," they become "a flame . . . blown cleanly out along the cool eternal dark" (p. 107). For Jason too the question of a sister's virginity is inseparable from incest; it cannot have escaped his attention that Caddy chose to call her fatherless child Quentin. Fearing that his niece is "just like her mother" (p. 159), he insists on at least a semblance of respectability, but his sanctions are no match for her kimono:

> I'll be damned if they dont dress like they were trying to make every man they passed on the street want to reach out and clap his hand on it. [pp. 139–40]

The three brothers, with very different degrees of self-consciousness, "want to reach out" to their sister. Strangely, doing so involves each of them in forms of more or less recognized miscegenation.

Benjy becomes "bluegum," and Quentin follows suit though in more articulate form. He contemplates sex with his sister and in so doing joins the other suitors, all of whom are "blackguards" (the epithet is carefully chosen and much repeated). Furthermore, Caddy's behavior strikes her brother as "black."

Caddy? Why must you do like nigger women do in the pasture the ditches dark woods hot hidden furious in the dark woods. [p. 57]

It follows that congress with her will darken those involved. A similar fear of racial crossing haunts Jason's recognition that Miss Quentin is of his "flesh and blood"; both Mrs. Compson and Caddy use this phrase when urging him to support his niece (pp. 110, 126), and in each case the wording triggers, within the space of a page, metaphoric acts whereby Jason is associated with a "slave" because he works so hard (in the second instance the epithet is his own). Once used, the term sticks – the "slave" Jason is attracted to his niece, whom he likens to "a nigger wench" (p. 114), believing that she "act[s] like [a] nigger" (p. 110) because "it's in her blood" (p. 140). Since he shares her blood, it is a short step from his claim that "blood always tells" (p. 110) to the recognition that what it tells may be a tale of mixed race. He does not take this step, however, perhaps because the blood that beats in his head gives him blackouts.

"Slave" thus joins "bluegum" and "blackguard" as covert forms of blackface, by means of which the brothers achieve displaced penetration of their sister. I've traced these submerged plots through the novel's verbal latencies to suggest how, for the brothers, the sister's hymen is also a colorline. In taking Caddy's virginity, no matter at what distance, each of them, metaphorically, turns "black." When the critical tradition sees these issues, it tends to psychologize them. The oedipal dragnet has been much run through Faulkner's preoccupation with incest. What generally results is some version of a primal scene in triplicate, in which brother challenges father by loving sister as surrogate for inadequate mother. Parts of the novel can be made to fit such a scenario, though not without strain, as in John T. Irwin's famously elaborate reading of Quentin's problems in terms of Freud's theories of narcissism. Irwin's case runs – because Quentin cannot accept as an object of love any "self" that does not resemble his own "self," he desires the sister, perceived as "*running out of the mirror*" (p. 50). Such mirroring reveals the goal of all infantile, regressive tendencies, narcissism included. It is the attempt to return to a state in which subject and object did not yet exist, to a time before the division occurred out of which the ego sprang – in short, to return to the womb, to reenter the waters of birth (Irwin).[35] I do scant justice to Irwin's ingenuities, though it should be possible to see from my summary how certain of Quentin's obsessions (mirrors, water, castration, repetition) could be set within a Freudian frame.

The problem with this Freudian reading is what such readings do to the black. Irwin describes the "negro resonances in Quentin's mind" as "the dark self, the ego shadowed by the unconscious."[36] To lodge the black in a universal unconscious is to remove him from Mississippi, though any reading of Jim Crow establishes that a fearful conjunction of race and sex disturbed the southern white imagination during what has been called the Radical era (1889–1915). Faulkner was born in 1897, Quentin in 1891, Jason two years later, and Benjy two years after that. The dates are less important than the fact that the creator and his characters grow out of a period of acute and specific racism, during which white and black sexuality became inextricable. Until the black, the virgin, and the incestuous brother are put into the Black Belt at the turn of the century, their centrality for Faulkner will not be understood. To make the case that Faulkner's founding deep-plots lie in the southern politics of race and gender (1890s–1910s), a brief history of that racial pathology is necessary.

To the conservative southern mind, the end of slavery (1865) proposed a key problem: how to position blacks in their organic place (at the bottom, as the hands of the system) without the educational benefits of the benevolent institution of slavery. "Freed," the black "child" (Sambo means "son of") could all too easily turn against the recently sustaining father (the antebellum planter as patriarch). By the mid-1880s the problem appeared to have worsened, in that a generation of young blacks were coming to manhood without the "civilizing" effects of slavery. Fear of falling agricultural prices during the early 1890s fostered scapegoating, as did the suspicion that northern politicians were threatening to break southern attempts illegally to exclude blacks from the ballot. All of which prepares the way for the rise of the Radical mentality, which signaled the South's "capitulation to racism"[37] between 1890 and 1915. Where the conservative sought to "protect" and "preserve" blacks by assigning them their proper place in the "natural order," the Radical was obsessed with the failure of that "order" – that is to say, he feared that the angelic black child of slavery, released from the school of the peculiar institution, was becoming the demonic black adult of freedom. To the Radical, the weaponry of Jim Crow (disenfranchisement, segregation, lynching) was the only means by which to subordinate blacks as they degenerated. One image focused the issue of black regression for the Radical: "the black beast rapist." Indeed, it can be argued that a sociosexual fantasy underpins much state legislation concerning segregation in the decades around the turn of the century. Joel Williamson makes the case that, faced with a deepening agricultural depression and the failure of political action to gain economic reform, white Southerners turned to racial action as an area in which they might at least appear to be managing their lives. He insists that Radicalism, as a system for thinking about black people, gained "absolute ascendancy"[38] in the deep South at this time. Neither Faulkner nor the Compson children would have escaped apprenticeship to its pathologies, and as Neil McMillen stresses, the years between 1889 and 1915 saw the most repressive Jim Crow activity in Mississippi's history. Repression modifies the repressors as well as the repressed:

> How much would white society have to change itself and white Southerners change themselves in order to keep black people down? When they were through with the Radical era, there was hardly a facet of life in the South in which the whites had failed to respond to the black presence, and the nature of that response gave Southern white culture in the twentieth century its basic shape.[39]

White self-revision turned on the image of the black male. The plot runs as follows: during the antebellum period, southern white males of the owning class idealized womanhood, building pedestals to raise the female gentry above the reality of interracial sex between slave women and slave owners. As the color line was criss-crossed in the quarters, so the pedestals soared at the plantation house. In the words of one southern historian, the white woman became

> the South's Palladium . . . – the shield-bearing Athena gleaming whitely in the clouds, the standard of its rallying. . . . She was the lily-pure maid of Astolat. . . . And – she was the pitiful Mother of God.[40]

By means of her propriety, husbands, fathers, and sons whitewashed their property and its sustaining institutions. However, the Cult of Southern Womanhood raised the standard of the unbreachable hymen precisely because miscegenation breached the color line throughout the prewar South. Plainly, if the iconic item was to withstand the iconoclastic force of the evidence, it needed support – support that white males found in the incest dream, institutionally reinforced by a high incidence of cousinship marriage among the plantocracy. Where the hymen stores the family "blood," protecting it from any risk of contamination through crossing, incest ensures that where crossing has occurred it shall be between like "bloods."

Even as the pathology whitened key whites, so it blackened key blacks, producing a mythological dark couple, the woman as a sexual "earth-mother" and the man as "black beast rapist." Emancipation had changed the obsessional map; freeing the slaves blocked white access to the quarters (contemporary observers agreed that misogenation between white men and black women was much reduced). In the white mind, because the "freed" man now served the libidinal black female, his nature shifted from child ("Sambo") to satyr. By definition, a satyr cannot be sated and, unsated, he will necessarily seek the white women earlier denied him. Within this pervasive fantasy, white men, having impeded their own intimacy with white women, project onto the black male extravagant and guilt-free versions of the sexual behavior whose ordinary forms they were declaring guilty and denying to themselves.

These more or less "untold stories" among which Faulkner was raised provide an effective prehistory for his narrative obsession with the triumvirate virginity, incest, and miscegenation. By 1915, Radicalism was dead as a political idea, but not before its plots had entangled those raised among its extremities – witness the sexual and narrative habits of the Compson brothers, each of whom attempts to enter his sister (or some version of her) in an incest that will shore up the integrity of his family and class but can do so only in blackface, because white potency is inextricable from black forms. Each attempt is severely punished (cannibalism among bluegums, Quentin's castration fantasies, Jason's headaches), while the hymen demonstrates its punitive resilience by its trick of regeneration, at least in the white male mind (Benjy's preference for events prior to 1909, Quentin's "innocest," Jason's contradictory faith in the integrity of his "blood"). What the brothers share is not attributable to a universal psychology (Freudian or otherwise) but to a historically specific regional pathology.

The problem remains, to what degree is this "conscious" or "unconscious" for the author and his characters? Eric Sundquist, who has done most to illuminate these questions, has no doubt that, in *The Sound and the Fury* at least, what matters is severely repressed:

> *The Sound and the Fury* does force this central issue [the depth of racial consciousness] back into the unconscious, for there is almost nothing . . . to indicate that miscegenation or its shadowy threat is an important feature of Quentin's psychological disturbance. One might say that *The Sound and the Fury . . . contains* the repressed that returns with increasing visibility over Faulkner's career.[41]

However, the "unconscious" need not necessarily be understood as an interior space; one might argue that repeated patterns of social action (Jim Crow, for example) geared to making and sustaining particular kinds of property (that of the southern gentry) will induce self-taught forms of forgetting.[42] If the unconscious is seen as a group-specific form of shared amnesia, its censors are historically shakeable. An individual's removal from the social pressures of the group may release him or her from what that group holds to be unthinkable, enabling a return not of the "repressed" but of forgotten social complexities. In this light, Quentin's removal from Mississippi to Harvard might be crucial.

III

The critical consensus blames Quentin for his memory on the grounds that it is repetitive, deeply incoherent, and rigidly fixed.[43] Behind the unflattering portrait lie two commonplaces: the first is that for all readers June 2, 1910, is oppressively the day of its narrator's death; the second assumes Quentin's inability to transcend the past by means of the present. Sartre's is merely the most famous statement of this temporal trap. Since "everything has already happened," Quentin can only and compulsively repeat a past that "takes on a sort of super-reality."[44]

I have my doubts about both assumptions. Quentin's day is filled with much more than provision for suicide; first-, second-, and third-time readers may well find that the flat-iron purchase pales in significance before the Boston Italian community, child abduction, court cases, and Caddy. Of course, the consensus might counter that the events of the busy day are directed to the terminal event, insofar as they replay obsessions centered on incest; because incest was Quentin's way of carrying himself and his sister beyond the "loud world," it follows that the plot requires the river bed. Such a case rests on a particular version of "repetition," one in which any event is a "substitute" bound by a chain of substitutions to an original object. So, for Irwin, Quentin's narcissism involves "an endless repetition of an infantile state."[45] It follows that New England replicates Mississippi because Quentin "makes present reality serve him as an analogue" for past realities,[46] which "he can only inadequately repeat" since they are finally deviant versions of an initial and absolute "infantile loss" (of mother or sister).[47] While not denying that the section features high levels of analogy, as Quentin moves rapidly between Boston and Mississippi (switching from Deacon to Roskus, from Bland to Ames, from the Charles River to a Jefferson "branch"), I would nevertheless argue that analogy need not mean "repetition."

Paul Ricoeur's work on metaphor prompts a reevaluation of what Quentin might take from the activity of temporal comparison. For Ricoeur, metaphor is frequently misread as an act of substitution, so that the phrase "majestic mountain" combines a decorative and a literal term, and the reader must paraphrase in order to recover the plain truth of the mountain. Some Faulknerians have tended to be just as literal about Quentin's temporal analogies; critical activity holds the present to be transparently decorative and concentrates on cleaning it away to reveal the fixed truth of the past. However, Ricoeur takes a tensional view of metaphor in which "impertinent predication" results from the interaction of the combined terms, in other words, the clash of the elements compared modifies their literal meanings. What results is not the obliteration of the thing referred to but its conversion into a "split reference" that confronts receivers of the metaphor with the requirement that they make and remake reality. To revert to the mountain, both royalty and the profile of Snowdon's north face need to be understood in relation to the network of assumptions about authority, grandeur, and land ownership informing their initial conjunction (mountains are rarely held to be "proletarian"):

> ... metaphoric meaning does not merely consist of semantic clash but of the new predicative meaning which emerges from the collapse of the literal meaning, that is, from the collapse of the meaning which obtains if we rely only on the common or usual ... value of our words. The metaphor is not the enigma but the solution of the enigma.[48]

When Quentin calls an Italian child "sister," he creates for himself an "enigma" within which the immigrant girl's proximity (her smell, for instance) and Caddy's remoteness (the odor of honeysuckle) both resist and yield to each other; their compatibility rests on incompatibilities of class, race, time, odor ... that will not simply lapse into resemblance (before passing from resemblance to "repetition"). Rather, the "sister" is a disturbing hybrid or "split reference" that creates, for Quentin, a conceptual need to challenge earlier versions of what sisters are and do. Where the southern sister could (at least for a time, and at least in Quentin's head) be subjected to a "flame" that would "clean" her hymen, her northern counterpart is dirtied with industrial fires (her face is "streaked with coal dust" [p. 89]). My point is that, on looking at the unnamed immigrant child, he does not see Caddy; he sees the collapse of what

Caddy meant to him. Whereas, in the South, the very idea of incest
involves a form of male cultural heroism – raising the standard of
the virgin – in the North, Quentin's return to that idea is deemed
child molestation, worthy of a six-dollar fine. The experience of "sister" as a "split referent" prompts a need for different terms that
will allow new thoughts on the connection displayed by the comparison.

On June 2, 1910, Quentin is prepared to recognize associative
openness (perhaps directed toward a future), where before he might
only have noted repetitive closure fixated on the past. The critical
custom of viewing history as *déjà vu* and of insisting on his "fear of
change"[49] consigns Quentin to a "timeless realm"[50] in which "the
story does not unfold"[51] and "no newness is produced, [and] no
difference can occur."[52] Yet Quentin's day has a plot, featuring
events that may transform their narrator. Indeed, June 2 might be
looked upon as the day when Quentin finds out so much that is new
that he has to challenge the key premises of his own culture; Deacon,
the Italian girl, and the country court are central to the challenge.
Quentin uses each as a surrogate through which, with increasing
insight, he revises his past. On the day before his last day Quentin
probably believed, as did his father before him, that the past was a
fait accompli. Mr. Compson defines "was" as "the saddest word of all
there is nothing else in the world" (p. 108), thereby paralyzing time
by insisting that all tenses take their form from a falsely inflexible
past tense. The rubric declares that history is absolutely determinate.

On June 2, in thrall to "was" and prepared to die for it, Quentin
learns, half by chance and half by curiosity, that the past can be
reinvented. His first act on getting up is to dismantle his father's
watch. Presumably he wants to escape from his father's model of
time, but its inner parts prove annoyingly well made and the watch
continues to tick. The events of Quentin's day revise the intellectual
substance of his initial symbolic act, so that the sound of clocks takes
on new meaning. By the time he returns to his room, paternal time
(or, indeed, grandpaternal time), that "mausoleum of all hope" (p.
47), inherited from his father and his father's father (or rather, from
a version of southern history), begins to sound inapplicable or "temporary." The word "temporary" punctuates the closing cadences of
June 2 and refers to a good deal more than Quentin's life. With it
the son insists on the flexibility of the past and casts his father's
determinate "was" as material for a dead language (*"Non fui. Sum.
Fui. Non sum"* [p. 106]). To perceive the father's position as archaic
requires detachment. Quentin distances himself from Mr. Compson
most effectively in their final conversation; I should point out that,

for me, this conversation never happened but is instead an imagined
dialogue. Asked, at the University of Virginia, "Did Quentin . . . actually have that conversation with his father about sleeping with his
sister . . . ?", Faulkner replied:

> He never did. . . . No, they [these words] were imaginary. He
> just said, Suppose I say this to my father, would it help me,
> would it clarify, would I see clearer what it is that I anguish
> over?[53]

If the words belong to Quentin, they can be read as a considered
device whereby he imitates the voice of his father, in order to expose
that voice, through parody. Which is not to say that Quentin is un-
fair; in the dialogue's initial phase, the father is given the strong
lines – making a humane bid to keep the son alive by pointing out
that time will change how he feels and implying that, in any case,
dead, the son can do nothing about "was." However, to stop here
would be to underplay the substance and tone of much that Quentin
makes his father say; it would seem that Quentin is to grow old
simply to learn that living is "staying awake . . . [to] to see evil done"
(p. 107) – done by a "dark diceman" who when he is not throwing
"loaded" dice is "floating" speculative "bond[s]" on a palpably
fixed market (p. 108). Heard with this emphasis, Mr. Compson becomes something of a fatalist for whom, in the larger scheme of
things, the death or life of a son can make no difference. After all,
given the dicing "gods," any initiatives (be they to suicide or a revised view of the sister) are deadened. Indeed, the father concludes
the conversation with an elegy to virtually everything:

> was the saddest word of all there is nothing else in the world
> its not despair until time its not even time until it was [p.108]

Quentin's Mr. Compson champions "was"; he can do nothing else
because, by his lights, "there is nothing else in the world." It follows
that time itself is determined by a past into which present and future
(tenses linked to action and anticipation) are simply subsumed ("its
not even time until it was"). All this is "sad," so sad that it might
have been better not to have been born, since despair is not, so far
as we know, a prenatal experience ("its not despair until time"). I
have exaggerated a tone in order to catch what I take to be Quentin's parody of his father's habits of mind and speech (fatalistic metaphors servicing tired aphorisms). Arguably, then, at the end of his
day, Quentin takes on his father's voice, precisely to counter both
its fatalistic tone and its celebration of "was" with a repeated inter-
jection of the "temporary" ("and I temporary"). "Temporary,"

here, refers to much more than one son's life; it is made to embrace all the assumptions of the father, from fate to manners, and from motives for suicide to the past itself. "Temporary" also modifies an earlier version of Quentin; if the dialogue is Quentin's, then the son who speaks in celebration of incest as an escape from "the loud world" is as redundant as the father for whom any change is no change (since it is prescribed by "the gods"). "Temporary" is the key to the conversation because it puts into time both the father and the son's atemporal casts of mind.

Once history can be seen as the activity of revision (because it is "temporary"), the contours of the past are unfixed. Tick and tock cease to be "the reductio absurdum of all human experience" (p. 47) and become a mechanical noise whose significance depends on the historian. Quentin is a historian who takes his sister as his subject.

Deacon gives him a first lesson in historical revision. Quentin makes contact because he needs a letter delivered to Shreve on June 3. However, the factotum is not in his customary haunts, and while looking for him Quentin reconsiders black/white relations in North and South. The sequence of his memories about racial exchange is revealing, being characterized by a rhythm of insight and evasion. In the post office, expecting to find Deacon, he recalls Deacon's fondness for "whatever parade came along" (p. 50). His memory slots its subject into a black type as lover of music, good times, and display and within a page similarly fixes two "boot blacks," "shrill and raucous" as "blackbirds." Quentin gives one a cigar and the other a nickel and leaves them, with the recipient of the cigar "trying to sell it to the other for the nickle" (p. 50). On this evidence Quentin is happy "to live in the fractured world of segregation,"[54] unable to learn from blacks whom he barely sees. Yet it should be noted that even here references to Deacon and to others of his color are ghosted by Quentin's self-conscious preoccupation with his own "shadow"; the black reflection cast by the white may in time take on a troubling racial tone. With Deacon still eluding him, Quentin catches a tram away from town toward the Charles River and discovers that "the only vacant seat was beside a nigger" (p. 53). Child of Jim Crow, Quentin speculates on verbal niceties – in the North "niggers" become "colored people" – and concludes

> a nigger is not a person so much as a form of behavior; a sort
> of obverse reflection of the people he lives among. [p. 53]

"Obverse" is essential here and should not be read loosely as a synonym for "opposite." Even in its more innocent forms, such as "counterpart" or "that which turns toward or faces the observer," the term suggests proximity rather than antithesis. The further we pursue the word, the closer Quentin perforce moves toward thought about racial interdependency; moreover, although in his statement blacks derive from whites (they reflect white behavior), the phrase "obverse reflection" in fact makes blacks "the front or principal surface" of white. Black primacy in the image is enhanced by the monetary meaning of "obverse," the "obverse" side of a coin being that "side of a coin bearing the principal image or inscription."[55] Earlier, for the cost of a nickel and a cigar, Quentin had turned two blacks into a vaudeville routine; here, at least implicitly, he senses that blacks are the not-so-hidden face of white wealth (a truism in the Black Belt). The conclusion, intimated by his usage, is that whites, in an important sense, are what blacks make. In the context of the troubling verbal latencies of "obverse," other words from Quentin's well-known statement become unstable. Take "reflection"; as Quentin debates comparative racial assumptions on a Boston tram, his mind slips from tram car to rail car and from North to South, seeking stable racial truths. The memory of "a nigger on a mule" (p. 53), seen from a standing train in Virginia, reassures him by providing an image of time-honored black deference. By working this strand of memory, Quentin can, in one sense, "raise the shade" that has fallen across his "reflection." In fact he does just that, he "raised the shade," let down the rail-car window, and played "Christmas gift" with the southern black (p. 53). For the price of a quarter thrown from the train, Quentin buys back a secure image of the Negro as "childlike," given to "reliability" and "tolerance" (p. 54). But even as Quentin reinscribes the color line (this black says "boss" *and* "young master" and is as well "static," "timeless," and serene), the tossed coin, spinning through a semantic atmosphere colored by the many meanings of "obverse," undoes his attempt. The "shade" (or shadow) on the mule may be as "timeless" as the land itself (according to Quentin, he "seemed carved out of the hill" [p. 53]), but the quarter with which Quentin buys Sambo back reintroduces a temporal note. "Obverse" is a word applicable to coins; in the case of American coinage, the "obverse" side "always bears the date, irrespective of the device." Monetarily speaking, the "front," "principal," "obverse," and by associative extension "black" side of Quentin's quarter is neither "static" nor "timeless." As if to underline the point, Faulkner breaks into Quentin's reassuring southern reveries when Quentin's black seat-mate on the Boston tram wants to get off, at which "Quentin swung [his] legs and let him pass." The unstable valencies of "obverse" inflect "pass," releasing a complex pun; light-skinned blacks may "pass" as white, a thought that, on a tram full of "mostly prosperous looking people," could encourage a Southerner to speculate as to how many "invisible" northern blacks have already passed their masters.[56] At the moment when he is "passed" by the black, Quentin smells the river; he dismounts and contemplates his fifty-foot shadow on the water, noting that, "Niggers say a drowned man's shadow was watching for him in the water all the time" (p. 55). If so, even in suicide Quentin will have to pass through a shadow ("shade," "reflection") cast in some part by a black story.

Some will object that I have made one or two words work much too hard. Certainly, linked latencies, no matter how numerous ("obverse," "quarter," "shade," "pass," "shadow"), may remain semi-secret to their user, unless the sequence of the narrative exposes what is half-hidden. Events in what I would call the "discover Deacon plot" culminate in an encounter during which the black tactfully demands that Quentin appreciate, through him, the political fullness of black experience as it transcends white definition. If we hear Deacon, blacks cease to be what white people make; instead, we expose the surface meaning of "obverse reflection" – that all black behavior derives from white behavior – as at best partial. Deacon turns the phrase upside down, so that, for Quentin too, its covert meanings become overt. After Deacon, "black" cannot mean what a child of the Radical era would have it mean, nor can the attendant term "shadow" escape redefinition.

Deacon has for forty years played servant to southern scholars coming to Harvard. His status as a "colorful" character stems in large part from his affection for costumes. Meeting trains from the South, he assumes an "Uncle Tom's cabin outfit," which later gives way to "a cast-off Brooks suit" (p. 59). His use of dress is calculated and displays a latent tendency to satire. At the station, despite the "patches" and talk of "young marster," Deacon is a servant who masters whites and displays that mastery to them, employing a white "boy" (his is the transferred racial epithet) as a beast of burden to carry student luggage. On June 2 Deacon's chosen guise is military, a fact that Quentin reads as a hangover from some "parade" earlier in the week. Military terms pervade their meeting (pp. 59–60): Deacon gives a "very superior officerish kind of salute" to a couple of freshmen, and Quentin recalls that he boasted a hatband taken from "part of Abe Lincoln's military sash"; Deacon inquires as to his appearance on Decoration Day, and Quentin assures him that in the veteran's uniform he looked good enough "to make . . . general." The list could be extended, but the point would remain that Deacon is doing something very significant with military signs that Quentin fails to read; his purpose comes directly into focus with his statement of changed political allegiance:

> Yes, sir. I didn't turn Democrat three years ago for nothing. My son-in-law on the city; me – Yes, sir. If just turning Democrat'll make that son of a bitch go to work. . . . And me: just you stand on that corner yonder a year from two days ago, and see. [p. 61]

Faulkner does not choose 1907 casually; in that year blacks might have given up on the Republican Party as a result of the political fallout from the much-publicized events in Brownsville, Texas, the previous year. In August 1906, three companies of the 25th Regiment, composed of Negroes, were involved in rioting in Brownsville; one citizen was killed, two wounded, one of them the chief of police. According to white townspeople, blacks "shot up the town." In November, acting on the report of a single southern inspector, President Theodore Roosevelt dismissed the entire battalion, without honors, disqualifying them from future military or civil service. One black commentator responded in 1908:

> A considerable fraction of Negro voters in the North and West will undoubtedly desert the Republican party on account of the stubborn attitude of the President. This may result in the defeat of his party and of the policies which bear his personal brand. So great a matter the Brownsville fire kindled.[57]

The matter did not go away: Deacon's reference may be to the Senate Committee report of 1907, which upheld the presidential handling of the affair, although Senator Foraker submitted a minority report denouncing the findings. Two years later, in 1909, Foraker forced through Congress an act establishing a court of inquiry to reassess the discharge. Many regarded the establishment of the court as "the most pointed and signal defeat of Roosevelt's administration."[58] It is within this extended context that Deacon's appropriation of military signs should be read; his bearing is a declaration of political allegiance to the disgraced black soldiers of Brownsville. His politics may be confused, since a shift to the Democrats commits him to the party of black disenfranchisement, at least in the South, but his reference to a son-in-law, once unemployed and now working, suggests that his purposes are more local and Machiavellian, involving access to labor. What matters, though, is not his political astuteness but his orientation to future purposes beyond Quentin's powers of definition; when a "servant" warns the "young marster" to look for him in a parade on May 31, 1911 (p. 61), the specificity of time and place pales before the tone of assertion. Deacon is unlikely to be party to Democratic electoral preparations for the three-cornered fight of 1912, but his statement in standard English, addressing future political action, declares him anything but "invisible," "Sambo," or "rapist."

Unable to face what he sees, Quentin runs South:

> suddenly I saw Roskus watching me from behind all his [Deacon's] whitefolks' claptrap of uniforms and politics and Harvard manner, diffident, secret, inarticulate and sad.
> "You aint playing a joke on the old nigger, is you?" [p. 61]

Quentin's anxiety is measured by the inappropriateness of his four chosen epithets. At this point, Deacon rather deserves their opposities: "immodest," "overt," "articulate," and "joyful," but he knows when he may have revealed too much and, eye-minded as to Quentin's troubled shift in attention, reassumes a southern Negro dialect along with its attendant subordination. Whatever his idiom, Quentin cannot make Deacon into Roskus, and his attempt to do so goes badly wrong, resulting in an attribution of complex purposes to a southern house servant. Deacon's effect can be measured by the "marster's" thoughts following his departure:

> "Yes, sir," he said. "I've had good friends."
> The chimes began again, the half hour. I stood in the belly of my shadow and listened to the strokes spaced and tranquil along the sunlight, among the thin, still little leaves. Spaced and peaceful and serene, with that quality of Autumn always in bells even in the month of brides. *Lying on the ground under the window bellowing.* He took one look at her and knew. Out of the mouths of babes. *The street lamps* The chimes ceased. I went back to the postoffice, treading my shadow into the pavement. [pp. 61–2]

A certain affinity between "belly," "bells," and "bellow" embarrasses Quentin's attempt to restore terminal calm. Quentin uses the chimes to make a point his grandfather might have approved, but time's inevitable passage refuses to become "the mausoleum of all hope" (p. 47), thereby consigning Quentin to the riverbed; instead it takes him to "brides" and to Benjy's insight at Caddy's wedding. On April 24, 1910, Benjy can see into Caddy's womb. Three months later, so too can Quentin, but he attempts to revise what he sees by playing sylvan historian; he improvises a Keatsian ambience, using the fall of light between leaves to suggest a "leaf fring'd legend" ruled by "peace" and "serenity," into which a "still unravished bride" might yet be called. But, post-Deacon, the "belly" of the Keatsian urn will deliver neither "slow time" nor a regrown hymen; indeed, Quentin's position in the "belly" of his own shadow is entirely problematic. With Deacon found, politicized, and partially recognized as such, Quentin's "shadow" – that is, his "obverse reflection," or black self – may yet be pregnant with claims quite at odds with those regional assumptions impacted in the emblematic virgin.

However, "shadow" could be read as appealing exactly to received rather than revisionist truths. Given that "shadow" is proximal to questions of impregnation, it might be said to summon the "black beast rapist" from the Radical prenarratives that constitute a crucial part of the Compson apprenticeship. Once the black rapist is loose in the associative mix, "shadow" performs like "bluegum" and "blackguard"; Benjy enters his sister as "bluegum," and Quentin, similarly blackened by a potent shade, uses Keats on Caddy to modify her sexuality. In each instance a brother perversely uses the "shadow" of the black rapist to bleach out what he perceives to be a sexual stain. Mr. Compson would understand the pathology because it rises from the interlock between virginity, incest, and miscegenation prevalent in the 1890s. But it should be remembered that the "shadow" falling across this particular passage is cast by Deacon, a northern and nonsexual figure. His shade (circa 1910) is more disturbing than any specter from the turn of the century, in that Deacon's ambitions focus on questions of politics and labor, whereas his orientation to the future challenges the ascendancy of "was" and so potentially opens Quentin to the recognition that his father's explanations are profoundly ignorant. At the last, Quentin aborts the revised self seen through his "guide mentor and friend" (p. 60) by treading his shadow into the pavement.

The Deacon sequence is rapidly followed by a second extended subplot of a revisionist kind, in which an Italian girl takes over as the "shadow." What distinguishes her from her predecessor is that she commits Quentin to events that will eventually force him to acknowledge the failure of his own historical reality, insofar as it derives from the cultural prenarratives concerning virginity, incest, and miscegenation. His recognition that his account of Caddy is inadequate negates the voice of his fathers and requires him to rewrite his own and their pathologies.

I run ahead of myself: first, the key details in the immigrant subplot in which the Italian "sister" is made bearer of Deacon's latent lesson. Quentin refers repeatedly to this sister's "black" looks, while his description of her face as resembling "a cup of milk dashed with

coffee" (p. 76) involves an epithet redeployed once only by Faulkner, in his account of the pastor of the black church as "of a light
coffee color" (p. 175). Matthews notes the connection, arguing from
it that "all foreign elements that threaten his [Quentin's] world order are in effect black"; he adds that during the day the "foreign"
proliferates, implying a future during which Quentin's fixed "ideal
of the South" can only further deteriorate.[59] Matthews thus deems
the suicide inevitable. Critical accounts frequently read "black" in
conjunction with "dirt" and link "dirt" with Mr. Compson's version
of women as "soiled." By these means Quentin is established as a
southern hygienist, the foolish champion of an impossible female
purity, embodying an archaic regional integrity.[60] What this case ignores is that "dirt," for Quentin, is not exclusively linked to women
as something that must be cleansed; the dirt on the Italian girl is
not the same dirt as that which stained Natalie and Caddy, rather,
it resembles "coal dust" (p. 89). Her smell, though dirty, does not
emanate from a sexual body but from a nickel, nor does it cause
Quentin to recoil (disgust belongs to the shopkeeper); instead, he
is curiously attentive to the odor of the coin in the child's hand:

> She extended her fist. It uncurled upon a nickel, moist and
> dirty, moist dirt ridged into her flesh. The coin was damp and
> warm. I could smell it, faintly metallic. [p. 77]

This "dirt" is not exclusively of the South, and in pursuing it Quentin encounters ethnic realities beyond his regional experience; the
Boston Italian community is industrial rather than rural.

His new "sister," in her difference, and in Quentin's ignorance
of it, challenges the idea of empedestalled southern womanhood,
an idea he learned at Mr. Compson's knee. Although a misogynist,
Quentin's father is first and foremost a failed idealist whose conviction that all women are dirty (whore) serves to remind us how, once
and for him, they must have been clean (virgin). So his rhetoric
renovates the cult of southern womanhood, even as it denigrates
women. Some account of that rhetoric may serve to show how far
an Italian guide carries Quentin beyond his culture's polarized account of the female:

> Because women so delicate so mysterious Father said. Delicate
> equilibrium of periodical filth between two moons balanced.
> Moons he said full and yellow as harvest moons her hips thighs.
> Outside outside of them always but. Yellow. Feet soles with
> walking like. Then know that some man that all those myste-
> rious and imperious concealed. With all that inside of them

shapes an outward suavity waiting for a touch to. Liquid putre-
faction like drowned things floating like pale rubber flabbily
filled getting the odor of honeysuckle all mixed up. [p. 78]

The passage occurs soon after Quentin encounters the girl and il-
lustrates perfectly why critics have read her as a replicant Caddy who
locks Quentin into "past realities."[61] Repetition appears to be the
order of the day as Quentin reconsiders his "old" sister's impregnation, only to end up in a verbal maze built by the father's voice.
Yet even here, before the Italian plot has evolved, there is hesitation.
Three sentences are interrupted, one of which hardly starts: "Outside outside of them always but. Yellow. Feet soles with walking like."
The reiteration of "outside" measures the extent of male exclusion
by women; given Quentin's virginity, the concluding "but" may cor-
rectively allude to his fear of impotence ("but one day . . ."), though
the syntactical break permits the conjunction a disruptive freedom –
for example, he might modify his exclusion were he to acknowledge
that he spied on his sister ("but at least I saw . . ."), while "but"
might be a synonym for "except" ("except on the occasion of incest"). In each case the hesitation, marked by the conjunction, precipitates Quentin from abstraction toward particularity: "women"
become Caddy, a transition that remains unmade because vitupera-
tion is more easily directed at a type than a person. "Yellow," in the
context of the evaded tension between generic "whore" and singular sister, refers not only to the color of the harvest moon (soon
to be discolored as the dried skin on the underside of feet, "soles")
but also to an implicit self-indictment: Quentin knows himself to be
a coward, even as he retreats into the verbal pleasures of an idiom
that no longer fits his reality. However, repeating the father has its
problems, and Quentin seems unable to finish a sentence. The father may be convinced that all women walk like prostitutes, but the
son can neither affirm nor deny the paternal simile. Quentin's inclination to specify would allow him to complete the phrase "with
walking like Caddy," but his sister, refocused through the Italian girl
standing at his side, is no longer a "whore" or a "virgin." Quentin
stops because events on June 2 have begun to suggest that sisters
deserve a new language. With the Italian narrative still nascent, hesitation does not become impasse, and Quentin reverts to repetition.
"Woman" remains a generic type – the whore full of "concealed"
clients. However, the new and troubling sibling will not go away;
instead she leads her adoptive brother into actions that will force
him to discard the assumptions through which he previously told
Caddy's story.

The main events of the Italian subplot are the arrest and trial, prior to which Quentin's habits of mind and language tended to warrant critical unkindness. His thoughts were often "intensely claustrophobic" and "almost impenetrably private."[62] However, his day, centering on the public accusation that he has molested a child, features a clear shift in mental habit. The accuser, Julio, is "brother" to Quentin, even as the supposed victim is a second "sister," but neither repeats past events. At every point, events leading up to the trial and the trial itself form an external re-presentation of an inner drama (the incest fable) in which southern tragedy, relocated, comes back as a northern farce that precipitates Quentin into historical revision. Externalization does not involve a return of the repressed but rather requires that Quentin see key scenes in the regional fantasy of his class, from below. Caddy, a somewhat soiled Palladium, becomes a dirty immigrant girl; the South's aristocratic champion, still "Galahad," albeit "half-baked" (p. 67), reappears in the guise of an Italian worker, as worried about wages as about family, while the judicial father – aptly named Squire – recomposes the southern patriarch as a barely literate figure who writes in something resembling "coal dust" (p. 86). The episode extends the lessons of the Deacon plot, lessons that disrupt Quentin's prenarratives and require that he recover what actually happened, released from its entanglement in the cultural prehistory of the Radical era.

My point is not that the occasion of the attempted incest "returns" but that Quentin finds it for the first time, and that as it emerges he discovers a very different brother and sister. The effect is tonally shocking; to turn from a pre-trial passage (such as the account of women as "vessels of periodical filth") to the ten or so pages of stark dialogue that follow Quentin's departure from court is like turning from the densities of *Ulysses* (the "Proteus" section) to the transparencies of Hemingway at his most minimalist ("Hills Like White Elephants"). Direct report cancels "chaotic first person effusion,"[63] in large part because the first person who emerges here is new to Quentin himself. The dialogue passage occurs as Quentin recovers from a fight with Gerald Bland; whether or not he is conscious, partially conscious, or unconscious during any or all of what he sees and hears is of less importance than the shock of Bland's blow to his head. The punch levels Quentin physically and intellectually, disabling those habits of perception through which he preserves a version of himself and thereby enabling revision of that "self." "Chaos" and "effusion," rarely as prevalent as critics claim, cease as Quentin breaks the structuring myths that have grounded

his account of "incest" and the "hymen," to find a different tran-
scription of his personal obsessions.

As Quentin becomes the historian of his own and of his region's
pathologies, he studies the new evidence without comment. I, however, shall briefly annotate the stunned silence of his historical discovery. Quentin comes to the branch in order to call his sister a
whore. Instead they talk, and motives emerge; the brother is physically jealous of Dalton Ames and wishes to take his place. Impotence
prevents him and provokes the substitution of a childish suicide pact
for the sexual act about which he knows so little:

> I held the point of the knife at her throat.
> it wont take but a second just a second then I can do mine
> I can do mine then
> all right can you do yours by yourself
> yes the blades long enough Benjys in bed by now
> yes
> it wont take but a second Ill try not to hurt
> all right
> will you close your eyes
> no like this youll have to push it harder
> touch your hand to it
> but she didnt move her eyes were wide open looking past
> my head at the sky
> Caddy do you remember how Dilsey fussed at you because
> your drawers were muddy
> dont cry
> Im not crying Caddy
> push it are you going to
> do you want me to
> yes push it
> touch your hand to it [p. 92]

One detail is particularly revealing; Caddy, ever practical, asks if
Quentin will be able to cut his own throat. Quentin's reply involves
an apparent non sequitur: "yes the blades long enough Benjys in
bed by now." Several elements are involved: Quentin invokes his re-
sentment of Benjy, who slept with Caddy until he was thirteen; fears
of sexual inadequacy tied up with the innuendo that all idiots are
sexual giants; and a glimmer of self-recognition. The evocation of
Benjy's howl has been one of Quentin's customary ways of voicing his
own confusion, and that all-obscuring noise is now silent. The knife,
like the howl, is a substitute. Like the howl, the knife falls away.

> dont cry poor Quentin
> but I couldnt stop she held my head against her damp hard
>   breast I could hear her heart going firm and slow now
>   not hammering and the water gurgling among the
>   willows in the dark and waves of honeysuckle coming
>   up the air my arm and shoulder were twisted under me
> what is it what are you doing
> her muscles gathered I sat up
> its my knife I dropped it
> she sat up
> what time is it
> I dont know
> she rose to her feet I fumbled along the ground
> Im going let it go
> to the house
> I could feel her standing there I could smell her damp
> clothes feeling her there
> its right here somewhere
> let it go you can find it tomorrow come on [pp. 92–3]

Lulled by Caddy and innocent memories, Quentin rests. The startling disjunction between the smell of honeysuckle and a cramped
arm can be simply explained as an interval of sleep; Caddy's sudden
"what time is it" may indicate an interrupted stillness. I propose
that Quentin's sexual response energizes this scene, that sleep re-
lieves him of guilt and restores his potency, and that he wakes with
an erection. Caddy resists his potency but does so in a way that balances between objection and response:

> what are you doing
> her muscles gathered

The linebreak could be understood conventionally, as marking a
division between speech and action; however, a passage that conspicuously omits the marks whereby such divisions are negotiated –
marks of punctuation and capital letters – may well foreground the
spacing of the text, causing readers to make meanings from textual
items (such as spaces) that are not otherwise particularly meaningful. In which case this break could be read as signaling a significant
pause, during which Caddy's body adjusts to changes in Quentin's
body – it appears that she is not gathering herself to sit or stand,
since Quentin rises first. "I sat up" is at once an embarrassed male
reaction and an attempt to disguise an erection. The duplicity is
contained in the knife play. Sleep rendered the symbol unnecessary,

so he "dropped it" and woke to discover the absolute redundancy of the substitute. However, the symbol is easier than the reality of standing straight and of his sister's gathering muscles; consequently Quentin fumbles. As they walk away Caddy seems sexually stimulated: "she walked into me . . . she walked into me again." Her arousal probably derives from an intermingling of thoughts about her lover and brother. What is clear is that Caddy (aged seventeen) departs to meet Dalton Ames in the woods, and that her eighteen-year-old brother goes with her. Whether she wants him there or thereabouts depends upon how "sat up" and "gathered" are disposed; she may be bumping into him because he blocks her path to the woods, or because she is flirting with him – both readings are possible and may even be simultaneous. To stress a mutual and confused arousal, as I do, is to appreciate that the physical actions and reactions of the brother and the sister constitute an erotics that both find troubling and yet exciting. Eventually, Quentin controls the contact:

> we crossed the crest and went on toward the trees she walked into me she gave over a little the ditch was a black scar on the gray grass she walked into me again she looked at me and gave over [p. 93]

However, when he tries to extend his control by holding her (a gesture with which he impedes her course to her lover and puts himself in the place of that lover), a tacitly sexual struggle ensues; "she was motionless hard unyielding but still" (p. 93). Caddy's refusal to fight – "I wont fight stop youd better stop" (p. 94) – involves a stillness that says "no" ("unyieldingly"); here, her muscles ("hard") are gathered to resist. But as soon as Dalton Ames arrives, forcing Quentin unambiguously back into the role of brother, Caddy redisposes her body. Safe and sexually alert, within Ames's shadow[64] and touch, she twice calls the departing Quentin back:

> I went back she touched my shoulder leaning down her shadow the blur of her face leaning down from his high shadow I drew back
> look out (p. 94)

Again, the reader is given bodies minus all but minimal speech. Interpreting flesh has its difficulties but does suggest just how fleshy the Quentin/Caddy liaison is. Quentin rejects a kiss whose meaning can be lodged anywhere between solace or "come-on"; whatever Caddy's motive, Quentin's extreme reaction ("look out") amounts to snatching his face and body away, a rejection that causes Caddy to request a meeting: "wait for me at the branch . . . Ill be there soon wait for me you wait" (p. 94). Her demand is complicated by the co-presence of two men to whom she has offered her face: "at the branch," Quentin will not be in the woods where Caddy intends to go with Ames, but by returning to the branch he will be returning to the scene of his and Caddy's problematic arousal. To meet the sister there might, arguably, be to fulfill a physical assignation. Whatever the case, on this summer night of 1909, Caddy loses her virginity to Ames, but not before she and her brother have prompted in each other a physically particular and emotionally difficult sensuality.

After such evidence, Quentin cannot retreat into his father's misogyny or its antithesis; to release Caddy from the trap of the "virgin/whore" is to discover his own and his sister's sexuality unmediated by his culture's "untold stories." The new evidence suggests that his sister was a confused girl, no more or less loving than many, and that he has been party to his family's misrepresentation and negation of her.

I have interpreted what is in effect the transcript of a dialogue that took place in 1909, and it has been my suggestion that, toward the middle of the day on June 2, 1910, Quentin, with scholarly perseverance, is likewise engaged. In fact he is being knocked down by Gerald Bland. The conversation at the branch, which I have read as part of Quentin's conscious attempt to revise his past, could be an uncontrolled flashback. The notions are not mutually exclusive. Thanks to the trial, Quentin knows what he is doing when he hits Gerald Bland. He repeats nothing, least of all anything compulsive; rather, he is claiming his past back for reappraisal. A punch thrown in 1910 recaptures the punch he wanted to throw at Dalton Ames in 1909 and wipes away months of misguided interpretation. The punch is not casual; Quentin strikes out at Bland, whom he has previously and parodically presented as a caricature of the southern gentleman (all "horses," "niggers," "women," and maternal approbation [p. 56]). The fight and lengthy mopping-up operations give ample time for the dialogue to be more than a flash of insight. Above all, the effect of the transcriptlike conversation on Quentin's monologue argues against any claims for it as the merely unconscious record of a moment.

After the fight Quentin's tone relaxes, and as his monologue draws to its close he describes actions as though at a considered distance. It is as if, having heard the obsessive pitch to his own voice, the speaker blunts its pathological edge and is therefore able to approach areas that previously he would have avoided. This tonal transformation is clear from single phrases. On a tram back to the university, the through-draft fills "with the odor of summer and darkness except honeysuckle. Honeysuckle was the saddest odor of all, I think. I remember lots of them" (p. 103). All morning Quentin has been nauseated by the memory of honeysuckle; by mid-afternoon he catalogues it among other smells and is undecided whether to grant it any special intensity. Quentin seems at several removes even from himself, with the result that he is prepared to comment dispassionately on his earlier stylistic habits:

> Sometimes I could put myself to sleep saying that over and over until after the honeysuckle got all mixed up in it the whole thing came to symbolise night and unrest I seemed to be lying neither asleep nor awake looking down a long corridor of grey halflight where all stable things had become shadowy paradoxical all I had done shadows all I had felt suffered taking visible form antic and perverse mocking without relevance inherent themselves with the denial of the significance they should have affirmed thinking I was I was not who was not was not who. [p. 103]

The memory is a nightmare that has been controlled. Previously it would have been returned to as experience; now its details are reported and weighed in a discursive structure, "neither . . . nor . . . all . . . all . . . all. . . ." His tone is tired, and he dismisses painful memory by underplaying the pain ("the whole thing came to symbolize"). The jumbled past tenses merely simulate an earlier style; having emptied "was" of its oppressive weight, Quentin can afford to look back on once tormenting phrases. Very soon he will consign phrases like them to the precise grammatical distinctions of a dead language: "*Non fui. Sum. Fui. Non sum.*" (I was not, I am, I was, I am not.) are the "Peacefullest words" (p. 106), because they possess the peace of a museum exhibit.

During the second half of June 2, Quentin obtains an abundance of what is effectively new information, arrived at via the dismantling of his own historical model. Time reemerges from the archetypes of a particular cultural pathology, and the creative responsibilities of the historian begin. Those responsibilities are finally beyond Quentin because, with the sustaining narrative of one "was" gone, he has no meaningful context in which to place his new information. At a loss for history, not oppressed by it, he kills himself. Lord Acton recommended that the historian rise above personal social and historical situations. Carried to its extreme, his suggestion reads like a suicide note:

History must be our deliverer not only from the undue influence of other times, but from the undue influence of our own,
from the tyranny of the environment and the pressure of the
air we breathe.[65]

Since so much of the "pressure" on Quentin stems from the "influence" of prenarratives rooted in the pathologies of the 1890s, it
might be pertinent to turn to Joel Williamson for some gloss on
Quentin's suicide; Williamson notes that for any white child of the
Radical era to break from his cultural apprenticeship may involve a
form of death:

> Southern white identity . . . was intimately bound up with the
> Southern white image of the Negro, however unreal that image
> might have been. To let that image go, to see black people as
> people, was a precarious and exceedingly dangerous venture
> that exposed the individual to alienation from his natal culture
> and to the loss of his sense of self. It was a matter of declaring
> essentially, "I'm not going to be me any more."[66]

Quentin makes this declaration. His recurrent debate about "was"
is reinflected by a revised cultural history, so that the past tense and
the first person pronoun are set in new relation. "I was I was not
who was not was not who" (p. 103) can be phrased, "I was. I was
not. Who was not? Was, not who," with the emphasis on "was" as
Sartre's murderous and "unchangeable burden." Reinflected, the
phrasing disperses the past along with the pronoun: "I was. I was
not. Who was? Not was . . . not who." The key both to this syntactical
shift and to the larger narrative revision is the black. However, in
the southern mind blacks are never alone, because "Southern white
culture, Southern white personality, and Southern white ideas on
race, sex and moral reality are inextricably intertwined. To change
one is inevitably to change the others."[67] By changing the black,
Southerners risk the destruction of their sense of self. Quentin lets
the black depart, particularly from the space of white sexuality, gains
a sister, and loses himself.

IV

Williamson asks:

> . . . how [does one] take the racism, the unreality of seeing
> black either as child or beast, out of the Southern mind without

killing the Southerner? How does one excise a functioning part
of the body and yet preserve the life of the patient?[68]

Faulkner responds that one cannot. However, he answers with only
part of his voice; what Quentin narrates is an absolute reversal of
Benjy's plot. Benjy wanted to keep Caddy innocent and beyond temporal change (the hymen);[69] Quentin struggles to free her, having
first tried to constitute her as the type "whore," a type that the third
of Faulkner's vocal inflections (called Jason) will recuperate and apply to all women of a sexual age.

The sections of *The Sound and the Fury* are locked in vocal contradiction. Faulkner is, quite simply, talking in several accents from
both sides of his mouth at once. For example, Benjy and Quentin
are at odds not only over sisters but over time. Benjy almost achieves
the past. Quentin almost achieves a future. To reach the third section is to hear a voice that holds both temporal poles together and
so is torn apart. Jason has no time for his father's times, being obsessed with cotton futures, yet he wants his father's times restored
insofar as he wishes to play patriarch to a kitchen full of suppliant
"niggers."

Initially, the three monologues and their confusions appear iso-
lated from one another, but reading and re-reading establishes filial
conflict, at which point collisions occur between preferred words.
Since "sister," used by one, refers both to a person and to that word
as it is spoken by the others, "sister" becomes double and treble
voiced. Of course, the brothers do not converse (Benjy cannot,
Quentin has stopped, and Jason, to all intents and purposes, talks to
no one but himself); rather, the reader becomes the location of a
dispute. What I am trying to describe is not "literary ambiguity" over
the meaning of a word, but a political conflict caught (care of the
reader) within a word's "semantic field," a term usefully glossed by
the linguist Vološinov:

> The word is not a tangible object but an always shifting, always
> changing means of social communication. It never rests with
> one consciousness, one voice. Its dynamism consists in move-
> ment from speaker to speaker, from one context to another,
> from one generation to another. Through it all, the word does
> not forget its path of transfer and cannot completely free itself
> from the power of the concrete contexts which it has entered
> . . . each member of the community . . . receives the word from
> another voice, a word full of that other voice. The word enters
> his context from another context, permeated with the inten-

tions of other speakers. His own intention finds the word already occupied.[70]

So defined, any term may be the site of historical dispute. Take the word "father"; it would be fair to say that Benjy's fretful modification of time does the father's work, insofar as the invention of Caddy as an unexchangeable purity (circa 1898) protects Compson blood from all forms of social incursion. Latent in Benjy's consciousness lies the possible rehabilitation of the voice of a father whose pathology is firmly rooted in the racial assumptions of the Radical era (1889–1915). However, Quentin uses the paternal voice and term, toward the end of that era of racial rage (1910), when "father" has passed through other contexts and into another generation. Mr. Compson may tacitly have renovated the "virgin" with all his talk of "whores," but Quentin quits the antithesis, along with its implied black, so that, by the end of his day the son no longer confesses to the father but judges that father an archaism unfit to face changing times ("and I temporary" [p. 108]).

To Jason, Mr. Compson always and paradoxically faced a northern future. Jason's father is primarily he who sold the pasture so that Quentin might go to Harvard – a figure who turns immovable property (Compson land) into movable property (a sum of money) and who further dictates that the sum be expended to gain northern credit in the form of status, a prestige that would promote the Compson name even as it diminished Compson substance. Jason's Mr. Compson tells a truth about the southern economy, a truth having no place in the world according to Benjy or to Quentin (prior, that is, to June 2, 1910); for them, dependencies of blood (familial and racial) have an absolute value. For Mr. Compson, they have a variable price; after all, this father agreed that his wife should take their daughter to the marriage market, so that the second son might receive his financial inheritance. The fact that the contract between southern property and northern capital breaks down, voiding Jason's promised job at the heart of northern finance (Herbert Head's bank), does not alter the point that neither land nor person lies outside the liquidities of the market. It is only apt that the father, according to Jason, should be claimed by liquid.

Seen from Jason's perspective and from 1928, the sale of the "pasture" becomes part of a revolution in southern land use. The pasture is turned into a golf course, leisure resource to a new mercantile class emerging from the old and persistent planter class. By 1946, in "Appendix. Compson: 1699–1945," Jason will have become self-consciously part of that class, but in 1928 his social trajectory is less clear. He spends his day caught between emergent and archaic class fragments, one minute working for a merchant while playing the New York market in cotton futures, and the next insisting on the patrimonial priorities of "blood" and "name." He resolves the contradiction by preserving his own past via what the historian C. Vann Woodward calls "the cult of archaism"[71] – that is to say, taking a paternal hint, he invests in "the Old South." At his mother's death in 1933, he becomes a successful cotton merchant, but not before supplying himself with necessary capital by translating his inheritance – the Old Compson Place – into liquid assets. The father traded with a nascent leisure industry; the son deals with would-be hoteliers, "chopping up . . . [the] oncesplendid rooms into what he called apartments" ("Appendix")[72] before selling the conversion as a boarding house. The father's golf course and the son's rehabilitated plantation are complementary sites, in which a new southern merchant class will play and stay, doubtless admiring "the Old South" as it springs from the heads of the new South's entrepreneurs.

Jason's "father" differs from Quentin's "father" as much as both differ from the "father" of Benjy, and the three fathers don't add up to one Mr. Compson (much less the repetitive oedipal papa). Once we realize that the word "father" means so many things, having such contradictory historical and political implications, then terms associated with the authority of the father ("virgin," "sister," "black"), along with their associative networks ("mirror," "water," "shadow"), will similarly split, turning the reader into the space where the vocal dispersal of the author takes place. Dispersal is exacerbated by Faulkner's choice of form. The three interior monologues represent a threefold immersion of his own voice in the vocal and cognitive peculiarities of other styles of speech. Read aesthetically they result in a modernist tour de force. Read historically, with an eye to Paul Goodman's observation that "a style of speech is a hypothesis about how the world is,"[73] the novel comes apart, torn by the very contradictions that tear the owning class from which Faulkner comes. Either reading delivers a difficult novel, but modernist difficulty can be solved by appeals to "suspended meaning," "the writerly text," "an open ending," and other descendants of that comforting lit-crit term "ambiguity." Historical difficulty bespeaks an altogether more intractable irresolution, best characterized by returning to the tension between narrators.

Each brother does very different things with the regionally iconic sister. Benjy turns her into a pure space, aptly represented by Faulkner as a Roman vase owned by an obsessed patrician. Quentin releases her from the constraints of "type" and so unstops time; as Frank Kermode notes, "types" are "those great instruments for the defeat of temporal flux."[74] Jason sells her, or at least embezzles what she has earned from the sale of herself, and hoards the profit. None of the brothers, with the possible exception of Quentin, can debate his version of the sister, sealed as he is within his own monologue. Nor does Faulkner supply a means to measurement, there being no section dedicated to Caddy; instead, Faulkner in late interviews repeats Benjy's space by claiming that "she was still to me too beautiful and too moving to reduce her to telling what was going on."[75] So, a narrative originating in a daughter's resistance to her father ("Your paw told you to stay out of that tree" [p. 24]) reaches no conclusion on father or daughter. Instead, Faulkner gives us difficult multiplicity.

The contradictions, which for me remain historical, can be relocated within Faulkner, through a notion of the author as a subject who "authors" himself by means of the story he tells; to adapt Auden, "how can I know who I am until I see what I write?" In which case, the authorial subject realized by *The Sound and the Fury* is an impossibly divided being: simultaneously the patrician (as three-year-old), the historian (as dead historian), and the investor (who cannot yet invest). Lacking authority, this author cannot reconcile himself to finishing the book as a way of coming to political terms with himself. Consequently, section four, nominally omniscient, provides no ending. I make no excuse for omitting April 8, 1928, from my account, as I believe that it has little to do with the novel. Dilsey's resilience, Shegog's brilliant offer of redemption, Jason's concluding exercise in arbitrary power can and have been used to build aesthetic bridges back to what has gone before – along the lines of "the full circle" (as at the first, so at the last, Benjy plus flowers),[76] the four-part symphonic structure,[77] the tightening web of Christian allusions.[78] Some bridges have been thematic – the black community beyond the white fragments,[79] disorder followed by Dilsey's simple order of universal Easter truths,[80] redemption after The Fall. . . . Many are the ways and insights, but none offers convincing answers to the novel's key historical questions: "Who is your father?" "Who is your sister?" "Of what use is your past?" These questions are cultural, and they produce the narrative. Because Faulkner cannot answer them, *The Sound and the Fury* is difficult, unfinishable, and torn apart by contradiction.

2

ABSALOM, ABSALOM!, *HAITI, AND LABOR HISTORY*

READING UNREADABLE REVOLUTIONS

I

In 1791 slaves revolted on San Domingo: "the world's richest colony"[1] was overrun in a black revolution whose forces "defeated the Spanish; inflicted a defeat of unprecedented proportions on the British, and then made their country the graveyard of Napoleon's magnificent army."[2] By 1804 the Americas had their first black national state, the independent republic of Haiti. In 1823 Thomas Sutpen left Virginia for the West Indies, where, in 1827, he put down an uprising among slaves on a French sugar plantation on Haiti. As due recompense, he married the owner's daughter and achieved a son (1829). The dates are important because they indicate that Faulkner has the hero of *Absalom, Absalom!* (1936) "earn" the properties upon which he will eventually base his plantation "design," improperly. There were neither slaves nor French plantations on Haiti in 1827. Faulkner's chronology creates an anachronism that rewrites one of the key facts of nineteenth-century black American history, in what looks suspiciously like an act of literary counterrevolution.

Those Faulkner scholars who notice urge "error"[3] – I am unconvinced. The Haitian revolution had lasting consequences for the slaveholding states of the South where, during the 1790s, white panics about slave revolts were endemic. Indeed, "Saint Domingo [became] the symbol for black liberation struggles throughout the hemisphere and touched off a series of new insurrectionary attempts"[4]: Gabriel Prosser in 1800, Denmark Vessey in 1822, Nat Turner in 1831; to turn to the major North American black rebellions is to discover allusions to Haiti.[5] Nor does the Haitian example fade with the onset of the Civil War. In 1864, in Natchez, ex-slave Mississippi soldiers in the Union Army reacted violently when the city's military commander tried to force freedmen to work aban-

doned plantations; a northern missionary, S. G. Wright, "trembled,"
fearing "blood equalling the day of vengeance in the island of
Hayti."[6] Mary Chesnut's diary entry for July 14, 1865, notes that "on
our place"

> our people were all at home – quiet, orderly, respectful and at
> their usual work. In point of fact things looked unchanged.
> There was nothing to show that any one of them had ever seen
> a Yankee or knew that there was one in existence.

However, she follows her reassuring observations with a piece of un-
attributed gossip: "We are in for a new St. Domingo all the same.
The Yankees have raised the devil, and now they cannot guide
him."[7]

In the South, "Haiti" is synonymous with "revolution," and
whether that be positively or negatively viewed it is not something
about which southern authors with an interest in antebellum history
lightly make mistakes. Moreover, the evidence of *Absalom, Absalom!*
suggests that Faulkner knows more than enough about San Domingo
to put its revolution in the right century. He knows that Haitian soil
is a cemetery on the grandest scale. Accounts of the colony's eigh-
teenth-century slave population vary, but historians agree that death
rates were extremely high; Rod Prince reckons the total number of
slaves imported between 1681 and 1791 at 864,000 and adds that
"some estimates have suggested that the equivalent of the entire
number of slaves was replaced every twenty years."[8] Faulkner notes
that the earth, "manured with black blood from two hundred years
of oppression and exploitation . . . cried out for vengeance."[9] He
knows that French planters were leading purchasers in the eigh-
teenth-century slave trade; C.L.R. James puts the figure for slave imports around 1789 at 40,000 a year,[10] a figure that translates into
Faulkner's sense of an island poised between Africa, ravaged by slav-
ers, and America, seat of "rational" slave production:

> a little island . . . which was the halfway point between what we
> call the jungle and what we call civilization, halfway between
> the dark inscrutable continent from which the black blood . . .
> was ravished by violence, and the cold known land to which it
> was doomed [p. 202]

It is likely that he knows that Vodûn (voodoo) was the initial language of revolt on San Domingo[11] (during the days prior to the
insurrection, Sutpen finds signs made from pigs' bones, feathers,
and rags, signs that he does not recognize as such [p. 203]), and
that the French territory was adjacent to a Spanish colony (Sutpen's

mother-in-law "had been a Spaniard" [p. 203]). Knowing even part
of this, he surely knows "1791"?

Why then pretend otherwise, when to do so implies that Toussaint
L'Ouverture's revolution didn't happen? The answer may, finally,
prove anything but counterrevolutionary. Consider the manner in
which Sutpen suppresses the anomalous uprising; on the eighth
night of seige

> he just put the musket down and had someone unbar the door
> and then bar it behind him, and walked out into the darkness
> and subdued them, maybe by yelling louder, maybe by stand-
> ing, bearing more than they believed any bones and flesh could
> or should . . . maybe at last they themselves turning in horror
> and fleeing from the white arms and legs shaped like theirs
> and from which blood could be made to spurt and flow as it
> could from theirs and containing an indomitable spirit which
> should have come from the same primary fire which theirs
> came from but which could not have, could not possibly have
> [p. 205]

Leaving aside the "maybe[s]" for a moment, it seems that Sutpen
triumphs by demonstrating "white supremacy." What he suffers establishes an absolute separation between white and black insofar as
their points of origin or "primary fire[s]" differ. White proves
stronger than black and causes black to vanish. However, allowing
that Sutpen said only that he "subdued them," the "maybe[s]" indicate that the fuller account derives from the story's line of transmission. The line is clear: Sutpen told General Compson (1835),
who told it to his son, who told Quentin, who tells Shreve (1910).
The options for anecdotal elaboration are several, but because it is
the General to whom we owe the detail of Haiti's bloody horticulture
and the General to whom Sutpen shows his scars (p. 205), it is probably the General who gives us the "spurt and flow" scenario. In
which case, two planters of similar social origin talking in 1835, four
years after the Turner rising,[12] combine to construct a story that
affirms their interest in clear-cut racial mastery, albeit an authority
tempered in rebellious fires. Given white "primary fire," insurrec-
tions will fail and revolutions fade. The supposition is General
Compson's, and the recognition that slavery is an undeclared state
of war, in which black revolution is a permanent risk, is Sutpen's.
His behavior as a slaveholder in Mississippi is eccentric but plain; on
a regular and ritualized basis he organizes and participates in single
combat with his slaves. While clearly the slave codes were designed
to police the peculiar institution on the understanding that black

conspiracy was a fact of planter life, and while it is certain that com-
pulsory pass-systems, complex patterns of surveillance, and "the
obligatory involvement of all white members of the community in
the implementation of the laws"[13] indicate an anticipation of unrest
on the part of what one historian calls "a strung-out society," it is
equally clear that anticipatory understanding among the masters remained deeply tacit. The region *was* strung out because the blacks
were "in the South in such numbers and in such manner as they
were. That manner was recurrently rebellious."[14] Yet few southern
planters, other than at times of disturbance, systematically viewed
their slaves as black Jacobins. To do so would have been to credit
them with a will quite beyond the capacity of a "chattel" or a
"Sambo." The peculiar institution peculiarly demanded that its
managers view their slaves as a threat but also, and simultaneously,
as children of limited will ("things" are will-less). This contradiction
produces the startling mood shifts of which planters were notoriously
capable. Genovese, discussing the slaveholders' need to love those
whom they made suffer, might be characterizing that state of mind
produced by having to trust those who are suspected:

> [Planters] could deny to themselves that in fact they did cause
> suffering, and could assert that their domination liberated the
> slaves from a more deprived existence. Such a view demanded
> "gratitude" [of the slave] . . . and an intimacy that turned every
> act of impudence and insubordination – every act of unsanc-
> tioned self-assertion – into an act of treason and disloyalty, for
> by repudiating the principle of submission it struck at the heart
> of the master's moral self-justification and, therefore, his self
> esteem. Nothing else, apart from personal idiosyncrasy, can ex-
> plain the ferocity and cruelty of masters who normally ap-
> peared kind and even indulgent.[15]

There is little of kindness in Sutpen, who has no time for Sambo;
and his moods, insofar as we see them demonstrated in his actions,
are changeless – he fights African Americans out of Haiti who are
physically his equal. As Haitians they embody that which the plantocracy most fears and must deny – the spirit of revolution. In the
aftermath of 1791, North Carolina passed a law prohibiting the entry
of all West Indian slaves over the age of fifteen, for fear that they
might incite a general slave rebellion; three years later (1798) Gov-
ernor Samuel Ashe, "seeking to suppress the ideology of the Haitian
Revolution," issued a proclamation urging that the landing of all
negroes from the islands be stopped.[16] To suspend the importation
of bodies is not to block news of their acts; as late as 1840, slaves in

South Carolina were interpreting information from Haiti as a projection of their own freedom.[17]

Sutpen imports his Haitian archaisms in 1832. In 1833 he appears
in Yoknapatawpha County, "takes up land, builds his house" (p.
305), and fights his slaves. The house is complete by 1835, but the
fighting continues, as far as I can tell, until about 1850. Sutpen's
persistent and systematized combat is without historical precedent,
as is Faulkner's dating of the San Domingo uprising. However, read
together these anomalies make absolute historical sense. Given that
Faulkner wishes to foreground the continuous potential for revolution within the institution of slavery, he needs Haiti, the only successful black revolution. Given that he wishes to characterize the
plantocracy as a class that suppresses revolution, he requires that his
ur-planter suppress the Haitian revolution and go on doing so. Had
Sutpen's "design" needed only "money in considerable quantities"
(p. 196), as Sutpen claims, Mississippi, as a rapidly evolving frontier
society, would have provided him with ample and historically accurate opportunities. Witness the career of Jason Lycurgus I, father or
grandfather of General Compson, who in 1811 entered Yoknapatawpha in possession of "a pair of fine pistols, one meagre saddle bag
. . . [and] a stronghocked mare";[18] it is doubtful whether Sutpen's
maritime wages amount to as much by the time he lands in San
Domingo (approx. 1820), but neither arriviste arrives with more
than a little, and both found dynasties. Furthermore, had Faulkner
merely wished to add "the capacity to quell slave insurrection" to
the list of "design" "ingredients" (p. 211), he could, with veracity,
have located his hero's first forays, during the 1830s, almost anywhere in the lower South – though South Carolina or Mississippi
would have been ideal, because with populations divided almost
equally between black and white,[19] opportunities for "impudence
and insubordination" were many, and always liable to induce violent
reaction.

My point is finally a simple one – in Sutpen's slaves Faulkner
creates an anomalous archaism; they are historically free and yet
doubly constrained, by a fiction (*Absalom, Absalom!*), and by a counterrevolutionary violence (Sutpen's) that is necessary to the workings
of the plantation system. Sutpen's fights give true title to each measure of labor control in the antebellum South. Southerners might
recognize that when Sutpen "enter[s] the ring" with one of his
slaves, he does so with "deadly forethought," not merely to retain
"supremacy [and] domination" (p. 21) but to enact the preemptive
counterrevolution, crucial to the authority of his class. Furthermore,
the fights are staged as a social education. Attended by white and

black (who form "a hollow square . . . white faces on three sides . . . black ones on the fourth" [p. 20]), the scenes in barn and stable are part of a class apprenticeship; Sutpen's son is required to attend at least once, and his daughters (white and black) watch illicitly. The origin of Sutpen's beaten slave allows Faulkner to posit the slave as black Jacobin (hence Haiti) prior to having the planter put him down. Of course, this cannot be openly acknowledged in any study of the imagination of masters, circa 1830–1850 (hence the suppression of "1791").[20]

Sutpen's belief in the abrasive primacy of his "primary fire" (p. 205) cannot entirely disguise the suspicion that, in getting into the ring in the first place, he has compromised his own "domination," that is to say his own "whiteness." James Snead notes how often in *Absalom, Absalom!* "white" becomes "black," or, in his terms, how frequently "Sutpen and blacks are twinned,"[21] this being conspicuously true of Sutpen and his "wild negroes" (p. 27): we are assured that they "belonged to him body and soul," yet despite being extensions of his will, *they* impose their bodily form on him, so that when they fight, they "should not only have been the same color, but should have been covered with fur too" (pp. 20–1); when they work, only beard and eyes distinguish the master, "the bearded white man" from the "twenty black ones"; all stand "stark naked beneath the croaching and pervading mud" (p. 28). Snead pursues the evidence of crossing in terms of miscegenation:

> These mergings would be less noteworthy if they did not culminate in Sutpen's merging with the one black whom he most wants to distance, his son Charles Bon.[22]

I, however, wish to pause in order to consider merger implications at the level of labor – after all, Sutpen works in the mud with his slaves (p. 28) and harnesses himself to the capstan of a brick kiln with his slaves (p. 27) in order to produce a property that is exclusively his own. His mastery (white), embodied in Sutpen's Hundred (*"Be Light"* [p. 4]), derives from the labor of the slave and is experienced as doing so by a master who almost made himself black to get his Hundred built. To turn from what Sutpen does in constructing a plantation to what he thinks he does (that is, to chapter seven) is to find evidence suggesting that his violent enactment of white supremacy explicitly contradicts his own fuller sense of master/slave relations. From what he tells General Compson, it is clear that he suppresses Haiti, to which one might add that he also suppresses Hegel. I say this because "Lordship and Bondage," chapter four of Hegel's *Phenomenology of Mind*, stands as a useful running-gloss on Sutpen's account of his childhood experience, particularly that of being turned away from a planter's door by a black butler.

Here is Hegel, considerably reduced. The Lord seeks absolute, because independent, authority. At the moment of his supremacy he is troubled because he recognizes, in objects through which he represents that supremacy (to himself), labor that is not his own. He knows that his Lordship depends upon the labor of the bound man:

> just when the master had effectively achieved lordship, he really finds that something has come about quite different from an independent consciousness. It is not an independent consciousness, but rather a dependent consciousness that he has achieved.[23]

The trauma of recognition involves him in an unpassable contradiction; the Lord must extract from his lordship the very materials that define it ("in order to become certain of [himself] . . . as a true being"[24]). Meanwhile, the bound man exists in an equally problematic relation to objects of labor; having experienced himself as a negation, or as nothing other than an extension of his Lord's will (one "whose essence of life is for another"[25]), he too is troubled because he recognizes, in the independent existence of those things made by his hand, the negation of his own prior negation by the Lord:

> Shaping and forming the object has . . . the positive significance that the bondsman becomes thereby the author of himself as factually and objectively self-existent.[26]

Such a moment is uncomfortable in that it requires that the bound man experience both the death of his dependent self and the emergence of an independent self:

> Precisely in labor, where there seems to be some outsider's mind and ideas involved, the bondsman becomes aware, through his re-discovery of himself by himself, of having and being a "mind of his own."[27]

Where the master risks his masterful "self" in the appreciation that the objects of his desire are the products of the slave's hand, the slave risks his abject "self" in the consciousness that his labor not only postpones the master's satisfaction but also produces an object "that is permanent" and remains "after the master's desire is gratified."[28]

Central to Hegel's understanding of "the forms of servitude"[29] are two notions: "recognition" and "death." "Recognition" occurs when a "distinct" self, whether bound or binding, comes to a "completer realization of self in another self"[30] – a process that involves loss "of its own [or initial] self, since it finds itself as an other being."[31] The "other" is, for the master, the slave and his works; for the slave, the "other" is simply his work. Hegel describes the moment of "recognition" as "death," since each self "risks its own life"[32] as it engages in "a life and death struggle" to "come outside itself"[33] into another. Politically speaking, masters must deny "recognition" if they wish to retain their goods and satisfactions. Slaves have several options along a more or less revolutionary spectrum; they can play dead – that is, they can pretend to be the chattels that they know themselves not to be; alternatively, they may pilfer, feign illness, and slow the pace of work,[34] or they can conspire and revolt. Whatever their decision, the bound have before their eyes artifacts that prove their independence. For Hegel, the slave's "recognition" derives directly from his works: "through work and labor the consciousness of the bondsman comes to itself,"[35] or as a freed man put it in the late 1860s, on learning that the Republican Party intended no redistribution of confiscated southern plantations:

> We have built up their houses and cultivated their lands . . . .
> if they were to pay us but twenty five-cents on the dollar, they
> would all be very poor.[36]

II

To return to Sutpen's methods of labor control: I have argued that his fights with Haitian slaves embody his recognition that slavery rests on a continuous repression of revolution. Yet in chapter seven, far from tracing the inception of his plantation "design" to a nascent sense of white supremacy, he roots that "design" on the interdependency of slave and master; the key image is a black butler's "balloon face." In 1835, as they pause from hunting the absconded French architect, whose recapture is essential to the completion of the dynastic house, Sutpen describes to Grandfather Compson the house upon which his house is founded. Just as a glimpse of Caddy's stained drawers, up a tree, is to *The Sound and the Fury*, so the boy Sutpen turned from the Virginian planter's door is to *Absalom, Absalom!*[37] What Sutpen tells the General is his own genesis (circa 1820), central to which is a black face, inside a white door, sending a poor white child around to the back:

> *But I can shoot him.* (Not the monkey nigger. It was not the
> nigger any more than it had been the nigger that his father
> had helped to whip that night. The nigger was just another

balloon face slick and distended with that mellow loud and terrible laughing so that he did not dare to bust it, looking down at him from within the half-closed door during that instant in which, before he knew it, something in him had escaped and – he unable to close the eyes of it – was looking out from within the balloon face just as the man who did not even have to wear the shoes he owned, whom the laughter which the balloon held barricaded and protected from such as he, looked out from whatever invisible place he (the man) happened to be at the moment, at the boy outside the barred door in his patched garments and splayed bare feet, looking through and beyond the boy, he himself seeing his own father and sisters and brothers as the owner, the rich man (not the nigger) must have been seeing them all the time – as cattle, creatures heavy and without grace, brutely evacuated into a world without hope or purpose for them, who would in turn spawn with brutish and vicious prolixity, populate, double, treble and compound, fill space and earth with a race whose future would be a succession of cut-down and patched and made-over garments bought on exorbitant credit because they were white people, from stores where niggers were given the garments free, with for sole heritage that expression on a balloon face bursting with laughter which had looked out at some unremembered and nameless progenitor who had knocked at a door when he was a little boy and been told by a nigger to go around the back): *But I can shoot him*. [pp. 189–190]

As Hegel might have put it, the self "has come outside itself"[38] with a vengeance. Three selves seem to be involved – the boy, the slave, and the master. The problem, contained in the slippery use of the third person pronoun "he," is how to tell them apart. Mapping the comings and goings produces a maze. Move one: "something" escapes the child, enters the black, and looks out with the eyes of the black. Move two: those eyes become the eyes of the owner as he watches from some "invisible place." It should be noted that all three figures are united within the eyes of the slave, whose tripartite gaze considers the boy only momentarily before recasting him as the representative of a "brutish" white tenancy. Move three: perhaps unsurprisingly, the narrator denies sight to the black. The identity of the narrator is elusive,[39] but because the story is told by one would-be dynast to another, we can safely locate the voice within a plantocracy for which the eye of any slave is a problem – it will be remembered that the blacks were forbidden to look directly into the eyes of the whites.[40] However, censorship proves difficult as the composite pronoun resists simplification. The "he," in "he himself," who sees his own family "as the owner, the rich man (not the nigger) must have been seeing them," retains threefold status (boy, black, master); three attempts to modify that interdependency, culminating in an entirely unnecessary parenthesis, add up to protesting too much. Far from taking the black out of the pronoun, the narrator fixes him there more firmly. What "he" witnesses is the genealogy of a class. Sutpen's father "fell" from the mountains of western Virginia to the Tidewater plain, from limited self-sufficiency within a yeoman class to limitless dependency within a tenant class. As poor white tenants the Sutpens are propertyless; that which they stand up in belongs to another, at least until the "exorbitant" debt is paid. As his father's heir Sutpen will have for "sole heritage . . . that expression on a balloon face." Move four: temporary recovery of status by the subject who sees – "[h]e himself seeing . . . as the owner must have been seeing" sees "that expression" on the black butler's face "bursting with laughter." Had the parenthesis stopped there we might safely have assumed that we had come full circle – the boy, having "come out of himself" (Hegel) in order to see himself as master and slave see him (a subject who is an object of contempt), returns to himself standing in front of the planter's door. However, the narrator cannot leave "that expression" alone. Instead, he restarts the cycle, this time with a "nameless" "little boy," soon to be progenitor of yet another who will come to the door . . . ad infinitum. Move five: vicious circling, whose logic would seem to run – Sutpen can never recover himself as an "independent being" (Hegel) because he will always see himself (and his class) from within "the balloon face." Sutpen "sublates": "to sublate," a verb used by Hegel as meaning both "destroy" and "preserve." As Sutpen moves back into himself as child at the door, he destroys what is not himself (black, master), only to recognize that he has preserved it within a new and modified self (boy, black, master). Ethnically speaking, the black has entered all available subject positions. Move six: exit again, toward the balloon, on the recognition that the emphasis has changed in two respects – the laughter, which up to this point had "distended" the balloon face that "held" it, bursts. In addition, the boy is "nameless." Sutpen no longer stands among "his father and sister and brothers." Instead, that part of him which "escaped" into the balloon face laughs at the class whose future is no longer his; the butt of the joke is Sutpen's "progenitor" – Sutpen himself, at the moment of knocking on the door, and prior to the complex witnessing of the "monkey nigger['s]" face. The social migrations

of Sutpen's "self" occur within a single parenthesis that, because it
is placed between a reiteration, takes the form of an ellipsis. The
ellipsis effectively contains and predicts the dynastic narrative of *Absalom, Absalom!* Sutpen will shoot "him"; that is to say, he will shoot
a master, contained in a slave, who is also Sutpen's future "self."
Neither the bracket nor its implied ellipsis can finally repress Sutpen's trauma over labor and its consequences. The labor lord's life,
in more ways than one, will turn on his lordship over labor. But I
run, riddling, ahead of myself. Here, it is necessary simply to stress
that the boy's experience is crucial, disturbing, and attended by
laughter.

But who laughs? Balloons can be made to bray and whinny by
releasing breath under pressure through their rubbery lips (we are
close to racial epithet). The breath and mouth are equally important
in this exercise. The epithet is undercut because, although the
breath depends upon the master (plus Sutpen), the laughter depends upon the mouth (the slave, plus Sutpen, plus the master).
Faulkner uses the balloon image three times in the space of four
pages, each time problematizing agency by implying the question:
"who empowers whom?" I have space only for one instance; spec-
ulating on the butler's effect, Sutpen recalls his father's "whipping"
of "one of Pettibone's niggers" (p. 187):

> He could even seem to see them: the torch-disturbed darkness
> among the trees, the fierce hysterical faces of the white men,
> the balloon face of the nigger. Maybe the nigger's hands would
> be tied or held but that would be alright because they were
> not the hands with which the balloon face would struggle and
> writhe for freedom, not the balloon face: it was just poised
> among them, levitative and slick with paper-thin distension.
> Then someone would strike the balloon one single desperate
> and despairing blow and then he would seem to see them flee-
> ing, running, with all about them, overtaking them and passing
> and going on and then returning to overwhelm them again,
> the roaring waves of mellow laughter meaningless and terrify-
> ing and loud. And now he stood there before that white door
> ... [pp. 187–8]

The hands are illusive. Three sets are in evidence: those of the captive, those of his captors, and an unidentified third pair; arguably,
the missing name is Pettibone, because he, as master, inflates the
balloon within which he lives. To damage his "nigger" is to damage
his goods; ergo, his hands struggle with those who would damage
his property. But why would white hands "writhe for [a] freedom"

they already have? The question is unanswerable unless, in the light
of the white door, it is recognized that the planter longs to be free
of suppressed dependency upon the sustaining but "unessential consciousness" of the bound man. The balloon face imprisons Pettibone
even as it empowers him. Given Sutpen's subsequent recognition
that from the perspective of the master his father's class is nasty,
"brutish," and long, it could be argued that white tenants avenge
themselves on their landlords by an abuse of lordly chattels.[41] Class
conflict might rage within the balloon (master against himself) and
around the balloon (tenant against master) while the balloon would
remain impervious. Sutpen's speculations, presumably annotated by
a narrator (witness "levitative"), grant the victim an impersonal pronoun; the pronoun, "it," may excuse the victimizers by rendering
their object less human, but equally, coming after a colon, and so
seeking to encapsulate the preceding clash of more or less identified
hands, "it" translates the "he" who suffers into a site where masked
forces of class "struggle" darkly. Who strikes whom remains obscure.
In conditions of such interdependency, blows are liable to fall an-
onymously ("someone") and to appear "despairing," because victimizers call themselves victims, and victims sense victory. The
laughter in the dark is as awkward here as that which "bursts" across
Sutpen's memory of the butler; moreover, its arc, described as the
motion of a deflating balloon ("overtaking . . . and passing and going on and then returning to overwhelm"), parallels Sutpen's sense
of self-evacuation under pressure from the butler's ballooning gaze:

> he seemed to kind of dissolve and a part of him to turn and
> rush back . . . like when you pass through a room fast and look
> at all the objects in it and you turn and go back through the
> room again and look at all the objects from the other side [p.
> 186]

Both instances involve dissolution on a scale tantamount to Marx's
"everything that is solid melts into air," where the solvent is not
capital but the complex breath of he who would claim mastery while
denying the labor that sustains him.

Almost enough of balloons, save only to add that the epithet
"slick," applied three times in these pages, is transferred in modified
form to the architecture of the plantation itself:

> that smooth white house and that smooth white brass-
> decorated door and the very broadcloth and linen and silk
> stocking the monkey nigger stood in [p. 189]

As "slick" becomes "smooth," with some prompting from the butler's "silk," so black becomes white, even as the entire edifice of the
plantocracy rises upon the unstable surface of black labor's face.

Grandfather Compson will later call Sutpen's problem "innocence" (p. 178); he is wrong. Sutpen's solution is innocence; his
problem is his disorientating insight into the dependencies of slave
production. What he sees is traumatic because it leaves him no possibility of an un-enslaved life. To state it at its most phenomenological, which is how Sutpen experiences it, he knows that what he
breathes is the breath of slaves, and that he will breathe it no matter
where he sits in the hierarchy.

His first move is to remove himself. He "crawl[s]" into a hole in
the ground, a "cave" made by a fallen tree where he sits "with his
back against the uptorn roots" (p. 188). His regression is twofold,
from human nature to nature, and from cotton production to self-
sufficiency (that of the hunter, the cave is a "den beside [a] game
trail"). Both removals are illusory. In the cotton South, the earth
itself is a fact of labor, whose meaning is inseparable from the dominant form of work. Sutpen knows this, at least in 1835, because he
prefaces his description of the cave with an earlier memory; as a boy,
he and his sister had refused to give way to a coach approaching
from behind – the black coachman swerved in time, but only just,
and Sutpen found himself "throwing vain clods of dirt after the dust
as it spun on."

> knowing now, while the monkey-dressed nigger butler kept the
> door barred with his body while he spoke, that it had not been
> the nigger coachman that he threw at all, that it was the actual
> dust raised by the proud delicate wheels, and just that vain [p.
> 187]

Faulkner shares Sutpen's evaluation; in a letter to Harrison Smith
(February 1934), he summarizes *Absalom, Absalom!* as follows:
"Roughly, the theme is a man who outraged the land, and the land
then turned and destroyed the man's family."[42] "Clod," "dust,"
"land". . . inorganic matter becomes an agent (whether as target or
destroyer) only because it is marked by human projects. As Sartre
puts it:

> I need only to glance out of the window: I will be able to see
> cars which are men and drivers who are cars . . . and instru-
> ments (pavements, a thoroughfare, a taxi rank, a bus stop . . .
> proclaiming with their frozen voices how they are to be used).
> These [are] beings – neither thing nor man, but practical uni-

ties made up of man and inert thing. . . . Later I will go down
into the street and become their thing.[43]

To apply this Parisian glance to the cotton lands of the antebellum
South is to see "clod" and "dust" as "beings" insofar as they are
"worked things"[44] that consequently issue imperatives and contain
futures. Virginian "dust" early in the nineteenth century is an en-
semble of human practices, chief among them slavery; but to Sutpen
on a dirt road, standing in it, the dust is that which will make him
its thing, least among its many things (lumpen labor). Of course, it
can do this only because, as the container of persistent practices, it
contains a sentence that some men have passed on other men.[45]
Under other systems dust issues alternative instructions, hence Sutpen's boyhood regression to memories of self-sufficiency. In the
mountains of western Virginia (circa 1807–20),[46] land was what you
hunted over; it "belonged to anybody and everybody" (p. 179), a
property in common from which men took only what they needed
and could hold on to. The dust in such places instructs, "carry a big
gun, since by your prowess shall your individual right to a portion
of that which is common be ensured." Sutpen's concern with the
"mountain man" who "happened to own a fine rifle" (pp. 185, 189,
192) obeys the imperative of these lands at this time. But Sutpen
also knows that among those who "eat" and "swap" there will be
those who "fence off a piece of land," and while they may not say
"this is mine" (p. 179), should they raise grain or perhaps even
tobacco on that land, the putative self-sufficiency of their household
production will at some point be implicated in a more general and
cotton-centered southern economy. Establishing exactly when the
readiness of a self-sufficient household to produce for a plantation
market ties the values of the householder to those of the planter is
difficult.[47] But Sutpen, with his back to an uprooted tree in 1820,
recalls mountains to which his "woodman's instinct" can no longer
return him (p. 184); furthermore, he is being recalled by Sutpen as
he hunts his plantation architect in 1835. The mountains of 1807
look irrelevant from the cotton lands nearly thirty years later, and
their values are anachronistic – small wonder that Sutpen tells General Compson that "his own rifle analogy" could not help with the
black butler (p. 192).

Very little can. Sutpen is forced to fall back on labor – almost all
that he has experienced – to take the "measure" of what he has
seen (p. 188). He catalogues the forms of work that he knows. Hunting (irrelevant). His father's Tidewater tasks, unspecified beyond
tenancy (irrelevant, since the butler does not bother to inquire after

the message that Sutpen carries from his father to the planter). His sister's brutal domestic work at the washtub (irrelevant; she is little more than things in process, "[a] shapeless . . . calico dress," an "old man's shoes," "pumping," though what she does strikes him as "the very primary essence of labor," in that it is "toil, reduced to its crude absolute" [p. 191]). The work of the master (inessential because slight, consisting of little more than receipt of drinks while in a "barrel stave hammock" [p. 184]). Indeed, so minimal is the master's labor that Sutpen speculates whether he who has a servant to put the glass in his hand and to pull the boot from his foot has others to chew, swallow, and breathe for him (p. 180).[48] If so, the master does not live. He is dead, and his servants do his living for him. The labor of the slave (essential, since the slave's services to the lord's body give that body its substance, "protect" that body [p. 190], and provide it with the vantage point from which it may dismiss, as irrelevant, the labor of surrounding bodies).

The implications of Sutpen's labor list appear plain; he who would be master must have "niggers and a fine house" (p. 192), which is why Sutpen goes to the West Indies. However, to be master is also to depend upon the labor that you dismiss, to be all but dead, and to rest enclosed in the head of a slave. Mastery on such terms is difficult. Sutpen becomes a planter in Mississippi (1835) only because what happens in Haiti (1827) allows him to repress what he saw in western Virginia (1820). Put tersely, Sutpen can raise the Hundred because, having experienced slavery as the suppression of revolution, he can, in his own defense, displace his knowledge that the master's mastery depends upon the body and the consciousness of the bound man. Again, Haiti is the key, but repression is not easy. The fights with the Haitian slaves (1835–50), read within this sequence, mark the return and control of repressed materials; only by "gouging" at the revolutionary eyes (p. 20) on the balloon face can Sutpen preserve the separateness of his "primary fire" (p. 205). Of course, in demonstrating that his whiteness does not depend upon blackness he contradicts himself, since to those who watch in the barn, his whiteness turns black:

> . . . and Ellen seeing not the two black beasts she had expected to see but instead a white one and a black one, both naked to the waist and gouging at one another's eyes as if their skins should . . . have been the same color [p. 20]

Sutpen constructs his integrity as master through a combination of violence and "innocence." The term, appealed to by most who tell the story, derives from General Compson and the conversation

of 1835, during which the General offers a detailed account of its
origin, rooting "innocence" in labor experience. Having returned
from plantation threshold to tenant cabin, the boy rethinks the
house servant's refusal to consider his father's message:

> And then he [Sutpen] said that all of a sudden it was not think-
> ing, it was something shouting it almost loud enough for his
> sisters on the other pallet and his father in the bed with the
> two youngest and filling the room with alcohol snoring, to hear
> too: *He never even give me a chance to say it. Not even to tell it, say it*:
> it too fast, too mixed up to be thinking, it all kind of shouting
> at him at once, boiling out and over him like the nigger laugh-
> ing: *He never gave me a chance to say it and Pap never asked me if I*
> *told him or not and so he cant even know that Pap sent him any message*
> *and so whether he got it or not cant even matter, not even to Pap; I went*
> *up to that door for that nigger to tell me never to come to that front door*
> *again and I not only wasn't doing any good to him by telling it or any*
> *harm to him by not telling it, there aint any good or harm either in the*
> *living world that I can do to him.* It was like that, he said, like an
> explosion – a bright glare that vanished and left nothing, no
> ashes nor refuse; just a limitless flat plain with the severe shape
> of his intact innocence rising from it like a monument; that
> innocence instructing him as calm as the others had ever spo-
> ken, using his own rifle analogy to do it with, and when it said
> *them* in place of *he* or *him*, it meant more than all the human
> puny mortals under the sun that might lie in hammocks all
> afternoon with their shoes off [p. 192]

I quote at length in order to emphasize the labor-based nature of
the trauma and to explore the manner of the coverup. As so often
on this day, agency is composite ("mixed up"). Sutpen receives
warning of his irrelevance – because of the irrelevance of his words
– from a voice whose status is unclear. The "something" that shouts
is not a "thought," and, given its apparent availability to others in
the room, appears to derive from outside the boy's consciousness.
Whatever shouts at him (his voice, an interior voice, the voice of
another or others) resembles "nigger laughing" and so in this context may well owe its origin to the problematic "balloon face." As
some "*thing*" carried on the master's/black's breath, addressing an
issue of labor, and identified most consistently by the impersonal
pronoun "it," it becomes a vocalization of the very "things" that
work produces. Because masters, according to the boy, don't work,
and because the voice declares that the labor of poor whites has no

substance, the "thing" that speaks is the work of the slave's hand. Other pronouns prove polyvalent; witness the "he" "which gave the boy no chance to say." Sutpen has earlier identified an italicized "he" as "(not the nigger now either)" (p. 191). However, his parenthesis occurs prior to the problems of "it," and consequently the pronoun ("he") retains its tendency to shift between planter and house servant, in which case the "he" whom Sutpen acknowledges as beyond harm is master and slave in the fullness of their interdependency.

Sutpen recognizes that he and his class cannot affect the master class; his recognition, involving a simultaneous acknowledgment that the substantiality of the master is inextricable from the works of the slave, is explosive. But Sutpen's term, "explosion," is modified in the telling. The labor materials so central to the boy's trauma are suppressed. The speaking "thing[s]" are silenced, and in their place "innocence" instructs. The awkward "it" is simplified so that "when it said *them* in place of *he* or *him*," "it," innocently renamed, refers to the planter as a class type whose unenigmatic properties are to be countered by possession of equally unenigmatic properties ("land and niggers and a fine house"). The modification is achieved in two swift steps: "explosion" is replaced by a synonym, "bright glare," whose emphasis falls less on damage than on illumination; brightness so obscures the work of dark hands that neither ashes (dark marks) nor refuse (refusal) remains. I am reminded of Quentin's equally hygienic "*Be Light*" (p. 4), where biblical reference and architectural expectation as to plantations and whitewash ally to obscure twenty Haitians and one master, united in labor and mud. Step two; in the space made by erasure a "monument" of overtly sexual design is raised, its shape both phallic and "intact." Gone is Sutpen's debilitating vision of slave production as the free passage of black bodies into white through labor. Instead, "innocence" grants male authority by expelling the black body from the white, which, cleansed of traumatic stain, may claim "integrity." Sex displaces labor to cast "integrity" as virginity, care not of Sutpen but of Rosa Coldfield; "intact" complements Sutpen's claim to have been a virgin on his wedding night (p. 200),[49] but its shape is hymeneal and echoes Mr. Compson's vision of Rosa's hymen-rampant:

> Perhaps she even saw herself as an instrument of retribution: if not in herself an active instrument strong enough to cope with him, at least as a kind of passive symbol of inescapable reminding to rise bloodless and without dimension from the sacrificial stone of the marriage-bed. [p. 48]

Asked (in 1862) by Ellen (her sister) to save Judith (her niece), Rosa (according to Mr. Compson) installs herself in the Hundred to await Sutpen's return from the Civil War (1865). More particularly she installs herself in the bed chamber, where her spectral slightness serves, in a metaphorical reworking, to heal her sister's hymen; the repair protects Judith by gathering her back (unborn) into the generic integrity of Coldfield womankind. This fantasy belongs to Mr. Compson (care of Quentin) but takes its preoccupations from the Cult of Southern Womanhood, which raised the standard of the unbreachable hymen in order to counter fears over miscegenation.[50] My point here, however, is merely to note just how far the antecedents of a single word – "intact" – have carried us from an "explosion" as it is used in 1820. Sutpen's experience is all too easily lost under the interpretive parentheses of his narrators. Mr. Compson and Quentin combine to translate labor fears into sexual fears, thereby producing a more local and manageable problem. Sutpen's sexuality *will* eventually bring his house down; it does not and cannot bring down the plantation as a system of production.

III

Of course, to blame narrators is to simplify Sutpen, who in 1861 can no longer afford to see what he saw in 1820. After Haiti, and with the Hundred built, he has to control his memory. However, his transition to full planter status remains awkward; for three years, between 1835 and 1838, with house built and cotton in the ground, he refuses to emerge through marriage into dynasty (p. 30) and instead uses his property against the grain of its imperatives. He retains himself in archaic form as "a fine rifle" (p. 185), employing his house as a hunting lodge. Implicitly, he is loath to commit himself to full slave production and to its peculiar form of mastery. In 1864, after twenty-three growing seasons, Sutpen may be said successfully to have pursued the public logic of his wealth; as a result, on entering General Compson's legal office to renew their conversation, he can deny his earlier insight, describing "the boy-symbol" as "just the figment of the amazed and desperate child" (p. 210).

To gloss – the practice of slaveholding has allowed him to repress his knowledge of the interdependence of slave and master. Further, three years into the Civil War, he is prepared to compound repressions by declaring a complete absence of class antagonism between slaveholding and nonslaveholding whites. Tenant and planter, upcountry yeoman and Black Belt lord elide as he tells his class ally how, were a "nameless" boy to come to his "white door" "now," "he would take that boy in" (p. 210). As one elected Confederate officer to another, with the war going badly and desertion particularly high among yeomen from the hill counties,[51] Sutpen needs a vision of southern unity. He, and every other planter, on "look[ing] ahead along the still undivulged light rays," hopes to see a Confederate future, with white "doors," "bigger" and "whiter" than their Virginian prototypes, still intact, and with at each of them, if necessary, a poor white child welcomed into an independent slaveholding republic. Without such images, planter hegemony, strained to the breaking point by 1864, could not hope to counter yeoman claims that this was "a rich man's war and a poor boy's fight."[52] Sutpen's reworking of the boy at the door is a piece of Confederate utopianism that still has resonance in 1910 for at least one grandchild of the plantocracy. Shreve interrupts Quentin's retelling to observe, "Dont say it's just me that sounds like your old man" (p. 210). Quentin extends the echo:

> *Maybe we are both Father. . . . Yes, we are both Father. Or maybe Father and I are both Shreve, maybe it took Father and me both to make Shreve or Shreve and me both to make Father or maybe Thomas Sutpen to make all of us.* [p. 210]

Given that his Harvard fees derive from the sale of some of his grandfather's landed property, Quentin is, in a very real sense, Sutpenmade, a product of planter efforts to ensure their class continuity.

Failure to hear Sutpen's insistence that the boy at the door would be admitted "now," in 1864, deprives the image of historical and political specificity. Dirk Kuyk rewrites 1864 as 1933 when, "in the midst of the Depression . . . plenty of nameless strangers were knocking at front doors" – so Sutpen becomes a New Dealer, seeking "to teach society the lesson that those lucky enough to have risen above brutehood should at least care about the feelings of the unlucky."[53] Further to the right stands Carolyn Porter's Sutpen, whose career, "conducted in the name of equality," is dedicated to "vindicating the American dream itself."[54] Both descend from Sutpen out of Cleanth Brooks, whose antecedents are Henry James's *The American* and Scott Fitzgerald's *The Great Gatsby*, as literary representations of a generically "American neurosis."[55] Sutpen, like Newman and Gatsby, is a self-made pursuant of an "abstract idea" that, because its form is "money" and its practice "the Protestant work ethic," may be said to be "a characteristically American aberration."[56] These Sutpens show scant concern for a dependent labor system; indeed, each celebrates "the idea that the cash nexus offer[s] a permissible basis for human relations"[57] – anathema to the antebellum planter. They are "capitalist entrepreneur[s],"[58] whose intense and various espousal of "human perfectibility" (Brooks),[59] "the principle of social equality" (Porter),[60] and radical egalitarianism (Kuyk)[61] must presumably be premised upon a thoroughly bourgeois faith in the individual as "free," "equal," and "autonomous."

Such Sutpens bear no traceable relation to the boy of 1820, or indeed to the man revising that boy in 1864. However, Brooks seems to have a point when he reminds us that Sutpen believes that his first wife will not object to being put aside, because he (Sutpen) "was willing to make a just and even generous property settlement for her benefit."[62] Brooks cites the cash nexus, and certainly there is much talk of "valuation," "schedule[s]," "compensatory amounts of time," and two-party agreements (p. 212). But this is not simply the language of bourgeois contract. Sutpen breaks his marriage when he learns that Eulalia is black; as a free black woman in the West Indies, she may freely enter contractual agreements, but were she to visit the South she would have to prove her "free" status and without proof would be designated a slave, sans contractual rights. Her child (as Haitian born) would similarly be "free" but required to prove it, and would therefore stand constrained by popular assumption. His ability to enter into contracts would be compromised, unless he chose to "pass." It follows that Sutpen enters into a contract with persons who, on racial grounds, in the antebellum South have no contractual rights. Sutpen omits to tell General Compson why he repudiates Eulalia, but knowing what Quentin and Shreve suppose about her antecedents, we may read his market lexicon both as inappropriate and as contrived to obscure racial trauma. Brooks misses the historical subtext. Sutpen's discovery that his first family is "black" marks the return of his childhood recognition that a white skin emerges from a laboring black body; whether that labor produces property as cotton or property as person is less significant than the fact that Eulalia's child is potentially a white dynast in a black skin. So read, "explosion" rather than "abstract" calculation informs the repudiation.

Brooks mistakes Sutpen's motives. Porter makes a stronger case for the structural nature of his "design." Her case runs . . . Sutpen's "dream of parental authority,"[63] far from tying him to Genovese's pre-bourgeois planters, typifies the degree to which he and they espouse market liberalism, since "paternalism" was throughout the first half of the nineteenth century another name for the nastier forms of bourgeois appropriation. Witness Andrew Jackson's fatherly removal of Indians, temporarily designated "docile children," as a prelude to being recast as underfed or dead. With "paternalism . . .

from the outset serv[ing] one interest . . . that of Capital," Porter's Sutpen, a "grandiose" father, "merit[ing] the analogy with King David implied by the novel's title," allows Faulkner to explore the self-contradicting logic of market paternalism which "logically dictates that fathers exile and repudiate their sons."[64] Her argument is worth stating more fully:

> As Faulkner explained, Sutpen was "a man who wanted sons and got sons who destroyed him" as a result of his failure to recognize that he was "a member . . . of the human family." Herein lies the central irony of Sutpen's dream of founding a dynasty. In the name of his patriarchal design, Sutpen ruthlessly violates the bonds of love and blood with stunning consistency. He repudiates one wife and refuses to recognize his eldest son . . . he turns one son into the murderer of the other. . . . Needless to say, these are not the acts of a benign paternalistic planter in a panama hat and a white suit; these are the acts of a character of mythic dimension in whose career is inscribed the history of America itself, revealing, for one thing, the irony of paternal authority in the name of which Africans were enslaved.[65]

But Sutpen is no kind of paternalist; he treats his Haitians as Jacobins, not as children. Nor, despite his interpreters, does he regard Bon as a son; in this instance, neither paternity nor miscegenation is *his* problem. Witness how he names his Haitian child; Quentin, citing his father and his father's father, notes:

> Father said he probably named him himself. Charles Bon. Charles Good. . . . Grandfather believed, just as he named them all – the Charles Goods and the Clytemnestras [pp. 213–14][66]

Bon: Good: Goods . . . the pun is cruelly obvious and is recognized as apt by a tradition whose authority over labor extended to the naming of new slaves, whether new by birth or by purchase. Planters were entitled to declare their title or property within a slave by naming that slave as they wished, and in so doing they deadened the slave's right by birth to human connections. Orlando Patterson describes this renaming as "natal death."[67] Sutpen does not deny his son his patronym, since Eulalia does not give birth to a "son" but to "goods," and in naming him as such Sutpen declares Bon dead and himself an "owner," not a "father." A residue of the psychic cost of this is contained in Faulkner's choice of name for Sutpen's wife; the root of Eulalia is Eula, Greek for joy – a term that threatens to release "good" from "goods"; "joy," however, is negated by a marital context in which the bride's "trick" (p. 218) of obscuring her origins prompts an additional letter (r), so that "joy" is tacitly canceled by Faulkner himself (Eula-liar). He calls Bon's grandson Jim Bond, in a complex nomination that underwrites my device of the additional letter. However, much more is involved. Quentin encounters the simpleton Jim Bond on his visit to the Hundred in 1909; after telling of that visit, he takes to his Harvard bed, "rigid" and silently quoting from "The Raven":

> "Nevermore of peace. Nevermore of peace. Nevermore. Nevermore. Nevermore" [pp. 298–9]

His choice is fitting, since Poe's poem features a talking bird that settles on "the pallid bust of Pallas"[68] to torment the poem's already disturbed narrator. Poe's selection of perch (referred to three times) is doubtless color-led – an "ebony" bird on a white head. Pallas euphonically yields "pallid" but is also another name for Minerva, goddess of wisdom, who, it is popularly supposed, sprang from the split skull of her father, Jupiter. Poe's black bird is an obscurely wise headache, and in quoting it Quentin may well be attending, through its choric word, "Nevermore," to the choric cry of another obscure blackbird. "Jim Bond," in the context of "The Raven," euphoniously yields "Jim Crow" because the semantics of the pun, "bond," have it so. "Bond," whether as "shackle" or "binding agreement," contains the idea of constraint. The name was presumably given at birth (1882), and although the network of Jim Crow laws, disenfranchising southern blacks, was not fully in place as a legal system until the 1890s, one of the first instances of such legislation was adopted by the Tennessee legislature in 1881.[69] Jim Bond is birdlike in another sense; he is that which cannot be caught. He can be heard, but Quentin and Shreve agree "they couldn't catch him" (pp. 300 and 302); further, Quentin admits on the novel's final page that he "still hear[s] him at night sometimes." Jim Bond may have vanished when the Hundred burned in 1910, but his howling persistence in Quentin's head (whether or not annotated as black wisdom liable to split white skull) provides Shreve with the pattern for his final and infamous joke:

> I think that in time the Jim Bonds are going to conquer the western hemisphere. Of course it wont quite be in our time and of course as they spread toward the poles they will bleach out again like the rabbits and the birds do, so they wont show up so sharp against the snow. But it will still be Jim Bond; and

so in a few thousand years, I who regard you will also have
sprung from the loins of African kings. [pp. 302–3]

Just as Minerva, having been eaten in fetal form along with her
mother, by Jupiter her father, sprang black and birdlike from the
paternal skull,[70] so Jim Bond, constrained to be little more than a
loud thing, will prove seminal, once it is recognized that his blackness, as that which gave substance to white bodies, also provided
them with their true patronym. The joke is metamorphic: Bond's
bleached-out bird, under pressure from "snow," transforms into se-
men, becoming a flutter in the "rabbit" loins of an African king. By
means of innuendo and contortion Shreve suggests that his and
Quentin's heirs (like Bon's before them) will eventually descend
from a great black father. His is a joke against white paternalism,
which turns the novel upside down in a manner owing much to
Sutpen's key recognition of 1820. Shreve, like the boy at the door,
though with different emphasis, points out that white "comes" from
black: an insight that allows him to retell the Sutpen story, in its last
and most minimal form, as a story of black paternity.

Quentin, still in bed, still "rigid" but now "panting," is shocked
– not by a reworking of the one about miscegenation (*"I'm the nigger
that's going to sleep with your sister"* [p. 286]); he's already heard that
earlier in the evening – but by his own response to the joke and to
the question that follows it: "Why do you hate the South?"

> 'I dont hate it,' Quentin said, quickly, at once, immediately; 'I
> dont hate it,' he said, *I dont hate it* he thought, panting in the
> cold air, the iron New England dark: *I dont. I dont! I dont hate
> it! I dont hate it!* [p. 303]

His reaction is automatic but not immediately meaningful. That
which he does not apparently hate – "the South" – appears too
generic to signify anything in particular.[71] What significance there is
seems, in the first instance, to reside in euphony. The rhythm of
denial precisely recalls Quentin's earlier use of Poe's negatives; he
offered five "nevermores"; Poe's raven croaked the word seven
times; Quentin gives us seven denials. Moreover, Quentin's two re-
iterations echo each other in their format, both consisting of two
phrases, one short, one longer, each staccato. I labor their affinity
because rhythm is not customarily considered a key semantic element outside a poem. Yet here, Quentin's denial, recalling his prior
use of Poe's denial, also calls into itself an awkward signifying chain
running from the raven and the crow, through Bond and Eulalia to
Bon, and so to Sutpen's designation of his "son" as "goods." If all

that falls into place as an archaeology imminent within the repetition, semanticizing its euphony, what is it that Quentin denies?

The manner of that denial is difficult, given that by saying "no" so often he seems to contradict himself, affirming his hate. But either way, affirm or deny, what object does he address? Of what southern thing or event does he think? My answer is unnervingly specific – "Bon," not as a person (fictional or real) but as an associative path through a collection of words, leading back to Sutpen's act of naming, that is, to the owner's translation of a nominal son into real property (Sutpen believes, quite literally, that he has "paid" [p. 220] in acres and slaves for Eulalia's labor and "goods"). As I have already argued, Sutpen's choice of the name "Bon" derives from and represses a prior event (the turning away from the planter's door). By calling the slave who "comes" from his own white body "goods," Sutpen disclaims his earlier vision of the master's white mastery emerging from the body of black labor. The term "Bon" proves to be less a name than a collection of verbal traces obstructing the trauma to which they refer. This "Bon" is what Quentin sees and does and does not hate. Paralyzed indecision is par for his circumstance; he retells Sutpen's story in 1910 because his Harvard place is paid for by the sale of ex–plantation land. His is a region where white bodies and accumulations "spr[i]ng" from the work of black bodies; to know as much is to know that you must deny it, should you wish to remain at Harvard, and perhaps alive.

Since "Bon" comes to mean so much, I had best reprise how so much meaning came upon it. My attempt to explain a single act of naming (Bon) led me to a small group of names (Bon, Eulalia, Bond). Attracted by the euphonies, puns, contortions, and distortions released by their conjunction, I find that I have discovered a labyrinth, zigzagging through space and time from Haiti to Harvard, and from 1820 to 1910.[72] My textual stratagems would be entirely pointless, and lacking in any functional relation to *Absalom, Absalom!*, without the instigatory force of Sutpen's traumatic experience in western Virginia. What he saw was, in effect, slave labor's primal scene, which scarcely happens before it is repressed, and to which no planter or planter's child or grandchild can give credence. He witnessed the simple and debilitating truth of slave production, that the master's body is made by the slave's work: a fact that casts ethnic interdependency as white dependency. It should be stressed that in the antebellum South sexual production literally resembled cotton production, insofar as both yielded a crop that could be taken to market. With the banning of the overseas trade in slaves (1808), miscegenation was always liable to become another way in which slaves made goods for masters. By naming Bon for property, Sutpen suppresses a trauma whose force continues to distort the working of the very word through which he attempted suppression. In pursuing "Bon" and its network of related names, I have produced an interminable decipherment that at any and every point risks reencrypting that story's unbearable truth.

IV

That "truth" would not trouble a capitalist. After my detour through "Bon," I return to what prompted it, to Carolyn Porter's claim that Sutpen's paternalism makes him a typical liberal capitalist of the first half of the nineteenth century. It is undoubtedly true that the antebellum planter was "deeply embedded in the world market,"[73] in that his products tied him to the western capitalist order. Cotton, sugar, and tobacco are the staples of Europe's midcentury consumer boom.[74] However, it is equally apparent that at the level of production, rather than those of distribution or consumption, his preferred labor relations are distinct from the labor relations of those with whom he trades. Indeed, the southern planter class stood in increasingly hostile relation to the northern bourgeoisie, eventually choosing "to wage a 'civil war' in order to break free from its political and economic ties within a bourgeois national state."[75] The bone of contention was slavery and the South's determination to defend its distinctive system of labor.

Because Sutpen's "design" is to become a planter, he is perhaps best understood through his status as a distinctive labor lord. Had he been a northern capitalist he would have paid wages, thereby declaring himself "independent" of his "free" employees, since in the bourgeois market place those who contract together, whether as purchaser or seller of labor, do so under the assumption that each of them is a "free" and "independent" unit. Contract is an institution that both separates and equalizes its signatories, or so the story goes; a contract to exchange wages for labor is at least nominally noncoercive, implying that those who sign do so "freely" and even "equally" insofar as both parties are property owners (one of the means of production [plant], the other of the means to labor [body]). "Everyone shall be free, and shall respect the freedom of others. . . . Everyone possesses *his own* body as a free tool of his will."[76] Such an agreement between "free" entities may grant them only "an equal opportunity to attain inequality"[77] but is premised on the existence of each party as the possessor of a "free," "equal," and "autonomous" will, expressed through property. Contract cushions the hirer; he need feel no dependence on the hired because contractually he purchases only a part of the laborer (his labor power) and may freely discard that part whenever it serves his own best interest to do so, not least because the hired hand is equally and contractually "free" to take his "independent" "tool" elsewhere.

Manifestly under slavery the bound laborer is not "free," and any suggestion that he might possess "rights" or "will," independent of the will of his lord, strikes at the working of the entire system because it threatens the grounds upon which the owner owns and uses the slave:

> When a slaveowner purchases a slave he or she acquires, not the use of the slave's labor-power – not, that is, only part of the slave's activities – but the slave's labor – all the activities in which the slave engages. The fundamental social relation of slavery is thus total, engaging the full personalities of the slave-owner and the slave.[78]

Bourgeois contract turns on "partial relations"[79] that direct the owner to ignore aspects of a worker's person or circumstance that are unrelated to production. Slave production turns on relations of personal dependency, which are "total,"[80] involving the whole life of masters and the whole life of slaves. Of course, the whole life of a slave is wholly negated if he or she is reduced to a chattel; nonetheless, even total subordination (without which basic precept slavery cannot work[81]) commits the owner to the whole life-as-living-death of the owned, in a way that bourgeois paternalism (freed by contract to be as finally irresponsible as it may wish) only pretends to do.

Planters were bound by ties of interdependency to their bound labor. They could and did disguise this fact in all manner of ways, but they could not and did not perceive their activities through the language of bourgeois individualism, because, as the Genoveses put it, "opportunities for individual autonomy" were limited in the antebellum South.[82] Which is another way of saying, contra Brooks and Porter, that Sutpen is no capitalist because he founds his design on relations quite other than those between capitalist and free labor:

> Slaves and masters . . . occupied the same social household. To the extent that this environment contributed to the individual identity of each, it contributed to their self definition relative to each other. The paternalistic forms it generated carried a far greater psychological force because of that common base, and the scope of autonomous identity and activity were re-

duced by the extent of mutual dependence. [the Geneveses][83]

Sutpen's vision of the consequences of mutual dependence as white dependency leads him away from paternalism as a language through which to address the relations of slavery. Paternalism does not suppress enough for Sutpen because, in its presentation of the master as "father" to an extended black family, it not only posits black gratitude in return for white responsibility but also implies filial rights, thereby contradicting "the principle of submission" lying "at the heart of the master's self justification."[84] Haiti allows Sutpen to go for total submission, becoming Judge Rifkin sans sensitivity, because having experienced a private revolution in Virginia and having enacted a necessary counterrevolution in Haiti, he can do nothing else – at least if he wishes to keep his property. Here is Judge Rifkin (circa 1829):

> The power of the master must be absolute to render the submission of the slave perfect. I most freely confess my sense of the harshness of this proposition. . . . But in the actual condition of things it must be so. There is no remedy. The discipline belongs to the state of slavery. They cannot be disunited without abrogating at once the rights of the master and absolving the slave from his subjection.[85]

The return of Bon to Sutpen is, for Sutpen, the return not of a son but of a slave. Sutpen has no apparent difficulty withholding his paternal acknowledgment because he does not see Bon as his child but as "goods." Indeed, it is as "goods" and not as a son that Bon threatens him; the threat derives not from miscegenation but from labor, since Bon reminds Sutpen of "the actual condition of things" under slave production – that every master and every master's son is a black in whiteface. My remark is not intended rhetorically – Faulkner stresses that Sutpen is "faced" (p. 220) with a "face" (p. 214). When he sees Bon ride up to the Hundred in 1859, he sees his own features on a male slave:

> ". . . and he –" . . . "– saw the face and knew . . . and Father said that even then, even though he knew that Bon and Judith had never laid eyes on one another, he must have felt and heard the design – house, position, posterity and all – come down like it had been built out of smoke" [pp. 214–15]

The form of their meeting is resonant of Virginia:

he stood there at his own door, just as he had imagined, planned, designed, and sure enough and after fifty years the forlorn nameless and homeless child came to knock at it and no monkey-dressed nigger anywhere under the sun to come to the door and order the child away [p. 215]

Except that to decipher, on the basis of what Sutpen knows, is to recover the butler, and to see what Sutpen saw in 1820. The recurrence of slave labor's primal scene revises the status and position of the subjects involved. The boy who *is* and *plays* Sutpen is a slave (black goods); the master who *is* and *plays* the "monkey nigger's" part is, despite his name (Sutpen), black goods. Faced with this, Sutpen has no option – he must turn the boy (and the insight) from the door, or lose the door. To extend the logic of the insight is to appreciate the extent of the "explosion"; should Bon marry Judith, not only will the Hundred be a materialization of black work but its inheritors will lose their euphemistic patronym (Sutpen), becoming goods (Bon) in name as well as in fact. As a result, the white master's nominal authority along with his nominal irony will vanish "like . . . smoke." As in the 1820s, so in the 1860s, Sutpen responds by using Haiti on Virginia, meeting revolutionary recognition with counterrevolutionary violence. Henry will kill Bon at his father's bidding, but in so doing he will kill that which manufactures mastery. Consequently, Henry vanishes to all intents and purposes as he pulls the trigger. He returns to a diminished Hundred *"to die"* (p. 298), a "wasted yellow face" with "wasted hands" who is "already a corpse" in 1909 because, as a planter who killed his own most vital part (labor), he has been a corpse since that act in 1865.

Critics who speculate on what might have happened had Sutpen let matters take their course, allowing Bon to marry Judith and become (in a region without primogeniture law) co-heir with Henry, miss the point. Brooks argues that had Jefferson somehow come to know that Bon was Sutpen's son, Sutpen – backed by property and the Coldfield link – could have outfaced the bigamy charge. Furthermore, by letting the community know that Bon was part Negro, he could have legitimized Henry's claim to full inheritance. By such means Bon might have been controlled, and the "design" realized intact. This works, if the design is simply "getting richer" (p. 209) after the manner of capital's "American dream." But Sutpen plans to accumulate by means of slave production, and consequently his accumulations are founded on a primary repression; repression of the fact that mastery is made by bound labor. Sutpen cannot keep this truth down; he therefore knows that, complete or incomplete, his design is vitiated. He tells General Compson in 1864 that if he does nothing, "let[s] matters take the course which I know they will take and see[s] my design complete itself quite normally and naturally and successfully to the public eye," what results will be "a mockery":

> a betrayal of that little boy who approached that door fifty years ago and was turned away, for whose vindication the whole plan was conceived and carried forward to the moment of this choice . . . [p. 220]

To vindicate that boy he had to repress what the boy saw, and to go on doing so for nearly half a century (the years of major slave production in the South). When that is no longer possible, when the unrepressed child (Bon, or "white" as "black" "goods") finally becomes father to the man (as his posterity), then the man as planter may as well be dead. If Sutpen lets "the design complete itself," care of Bon, he must witness his own dynastic body become what it always was – black property.

Sutpen considers his design "a mockery" (p. 220) because it rests on an "initial mistake" (p. 219) that is the "sole cause" of its failure (p. 218). In this he is right, except that he nominates the wrong "mistake," directing the General's attention, at least in 1864, to the Haitian marriage. Bon, although he never quite says as much, becomes Sutpen's way of repressing his own founding narrative. Sutpen's "mistake" lies here; he uses miscegenation, barely confessed in 1864, to mystify labor fear, more fully confessed in 1835. The earlier story is deeply disruptive of planter properties, and in 1835, less committed to those properties, he almost said as much to the General. However, neither then nor thirty years later can he bear full witness to the boy's insight into the labor facts of the master's matter.

As a labor lord, Sutpen cannot let the revolution in his own consciousness be readable to himself or to others. In this, at least, he is successful; his labor trauma passes almost unremarked upon by interpreters in and outside the novel. While it is fair, therefore, to say that repression delivers the goods both cognitively and politically, it must be added that Faulkner marks Sutpen's chief repressive device (counterrevolution care of Haiti) as a mistake. To put it crudely, repression in Haiti in 1827 is, quite literally, an impossible counterrevolution. Interpreters should not have been misled, yet it remains entirely understandable that they were and are. It will not have escaped attention that *Absalom, Absalom!* is almost unreadable; as a record of an attempt by a planter and his class descendants to tell the

story of planter accumulation it is the product of characters who, in
order to live with themselves and their properties, have to make
themselves more or less unreadable to themselves and to others.
Repression, cognitive and political, is their cast of mind, yielding
stories that contort, distort, evade, and displace what they know.

It would be a mistake to read the novel's difficulty as raising primarily epistemological questions; while readers must ask, "Who
knows what, when, and how?" this should not – critics to the contrary[86] – induce a crisis of knowledge culminating in some form of
the unanswerable question "How can they (or we) know at all?" In
Absalom, Absalom!, a novel designed to explore a repressive class "design," difficulty begs the altogether more answerable question "How
can those who know so much, repress so much of what they know?"
As with most things in this novel, Sutpen is there first. Apparently
motivated by a desire to make himself intelligible, he holds two conversations, separated by thirty years; however, the former, a story
about labor experience, is so concealed under the latter, a story
about marital "innocence," that decypherment leads to encypher-
ment. Mystification depends upon overlap. Were the two stories
manifestly different, the second would not encrypt the first. However, because the second half of Sutpen's conversation appears to
continue the first, right down to starting at the point where the first
part ceased (the marriage), distortion can occur under the guise of
resolution. So, one "error," the Virginian decision to become a labor lord when the consequence of such lordship is perceived as
bondage, becomes another, the Haitian decision to marry a woman
whose "Spanish" mother is found to have been "black." Similarly,
one child at the door (Sutpen), subjected to labor trauma, becomes
another child at the door (Bon), subjected to another and familial
trauma. In each instance, affinity disguises the degree to which Sutpen's narratives are collusively cryptic. For example, although it is
true that a master's sexual abuse of a female slave results in large
part from the more general condition of slave labor,[87] miscegenation
cannot be said to express the essence of that condition. Yet the in-
terference of Sutpen's two stories, one with another, promotes a
reading of Bon not as "goods" but as miscegenated son. Alternatively, although it is true that the history of the Sutpens is familial,
in the South the family as "household"[88] always extends beyond the
family as oedipal unit; which is simply to say that Sutpen, "the father," is also a man who does not take sugar in his coffee, who fights
slaves, who allies with merchant capital, and who is an elected Confederate officer. Yet because the link between Sutpen, parts I and II,
appears to be Eulalia as wife and mother, rather than Eulalia as route

to slave properties, Freud and not Hegel has provided the prevalent critical glossary to the novel.

It remains the case that if the labor truth is missed, it is because Sutpen would have it so. He tells his second story in order to avoid unbearable truths in his first. Because he renders himself unreadable, it is perhaps understandable that so many have compounded his unreadability. The nature and consequence of their collusive repression is the substance of another essay on *Absalom, Absalom!*

3

ABSALOM, ABSALOM! *AND*
ROSA COLDFIELD

OR, "WHAT IS IN THE DARK HOUSE?"

I

In 1865 Henry Sutpen shoots Charles Bon dead at the gate to Sutpen's Hundred. In 1909 Rosa Coldfield tells Quentin Compson what
she knows of that death and the events that follow it. I offer the
dates merely to indicate that Rosa has had forty-four years in which
to get her story straight and yet remains capable of statements such
as, "*for had I not heired too from all the unsistered Eves since the Snake?*"[1]
and "*I became all polymath love's androgynous advocate*" (p. 117).
Whether or not one deems her phrasing poetically dense (apt perhaps in an elegist) or transgressive ("a challenge to what we might
call the paternal phallic authority of a text's meaning"[2]), the upshot
is mystification.

Rosa has nominal grounds for obscurity; before breaking into the
Hundred in 1909 and talking to Henry, she apparently does not
know who the murder victim is, beyond his being Henry's university
friend and Judith's suitor. However, as Eric Sundquist persuasively
argues, when she enters the Hundred to confront the corpse, she
appears possessed of a covert account of Bon's identity. Faced with
Clytie, blocking her way to the stairs and to the body in Judith's
bedroom, Rosa "*crie[s]*", "*And you too? And you too, sister, sister?*" (p.
112). Since she specifically does not address the term "*sister*" to
Judith ("*and not to Judith, mind*") but to Clytie, and to Clytie's face,
"*which was at once both more and less than Sutpen*" (p. 112), it follows
that Rosa recognizes Clytie as sharing a sister's relation to Bon. Sundquist assumes that bone structure or expression or both are the give-
away:

> And why should not Rosa, the fever of her vicarious life driving
> toward that recognition [of miscegenation], see now in Clytie's

darkened face what we are to imagine Quentin sees half a century later?[3]

Leaving aside whether or not Quentin discerns Bon's familial status from Clytie, prior to his seeing Henry in 1909, there is something, if not wrong, then missing, here. Neither Clytie's expression nor her bone structure tells Rosa anything about Bon; the former, Rosa describes as "*rocklike and firm,*" insisting that the face that faces her has neither "*sex [nor] age*" and has from birth remained that of a "*sphinx*" with "*no change, no alteration in it at all*" (p. 109). Signals, there are none. And because Rosa reiterates that she never saw Bon, Clytie's features are similarly mute. Rosa simply cannot have read the Sutpen connection to Bon from Clytie's face. If we are to believe Sundquist, the creativity of Rosa's sexual imagination, triggered by the sisterhood of Judith and Clytie, in a context of pervasive misceg- enation, is sufficient to establish the missing link. Rosa knows that Bon is Sutpen's son because white planters have a habit of fathering black families.

I too believe that Rosa knows. She does, after all, refer to the murder as "almost a fratricide" (p. 10), a phrase whose reservation may be inflected one of two ways, either as indicating that the friend- ship of Henry and Bon is close to brotherhood, or as suggesting that when a white brother shoots a black brother, he commits partial fratricide since a slave "brother" is a contradiction in terms, a slave being a "thing" that is already socially dead.[4] I hold to the second inflection but do not believe that expectation of miscegenation is Rosa's route to that inflection and to the knowledge that it implies.

Rosa tells Quentin how, aged three and on the road to church, she remembers first seeing her sister Ellen and the Sutpen family:

> this is the vision of my first sight of them which I shall carry to my grave: a glimpse like the forefront of a tornado, of the carriage and Ellen's high white face within it and the two rep- licas of his face in miniature flanking her, and on the front seat the face and teeth of the wild negro who was driving, and he, his face exactly like the negro's save for the teeth (this because of his beard, doubtless) – all in a thunder and a fury of wildeyed horses and of galloping and of dust. [p. 16]

Because Henry's and Judith's faces replicate their father's face, all three faces necessarily find themselves in the face of the slave. The passage of the three Sutpen faces into the face of the bound man grants to the generic Sutpen face, at the very least, a disputed gen- esis, either in white paternity or in black labor. Arguably, since three comply to one, the dispute is resolved in the slave's favor. It follows that black work, and not the white father, founds the dynasty – it follows, that is, if Rosa's initial and traumatic glimpse is read through the stencil of Sutpen's Virginian labor trauma; her reference to "the driver" as "looking exactly like a performing tiger in a linen duster and a top hat" (p. 16) inclines that way. A euphonic side step separates "performing tiger" from "monkey nigger," a step that, if taken, places Rosa's recognition within the organizing purview of Sutpen's founding narrative in Virginia. Whether Rosa is three (1848) or twenty (1865) or sixty-four (1909), she in some sense *knows* that the story of Sutpen's house starts in the work of slaves and not in their sexuality.

Alerted by Wash Jones to Bon's killing, Rosa rushes to *"my sister's house"* (p. 107) through a landscape marked not simply as property but wherever possible as Coldfield property. Having *"locked the house,"* she passes *"Ellen's . . . flower Howe, beds"* (p. 108) and does so while wearing inherited garments (whose various sources are noted [p. 107]) and riding in *"our buggy,"* harnessed to a mule *"which was not his* [Wash Jones's]" (p. 107). Possession preoccupies her. I have listed proprietorial intimations from the first two pages of her extended monologue (chapter five). Moreover, she is aware that the very words with which she tells her story come to her second and third hand, having been occupied by others; *"they will have told you doubtless"* is twice repeated, on that first page. It should be remembered that Rosa rides to the Hundred to keep her word to Ellen, by saving Judith; she will attempt to do so by becoming Judith's mother, that is by marrying Sutpen. Her monologue is a marriage narrative, albeit thwarted, and as such it is a story about taking possession of a plantation house, a house that those subjected to the primal trauma of slave production know (at some level) to be "Nigger sweat."[5] That Rosa knows as much is evidenced by her own account of her entry into Sutpen's Hundred in 1864. And it is from this recognition that her knowledge of the facts of Bon's birth derives its meaning. But first the analysis.

Rosa's *"sister's house"* is neither Sutpen's nor Ellen's, as Rosa enters it. It is Clytie's, to such a degree that the body of the slave and the body of the house become coterminous, rendering Rosa's attempt to reach Judith's bedroom a latent act of bodily penetration. Rosa forces entry, in effect, to master the slave by reaching and laying claim to Judith, that vessel through which planter property will be exchanged. Judith's bedroom contains in Bon's body, in Henry's absence, and in Judith's implied widowhood evidence of a violent rupture in the pattern of white dynastic inheritance. Acting on behalf of Ellen, whose marriage first linked merchant capital to planter properties, Rosa cannot achieve her goal because the very properties that she seeks to protect (the properties that grant the master his mastery) no longer appear to be held in the master's name and are, therefore, temporarily unavailable for repossession.

I am reading the first act of Rosa's monologue as a class allegory, but before exploring its outcome I had best establish textual grounds for that claim. Rosa's perception of the house as a body is clear from a network of allusions; it is a *"skeleton"* (p. 109), capable of speech (p. 110), whose architecture grows from Clytie's form:

> *that body . . . seemed to elongate and project upward . . . a brooding awareness . . . which created . . . that bedroom long-closed and musty, that sheetless bed . . . with the pale and bloody corpse in its patched and weathered gray. . . .* [p. 110]

The house and its corpse are the things that Clytie made. Moreover, that part of Clytie which *"seemed to elongate"* contains no white or Sutpen part, because, so Rosa says, it was *"inherited from an older and a purer race than mine"* (p. 110). If the Hundred with its corpse becomes that which grows from an African slave's body, it is as an African slave, and as an African slave only (and not as Sutpen's daughter), that Clytie makes the plantation and makes it as the container of that which counters the capacity of its owner to retain and pass on his properties.

Rosa, ever fantastical, casts Clytie's refusal (*"Dont you go up there"* [p. 111]) as a slave revolt. She does so because she knows that the *"older . . . purer"* and more revolutionary *"race"* from which Clytie and the Hundred rise is identifiably Haitian. Rosa tells Quentin, at the outset of their first conversation, that Sutpen's original slaves "may have come (and probably did) from a much older country than Virginia or Carolina but it wasn't a quiet one" (p. 11). To be older than Virginia is to be located outside the slaveholding South; to be unquiet is to be Haiti. Rosa dare not say as much, since to name the place would be to declare the house both black and unstable.[6] Nonetheless, if Rosa knows that Bon is Sutpen's son ("almost a fratricide") and knows that he is a son out of the unmentionable Haiti, then she can almost certainly deduce that the body on Judith's bed is black; after all, she characterizes the corpse and its situation as an *"elong[ation]"* of Clytie's African body, itself a body made by a white planter on a black Haitian. Such knowledge, when seen as growing from the Haitian aspect of the *"nigger"* at the door,[7] involves Rosa (the planters' would-be champion) in the potential recognition that because planters, their properties, and their children are all *"project[ions]"* from the body of slave labor, those planters and their children are necessarily blacks in whiteface, whose black and Jacobinical part will rise up and defeat them. Bon's death effectively cancels Henry as inheritor and is the death of Judith's will to mother heirs.

Rosa cannot face her own vision of white dependency. Even as she hears what the "dark house" has to say, she applies whitewash by transferring ownership:

> *'Dont you go up there, Rosa.' That was how she* [Clytie] *said it: that quiet, that still, and again it was as though it had not been she who spoke but the house itself that said the words – the house which he had built, which some suppuration of himself had created about him as the sweat of his body might have created, produced some (even if invisible) cocoon-like and complementary shell in which Ellen had had to live and die a stranger, in which Henry and Judith would have to be victims and prisoners, or die.* [p. 111]

Nominal title goes to Sutpen; it is he who speaks through the house that was briefly called Clytie. But Rosa restores the master to mastery by returning his house, only to raise the awkward question of labor. If the house is *"sweat,"* who did the sweating? *"Suppuration"* gives the labor to Sutpen, who, since he is most typically a *"demon"* in Rosa's eyes, might be expected to perspire poisonously. But, again, the path to entitlement is troubled. No sooner has the sweat crystallized as the very image of "white" property, a *"cocoon,"* than the term releases a claim to alternative title: *"coon"* troubles the coherence of Rosa's effort to see the house as the embodiment of Sutpen's will.

Rosa's monologue, presumably against its own better judgment, generates, in its unstable semantics, the recognition that the Hundred is the site of a clash of wills. Again, Hegel provides explanatory gloss; according to "Lordship and Bondage," a master's property is both that through which a master exemplifies his mastery and, as the labor of the bound man, the slave's route to the recognition that since the works of his hand make the owner what he is, those works make him (the bound man) far more than a will-less extension of that owner's will. Things produced under slave production necessarily become split things whose double articulation can never wholly cease, because if the owner finally and completely suppresses the vocal body of the slave, he puts at risk that which constitutes his person. Rosa works hard to give Sutpen back his things, by seeing the Hundred as the materialization of his singular will, but caught in Clytie's gaze she cannot escape the corrective viewpoint of the slave. Time and again, when she addresses the house, she is unsure to whom she speaks; similarly, when she hears the house speak, she cannot decide who owns the voice. One instance must make my point: Rosa's headlong rush into the hall is stopped by Clytie's touch:

> *Yes, I stopped dead – no woman's hand, no negro's hand, but bitted bridle-curb to check and guide the furious and unbending will – I crying not to her, to it; speaking to it through the negro, the woman, only because of the shock which was not yet outrage because it would be terror soon, expecting and receiving no answer because we both knew it was not to her I spoke: 'Take your hand off me, nigger!'*
>
> *I got none. We just stood there – I motionless in the attitude and action of running, she rigid in that furious immobility, the two of us joined by that hand and arm which held us, like a fierce rigid umbilical cord, twin sistered to the fell darkness which had produced her.* [p. 112]

Rosa apparently addresses the house and speaks, therefore, to two potential proprietors – to Clytie's African/Haitian part, or to Sutpen. Resolution involves deciding whose hand *"check[s]"* whose *"will,"* since the hand and implied ear belong (at least initially) to one and the same presence. However, the *"unbending will"* cannot be ratified until ownership of the house is decided. If *"it"* is Sutpen, various attributions fall neatly into place: his *"hand"* is male and white and has a way with horses (witness Wash Jones's habit of casting "the kernel" as an equestrian statue [p. 226], and the Colonel's own fatal preoccupation with foals [p. 229]). Moreover, Rosa, we are to discover, is intent on matrimony; she wants Sutpen's hand on her arm. Consequently, the pun on the *"bridle"* contains an impacted narrative. Rosa is engaged to Sutpen until he tries to treat her like a stock animal, at which point she quits him and his house, refusing to be what Milly becomes, "a mare" (p. 231). However, talking to Quentin in 1909, she may sense how close she was in 1866 to being a beast for breeding purposes, or a bride contained in a *"bridle."* Despite all this, Sutpen cannot be fitted up as *"it,"* because there is no compelling reason why Rosa should call him *"nigger!"* A case can be made; one might argue that in the second paragraph *"it"* is described as *"fell darkness,"* a phrase that if taken as referring to Sutpen might just be part of Rosa's general demonizing, in which case *"darkness"* turns demonic, drawing "The Fall" from *"fell"* and placing *"nigger"* as just another synonym for Satan. But such usage sounds slack in a novel preoccupied with the niceties of racial attribution. Furthermore, if the *"darkness"* is Sutpen, then I can find no way to explain its maternal relation to Rosa and Clytie. Perhaps Rosa has been carried toward imprecision by her own rhetorical energy? Sutpen *does* "produce" Clytie, who between 1864 and 1866, by dint of co-residence, loosely becomes Rosa's "*sister.*" But the umbilicus stumps me.

As a "thing" made by slaves, the house has another latent proprietor. If the "*it*" addressed by Rosa refers to Clytie's African/Haitian antecedents, the umbilicus can be attributed. Sutpen imported a number of slaves from Haiti, among them two women, one of whom was Clytie's mother. Again, much though not all falls into place if Rosa's addressee is the body of slave labor. As Haitian, and therefore capable of revolution, the "*dark*" body from which Clytie comes is a body Rosa must fear. So, even as she is produced (birthed) by a slave's "*hand and arm*" (instruments of work), and in labor terms "*twin[ned]*" and "*sistered*" to a slave upon whom she depends, she must seek to break that hold. (The umbilical tie is "*fierce and rigid.*") Rosa's "*Take your hand off me, nigger!*" now has a clear subject; she cries through Clytie, as a slave, to that embodiment of all those slaves, "*it*" as the work of bound hands. But with this identification, too, there is a problem: "*it*" seems to elude its new subject – the house as slave labor – because its "*hand,*" we are told, is "*no negro's hand.*" However, the problem is resolved once one recognizes that the "*will*" need not belong to Rosa. Certainly, "*bitted bridle-curb*" works if the hand is read as Sutpen's seeking to curb Rosa's will in marriage. But, in a context of slippery attributions, "*will*" too cannot be granted a single subject. Initially, the circumstance in which the passage is framed – Clytie's hand stopping Rosa's rush – casts Rosa as possessor of the "*furious will.*" But "*bit,*" "*bridle,*" and "*curb*" are all instruments used to constrain slaves.[8] Sutpen's hand (not "*negro,*" not "*woman*") remains in play, but as the hand that checks and guides the peculiar institution. In which case, the "*will*" belongs to the slave as Jacobin, and its touch, enacted by Clytie's Haitian "*part,*" elicits from Rosa predictable "*shock,*" followed by intimations of "*outrage*" and "*terror,*" should Sutpen's checks fail.

Rosa stops "*dead*" because the "*dark house,*" as the elongation of an African/Haitian's "*body,*" *and* as the body of Sutpen's property, is simultaneously her point of imminent access to proprietorial mastery *and* yet also the locus of the imminent death of that mastery. Like Rosa, the reader is caught in a standoff between two claims to possession, focused on the attribution of "*it.*" I should reiterate that Rosa's paralysis results directly from what I have elsewhere called the trauma of slave production. Rosa and Clytie reenact Sutpen and the "*monkey nigger*" and recall her three-year-old vision of Sutpen and the "performing tiger," precisely because such scenes receive their form from a primary scene latent in slave property as the locus of an unbearable contradiction (for "contradiction" read: an untenable and so untellable structural instability[9]).

Rather than think something that she cannot bear to think, Rosa finds a more manageable image than that produced by the divided house as it touches her body through Clytie's hand. She brings to mind a time when objects could be clearly identified and owned. Even as "*we* [Clytie and Rosa] *stood there*," she recalls a clear distinction between the Sutpen household and the Coldfield house;[10] as children, Judith and Clytie played with the same "*objects*" and were rumored to share "*pallet*" and "*bed*," whereas Rosa was taught not to play with their things. Coldfield, the merchant who manumitted the only two slaves he was briefly given in payment for debt, distances himself and his children from the awkward interdependencies that typify slave production. As his daughter, Rosa has been instructed to stand back from those things that cannot be alienated from the black work that made them to the bourgeois price at which they will sell. Rosa deploys her class apprenticeship to block what she has sensed at the threshold to the Hundred, making herself less intelligible to herself and to Quentin. Self-censorship works insofar as her trauma recedes:

> Even as a child, I . . . under[stood] . . . to shun the very objects which she [Clytie] had touched. We stood there so. And then suddenly it was not outrage that I waited for, out of which I had instinctively cried; it was not terror: it was some cumulative over-reach of despair itself. I remember how as we stood there joined by that volitionless (yes: it too sentient victim just as she and I were) hand, I cried – perhaps not aloud, not with words (and not to Judith, mind: perhaps I knew already, on the instant I entered the house and saw that face which was at once both more and less than Sutpen, perhaps I knew even then what I could not, would not, must not believe) – I cried 'And you too? And you too, sister, sister?' [pp. 112–13]

Armed with her Coldfield distinctions, Rosa tries to stop talking to the house as a place of embattled wills. Once again she appears able only to name her addressee (in 1865) as a "*hand*" – a hand, moreover, that does not, here, in any simple sense, belong to Clytie, since Rosa draws a clear distinction between "*it*," herself, and the slave. Rosa's earlier inability to determine who finally owns this hand meant that "*its*" objects continued to be disputed (for as long as "*it*," in the largest sense, remained a possessive pronoun without a possessor). Rosa has, therefore, to tie her own tongue, in the interest of her sister's property. This she will achieve by shifting her attention from "*it*," as the house the hand made, to "*it*" as one object in the house. By focusing on Clytie's Sutpen part, at the cost of Clytie's "*older and purer*" Haitian element, she can turn the unresolvable labor question (of who made the Hundred and its associated goods) into the altogether easier sexual question of who made Bon and Clytie.

It follows that, at one level, Sundquist reads Rosa's exclamation, "*you too, sister, sister?*" correctly, as suggesting

> not only that Clytie is clearly Judith's sister . . . and not only that Clytie, like Rosa, may be vicariously in love with Bon, but also . . . that Bon is Clytie's brother, and that Bon is black.[11]

To recap, for Sundquist, the historical context of pervasive but scarcely admitted miscegenation, allied to a sexually curious nature, is Rosa's route to knowledge. In contradistinction I contend that Rosa's cry addresses a newly sexualized subject and that her monologue up to this point has been about something else – not about Bon's familial body but about planters' goods (of which Bon is but a small part). Sundquist, for all his illuminations, misses a crucial switch in Rosa's attention, a switch by means of which she finally renders the contentious "*hand*" and its things "*volitionless.*" Rosa's amputation of "*will*" from "*hand*" is a Coldfield trick, involving a repression of the interdependencies of slave production characteristic of those who would be bourgeois. Rosa's brief regression to her proto-bourgeois childhood enables her to still her own "*terror*" and "*outrage*" over the recognition that black work continues to be present in white property.

In effect, she begins by telling one story (about a hand) only to end up telling another (about a face). One way of showing how she overlays one subject with a different and more manageable subject would be to return to the question of the identity of the "*it*" to whom she speaks. Take, yet again, the parenthetical statement

> *perhaps I knew already, on the instant I entered the house . . . which was at once both more and less than Sutpen, perhaps I knew even then what I could not, would not, must not believe*) –

I have cut the phrase "*and saw that face*," marking its location with an ellipsis; my contention is that the phrase and the face are secondary and that what traumatizes Rosa is the house, which, as soon as she enters it, she experiences as both Sutpen's and as that which belongs to the body, and more particularly to the hand, of the African/Haitian slave. By putting "*that face*" back I follow Rosa's wish to avoid *"terror"* by turning away from the subject of labor and toward the finally less founding issue of miscegenation. By moving from *"hand"* to *"face,"* Rosa shifts from the instrument of labor to one site of genealogy, thereby reading Clytie (and, by extension, Bon) out of their revolutionary Haitian past and into their miscegenated southern present. At which point, they are indeed *"victims,"* but Rosa's lapse of memory is complicit in their victimization because it deprives them of their revolutionary antecedents. Without *"and saw that face,"* Rosa's parenthesis, while appearing to modify that to which she *"cried,"* in actuality marks the spot where she changes the subject by bracketing and repressing both the traumatic object (*"the house"*) and the instant of trauma (her entry into it). With *"and saw that face"* restored, the reader may, like Sundquist, fall for the articulated cry with which Rosa distracts herself, as she uses the issue of miscegenation to bury that which she knew that *"on the instant . . . [she] entered the house"* she must not *"believe,"* and which therefore remains silently encrypted in a bound man's hand, and altogether less traceable in a cross-bred face.[12]

The case for encryptment rests on the assumption that "Haiti" exists as an unstated presence within Rosa's imagination. Historically, as a compulsive eavesdropper (p. 116), presumably on planters and their associates, she cannot but have heard mention of San Domingo, since, as Alfred Hunt makes quite clear, the revolution was "a lesson" planters "never forgot."[13] Textually, it is fair to assume that she picked up what General Compson knew and passed on, particularly since, in 1909, she identifies Haiti as the source of Sutpen's property in slaves, though she cannot bring herself to name the place. Such knowledge indicates that Rosa does not need Clytie's face to tell her who or what lies dead on Judith's bed, since the word "Haiti," allied to an unacknowledged son, and a Spanish wife set aside, are clues enough.[14] At some level, Rosa expects the not entirely shocking return of the Haitian claimant. That she cannot say as much is a measure of her singular class ambitions in 1865.

In 1838 Goodhue Coldfield agreed to a marriage between his daughter Ellen and Thomas Sutpen. In economic terms the match signals an alliance between merchant capital and planter accumulations. Indeed, at around that time, Coldfield and Sutpen do speculate together. The terms of their speculation remain obscure but seem to involve Coldfield's merchant "credit" and a "bill of landing" made out to Sutpen's name (p. 211). The scheme typifies the merchant function within a slave economy, since although the planter's wealth derives from slave production it is realized in the world market. For valorization to occur, merchants must act as mediators, facilitating import and export between dissimilar worlds. However, although Coldfield mediates, allowing Sutpen to bring in the bourgeois trappings of his nonbourgeois house, he refuses to take his cut, being convinced of the illegality of Sutpen's scheme. In effect, Coldfield withdraws from the regional version of his own class function as the parasitical link between pre-bourgeois and bourgeois economics. His refusal to "adjust. . . . [his] interest to those of the prevailing ruling class"[15] leaves his stock "small" and his trading "close" (p. 65). Rosa's adolescence is the product of her father's decision; between 1861 and 1864 she keeps his store and is, according to Mr. Compson, a perambulating inventory of its ever-diminishing contents (p. 65). By her own admission, she is *"competent"* only to *"reach a kitchen shelf, count spoons, and hem a sheet and measure milk"* (p. 117), since from the ages of sixteen to nineteen she has had to watch Coldfield goods, unreplenished and looted, shrink drastically, while she administers her father's further withdrawal from the Confederacy and from life. Mr. Coldfield's suicide in a self-sealed attic takes three years, during which time his daughter learns to cook and to compose "odes to Southern soldiers" (p. 65). She probably does both while wearing the "cast-off . . . silk" of her infrequently seen sister. Her writing inclines to the "silk" and to the planter cause, while her cooking sustains her father's disaffiliation from that cause. The death of her father releases her from much of the cooking and, if the output of odes is to be trusted (a thousand by 1885), also releases her from her divided class apprenticeship. So when Bon dies (1865), Rosa, equipped with her deathbed promise to Ellen to save Judith, moves with single-minded purpose to take up her sister's role as plantation mistress.

Rosa goes to the Hundred as her niece's guardian and as her brother-in-law's future wife; she goes, therefore, as one who has claims on Sutpen's goods and chattels. If so, she understandably wishes to inherit stable properties, not objects marked by slave labors' primal scene. Consequently, she deploys an intimation of a rumored story about Thomas Sutpen and miscegenation to obscure, to herself and others, the continuing presence of the black hand in the white house. Her choice of story is apt, given that she enters the house not simply as she who would marry its master but as the would-be seducer of its only available heir (Judith). With Bon semi-acknowledged as a black Sutpen, Rosa's case (at least in her own mind) for a place in Judith's bed is strong. She replaces an unsuitable suitor. Her case, however, cannot be openly declared, since acknowledgment of Bon, either as *"nigger"* or as Sutpen's son, might further sully the name with which Rosa seeks alliance.

I run, schematically, far ahead of myself, leaving several claims lacking textual grounds. I do so because I cannot stress enough, first, that prior to 1865, Rosa knows exactly who Bon is; and second, that in 1865, she has class-based reasons for deploying that knowledge in a minimally articulated form. My schematics may also serve to outline a pattern of motivation from within which to read the rest of Rosa's famously convoluted yet compositionally straightforward monologue. It may seem disingenuous to claim clarity of composition for chapter five, having just spent 5,000 words struggling with the first episode of that chapter; but once it is recognized that Rosa's goal is planter property, and that consequently the structural imperatives of that property condition what she has to say, then the larger form within which she says it grows clear.

Chapter five is a strategic discourse in five acts. The first act, which takes Rosa to the foot of Sutpen's stairs, might be variously entitled "Breaking and Entering" or "The New Mistress Takes an Inventory"; the second should carry Rosa's own description, "The Summer of Wisteria (A Plantation Romance)"; with due attention to tonal contrast, it is followed by "The Funeral of an Heir," which both prefaces "The Master's Return" and prompts "The Master Finds a Mistress" (or, perhaps, "The Mistress Finds a Master"). Though it lacks panache, a generic title for the piece might be, "The Renovation of a Plantocracy." I would emphasize that while Sutpen does the repairs, Rosa writes the script.

My scenario is at considerable odds with current critical responses to Rosa Coldfield. Recent studies cast her as a heroine designed by French cultural and feminist theory. I refer to the considerable scholarship of Kauffman, Coleman, O'Donnell, and Gwin, whose accounts, though various, share the assumption that Rosa is subversive. So, for example, her capacity to slip between male and female, paternal and maternal roles, "mothers" the liminality of a novel in which "slippage" becomes "a structural component of the artistic process of the text itself."[16] "Slippage" (Coleman) turns rapidly to "flood" (Gwin) as, by means of Kristeva and Cixous out of Lacan, the fluidity of Rosa's transgressive body is translated into the body of the "hysteric" (O'Donnell and Gwin), or of the madwoman in the attic of the southern fathers (Gwin):

Rosa's voice, both excessively prolix and obfuscatory . . . act[s] as a kind of textual noise . . . proxim[ous] to the "before" of speech and language . . . which in Kristeva's terms . . . "rupture[s] and articulate[s] and precede[s] evidence, verisimilitude, spatiality and temporality." . . . She is close to all that

precedes and threatens to undermine the hierarchies, prohibitions and lines of succession Sutpen wishes to establish as the
conditions of his domain. [O'Donnell][17]

or:

> the unrepresentable, mad text of Rosa Coldfield . . . exposes
> the "repressive assumptions" of all narrative and all theory
> which fails to hear its own unconscious voice. . . . I am search-
> ing for *that* Rosa inside a dark bisexual space between the mad-
> ness of the phallic order and its transference to the woman
> who must speak it, and who in the process of speaking . . . finds
> herself constituted as the otherness it imposes upon her.
> [Gwin][18]

Whether one grounds this fluidity in Kristeva's desire for the pre-
oedipal or in Cixous's bisexual desire is finally a theoretical nicety,
since either option distracts from Rosa's founding desire for her
"*sister's house.*" Removed from her own Mississippi narrative about
the coming into being of planter property, she is made to figure
Anywhere, in a universal story about the origin of a generic "subject." Each of the accounts makes available intriguing matters of
emphasis, but their theoretical agenda leads all of them to mistake
Rosa's goal. Rosa Coldfield does not seek to bring down the mansion
of Patriarchy (self, phallus, and signifier) but to live in a planter's
house. To that end her voice experiences the contradictions endemic to that desire; but at each stage of her monologue, and with
a kind of sweet reason, she negotiates those contradictions in ways
that will maximize her claims to possession.

II

Take Act II, "The Summer of Wisteria (A Plantation Romance)";
having been denied access to Bon's body on Judith's bed, though
not to the house, Rosa tells a "*fairy-tale*" set in a "*garden*" (p. 118),
by means of which she gains covert admission to that bed, while
displacing Bon from imminent occupancy. During the summer of
1861, her father having gone "*away on business*" (p. 117), she is left
in her sister's care. In June of that year, Bon courts Judith, at least
according to Ellen; and Rosa courts Judith, through Bon, at least
according to Rosa, and at least some of the time.

The story is not without its twists, but the main plot strands run
as follows: Rosa haunts the couple, noting "*obliterated*" footprints on
sanded paths and tracing invisible thigh prints on a "*nooky seat*" (p.

119). The prints in question are "his" but only as a route to "hers."[19] Bon is the means to Rosa's desire, since by becoming him she can enter Judith. Her proposal is explicit, climactic, and made in triplicate to Judith:

> 'Let me sleep with you'. . . . 'Let us lie in bed together while you tell me what love is'. . . 'Dont talk to me of love but let me tell you, who know already more of love than you will ever know or need.' [p. 119]

The final declaration brings "The Romance," dramatically, to a close, being followed immediately by "Then my father returned and came for me and took me home and I became again . . . nondescript" (p. 119). But even an intrusive father cannot entirely interrupt coitus. It is timorous to argue, as does Rosemary Coleman, that Rosa offers Judith "non genital, whole body, androgynous love"[20] via her dress making and housekeeping – the genitalia are apparent and male. Nor is it useful to suggest that her love is characterized by "deferment," because although "her words substitute for . . . lovers" it cannot follow that they "safely defer the satisfaction of her desire,"[21] as John Matthews claims, when evidence of emission is available in the text.

At fourteen, Rosa's sexuality is embryonic, problematic, and inclined to horticulture. That is to say, when Rosa represents her sexuality she does so through agricultural metaphor, though even here her emphasis is male:

> I will not insist on bloom, at whom no man had yet to look. . . . Nor do I say leaf – warped bitter pale and crimped half-fledging intimidate of any claim to green which might have drawn to it the tender mayfly childhood sweetheart games or given pause to the male predacious wasps and bees of later lust. But root and urge I do insist and claim, for had I not heired too from all the unsistered Eves since the Snake? Yes, urge I do: warped chrysalis of what blind perfect seed: for who shall say what gnarled forgotten root might not bloom yet with some globed concentrate more globed and concentrate and heady-perfect because the neglected root was planted warped and lay not dead but merely slept forgot? [pp. 115–16]

The female forms ("bloom" and "leaf"), attractive to penetrative attention, are dispensed with. The "root" (or male form) is insisted upon. Grounds for the claim are obliquely significant. " "[H]ad I not heired" might be understood to mean "was I not descended from," in this case, "all" lapsarian women (when Eve, prompted by the Snake, falls from the Garden she becomes Adam's wife and is, therefore, "unsistered"[22]). However, "heired" is an active verb, which, in the context of "*root*," "*Snake*," and "*warped chrysalis*" (all variously penile), could transpose Rosa's neologistic usage into a deviant paternity claim – that is, "had I not inseminated and made heirs of . . ." In which case her descendants would indeed be extensive ("*all*"), since, given the co-presence of Eve and the Snake within the inquiry, Rosa's phrase claims Adamic sexual status. But one need not look "*too far*" along the genealogical line to find the Eve in question. Judith is in the garden and doubly "*unsistered*"; in 1861 her brother (Bon) is no longer treating her as a sister; and, after 1864, she is "unsistered" by her brother's death. I contend that Rosa wishes to penetrate Judith in the garden (at the risk of quoting myself, "had I not inseminated Judith?"). Insemination would ensure both that Rosa occupy the garden (becoming heir to the property) and that she oust the evil suitor (Bon as Snake). Furthermore, the presence of Rosa's Adamic claim within the network of semantic options renders "*warped chrysalis*" complexly penile. At once infantile and innocent, the "*chrysalis*" is a diminutive synonym for the claimed "*root*." Its relationship to that "*root*" is explored after the sentence's second colon, where it is cast as the "*globed concentrate*" and "*heady-perfect*" expression of rootedness. Reading back across the sentence from the essentialist account, the reader sees that the "*chrysalis*" is not the product "*of*" the perfect seed but is itself capable of seminal perfection. Equipped with such a "*root*," Rosa can, within three lines, clarify her position: "*That was the miscast summer . . . I lived out not as a woman, a girl, but rather as the man which I perhaps should have been*" (p. 116).

Rosa has the means, Rosa has the motive. Evidence of penetration survives the interrupting father; as a coda to her Romance, Rosa speculates on its residue:

> – *and yet I gave it* [love]. *And not to him, to her; it was as though I said to her, "Here, take this too. You cannot love him as he should be loved, and though he will no more feel this giving's weight than he would ever know its lack, yet there may come some moment in your married lives when he will find this atom's particle as you might find a cramped small pallid hidden shoot in a familiar flower bed and pause and say, 'Where did this come from?'; you need only answer, 'I dont know.' "*
> *And then I went back home and stayed five years, heard an echoed shot, ran up a nightmare flight of stairs and found –*
> *Why, a woman standing calmly in a gingham dress before a closed door . . .* [p. 120]

What Rosa "*gave*" is recognizably to be found in a "*bed*"; that she transposes her proposal from sheets to soil should not disguise the nature of the *"particle"* in question. Found after talk of *"giving's weight,"* *"love,"* and *"pallid shoot,"* Rosa's gift is a male emission of measurable potency. Consider its qualities: as the first *"seed"* it takes seminal priority over that of other lovers; its position between types of *"bed"* elides the body of the master (represented by the body of his daughter and genealogical guarantor) and the body of the master's land. Rosa's *"seed"* marks both and is latently murderous; Henry's *"echoed shot"* disposes of the unsuitable suitor, but only after Rosa's hidden *"shoot"* (containing and echoing *"shot"*) has already done for him, sexually.

Means, motive, a scene of crime . . . "The Summer of Wisteria" has them all. There is, however, a disruptive subplot. Even as Rosa writes Bon out of Judith's bed, she writes him into her own conception, claiming of his visit to the Coldfield house on New Year's Day 1860 (a visit she missed): *"it was as though that casual pause at my door had left some seed, some minute virulence in this cellar earth of mine"* (p. 117). Rosa's habit of viewing herself as a fourteen-year-old egg gives a gynecological slant to her cellarage, casting it as *"a lightless womb"* in which she *"lurks[s]"* *"long overdue"* (p. 116). She reiterates, *"There must have been some seed he left . . ."* (p. 117). Bon, sight unseen, becomes her metaphoric father;[23] moreover, her account is filled with ethnic intimations; he is, time and again, *"that shadow"* emerging from a *"shadow realm"* (p. 118). Because he is also metaphorically present at Rosa's conception, it is entirely logical that he colors what she knows:

> [I] acquired all I knew of that light and space in which people moved and breathed as I (that same child) might have gained conception of the sun from seeing it through a piece of smoky glass [p. 116]

Rosa, ever horticultural, owes her *"conception"* to the *"sun."* A pun is, at one level, a metaphoric convergence induced by a sound; as "son" but still *"smoky,"* Bon features here as the seminally dark father.

Of course, more generally, the *"seed"* in question can be read as the genesis of Rosa's idea for a romance, since Bon, in his role as Judith's companion, prompts her aunt's literary endeavor. However, because Rosa's narrative habits incline to the subterranean networks and divided referents of metaphor, it is difficult to edit out so consistent a latency as the one about Rosa's descent from Bon.

How, then, to account for it? Bon "fathers" Rosa's Romance – a story designed to write him out of the claimant's bed by making a space for Rosa there in his stead – but as Rosa's father he nullifies her displacement of him by returning as that which defeats her attempt to lodge a *"perfect seed"* inside the vessel of Sutpen's property since, if Bon fathers Rosa, and Rosa leaves a seminal deposit on Judith's *"bed,"* that deposit is also marked by his *"shadow."* I would emphasize that the subversion of the master narrative of "The Summer of Wisteria" by its subplot may well derive from the placing of the Romance. Act II, the love story, is interpolated into Act I exactly where Judith appears *"before the closed door"* and Clytie lifts her hand (p. 114). Immediately prior to this point, Rosa, in Act I, had chosen to suppress her knowledge of the primal scene of slave production (the black *"hand"* in the white house, which she *"could not, would not, must not believe"*) by shifting her attention to those intimations of miscegenation about which she has long since known. "The Summer of Wisteria" is, therefore, a structural consolidation of her repression of labor trauma, in that it distractedly whispers of sexual crossing while dispersing even that threat by discovering white lovers. One threat overwrites another and greater threat; but, as with any palimpsest, traces of what has been written over remain discernible. Although Rosa, simultaneously and with great ingenuity, stabilizes Sutpen's goods and establishes sexual claim to those goods, her story continues to be stalked by the ghost of Haitian paternity in the cellarage (as subplot and metaphoric option). "Haiti" is doubly neutralized (as Bon and as paternity); yet the very word that obstructs it, *"seed,"* at cross-purposes with its own intended lie, releases ambiguities that *"shadow"* Rosa's sense of her self at exactly that point where she "enters" the master class. Bon, at a low but semantically disruptive level, may claim paternity in Rosa because of her own forbidden recognition that with the merchant/planter alliance fixed (through her "marriage" to Judith), the foundations of her father's house (like those of the Hundred) will derive from a horticultural *"seed"* tended by black labor.

III

Acts III to V can wait. Exasperated by exegesis, I turn to theory, in part to salve my reader's patience. In this section I shall try to explore some implications of a narrative habit shared by Rosa Coldfield and Thomas Sutpen. Both tend to double articulation because each, disconcertingly, talks about one thing (miscegenation) as a means not to talk about another (labor). Their styles of speech contain a historical hypothesis,[24] discussion of which may usefully be prefaced by remarks from Walter Benjamin's "Theses on the Philosophy of History" (1939):

To articulate the past historically does not mean to recognize it "the way it really was" (Ranke). It means to seize hold of a memory as it flashes up at a moment of danger.[25]

Benjamin's dangerous moment contains two times, neither of which is time past, "the way it really was." Instead, "articulation," under threat, is possessed by memory in the form of an "unexpected . . . image"[26] that expresses a new relation to a past that has itself been reconceived in that instant, and through the exigencies of the moment of danger. Gone, for Benjamin, is an extant and prior past. Gone, too, is a traceable continuum between such a past and an extant and subsequent present. What he describes is a drastic lacuna in temporal sequentiality, and so in historical causality. "To articulate the past" under such conditions is to experience writing or speech about history as the site of a process staged across two times, in which those times clash so violently that the past cannot remain "as it was" any more than the present can stay "as it is." Instead, each is discovered through the other in a form that "makes the continuum of history explode."[27]

To return to *Absalom, Absalom!*, and more particularly to Thomas Sutpen aged fourteen at the planter's door, and to Rosa Coldfield aged three outside Jefferson's church. Both experience what Benjamin might call an "arrest"[28] of thought or "cessation of happening"[29]

where thinking suddenly stops in a configuration pregnant with tensions, it gives that configuration a shock, by which it crystalizes into a monad.[30]

"Monad" is difficult, but clearly counterposed to "continuum." I take Benjamin to mean a unity achieved through rupture (or the "cessation" of continuity) in which configured temporal elements cancel one another, while preserving what their clash releases from each of them – alternative forms of realization. For example, Benjamin alludes to Robespierre dressing the French Revolution in togas; plainly, Benjamin's Robespierre does not re-create classical Rome in late-eighteenth-century Paris, nor does he cast the revolutionary capital as an ancient republic. The issue is not reincarnation but a revolution in the received temporal scheme of things.[31] More, however, is involved; when Benjamin talks of time, he tacitly and pervasively sees the temporal as a made thing, that is to say as an organization of time resulting from particular social choices and denials. Consequently, any "moment" contains within it victors and victims, albeit transcoded firstly into decisions about who shall do what with time, and second into a "naturalized" order of temporal units (which exactly disguises the power over time that has gone into making that temporal scale). Robespierre's cognitive costume drama involves what Benjamin calls a "tiger's leap into the past" that doubles as a "leap into the open air of history"[32] presumably because the revolutionary leader recognizes that both ancient history and his own revolutionary project are "incomplete"[33] without each other, since his revolution gives new form to Rome's republican impulse, even as his revolutionary procedures may find, within themselves, alternative figurations of themselves, through the redrawn stencil of the classical "image." The "air" of history is, indeed, openly dangerous when the past is no longer "what it was," and the present can, consequently, no longer be "what it is."

The "danger" within the temporal moment or "monad" devolves from the key notion of "incompleteness." In his essay "Edward Fuchs: Collector and Historian" (1937), Benjamin observes, "for historical materialism the work of the past is incomplete."[34] The remark elicited a considered rebuke from Horkheimer:

> Your formulation can certainly stand as is. I have but one personal reservation. . . . The pronouncement of incompleteness is idealistic if it does not incorporate completeness as well. Past injustice is done and finished. Those who have been beaten to death are truly dead . . . so the injustice, the terror, the pain of the past are irreparable.[35]

Not for Benjamin, or at least not for his historical materialist. Benjamin replied by drawing a distinction between winners and losers, noting that for the loser of a trial or war, "events are truly concluded" since "for that person *any avenue of praxis has been lost.*"[36] It follows that the "completeness" of the loser's loss of praxis belongs to (inhabits and enables) the winner's "lifework"[37] or praxis (we are close here to Hegel's "Lordship and Bondage"): a state of affairs that the memory work of the historian can and should undo, as it realizes in the writing of history (or conception of time) that the victim's refusals can still be made to count against the victor's versions and the continuing social practices that they inform and stabilize. As Benjamin puts it in the *Arcades Project*:

> history is not only a science but equally a form of remembering. What has been "established" by science can be modified in remembrance. Remembrance can make the incomplete (happiness) complete, and render the complete (suffering) incomplete.[38]

The concept of "incompleteness" allows the historical materialist to "brush history against the grain"[39] because it prompts a doubly explosive recognition: that any "moment" is a potential "monad" (or "configuration pregnant with tensions"[40]) and that all present moments "enjoy" their form only because they have imposed "completeness" on what has gone before:

> A historical materialist approaches a historical subject only where he encounters it as a monad. In this structure he recognises . . . a revolutionary chance to fight for the oppressed past. He takes cognizance of it in order to blast a specific era out of the homogeneous course of history – blasting a specific work out of the lifework. As a result of this method the lifework is preserved in this work and at the same time cancelled; in the lifework, the era; and in the era, the entire course of history.[41]

Setting aside the mystifying speed with which Benjamin totalizes the "explosion," I would like to gloss his notion of cancellation and preservation; my gloss (care of Hegel) departs from the emphasis on work. Benjamin has two kinds of work in mind – the work of memory, and the work of the victim that memory recovers from the "lifework" of the victor. The act of remembering constitutes a refusal to ratify what has previously been lost – that is, the loser's praxis, as lost for all time within the victor's appropriation of it. What the radical historian cancels is the victor's appropriation of the victim's work. What he or she traces and preserves, in exactly the same worked object (be it an artifact, a text, a historical treatise, or a corpse), is the victim's wasted alternative "lifework." The explosive trick is to recast the inert works (or "things," generally turned into properties that bolster the "lifework," "era," and "history" of the victors) into processes of labor. So perceived, these works become locations at which different forms of praxis contend, and from which alternative outcomes, "era[s]," and "histor[ies]" might have been possible. Benjamin expects the radical historian to acknowledge that the nominally "completed" past contains, in its wasted praxis, a claim on the present; a claim that the radical historian will meet by reopening the unhappy past in such a way that its right to happiness and "incompleteness" will transform how the present perceives itself as being.

Which is all very well for Robespierre, but what of those memory workers who have a positive interest in keeping the work and temporal options of the victim firmly closed? Thomas Sutpen makes himself a plantation master, and Rosa Coldfield all but contrives to become mistress in the same house, yet both are subject to temporal emergencies during which the glimpse of repressed (black) "work" within their own (white) "lifework" is exposed.[42] Nor can they forget their monadic moments. In 1835, Sutpen pivots the story of his "lifework" on what contradicts it in 1821. In 1909, Rosa turns 1848 into her own year of revolution and then brackets her "lifework" within it by declaring that what she saw at the church door was not only her "first sight" of Sutpen *en famille* but that it will be her last, since she will carry it to her "grave" (p. 16). It is in the best interest of neither character to recall these moments because, in each case, the moment in question disrupts the preferred class trajectory of the speaker.

Yet Benjamin's insights and structures continue to be revealing in these less than radical contexts. Witness Sutpen turned from the planter's door, according to "Theses on the Philosophy of History." The boy walks to the door equipped, albeit semi-cognitively, with a "lifework" of debased self-sufficiency, learned among the west Virginian yeomanry. He turns away, "blasted" not merely by the knowledge that what he worked to make himself is irrelevant outside the mountain enclaves but by the further recognition that the "work" that he will do can add up only to a "lifework" of mastery that is "pregnant with tensions" because excruciatingly subservient. Ditto, structurally speaking, for the three-year-old at the church door; Rosa looks for Ellen, expecting one kind of family (located in patrimonial genealogy) and experiences quite another (dislocated by labor interdependencies). In each case a "monad" forms from which neither character recovers. Subsequently, Sutpen and Rosa lead lives more or less committed to the plantocracy, yet each remains internally divided by a single moment in which recognition of the laboring presence of the slave "shatters the continuum of [their] history."[43] That moment is forbidden and repercussive.

Why "monads" might feature in deeply conservative memories may be apparent from Benjamin's stress on "danger." For the historical materialist, "monads" are everywhere because "the tradition of the oppressed teaches us that 'the state of emergency' in which we live is not the exception but the rule."[44] To live as an owner within the slave system is to live in awkward proximity to "the tradition of the oppressed." As the historian James Oakes puts it, "by seeing up close what it meant to be a slave, the child [of slaveholding parents] grew up to appreciate in a unique way the full meaning of human liberty."[45] "Liberty," learned from the object lesson of the slave, is liberty understood as a product of repression – that is to say, as freedom that has to be policed because it is under threat of extinction. Why else should Sutpen fight his Haitians, or Rosa react so

intensely to the touch of an African hand? Given Sutpen and Rosa's
labor circumstance, a tendency to monadic moments is to be expected. Given their propertied ambitions, denial is *de rigueur*. Which
may explain something of their styles of speech. Both incline to extended monologue, and both are duplicitous. In speaking their histories at length, they each engage, quite literally, in doublespeak.
Sutpen tells one story only to hide it under another; Rosa tells contradictory stories at the same time, with the stylistic result that they
talk in order to hide what they are talking about in their talk – and
since they can neither face up to nor face down what it is they almost
articulate they prove almost unstoppable, casting themselves into interminable sentences that serve to create them as enigmas. But I
must guard against slipping back, too soon, into exegesis. My concern here is for the temporal and historiographic implications of
this shared style of speech.

On the grounds that psychoanalysis has been seen as permanent
testimony to a failure of communication,[46] I turn, with some reservation, to the psychoanalytic tradition for further ways of reading
double articulation as it addresses the time of trauma. At the center
of Freud's account of trauma is the troubling sense that we are summoned, by the primal scene, to "a *rendez-vous* . . . with a real that
eludes us."[47] For example, when Wolf Man, aged one and a half,
witnesses parental intercourse, he lacks the knowledge to understand
what he sees; the shock is deferred, requiring a second event to
release its force. As Freud puts it:

> At the age of one and a half the child receives an impression
> to which he is unable to react adequately; he is only able to
> understand it and to be moved by it when the impression is
> revived in him at the age of four; and only twenty years later,
> during the analysis, is he able to grasp with his conscious men-
> tal processes what was then going on in him.[48]

The first "impression" is a "shock without affect" which takes form
only as an "after-the-fact-effect"[49] at the time of its "revival." But
for the four-year-old, understanding leads only to misrepresentation,
that is to the creation of a defense against understanding (his infantile neurosis). And not until analysis does the trauma receive its
meaning and become an event. As Lacan observes, "the event remains latent in the subject,"[50] inducing a complex temporality in
which "the subject is always in more than one place at any time."[51]
The deferral of the "*rendez-vous*" with trauma is then "a product of
the excessive character of the first event which requires a second
event to release its traumatic force."[52] Much of what I have tried to

say about Sutpen and Rosa might be boiled down to the statement
that wherever they are within the plantation economy, they are respectively in 1821 and 1848 as well, since their region's regime of
accumulation surrounds them with evidence that can at any and
every point threaten to release the excessive and shocking character
of those first events.

But even the phrase "first events" is problematic within this temporal model, because where subjects are caught in "the tension between the old scene and the recent scenario"[53] they never feel the
initial shock directly but only through later representations in memory. As Derrida might put it, they are afflicted with "a past that has
never been present."[54] His case would seem to run: the present may
command reiteration of the past (particularly of the traumatic past),
but each iteration involves the recovery of a reality that is different
and that in its difference renders absent that which it insists must
be brought to presence. We are close here to historicity according
to Derrida; in *Dissemination* he speaks of "a series of temporal differences without any central present, without a present of which the
past and the future would be but modification."[55]

I have advanced this far along a path that I believe to lead away
from Faulkner because it makes possible certain insights into the
kind of history Rosa and Sutpen seek to tell. Both address a social
trauma that menaces their own legitimacy and as a result are unable
to react adequately to what they see, which therefore remains imminent rather than present. However, Derrida to the contrary, their
trauma is "centrally" imminent. While it is the case that in *Absalom,
Absalom!* as a whole, and more particularly in chapters five and seven,
continuum is at best patchy, and causal relations are elusive, nonetheless a single structural trauma unites its key narrators. The striking differences between what Sutpen sees in 1821 and what Rosa
sees in 1848 should not disguise the fact that both see what they see
at a shared social site, created by a particular conjunction of power
relations within the plantation regime of accumulation. Various
slants on that point at which master faces slave and sees his own
mastery slip toward dependency orient the narrative, casting past,
present, and future within a set of causal imperatives designed to
realize stories that will occlude their own most crucial and damaging
insights. Which is *not* to say that Rosa and Sutpen are at liberty to
fabricate whatever past most meets their current class needs. They
are constrained by the presence of an unthinkable structural fact as
it elusively organizes and informs their best efforts to tell a story that
might finally enable them to think about something else.

I have used Benjamin to cobble together a critique of the groundless nature of trauma as it is perceived within the psychoanalytic tradition. To return briefly to my source, "Theses on the Philosophy of History; although the "monad" allows neither the past nor the present to remain in received form, its reconfiguration of temporal relations is grounded in an emphasis on the victim; "not man or men but the struggling oppressed class itself is the depository of historical knowledge."[56] Benjamin's historian is "nourished" by "the image of enslaved ancestors" whose wasted praxis constitutes his "depository";[57] a buried past, which precisely because it is the past "the way it was forbidden to be," is to be found buried at points of resistance within the praxis of the victor's structures of oppression. Benjamin emphasizes "class" to indicate that a structural understanding of the processes of power (particularly as they confront labor) is some guarantee that memory work will result in truth (whose criteria are historical discontinuity and social "incompleteness"). The analyst and analysand whom I have devised from Freud, Lacan, and Derrida have no such guarantee. Truth, for them, remains finally unintelligible and probably uninteresting; analysis leads to the framing of an interpretive elaboration in which two (or more) moments are articulated together, adding up to what is finally a hypothetical account, through which the subjects make their destinies in more bearable forms. Any measure of truth is therapeutic, being dependent on whether or not the stories work, relieving the analysands of their symptoms.

Because I am concerned to establish the truth of *Absalom, Absalom!* as a narrative about history, the psychoanalytic can help me only so far toward an understanding of what I have been calling the novel's habit of double articulation. Let me gloss what the talking cure might have to say about Rosa and Sutpen's strategies for noncommunication. They speak in order to make present a particular social catastrophe that threatens their stability, yet even as they speak they obstruct what they seek to reveal. What is being blocked is a structural circumstance of slave labor. Their monologues are, therefore, generated by an impulse to make present a historical trauma whose presence must elude them. In temporal terms, they are haunted by the imminence of a past moment that they cannot make fully present – not because of a metaphysics of absence but because of certain economic and political decisions taken by their class. To put it crudely, their troubled sense of time derives not from the fact that a past event has gone absent with many traces but from their chosen role as victors within a particular structure of oppression[58] – a role that requires them both to experience and to deny their own dependency upon a labor force that resists them at almost every turn.

The presence, rather than the absence, of the traumatic moment divides them.

In narrative terms, that moment, despite being largely a matter of exegetic conjecture, instigates the speakers' structural stratagems. For example, Sutpen's conversation with General Compson is divided into two parts by a thirty-year intermission; during the break, Sutpen decides to tell the story of his later years in a way that will obfuscate the central episode of his account of the early years:

> telling Grandfather that the boy-symbol at the door wasn't it because the boy-symbol was just the figment of the amazed and desperate child [p. 210]

As I have argued earlier, he tells the one about the boy at the door again, but differently, in order to interrupt and repress his own labor trauma – an experience that has compelled his labor practices for the past thirty years. Rosa, too, deploys intermissions. Forty-four years separate the shot in 1865 from her fullest account of the shot (in 1909), though her fluency suggests that she has been living with the shot, if not telling its story, at all points in between. Because both moments reproduce and obstruct a social situation that first "struck" Rosa in 1848, each necessarily tells again, though differently, that initial resistance to meaning at the church door. More typically, Rosa manifests Sutpen's rhythm of reiteration-as-interruption at a local rather than a general syntactic level. Almost any of her sentences is a sliding scale of approximations, during which subject, verb, and object are often so transected by modifiers that their referents disturbingly intersect – even as, in 1848, the profiles of a white owner and a black worker slid toward contention.

Clearly, in stylistic terms, what remains unsaid stays unspeakably close to the surface of the speech of both speakers. There is, perhaps, no need to rehearse the crossed semantic valencies of Sutpen's use of "it" and "balloon," or of Rosa's reference to "*bridle*" and "*seed*," as they activate narrative latencies to tell the truth of one traumatic moment by lying about it. What should by now be remorselessly apparent is that throughout both monologues words become the locus not simply of a textual but of a social controversy. Slave labor is that controversy's core, affecting every aspect of its articulation, from temporality to poetics. The trauma may only indirectly be what the words are about; yet it is traceably *in* the working of the words as they split their referents, and divide their user's consciousness, on the extremities of an inoperable labor contradiction, before negotiating the ensuing clash of interests. Which is why the words demand such close attention. Those words are often semantically ambiguous because their speakers tell stories that are forced into existence by the tellers' need to mediate contradictions within that system of production that grounds their sense both of themselves and of their reality. A brief account of that system, and of its continuing urgency for Faulkner during the early thirties, as he writes *Absalom, Absalom!*, will be the substance of a later section. But, before then, I must step back from history, and the theories it excites, to exegesis and to Rosa Coldfield's last "Acts."

IV

Acts III to V remain. I shall sketch how each allows Rosa to constitute herself through the mediation of an almost unconfessed but persistent labor trauma. Act III ("The Funeral of an Heir") is short and to the point. Concerned to take possession of Sutpen's goods and heirs, and to cleanse them of elements of ethnic resistance, Rosa continues with her displacement of Bon from Judith's bed into the grave. His progress is superficially swift. Rosa sees the coffin built, acts as a pallbearer, witnesses the funeral, and, in conclusion, notes, "*and he had never been*" (p. 123). She is so confident as to his erasure that, at the outset, she all but repeats Sutpen's decisive repression of "son" into chattel via a chosen name "Bon" (good . . . goods). For Rosa, Bon gone without "*trace*" (p. 120) is little more than "*some esoteric piece of furniture*," desired by Ellen for Judith. Unfortunately, in rendering him inanimate ("*not . . . man*"), she allows him as "*vase or chair or desk*," to cast a "*shadow*" (p. 120) – a term that fails to hide that which Rosa seeks to excise. As a result, "Haiti" seeps associatively from "*shadow*" back into the very fabric of the master's house (recalling the difficulties of Act I), so that "*[his] shadow . . . his very impression (or lack of it) on Coldfield or Sutpen walls held portentous prophecy of what was to be, –*" (p. 120). Rosa's version of Sutpen's word play goes badly wrong; instead of constraining Bon, it allows "Haiti" to escape through "Bon" into the very "goods" that Rosa would inherit. Predictably, she does not complete the "*prophecy*"; without pausing, and quite literally on the dash, she changes the subject from goods to trousseau. Having taken Bon's place in Judith's bed, she shifts affection from live heir to dead claimant and does so, once again, through the medium of Judith's body, by insisting that Judith's four years of "*love*," "*hope*," "*waiting*," and trousseau preparation were not Judith's but her own (p. 119). Weinstein intriguingly notes that Bon is Rosa's route to Faulkner's "most audacious fantasy":

that black is more beautiful than white, that the unconscious desire for miscegenation lurks deep within the white psyche. Bon represents in his lithe body and unfailing civility the novel's inadmissible desire for racial union, a desire that compels even so recalcitrant a Southerner as Rosa Coldfield.[59]

Intriguing, but insufficiently so. Weinstein misses the dash ("; –"), in this instance the mark both of censorship and of seepage. To recap, through Rosa's botched repetition of Sutpen's initial pun, Bon's Haitian "*shadow*" is allowed to mark the walls of the Hundred. The repressed energy of the traumatic undernarrative, whispering through the single word "*shadow*,"[60] reaches back along an implied verbal chain ("*shadow*," "*Bon*," "goods," "*prophecy*," "Haiti") toward an extralinguistic event (Rosa's revolution of 1848, itself a version of 1791), forcing from Rosa the equally subterranean acknowledgment that if she wishes to be Sutpen's heir (by becoming Judith), she must also take into herself, and somehow contain, the unspoken Bon/Haiti connection. In other words, she who would be mistress in her "*sister's house*" has, at some level, to countenance miscegenation not as "desire" but as a way of managing the African claim to the house and goods that would make her a mistress.

As with Sutpen, so with Rosa, a secondary crisis (miscegenation) is deployed to censor a primary trauma (labor), with the result that while the master narrative of Act III proceeds apace to bury Bon, a subnarrative, with equal alacrity, engineers his resurrection (as sexual body), but only to ensure his repression as the body of labor. Let me explain – to dispense with Bon and his several threats, Rosa must get him out of the house and into the ground, but throughout Acts I and II she used "house" and "ground" as metaphoric representations of her own body. She was variously, it will be recalled, a "*cellar*," a "*tenement*," a "*corridor*," a "*door*," while her horticultural extensions were legion. Her reasoning was proprietorial; metaphor allowed her to stake a claim to the master's estate. Marx indicates that an elision between land and owner is commonplace among landholding classes – "the land is individualized with its lord, it acquires his status. . . . It appears as the inorganic body of its lord"[61]: an idea of which Rosa takes metaphoric note. However, as Max Black points out, any instance of metaphor consists of both a "focus" (the particular metaphoric term) and a "frame" (or network of words "focused" by the initial term); he adds that the frame's net may extend from the immediate context of the focal term to the outer limits of the work.[62] Consequently, when Rosa watches Bon's body lowered into the *"gashy earth"* (p. 122), her phrase by metaphoric inference is anatomically concise – Rosa takes Bon into herself, sexually. However, desire for goods, rather than desire for miscegenation, is uppermost in her mind, organizing the layered implications of the metaphor to comply with the needs of Act III's master narrative. While it is the case that *"gashy earth"* represents Rosa as a "split referent"[63] – a body both sexual and proprietorial – the disposition of that division turns on the implied word "die." To penetrate Rosa, Bon must "die" or enter the *"earth"*; he may be aroused ("die"), and he may arouse (*"gashy"*), but on entry he takes from the *"earth"* a mortal wound ("gash"). Within the logic of the metaphor's "frame," the consummation of miscegenation results in the death of Bon, whose bid for sexual possession effectively terminates the provenance of his Haitian counterclaim to the body of the estate.

With Bon's several implications severally buried, Rosa may conclude "The Funeral of an Heir" with the emphatic observation *"three women put something into the earth and covered it, and he had never been"* (p. 123). Yet *"something"* weakens her emphasis, since there is something about *"something"* that eludes the erasure of having *"never been."* Nominating exactly what escapes is difficult, but I want to argue that, despite burial, *"something"* about Bon is not dead, and that by refusing censorship it continues to live in Rosa's *"earth."* If *"gashy"* is to be believed, the revenant is not primarily sexual (i.e., some figuration of Weinstein's "inadmissible desire for racial union" still troubling Rosa). During what I would call Act IV, Rosa returns to the pall of silence that she, Clytie, and Judith have cast over the body in the bed and grave; *"But not once did we mention Charles Bon"* (p. 127). She recalls that Judith made two visits to clear leaves from *"that mound vanishing slowly back into the earth, beneath which we had buried nothing"* (p. 127). But if the grave is empty, then, by extension, the coffin was empty (Rosa did try *"to take the full weight . . . to prove . . . that he was really in it. And I could not tell"* [p. 122]).

Where, then, is Bon? All that occurs to me, since *Absalom, Absalom!* is not "A Rose for Emily," is that he is inside Rosa. Bon is a revenant living among the inferences of Rosa's narrative – which is to say, he haunts her lower semantic levels, because he survives within the contradictory situation in which she finds herself in 1865, laying proprietorial claim to a white house that blacks built. Bon lives in Sutpen's house and ground as labor's counterclaim to those properties that embody Rosa's willed membership of the master class. Ergo, Bon lives inside the goods that *are* Rosa. Because she must continue to suppress her revolution of 1848, and because that rev-

olution is recursive within slave production, Bon (who is simply another instance of that demanding trauma) must be buried only to
rise again. *

To backtrack briefly to Hegel, for whom the master's mastery depends upon the laboring presence of the slave: should the master
abjure that dependency and negate the slave, allowing him no independent consciousness, then the master will find himself en-
meshed with a dead thing (a nonconscious being). He, having
deprived himself of the very goods and recognitions that represent
his lordship, will discover himself to be close to death. Yet Hegel's
lord takes the risk, because, despite his need of the other's works
and recognitions, he seeks to be absolute in his independence.
Hence Rosa, care of Hegel and caring for Sutpen's goods, extin-
guishes Bon (as she extinguished Clytie's *"older . . . part"*), while
granting him a half-life in the form of a structurally necessary
"something" (who is also *"nothing"*), troubling the lower reaches of
her consciousness (and, consequently, the outer semantic reaches of
her prose). Bon's death and resurrection, within the substance of
Sutpen and Rosa's goods, is necessary to Sutpen and Rosa's survival
as owners. The very last thing required by Rosa's "structure of feeling"[64] is a body as irrefutable evidence of death. Confronted with
Bon's corpse, she would be in Henry's position as he pulled the
trigger, attendant at her own death or at least at the demise of the
goods that make her mastery.

If this sounds like fantasy, it nonetheless accords exactly with the
particular requirements of Rosa's situation in 1865 (and, as I will
later argue, in 1909), as well as with the imperatives of the plantation
economy. Plantation property requires that Bon be killed and reviv-
ified by Rosa (as the plantation's keeper) in perpetuity. Witness her
denial of his death even as she describes his grave – a denial that
turns on her translation of the sound of the shot that killed him
into a sound that marks his survival inside the Hundred:

> . . . that mound . . . beneath which we had buried nothing. No, there
> had been no shot. That sound was merely the sharp and final clap-to of
> a door between us and all that was, all that might have been – a ret-
> roactive severance of the stream of event: a forever crystallized instant
> in imponderable time accomplished by three weak yet indomitable women
> which, preceding the accomplished fact which we declined, refused,
> robbed the brother of the prey, reft the murderer of a victim for his very
> bullet. That was how we lived for seven months. And then one afternoon
> in January Thomas Sutpen came home; someone looked up where we
> were preparing the garden for another year's food and saw him riding

up the drive. And then one evening I became engaged to marry him. [p. 127]

Rosa makes a metaphor from a sound; the gunshot is not *like* a slamming door, it *is* the slam. By metaphoric means, she commits a massive "impertinence"[65] against the literal facts, keeping Bon quasi-alive (and so quasi-dead) on behalf of the structure of plantation facts (and, incidentally, on her own behalf as their creature and temporary owner). Once again, the issue is only superficially one of miscegenation; for although Clytie and Judith do, within Rosa's structurally realistic metaphor, love and preserve their black half-brother, they more importantly keep alive that which guarantees the fabric of the house – Bon, as the partially acknowledged presence of black resistance within that house.[66] Act IV ends, quite properly, with the return of he who would *"begin at once to salvage"* the Hundred (p. 124), the systemic core of which has been restored by its three caretakers.

When I first thought of Rosa's monologue as a drama in five acts, I took "Awaiting the Master's Return" as my fourth act's title. I now prefer "A Caretaker's Diary," since although the substance of the act is the seven months during which Rosa, Clytie, and Judith *"waited for him"* (p. 124), their "waiting" is made synonymous with "keeping" as Rosa lists the activities through which the women preserve what Sutpen built; *"We kept the house,"* *"we kept the room,"* *"we grew and tended and harvested"* (p. 125). Tasks proliferate, and the three nominally become *"one being"* (p. 125) dedicated to the structure of the Hundred.

Act V can begin as soon as their dedication pays off, by getting Bon out of the ground and back into the house. Once the formational essence of the Hundred is rehabilitated, the master has *"something"* to redeem, and the would-be mistress has *"something"* to marry. Rosa announces her engagement, at the end of the paragraph that details Bon's revivification, in a brief sentence beginning with a conjunction, because the entire logic of Acts I to IV bespeaks her determination to possess the house and contents by any means necessary, among them marriage to its master.

Her bid fails, nominally because Sutpen suggests that they "breed," indicating that marriage will depend upon the production of a male heir. On being treated like a *"bitch dog or a cow or mare,"* Rosa *"came back home"* to Jefferson (p. 136). But, as so often, Rosa's words work toward a rather different story at their lower associative levels. Take her account of why she watched him try to reverse the Civil War, *"fighting . . . against the ponderable weight of the changed new time itself"* (p. 130), by restoring, along with the integrity of the Hundred, that of the South as a plantation economy. She listens as he defies the Whitecaps:

> *telling them that if every man in the South would do as he himself was doing, would see to the restoration of his own land, the general land and South would save itself* [p. 130]

She responds as he reabsorbs the inorganic body of the estate into his person, "*a part of him encompassing each ruined field and fallen fence and crumbling wall*" (p. 129),[67] so that the title of the estate and the person of the patriarch are one.

Historically, from the perspective of 1909 and 1934, Sutpen is a realist. The plantation system *did* persist throughout the second half of the nineteenth century and for the first half of the twentieth. This is not the place to elaborate on the continuities between chattel slavery and sharecropping, save to say that the latter imposed severe restrictions on black labor. In Jay Mandle's summation, "confinement more than opportunity characterized the labor market" of the postbellum South.[68] Charles Johnson, in his sociological survey of black tenants during the early thirties in Tennessee, remarks:

> Patterns of life, social codes, as well as social attitudes, were set in the economy of slavery. The political and economic revolution through which they have passed has affected only slightly the social relationships of the community or the mores upon which they have been based. [*Shadows of the Plantation* (1934)][69]

Sutpen's historical astuteness is less relevant, here, than Rosa's reaction to it.

> *the child* [Rosa] *who watching him was not a child but one of that triumvirate mother-woman which we three, Judith Clytie and I, made, which fed and clothed and warmed the static shell and so gave vent and scope to the* [Sutpen's] *fierce vain illusion and so* [I] *said, 'At last my life is worth something, even though it only shields and guards the antic fury of an insane child.' And then one afternoon . . . I looked up and saw him looking at me.* [p. 131]

Given a sustained contextual homology between landowner and land, it would seem that Rosa's landed body "*vent[s]*" the "*child*" Sutpen. Yet, three pages earlier, the same "*gashy earth*" (p. 122) absorbed Bon, whose sexual residue in Act II quickened Rosa's "*cellar earth*" (p. 117). "*Shell*" and "*shield*" may, at first sounding, lack horticultural and gynecological edge; but during "The Summer of Wisteria" Rosa likened the "*lightless womb*" of her childhood to an ocean bed, cruised by *"blind subterranean fish,"* cast into which Bon's *"seed"* (p. 116) became *"that insulated spark whose origin the fish no longer remembers"* (p. 116). Oceanography allows that Bon's *"spark"* in Rosa's *"shell"* may be Sutpen's source. If so, the genealogical ramifications are complex, since Act II's subplot proposes Bon as Rosa's father, whereas in Act III his *"seed"* enters her more directly. Resolution is less important than the recognition that Rosa cannot escape her sense that the *"shell"* of slave property, be it embodied in the land or in the land's owner, takes its severely repressed genesis from a black *"seed."*

"Seed" grants Bon paternity or grandpaternity in his own father and serves to delight those of oedipal persuasion, because it allows the son to avenge "the primal affront . . . suffer[ed] at the hands of the father . . . the very fact of being a son – of being the generated in relation to the generator."[70] Nor should an incidence of filial vengeance occurring within a daughter's consciousness give pause to the psychoanalytically committed because, as Minrose Gwin has argued, "held in patriarchal arms . . . [and] foaming silently in front of the father's house . . . [daughters] become the feminine space that male narrative writes itself upon."[71] Except that, through it all, *"seed"* retains its link to "cotton" because the point at issue is the maintenance of a house dependent upon a cotton monoculture. Pursuit of the sexual code disperses the labor link and is encouraged by Rosa, who twice makes the tacit presence of Bon's *"seed"* the immediate occasion of Sutpen's proposal. *"And then one afternoon I looked up and saw him looking at me,"* echoes and retains, by recalling, *"And then one evening I became engaged to marry him"* (p. 127). Both instances of the conjunctive usage occur in response to Bon. At the end of Act IV, the three women resurrect him and prompt the master's counterproposal. Here, the same *"triumvirate"* deploys Rosa as a surrogate *"mother"* into whom Bon *"comes"*:

> turned twenty true enough yet still a child, still living in that womb-like corridor where the world came not even as living echo but as dead incomprehensible shadow [p. 131]

Predictably, the seminal presence is doubly disguised. Rosa's *"world"* turns on the *"echo"* of the shot that killed Bon, a shot whose fatality she has just denied (*"No, there had been no shot"* [p. 127]). Yet the *"echo"* does not *"live,"* assuming instead a second and shaded guise; that *"shadow"* which is *"dead"* is "ghostly" and may in whitened shape elicit a *"child"* from the *"mother-woman"* into whom it passes. Again, the presence of the slave's *"seed,"* albeit in dislocated form, elicits an immediate negation from the master. Sutpen must (re)impregnate Rosa to erase from her "*shell*" the mark of another.

Hegel offers the best gloss on Rosa's deeper and nonsexual sense of Sutpen's timing. On the two occasions when Rosa tries to tell Quentin about Sutpen's proposal, she takes her own person (as body and estate) to be the focal point of a struggle to the death between a master and a slave. Rosa makes herself the prize. Because she is of the owner's party, she must negate the slave's struggle and accept the master's proposal. But, because she is of that party, she must not entirely deny the slave's opposition, since, as Jessica Benjamin has Hegel say, "if we fatally negate the other, that is if we assume complete control over his identity and will, then we have negated ourselves as well."[72] Because Rosa conceives of herself within the formative tensions of slave production, she must accept the master's domination, while simultaneously recognizing (though in encrypted and barely traceable form) the slave's resistance to it.

Nor does her eventual rejection of Sutpen release her from a tension that has been with her since 1848. Her closing remarks to Quentin in 1909 indicate that her denial of Sutpen's death in 1869 still stands: "*you're not dead; heaven cannot, and hell dare not, have you*" (p. 139). Without a place in heaven or hell, Sutpen is forced to live, presumably forever, on earth. But even here Rosa insists on displacement; responding to Jefferson's rhyme, "*Rosie Coldfield, lose him, weep him; caught a beau but couldn't keep him,*" she objects:

> *I never owned him . . . I mean that he was not owned by anyone or anything in this world, had never been, would never be, not even by Ellen, not even by Jones' granddaughter. Because he was not articulated in this world. He was a walking shadow. He was the light-blinded bat-like image of his own torment cast by the fierce demoniac lantern up from beneath the earth's crust and hence in retrograde, reverse; from abysmal and chaotic dark to eternal and abysmal dark completing his descending (do you mark the gradation?) ellipsis, clinging, trying to cling with vain unsubstantial hands to what he hoped would hold him, save him, arrest him — Ellen . . . myself, then last of all that . . .* [Milly Jones]. [pp. 138–9]

At the nub of her objection to "*owned*" is her sense that Sutpen was so much the "owner" that he could not be held in forms of dependency, a conviction that disabuses the term "*owned*" of any inference of "property," in an evacuation that releases Sutpen from the pattern of denied dependency that characterizes the owner's version of slave "goods." As he who cannot be "*owned*," Sutpen is beyond "*articulation*," or dependency upon language: a judgment that shifts "*owned*" from carnal to cognitive knowledge but that also encourages a reading of "that which cannot be spoken distinctly" as "that which cannot be owned up to or confessed." In which case, Rosa's momentary implication that her summation of Sutpen is to consist of an "omission" in the form of three dots (or an "*ellipsis*") is immediately countered by the suggestion that any such gap would mark the site of a "secret."

Reading for the secret involves reading against the grain of the rhetoric of hiding that secretes it and toward that secret whose history has generated her own and Sutpen's existence. As usual, Rosa works to block understanding while obliquely indicating the source of her distress. The demonizing with which she framed the opening of her monologue returns, prompted by a contradiction: "*he was not articulated. . . . He was a walking shadow.*" By this stage in chapter five, "*shadow*" is "*articulate,*" functioning as a synonym for "black." Faced with what amounts to a summary breaking of her own code, Rosa *must* mystify, casting Sutpen across a trajectory borrowed from Milton,[73] into an "*ellipsis.*" However, Sutpen's black goods (albeit on the brink of omission) continue to trouble the terms that would exclude them ("*owned,*" "*shadow,*" and "*ellipsis*") and, presumably, will continue to disturb Rosa's language for as long as the house that carries Sutpen's name remains, for her, a site of encrypted labor conflict (Act I).

Rosa ends Act V with the denial that Sutpen is dead and the insistence that "*There's something in that house*":

> Something living in it. Hidden in it. It has been out there for four years, living hidden in that house. [p. 140]

Henry Sutpen is the most obvious candidate, but Rosa recruits Quentin to check the contents, in a darkened reprise of her journey of 1865. During her monologue Rosa has in some sense been Henry's agent. He shot a miscegenator; she, having purged the miscegenator's "*seed*" (Act II), buried the corpse (Act III). Where Henry's action destroyed planter substance and was tantamount to suicide, her fantasy retains Bon's presence, granting structural substance to property for which she cares (Act IV). Yet she has also conspired against Henry's interests, seeking to impregnate Judith in order to affirm her own hold on the Hundred (Act III), while her engagement to Sutpen, had it produced a male heir, would effectively have nullified Henry's claim. So, despite similarities, Henry is Rosa's rival, because, until his return, she, as Ellen's sister and the sole surviving white claimant, was technically mistress of the Hundred. Her fantasy had its sustaining object. Because Henry threatens that object he must be removed, though her four-year delay indicates Rosa's mixed motives. But of course what has sustained the fantasy for forty-four years, and indeed for sixty-one years (since 1848), is not a dispute between white claimants but the original and denied dispute between white masters and black workers (first bound and then nominally free) over the "goods" produced by the plantation economy. Rosa's life and utterance pivots on this dispute. Consequently, she needs both to visit and celebrate Henry as a class hero who went about his father's counterrevolutionary business and to identify and incriminate him as a class rival whose murderous act simplified the unbearable relation from which the Hundred, and she as its mistress, arose and took their peculiarly southern forms.

4

THE PERSISTENCE OF
THOMAS SUTPEN

ABSALOM, ABSALOM!, *TIME, AND LABOR DISCIPLINE*

I

Seventeen-ninety-one and 1848 are years of revolution; but why in 1934 should Faulkner create and indulge witnesses who would deny that fact? In conversation with General Compson in 1863, Thomas Sutpen suppresses his recognition that to be master is to rest enclosed in the Jacobinical head of a slave. In 1909, Rosa Coldfield delivers a philippic, in preparation for forty-four years, turning on her refusal to acknowledge that the darkness of the "dark house" derives from the instability of the black labor from which it and she take their form. Sutpen was born in west Virginia in 1807 (or thereabouts), while Rosa Coldfield was born in 1845 in Jefferson, Mississippi; they were apprenticed to the peculiar institution, and their denials are therefore perhaps understandable. What is less so is why Faulkner should be interested in evoking and compounding them.

Sutpen's story is nothing if not persistent. Its line of transmission extends from the first gossip at his appearance in Yoknapatawpha County (1833) to Quentin's last denial in "the iron New England dark" of 1910. Why go on so, when Lincoln's Emancipation Proclamation of 1863 declared three million slaves "free," and the crucial dependencies of slave production were radically reconstructed between 1863 and 1877?

Eric Foner's recent study of that reconstruction calls it "America's unfinished revolution,"[1] and to read the historical documents surrounding tenancy during the mid-thirties (as Faulkner wrote *Absalom, Absalom!*) is to recognize that the New Deal constitutes the South's "Second Civil War,"[2] another revolution from without, initiating a second and more radical reconstruction of southern labor. Faulkner *has* to go on telling the one about Thomas Sutpen, partic-

ularly from 1934–6, because, during those years, the southern owning class finally gave up on its long counterrevolution, running
arguably from Haiti in 1791 to the Agricultural Adjustment Act of
1933 (AAA), years during which owners resisted attempts (from
slave revolt to Civil War) to translate the bound laborer into the free
employee. They struggled on behalf of dependency in the face of
autonomy, seeking to preserve their status as masters rather than as
employers. To put it reductively, from 1791 to 1933, the planter
demands some version of what Mark Tushnet calls the "total relations" of slavery.[3] The names change; the tethers that bind are modified, but the goal remains – a system of production turning on
relations of personal dependency and involving the whole life of the
slave (tenant) and the whole life of the master (employer).

In 1935, Johnson, Embree, and Alexander surveyed cotton tenancy and concluded:

> The status of tenancy demands complete dependence; it re-
> quires no education and demands no initiative, since the land-
> lord assumes the prerogative of direction in the choice of crop,
> the method by which it shall be cultivated, and how and when
> and where it shall be sold. He keeps the records and deter-
> mines the earnings. Through the commissary or credit mer-
> chant, even the choice of diet is determined. The landlord can
> determine the kind and amount of schooling for the children,
> the extent to which they may share benefits intended for all
> the people. . . . He controls the courts, the agencies of law en-
> forcement . . . and can effectively thwart any efforts to organize
> to protect their [the tenants'] meagre rights.[4]

Or, as an Arkansas sharecropper put it in 1939, "De landlord is
landlord, de policeman is landlord, de shurf is landlord, ever'body
is landlord, en we ain't got nothin."[5] Of course, to preserve "total
relations" (even at the level of class fantasy) is to be liable to the
trauma inherent in them; witness Thomas Sutpen, Rosa Coldfield,
and Sutpen's postbellum witnesses. I stress that, with the exception
of Shreve, those who tell Sutpen's story are, in class terms, his inheritors – General Compson is a planter (it is he who "loaned"
Sutpen his first seed cotton); his son practices law but does so from
a house founded on slave wealth, and it is a portion of these monies,
released by the sale of Grandfather Compson's pasture, that sends
Quentin to Harvard. Each narrator depends upon a labor culture of
dependency capable of delivering traumatic "goods," and distinct
from the "partial relations"[6] of the bourgeois marketplace. There,

the independent employer of nominally "free" labor is unlikely to suffer the wounding recognition that the level of his own dependency upon the work of his workers makes him little more than an extension of their collective body.

The much-told Sutpen story is substantially retold between 1909 and 1910, to be effectively collected by Faulkner from 1934 to 1936. But, to return to my initial question, why, in 1934, start collecting the suppressed recollections of a revolution suppressed? Blandly stated, the answer can be found in the ever-falling price of cotton and in New Deal attempts to restrict overproduction of that staple. In 1933 the Agricultural Adjustment Act responded to a world market for cotton, glutted with twelve and a half million unsold bales, by offering southern landowners between seven and twenty dollars an acre (depending on estimated yield) to plow their crop under. Fifty-three percent of the South's cotton acreage went out of production. Because a sharecropper, cropping on a half-the-crop agreement, would by rights receive half the federal payment for the sacrifice of any of his acres, it paid the landowner not to sign sharecropping contracts for the following year. Instead, landowners might hire the same cropper on a wage, pay him to plow the crop under, and reap the entire subsidy themselves. Between 1933 and 1940 the southern tenantry declined by more than 25 percent, while the number of hired laborers increased, though not proportionately, since landowners might simply evict any unnecessary "dependents," enclosing their "farm" to produce larger units, more viable for mechanized agriculture.[7] Eviction, enclosure, and drastically increased tenant mobility are the visible marks of a structural change, as sharecroppers are made over into cash workers, "free" to be under- or unemployed in a region where dependency is finally ousted by autonomy as a cultural dominant.[8]

On July 26, 1934, seven blacks and eleven whites met on a plantation just outside Tyronza, Arkansas, to form the Southern Tenant Farmers' Union (STFU), as a direct response to the tide of eviction prompted by the "freeing" of the region's labor. By the end of 1935 the STFU reported a membership of 25,000 scattered across six states. Two strikes to raise picking prices, one in 1935 (successful) and another in the following year (broken), turned the crisis of tenancy into a national issue:

Largely because of the headlines, newsreels and radio broadcasts stimulated by the STFU's struggle in the Arkansas Delta, the problem of farm tenancy had become a leading topic of discussion across the country.[9]

Press demand for images of the ruined peasantry prompted Roy Stry-
ker, head of the Historical Section of the Farm Security Administration, to exhort his photographers to "make a big drive on tenancy pictures."[10] They photographed the misery consequent upon
systematic removals, but as Paul Schuster Taylor (economist and
co-author with Dorothea Lange of *An American Exodus* [1939]) put
it in 1937, emiseration was a symptom of the "greatest revolution
since the Civil War . . . [in] the cotton sections of the South."[11]
The historian Jonathon Wiener makes a similar point when he
notes that the influx of federal subsidy checks induced greater transition than the influx of federal troops.[12] And Donald Grubbs
continues the trope by describing the Farm Security Administration's 1937 attack on "tenancy['s] . . . version of slavery" as a
Second Reconstruction.[13] I add merely that what was, by the mid-
thirties, perceived as a radical restructuring of labor was in actuality
only the final phase of a far longer revolution, aimed at freeing the
bound.

Of course, the transformation of a laboring class is necessarily the
co-transformation of the class that binds; yet from 1791 to 1933
southern landowners most typically showed little inclination to release themselves from their dependency upon dependent labor. Why
should they? As Gavin Wright suggests, by protecting their low-wage
economy and preserving the separateness of their region's labor
market, they (at least until the declining international price of cotton in the 1920s) maintained reasonable returns on minimal investment.[14] They had little to invest; with up to 60 percent of their
antebellum capital tied up in people's bodies, Emancipation came
as a massive devaluation of planter assets, leaving them only their
land, whose value plummeted after the war.[15] Without capital to pay
wages, but with land ready to plant, landowners had to negotiate the
reattachment of freedmen to that land. Sharecropping emerged as
the eventual solution, a labor pattern that remains regionally typical
from the end of Radical Reconstruction to the close of the New Deal.
Sharecroppers and tenants were a far more important labor source
on plantations than wage workers; in 1909, more than 70 percent
of plantation land was operated by tenants and croppers, a figure
that probably underestimates their prevalence in the production of
cotton (a survey of 1920 has more than 80 percent of cotton land
farmed under some form of tenant agreement).[16] In the 1930s, com-
mentators described tenants as "virtual slaves,"[17] held "in thrall,"[18]
subjected to "almost complete dependence,"[19] and "incapable of
ever achieving but a modicum of self direction."[20] They were wrong:
"freedmen" who farmed on shares were not slaves, but nor were

they "free." Dependency, not autonomy, defines the social relations through which they were required to live their lives, at least until the AAA pushed labor from the South and increased the bargaining power of those who stayed. Between 1930 and 1940 the number of black southern sharecroppers declined by almost a quarter, in an outmigration that Jay Mandle equates with the final "undermining of share tenantry."[21] He notes that "deference became increasingly anachronistic and irrelevant [as] . . . labor market relations began, for the first time, to resemble real negotiations"[22]: real, presumably, in that employer and employee both negotiated from assumptions of autonomy. Where "dependency" and its synonyms, "deference" and "paternalism" once stood, "autonomy" and its poor euphemisms "freedom" and "equality" stand, at least by the end of the 1930s.

Absalom, Absalom! is a novel about dependency both as a fact of labor and as a consequent mental fact for the owning class. Faulkner wrote the novel between 1934 and 1936 because during those years a dependency culture and its labor base were dramatically exposed as economically archaic. Which is not to say that peonage did not exist in the South until well into the 1950s and beyond,[23] or that deference and paternalism vanished in 1940; it is merely to argue that dependency, and its foundation in a peculiarly southern system of production, is no longer a regional typicality[24] by the end of the 1930s. I am aware that, in my struggle to locate Absalom, Absalom!'s substance and moment in the termination of a lengthy counterrevolution, I have skated diagrammatically over disputed historical areas, which I had best now fill in.

Central to the historical debate is the rate of new class formation in the postbellum South. Even "half a revolution,"[25] "unfinished,"[26] has considerable structural consequences. The Civil War turned masters into masters without slaves, but it left them with their plantations. At the same time, chattels became "free" and human; but, because the war settlement did not invoke a redistribution of land to ex-slaves, and because most "freedmen" acquired no property under slavery, "freedmen" were without means and found their employment chances in the hands of ex-masters. In such circumstances, it may be difficult for the landlord to accept that he is no longer a labor lord. Slavery was "a shattered world,"[27] but the new class structure that replaced it bore limited relation to Radical Reconstruction's free-market dream. Foner notes:

Former masters and former slaves inherited from slavery work habits and attitudes at odds with free labor assumptions . . . and

both recognized . . . the irreconcilability of their respective interests and aspirations.[28]

Landowners sought prewar levels of control but had to reorganize
production fast or face bankruptcy. Freedmen wanted autonomy but
had as a lever only their capacity to work. Consequently, northern
hopes for the development of wage labor in the South proved
fragile; freedmen were sufficiently "free" to resist gang labor and
vagrancy acts, but lacking capital they were not "free" enough to
avoid being bound in yet another peculiar institution – the institution of sharecropping.

Share wages differ substantially from free wages. The owner contracts to pay his laborer at the close of the growing season; payment
takes the form of a predetermined share of the crop. Should the
yield be low, or the international price of cotton drop, or the market
be glutted, the cropper may not make enough to pay the merchant
who has "furnished" his seed and sustenance on credit for the year
– in which case, the tenant becomes a peon insofar as he is bound
to labor to pay the debt.[29] A study of black tenants in Alabama in
1932 estimated that only 10 percent received any cash for their
year's work, with the remainder "breaking even" or "going into the
hole."[30] With labor immobilized by such means, the debt holder –
be he the merchant, or the planter, or both as one – exerts an
absolute authority over the laborer. Jonathon Wiener argues that
because owners maintained "involuntary servitude" as "the special
form of Southern wage" from Reconstruction to New Deal, they
cannot be spoken of as "classical capitalists."[31] Eric Foner, less emphatic, speaks of the South as "a peculiar hybrid – an improvised
colonial economy integrated into the capitalist market place yet with
its own distinctive system of repressive labor relations."[32] Mandle
specifies the distinction, arguing that "the plantation mode of production" (turning on labor "confinement") is a better analytic device for interpreting postbellum economic underdevelopment and
racial etiquette than "the capitalist mode of production."[33] He emphasizes how much of capitalism is missing from the South, at least
until the early forties. The South is not a free labor market, nor does
"bourgeois individualism" (shadowed by "merit" and "universalist
principle") carry much weight in a region where "subordination
and paternalism typify relations between white and black."[34] Capital
thrives on expectations of rapid economic change and technological
transformation, but technological stagnation typifies the production
of cotton.

There is much to say for establishing a structural divide between northern capitalist and southern landowner. In the North, capital developed sequentially after the Civil War; enhanced mechanization intensified labor divisions and increased surpluses, which in turn prompted competitive investment in technology. Innovation raised output, and the threat of overproduction ensured a "high-wage" economy in which workers doubled as consumers. Capitalists, too, had to change, converting their "captaincy" from industry to consciousness,[35] in order to maintain consumption. Almost none of the terms, in my potted trot through the Gilded Age toward Partial Fordism, apply in the South, where landowners had little interest in transforming their workers or their technology or themselves, since sharecropping guaranteed a low-cost labor force tied to the land and delivering a reasonable profit for as long as cotton prices remained high.[36] Moreover, mechanization appeared redundant in the context of a large and "bound" labor force. Indeed, machinery would only disrupt a social and political order founded on the owner's capacity to pay low across the board; that order "constituted a fully formed system"[37] whose difference from northern "classic capitalism" rested on labor-repressive production, enforced by state restrictions on the mobility of workers.

Mandle puts the separatist case emphatically; others are of a gradualist persuasion, defining the postbellum South as a capitalist society in a state of malfunction. For Harold Woodman,

> the New South might best be seen as an evolving bourgeois society in which a capitalist social structure was arising on the ruins of a pre-modern slave society. It was going through a process of social change, of modernization, that the rest of the nation had gone through half a century or more earlier. But where the rest of the nation had made the change with a social and political structure and an ideology that generally supported such changes, the postwar South was going through the change with the remnants of a social and political structure and an ideology that had been antagonistic to such changes.[38]

Yet the sheer resiliency of the "ruins" and the antagonisms generated within the share-wage system suggest that Woodman's "remnants" deserve Mandle's designation as a distinctive "mode of production" – a mode in which neither owners nor laborers were "free." Because the laborer could not realize his "wage" until he cashed in his crop ("the long pay"[39]), he was bound to the land for at least a year, during which time the landlord sought "unlimited power over the productive energies of the cropper and his family";[40] or, in the words of Charles Johnson, writing in 1934, the planter "demands an unquestioning obedience to his managerial intelligence . . . the right to dictate and control every stage of cultivation; [he] cannot and does not tolerate the suggestion of independent status."[41] What Johnson misses is that while "policing" at this level ensures that the tenant stays "known,"[42] it also ensures that the knower knows little else, thereby rendering himself liable to the damaging recognition that he depends upon his dependents.

Whether one views Johnson's "tradition of dependence"[43] as the result of a distinctive system of production or as the remnant of a remnant, it *is* clear that "dependency" is both all-pervasive and much-disputed within the agricultural South from Redemption to New Deal. Two examples must demonstrate my meaning. For Foner, black tenants were "a disenfranchised class of dependent laborers";[44] Wiener speaks of "involuntary servitude,"[45] and Peter Daniel of "peonage" and "virtual slave labor."[46] Yet the same people, according to Woodman, are learning to be free laborers,[47] while for Barbara Jeanne Fields they are "the next thing to wage hands."[48] The party of the "remnant" takes heart from evidence of considerable, if localized, cropper mobility – on the grounds that he who is "free" to move is loosely "bound."[49] Yet mobility may be read two ways: from below, as evidence of cropper resistance, whereby former slaves and their descendants "run away" each year (from bad to bad), thereby setting themselves apart from their forebears in bondage.[50] Alternatively, from above: because tenant debts were more often contrived than real, a landowner might "keep" or "let go" whomever he wished, being motivated by "a planter's principle, best summarized as the endless quest for the perfect (that is the perfectly subordinate) laborer."[51] I would add that neither emphasis translates mobility into evidence of a regional market in "free" labor. As with mobility, so with the share contract itself, the agreement was the site of dispute. Settled on in the immediate aftermath of war, it might appear even-handed, granting freedmen a degree of autonomy and landowners a degree of control; that degree depends upon who reads the contract: from below, "freedmen insisted that their working on shares made them partners . . . and, indeed, had a voice in decisions concerning production."[52] From above, managerial prerogative lay with whoever held the debt, and because the cropper, more often than not, "furnished" out of the landowner's store on credit whose interest ran from usury to larceny,[53] the prerogative of that debt might be absolute.

II

A year after finishing *Absalom, Absalom!*, Faulkner wrote "Barn Burning" (1938), a story detailing two "crimes" against property – a rug and a barn – whereby a tenant seeks to command a degree of 'freedom' and mobility within a sharecropping agreement. Narration is in the third person, but the story is told from the viewpoint of a key witness, the tenant's ten-year-old son. Named for the polarities of a class war conducted within the parameters of dependency, Colonel Sartoris Snopes predictably sees his father's "offenses" from above and below simultaneously and so is torn apart. Like Sutpen before him, the boy has a crucial experience at the threshold of a white house. Ab Snopes takes his son to Colonel DeSpain's plantation for a lesson in labor relations, pointing out that the boy had best hear his father, "have a word with the man that aims to begin . . . owning me body and soul for the next eight months."[54] The pronoun is capacious, since a landlord operating share wages assumes that his contract with a titular head includes the labor of his kin. The boy – shown variously splitting wood, plowing, and handling stock – is, therefore, part of the "me" that DeSpain aims to dispossess. No words are exchanged (DeSpain is away), but unlike Sutpen the boy and his father penetrate the big house or, more particularly, rape a rug. Faulkner focuses the tortuous interdependencies of the landlord/tenant contract through one object; the rug, "blond," French, priced at a hundred dollars, and a part of Miss Lula (or at least of "her house" [p. 316]), is palpably gendered and subjected to the attentions of Ab's boot:

> He just stood stiff in the center of the rug, in his hat, the shaggy iron-grey brows twitching slightly above the pebble-colored eyes as he appeared to examine the house with brief deliberation. Then with the same deliberation he turned; the boy watched him pivot on the good leg and saw the stiff foot drag round the arc of the turning, leaving a final long and fading smear [p. 12].

The anatomical markers are crudely deliberate, as is Miss Lula's "hysteric . . . wail" (p. 312) at the Snopes withdrawal, but the offense is complex in ways that finally elude the tenant's "deliberation." Ab is autochthonous and his foot is his synecdoche. Autochthony, most famously borne by Oedipus, whose name means "swollen foot," is the state of having sprung from the soil (proverbially "a son of . . ." same) and is often signaled by a clubbed or wounded foot. In Ab's case the wound owes something to Achilles (being received in the heel from a Confederate musket [p. 315]). The insurgent foot is classically weighty but carries a mixed message; Oedipus killed his father (and Ab confronts a paternalist employer, whose class has a nominal claim on his son's paternity); Achilles' heel was his death (but Ab, at least in the matter of the rug, leads with his spoiled foot – a step that within the confines of the story may be the death of him). The limb, whatever the import of its pedigree, "seemed to bear (or transmit) twice the weight which the body compassed" (p. 311) and is both a pivotal point ("compass" and "arc") and a contradictory part (his is a "stiff . . . limp" [p. 10]). Centered "in the center" of the rug – a token both of the planter's house and of his wife – Ab "pivot[s]" in an "arc" that at once "[en]compass[es]" and soils DeSpain's goods. Usage here is odd on several counts: "compassed," in a geometrical context, suggests "to encompass"; so . . . Ab's foot carries twice the weight of that which his body (or gaze) encompasses. The enhanced body weight is easily explained; tenant plus planter property equals a load. The equation turns on "compassed" or its synonym "to encompass" . . . "to draw a circle round," "to surround with friendly or unfriendly intent," "to take the measure of" and therefore to understand or possess. Read this way, Ab's boot, bound to the soil, of which it is the son, takes vengeance with the soil on those items that have been raised upon and stolen from the soil.[55] The planter's household, founded on a version of bound labor, rests on the tenant's foot and is an extension of his body, and Ab knows it. The assault complete,

> [h]e stood for a moment, planted stiffly on the stiff foot, looking back at the house, "Pretty and white, ain't it?" He said. "That's sweat. Nigger sweat. Maybe it ain't white enough yet to suit him. Maybe he wants to mix some white sweat with it." [p. 312]

At this point Ab is a demotic Hegelian. For Hegel, the bound man (whose essence is to labor for another's will) is liberated by the objects of his labor, because in the independent existence of those things that *he* has made, he discovers himself as having "a being and a mind of his own."[56] However, Hegel did not have a son called Colonel Sartoris Snopes, nor did he appreciate that men united in bondage might be divided by race. Ab knows that the house and its contents derive from him, or at least from his class, but he turns the class against itself by refusing an alliance in sweat with the black body of tenancy. Indeed, Ab deploys one version of that black body to enhance the impact of his attack on the great house, the "it" that he declares "pretty and white," even as a woman "wail[s]," may refer beyond the house to the "pallid," "blond" rug. Ab's stiffness is black, in Ab's version of Lula's mind, in direct proportion to the extent that his assault has a sexual edge; in the 1890s, when the story is set, the currency of the notion of the African American male as "beast" or "rapist" darkens Ab's rigidity.[57] However, by blacking up sexually, Ab disables himself in class terms (the boot finally fits Achilles). To draw a racial line in sweat, when the body of your class is predominately black,[58] is, to say the least, to shoot yourself in the foot – a self-mutilation indulged by the Farmers' Alliance during the 1890s.

Ab's foot is complicated[59] not only by its classical freight and ethnic complexion but also by its implied witness – the nominally divided son – to whom the "prints" of the father's "stiff foot" appear "machinelike" (p. 311), a simile from the landlord's party, neutralizing the tenant's will by declaring him a mechanical man, incapable of insubordination. However, the boy is in two minds; remember that his father's foot both suffers and issues the weight that it carries – I had best quote the problematic phrases again, "the foot which seemed to bear (or transmit) twice the weight which the body compassed." "Transmit," implying that the planter's house issues from the tenant's dirtied boot, is bracketed as an afterthought, priority being granted to the politically less troubling sense of the tenant as one who "bear[s]" or suffers. The son, quite literally, cannot balance his father out, being unable to hold, in a single thought, the contraries of the tenant as victim and the tenant as agent; hence the ungainly phrasing, the seeping parenthesis, and the resonant subsemantics. Eventually, the boy makes a decision; he betrays his father in the act of burning DeSpain's barn and by making himself the planter's ally denies himself a class home among the tenants.

Sutpen went to Haiti. Colonel Sartoris Snopes runs, vanishing from the story and from the Snopes canon.[60] The manner of his departure is significant; at dawn, backed up against a tree and unsure of whether DeSpain's shots in the dark have rendered him patricidal, he drops the familiar "Pap" and uses "Father," applying a possessive to the man whom he has dispossessed of political agency. "Father. My Father, he thought. 'He was brave!' . . . He was in Colonel Sartoris' cav'ry'" (p. 24). By converting a lonely labor radical into a minor equestrian statue, having just been knocked down by DeSpain on a "galloping mare . . . in furious silhouette against the stars" (p. 24), Colonel Sartoris Snopes denies one patrimony (Snopes) by affiliating it to another and inappropriate line (Sartoris/DeSpain).

Faulkner knows what the boy does not know, that Ab went to war for "booty . . . enemy booty or his own" (p. 25). A Confederate shot him through his boot, and his boot writes dirty truths in DeSpain's hall. Much about this story reverts to the troubling foot, perhaps because during the 1890s, as in the 1910s, when the boy recalls his father's acts, tenant mobility, however impaired, is central to tenant resistance. Indeed, by 1938 mobility had become exodus as evicted tenants moved North in a black diaspora.[61] In effect, at the story's close, on foot and on the road, Colonel Sartoris Snopes is a ten-year-old migrant laborer. He leaves "a little stiff" and choired by "whippoorwills" (p. 25). Neither endnote is casual; the boy imitates his father's signatory step, "but walking would cure that," not least because his "will" is broken – breakage stems directly from an inability to understand the meaning of fire in his father's hands. Moving between cropping for Harris (whose barn has burned) and cropping for DeSpain (whose barn will burn), the family has a fire, "a small fire, neat, niggard almost, a shrewd fire" (p. 7). "Niggard" is repeated three times within the space of a page, but the narrator assures us that neither the boy nor the man he becomes reads the shrewdness in the pun, although "he had seen those same niggard blazes all his life" (p. 8). Omniscience translates:

> he might have divined . . . that the element of fire spoke to some deep mainspring of his father's being . . . as the one weapon for the preservation of integrity. [pp. 7–8]

Flame, to Ab Snopes, is almost black, as "niggard" is almost "nigger" – almost but not quite. Faulkner pushes the point by attaching a literary name tag to Ab's ubiquitous frockcoat; summoned from the "niggard blaze," the boy sees his father "against the stars . . . a shape black, flat, and bloodless as though cut from tin in the iron folds of the frockcoat" (p. 8). Any reader as well versed in Conrad as Faulkner will appreciate the theft; Ab, by flame and intertext, is all but a "Nigger," given that the crew of the *Narcissus* first appear against that vessel's "illuminated doorways," "very black, without relief, like figures cut out of sheet tin."[62] What is interesting, here, is that the association cannot be fully articulated. Even though Faulkner writes after the interracial activities of the Southern Tenant Farmers' Union (1934–7), he senses that a white tenant who destroys a planter's goods cannot do so in the name of his *whole* class, because that acknowledgment would render his class body more black than white. Recognition is blocked ("niggard" is not "nigger"), not least because of the resilience of dependency, and its key trauma, grounded in the institutional persistence of bound labor.

Again, Hegel offers a way into Ab's failure to achieve the relative independence of full class consciousness; were he to negate the landlord, who "owns" so much of his disputatious "body and soul," he would destroy himself, because labor conditions require that his body and soul seek recognition through that landlord. Apprenticed to dependency, as a structure of feeling arising from "the plantation as a system of production," the tenant who resists is necessarily a king-killing Oedipus with an Achilles' heel. Ab's "stiff" boot will always be "limp" – particularly because his preferred weapon is dou- ble-edged: "fire" grants him moments of "integrity," which are also small deaths, in that he who diminishes his lord diminishes himself. A vocabulary of diminution ghosts Ab, who is variously "less" than human – "wiry" (p. 4), "flat," "bloodless" (p. 8), and "depthless," his coat the color of "old house flies" (p. 11), his hand "a curled claw" (p. 11), and his track, purged from DeSpain's rug, "lillipu- tian" (p. 14). In this aspect he resembles Prometheus, whose interest in flame leads to repeated and liverish diminishment. Ab's fire is, we are told, his "living fruit," the root of his "integrity," but insofar as Ab (né Prometheus) may wander allusively through a Garden out of *Genesis*, his plundered "fruit" involves a Knowledge that will ex- clude him from intimacy with the Lord. So stenciled, "fire" is am- bivalent, ensuring an expulsion that will merely "free" him to migrate to another landlord, while exposing him to an entirely more intimidating social mediator.

The black most typically found in the "niggard" flame during the 1890s is a lynched victim, but the "niggard blaze" is, for Ab, a "liv- ing fruit" and not a "strange" one in that fire is his means to in- dependent existence, however brief. Whether or not Faulkner uses "living" in "living fruit" as a conscious antonym, summoning "strange fruit" into a semantic mix, I cannot determine. Lewis Al- len's song "Strange Fruit" was first sung by Billie Holiday at Café Society, an interracial Greenwich Village club, early in 1939.[63] Whether Allen is the title's source, or whether he borrowed a phrase current in the late thirties, a phrase perhaps available to Faulkner, I have been unable to discover. But finally, aside from academic pride, the footnote doesn't matter. A "niggard blaze" in the 1890s, recalled in the 1910s and recorded in 1938, must contain among its semantic embers a charred black body; that such a body, buried in the subsemantics of "niggard," may have been "living fruit," or more particularly, "the living fruit of nights passed during . . . four years in the woods hiding from all men, blue or gray, with his strings of horses" (p. 7), is both a charged and heavily disguised recogni- tion. There is little here to go on, and a great deal to find. Does Faulkner imply that the Civil War teaches Ab two things; to burn a parsimonious flame, and to preserve white supremacy by fire as the only "fruit" he is liable to take from a bound life? Or, alternatively, does Ab learn from a war on the run, during which he "admitt[ed] the authority . . . [of] no man or army or flag" (pp. 24–5), that the ally to be found in the fire is the "nigger" as runaway – or the black who refuses tenancy, and, as part of an exodus (running from the 1890s to the 1930s), seeks "autonomy" under "free" wage labor in the North?

I have unearthed semantic scraps, socially grounded, but tenuously so. The cultural dominant, "dependency," ties "niggard" to white supremacy, while tenant resistance orientates it to diaspora. Finally neither inflection is fully articulated, and "niggard" joins

> all those vague and undeveloped experiences, thoughts, and idle, accidental words that flash across our minds. They are all of them cases of miscarriages of social orientations, novels without heroes, performances without audiences. They lack any sort of logic or unity.[64]

Illogicality lies not in the words but in the social conditions through which they are semanticized. Glossed by the linguist Vološinov, "niggard" is "a novel without a hero" because neither Ab nor his son is sufficiently at liberty to read barn burning as an act committing them to the black tenant as the mediator through whom they may discover their full class "integrity." Consequently, "niggard" is charged with impossible ethnic alliances, with class betrayals underrealized, and with unresolvable social contradictions. The word is induced by Faulkner's sense of a revolution resisted even as it is completed; in the 1890s a "niggard blaze" contains "strange fruit," although Ab's racism is relatively low-key, involving the epithet "nigger" used, significantly, "without heat" (p. 11). By 1938, thanks largely to the activities of the STFU, "niggard" foregrounds the radical ethnic option; but Ab strikes for himself, and his mobility lacks the dimension of migration. Admittedly, the story ends with his son as a displaced migrant, but that son's name highlights the cultural resilience of dependency even as it gives way to autonomy born of waged work.

Which leaves the question I should have asked in the first place; why does Ab name his youngest son Colonel Sartoris Snopes? Whether the conjunction of nominal opposites (as nominally opposed as master/slave, landlord/tenant) involved irony – pulling the master down into the class whose labor raised him up – or simply commanded notice is in the last instance irrelevant. Either version (and both are structurally required) declares the interdependence of Snopes and Sartoris by lodging them in a single body (even as the bound man's body is inhabited by the master's will, and the master's body is the vessel of the bound man's labor). However, from the perspective of the late thirties, the name is an anomaly; federal programs, prompting the collapse of the share wage, have loosened the structural glue binding the body of the lord to the body of the bound man. Consequently, the boy's names are forced historically apart. Betrayal cancels "Snopes," but migration North renders "Colonel Sartoris" a liability. The name, and the tradition of dependence that it encodes, will dissolve in the solvent of waged work.

"Barn Burning" is very much an afterword to *Absalom, Absalom!* Written out of Faulkner's despair over modernization (confronted through *Pylon* [1935], which he wrote while writing and rewriting Sutpen's narrative), the story explores the limited patterns of resistance within the cropping contract. In this it differs from *Absalom, Absalom!*, being a view from below, but story and novel share a single trigger – the breaking of the plantation system of agriculture, and the attendant exposure of "dependency" as a cultural remnant, no longer useful to a dominant class, finally forced to revolutionize itself, and moving from "pre," or "quasi," to "full" bourgeois status.

I must revert briefly to the historical narrative. My case has been that, at least in the agricultural section, and at least until the late thirties, owners were not a bourgeoisie. The planter's concern with the maintenance of repressive social relations, as a means to a low-wage economy, marginalized those props to the bourgeois world – individual freedom and consumerism. Consequently, the planter was a bourgeois in an impacted state of development. In this the South differed strikingly from the North, whose modernization had had the ideological backing of the dominant institutions. For some historians of the South, "modernization" is complete by the thirties. Jack Kirby points out that by 1934 the average income of planters was on a par with that of white-collar professionals (physicians, attorneys, and dentists). He therefore concludes that "planters were of the modern world. Their tenants to varying degrees were not."[65] His distinction ignores the degree to which the very process of maintaining a peasantry casts the maintainer in a pre-modern mold. He who preserves longstanding prohibitions, denying access to debt book or mystifying market procedure, does so to perpetuate a dispensation that has been naturalized by time, in the light of which he who commands service is liable to see himself, aristocratically, as more a master, a father, and a lord than a farmer. The planter, equipped with the share wage agreement, continued to be (in Woodman's terms) an antagonistic remnant liable to resist his own modernization.

Absalom, Absalom! is forced into existence from the collapsing center of this labor structure. Situated at the commercial edge of the owning class[66] as its counterrevolution fails, and prompted by cumulative evidence of eviction, exodus, and tenant unrest, Faulkner anatomizes the long last days of an archaic structure of feeling. In 1939, Steinbeck has Tom Joad famously kill a Company man with an instrument of labor (a pick handle). In 1936 (and 1869), Faulkner's Wash Jones executes his landlord with a scythe, thereby ensuring a critical reputation as Father Time. But a scythe is a tool, and the murder an act of labor upheaval performed with one working implement and compounded with another. Jones cuts the throats of his granddaughter Milly and of her unnamed daughter by Sutpen with "the butcher knife . . . the one thing in his sloven life that he was ever known to take pride in or care of."[67] Having severed the genealogical continuity of one strain of the master class, he runs, scythe to the fore, into the guns of the "men of Sutpen's own kind" (p. 232), those who "set the order and rule of living" (p. 232). Wash's exit is an early incident in an underdeclared class war. At the time, in 1869, dependency has been redeemed as the "order" of life, and consequently resistance is suicide – so, in scything Sutpen's family tree, Wash necessarily butchers his own. However, by 1936, the "rule" of the planter class is all but over; perhaps because Faulkner casts Wash's "crime" back in time, its incipient status as a labor revolt is critically missed.

Like "niggard" in "Barn Burning," the scythe, knife, and Wash's use of them have to be read from at least two temporal perspectives. Viewed from 1869, they add up to a domestic killing, after which Wash imagines all the voices "murmuring":

> *Old Wash Jones come a tumble at last. He thought he had Sutpen, but Sutpen fooled him. He thought he had him, but old Wash Jones got fooled.* [pp. 232–3]

Recalled in 1909, as Mr. Compson tells Quentin the story, and with southern labor quiescent (though given to localized resistance over enclosure[68]), Wash's "motive" may just contain a class dimension; like Colonel Sartoris Snopes (after him), Wash is bound to an equestrian statue, "the fine proud image of the man on the fine proud image of the stallion" (p. 230), by means of which "apotheosis . . . beyond all human fouling" (p. 232), the tenant is drawn into the master's mastery. "Apotheosis," *canonization*, or *deification* also involves notions of "ascension" and "resurrection." Wash, who during the war claimed to stand in the master's place ("I'm looking after the Kernel's place and niggers" [p. 225]), and who ever after remains "somehow mixed up and involved with galloping hooves" (p. 230), considers himself caught up in the ascendant of Sutpen's plan to resurrect the Hundred:

> *Maybe I am not as big as he is and maybe I did not do any of the galloping. But at least I was drug along where he went. And me and him can still do hit and will ever so, if so be he will show me what he aims for me to do.* [p. 231]

Unsurprisingly, their sharing extends to birth; "they were of the same age almost to a day."[69] Yet, on hearing the master refer to Milly as a "mare" (p. 231), the tenant recognizes that he and his are merely the "stock," or goods and chattels, through which masters sustain mastery. As a result, in Hegelian fashion, Wash experiences "negation," "maybe feeling no earth, no stability . . . maybe not even hearing his own voice" (p. 231). His death, structurally, will provoke the death of the master. Murder follows. Resting from his labor, Wash concludes:

> *Better if his kind and mine too had never drawn the breath of life on this earth. Better that all who remain of us be blasted from the face of it than that another Wash Jones should see his whole life shredded from him and shrivel away like a dried shuck thrown onto the fire.* [p. 233]

Corn is "shucked"; "shredding" involves a removal of outer leaves – in the context of labor instruments, these processes, and Wash's metaphoric allusion to them, denote the degree to which he recognizes that, as a tenant, he has been no more than a quantity of disposable labor. Gone is the bound man's deference. Released from within the master's body (or at least from servicing that body as servant, groom, and pander), Wash stands "free" and on the edge of class consciousness. He speaks of *"kinds"* and will act from a desire to prevent his own condition from becoming "typical." Which is to say, Wash is no longer the subject of local gossip ("murmuring"), but one of many who seek, in Engels' terms, to transform "the laws and perspectives of future social development"[70] by stopping *"another Wash Jones"* coming into being. Though it is significant that, even now, he cannot conceive of the independence of his class; plantocracy and tenancy, having lived as one, will perish as one.

So inflected, the killings are part of a class scenario. I would emphasize, however, that "Father said" is choric to this version, and that Mr. Compson is fond of the word "maybe." In 1909, with the plantation system of production firmly in place, *class* antagonism is perceivable only through the veil of particular and particularizing interdependencies. However, from 1936, the year of the STFU's second strike, of President Franklin Roosevelt's appointment of a Presidential Committee on Farm Tenancy, and of violent tenant evictions throughout the Delta,[71] scythe and butcher knife become weapons in a class war, and the veil of dependency is torn.

III

Faulkner first wrote the Wash Jones story in 1934 (as "Wash"); it therefore prefaces his work on the novel into which it passed, indicating that, from the first, Faulkner thinks about Sutpen through the issue of the binding and unbinding of labor. With Wash as "foreword" and "Barn Burning" as "afterword," it is difficult *not* to read *Absalom, Absalom!* as Faulkner's most sustained exploration of "dependency," its persistence and demise.

However, both stories leave out the bound black man and in so doing avoid the problematic heart not simply of the plantation system but also of the owning class – their very "good" and goods. Consequently, neither offers more than a diagrammatic stencil of the matter that makes Sutpen. Bon – his "good" and goods – is a body repeatedly declared missing and yet, as repeatedly, made central. I have argued that his highly visible quasi-invisibility expresses a labor fact; or, more particularly, the traumatic inability of the members of the owning class to constitute themselves *as* owners without expelling black labor from their mastery (or goods) while simultaneously retaining black labor, in a denied form, at their structural core (or good). Bon, consequently, represents the contradictory essence of "dependency" – a "character" who is not only a black in a white face (miscegenation), but who is also a white master doubling as a black slave (labor trauma). Faulkner's primary concern is with the latter, hence his choice of name; Bon, or "good" (the master's "good" or masterful integrity), which good resides in "goods" as they are shaped by black work. So named, Bon is not just another tragic mulatto. Because it is essential to dependency that the white master all but deny his black structure, the pun remains virtually silent. Furthermore, we never know for sure whether Bon is black, or whether he knows that he might be black. But ignorance, here, is not an epistemological problem; rather, it is Faulkner's way of exposing the haunted and doubled nature of planter ascendancy, and of the labor trauma from which it and *Absalom, Absalom!* arise.

Nonetheless, given the prevalence of the trauma in the novel, I would argue that we *do* know that each of the narrators (bar Shreve) knows exactly who Bon is. Which is to say not only that the eyewitnesses recognize Bon but also that the secondary sources inherit their recognition, knowing, from the first, that Bon is Sutpen's black son. However, as heirs both to Sutpen's story and to his "goods," they are bound almost to deny it. "Almost" is the key here, since, to return for a moment to Hegel, via Jessica Benjamin,

> if we fatally negate the other, that is if we assume complete control over his identity and will, then we have negated ourselves as well.[72]

For "negate" read "deny." For "other" read "Bon." For "assumption of complete control" read "casting Bon as white and only as white." And for "self negation" read "the lapse of class consciousness attendant upon *complete* denial of Bon's blackness." Revised to suit the class position of those who narrate *Absalom, Absalom!*, Benjamin's statement reads, "If we fatally deny Bon, that is, if we cast Bon as white and only white, then, by way of our complete denial of Bon's blackness, we have denied what is structurally central to ourselves as a class" . . . which is something no southern narrator is, at any stage, able to do.

Addressing racial and sexual stereotyping during the Radical era, Joel Williamson asks:

> how [does one] take the racism, the unreality of seeing black as either child or beast, out of the Southern mind without killing the Southerner? How does one excise a functioning part of the body yet preserve the life of the patient?[73]

Transposed to the context of bound labor, his questions are still more exacting; the argument would run – since the work of the variously bound black body produces the substance of the white body, even to speak of excising the black and "functioning part" is to extinguish the white body. But since the white body derives from the black, while retaining black in secret forms, Bon must be both "black" and kept back by his narrators.

The claim that Bon is peculiarly "known" by all narrators (bar Shreve) carries the consequence that their various versions, to a degree consciously, misrepresent him. To read their accounts as structured around calculated error and informed distortion is, firstly, to recover from distortion the labor trauma which that distortion seeks all but to bury; and, secondly, to recognize that the double articulation, which is the shared form of distortion, reflects a class imperative among the distorters. Or, to put it another way, to know that the narrators *know* may be to trace how a pervasive trauma produces a prevalent aesthetics, which intimate a shared politics.

But to make any of this stick, I must first prove that everyone (bar

Shreve) knows about Bon from the start. I am uncomfortable coming on, if not as a detective, then as Cleanth Brooks, since the pursuit of clues as to who knows what (when, where, and how) is always liable to trip the novel into an epistemological regression – a bolt-hole down which I do not wish to vanish, given that it has been my case that readers find time for an epistemological crisis only because they miss the more material crises of class and ethnicity. But, for a moment, to play Brooks . . . his scrupulous notes, attached to *William Faulkner: Yoknapatawpha Country*,[74] have trained the critical tradition in detection, as a result of which the across-the-board assumption is that no one knows (bar Sutpen) until Quentin knows. There is some dispute over when he finds out, but the tacit consensus has it that Henry tells him, somewhat elliptically, on the night of his own visit to the Hundred as Rosa's attendant in 1909. Brooks proposes Henry as source because only Henry is in a position to know and to pass on the knowledge that Bon is his black half-brother. Variants have emerged: Sundquist argues forcefully that, although Quentin learns on that night in 1909, he does so not from Henry upstairs but from Rosa at the door – as Shreve puts it, "she didn't tell you in the actual words because even in the terror she kept the secret: nevertheless she told you, or at least all of a sudden you knew –" (p. 280). Stonum was there first,[75] but Kartiganer modifies the case, arguing for Quentin as late-developed face reader in order to protect him from a charge of hypocrisy. This is Kartiganer's case; if Quentin already knows about Bon's identity (signed, sealed, and bespoke care of Henry) while talking with Shreve, he is a "hypocrite of psychotic proportions."[76] Ergo, he learns from Clytie's face (1909) but realizes what he knows thanks only to Shreve's words (1910). Radloff confirms, but only to fix on a different clue; Clytie didn't do it, the discourse did. Here is Radloff; since the narrators know the past "only . . . through the mediation of the oral tradition," it is through that "heritage," along with its " 'silent' context of intelligibility," that they realize "possible ways of telling." So, "when Quentin speculates that Bon has Negro blood he allows the subterranean power of his heritage to speak through him, for his heritage is based on the inequality of the races."[77] If the "heritage" did the telling, then, since Radloff fails to ground talk in a historically located conflict (aside from "race" understood through generic "conflict"), it did it nowhere in particular and through no particular means. Only a short step separates Radloff, with his discourse evidence, from the "know nothing because nothing can be known" school of non-detection.

Watching the detectives skirt an epistemological void has its pleasures, but these are limited. Detection seems stymied on an undenied lack of "direct evidence."[78] Brooks comes up with some missing words (Henry's) for which Stonum substitutes phrenology (Clytie's); Kartiganer supplements the bones with transcribed words (Shreve's), while Radloff brings in "discourse." The haul is evanescent because taken from misguided places at the wrong times (variously, the Hundred in 1909, the Harvard study in 1910, and southern talk, anytime and any place). Haiti would be my bet; or, more particularly, Haiti in 1791 – recast as Haiti in 1827. Taking Faulkner's "error" over the date of the Haitian revolution to be calculated, I assume that Sutpen's claimed suppression of an uprising on that island in 1827 is believed by all who hear it (excepting Shreve, who appears indifferent to whether Bon was born on Haiti or Porto Rico [p. 239]). We know from the historical record (grounds already established) that Haiti, in the plantation South, is synonymous with black revolution. We know, from Grandfather Compson, that Sutpen first notices his wife as a "shadow" thrown by gunfire against the wall of a Haitian plantation – the image is twice repeated (pp. 199 and 200). We know, from the same source, that Sutpen's first wife had a "Spanish" mother. We know also that Grandfather Compson is no fool in the ways of planters (he did, after all, do rather well among them). He can put Haiti, a Spanish wife (set aside), and a part–Spanish/Haitian son (denied) together and come up with a black claimant.

The evidence that he does so is in his words. But unlike Brooks' words, these are not missing; instead, they are obstructed by other words that constitute their hiding place. So, I offer in evidence key words that are systematically marked by what they don't quite say. Exasperated, a devil's advocate might here interject: who is *he* to claim a detective's credentials . . . his stuff is more speculative than any of the absent evidence already on the table . . . hypothesis won't catch the "nigger in the woodpile" (Mr. Compson's phrase [p. 56]), any more than it will apprehend those who claim not to know that he is there. In my defense, I submit that these words in hiding may stand as material witnesses because, unlike Radloff's versions of "discourse," their "secrecy" is given a semantically traceable meaning by their particular passages through the trauma inherent in the institution of bound labor.

Much of what follows is juridical; I shall effectively summon witnesses and sort testimony. Because I am concerned with those whose evidence frequently compounds Sutpen's initial act of false witness, I am necessarily skeptical about what they have to say. Consequently, my inquiry will address the inferential, the tangential, the parenthetical, the unexpected pause, the slip, the dash . . . in other words, those often out-of-the-way areas of speech where a witness may trip, revealing what he or she would rather not say. Of necessity, I shall sound finicky. For this I apologize, offering in scant compensation the assurance that I will do my best to keep order in the critical court of my own invention.

A resumé of the background to the case may be useful. Sutpen has a secret – the labor trauma central to his first conversation with General Compson in 1835 (hereafter known as Sutpen I). He also has reasons for keeping the secret – his goods and his integrity as a master – as well as a means to secrecy, the double articulation achieved by his second conversation with the General in 1864 (hereafter known as Sutpen II). He transmits his secret in its quasi-articulated, quasi-digested form to his friend and fellow planter. They enter a quasi-silent partnership, rooted in class interest and dedicated to preserving the secret almost intact. General Compson, sharing Sutpen's reasons, hands the secret to his son, and so on. . . . At least until the reason for transmission, the particular structure of property and property holders generated by a tradition of bound labor is canceled by a revolution in labor forms. In the absence of the social structure that generated the secret – that is to say, with the black expelled from the white body (by wage and diaspora) – the secret can at last be spoken. But not by those apprenticed to its peculiar form of accumulation; they, and I include all the narrators (save Shreve), remain transgenerationally haunted by that which they can neither ignore nor confess.

My summary lacks a linguistic dimension, offering no account of why a problem of work should manifest itself as a problem in language. Labor takes a linguistic turn once it is perceived that Sutpen I is an unbearable referent, involving a specific intersubjective situation between white owner and bound black – a situation that, because it is unbearable and yet constitutive of white mastery, becomes *the* referent from which a master class arises, and to which each master and every instance of his property *ought* to be referred. Sutpen II is, therefore, inevitable – the signifier that exists to represent, and yet to deny access to Sutpen I, the signified as secret labor trauma. I shall risk glossing my own gloss in the hope of clarifying a murky circumstance; knowing what they know (that they are blacks in whiteface), masters and their heirs must make themselves white, while retaining *and* refusing their own black part. Their process steps laterally into language because it involves deploying words both to obstruct access to the fullness of their knowledge and yet also to act as guides to the location of that disruptive meaning.

But I have been here before, perhaps rather too often. So, back to my initial witness, and to the question of hard evidence in the case of what General Compson does and doesn't know. I offer the first Mrs. Sutpen as "shadow." In 1835, Sutpen tells Grandfather Compson about "the besieged Haitian room":

> (and now Grandfather said there was the first mention – a shadow that almost emerged for a moment and then faded again but not completely away [p. 199] . . . so that Grandfather said it was like he had just seen her too for a second by the flash of one of the muskets [p. 201]

Eulalia first takes the eye, of talker and listener, as a dark form virtually materializing between revolt and its suppression. Her Spanish mother joins "shadow" as a cryptic clue to Eulalia's Jacobinical blackness. Grandfather Compson notes that Sutpen spoke of "the old man's wife [having] . . . been a Spaniard" (p. 203), "as you might flick the joker out of a pack of fresh cards" (p. 203). The simile is not casual; it alludes doubly. First, to the General's earlier sense that the West Indies are the element in Sutpen's story picked by "Fate" as a "blackjack" (p. 194). Second, to the context of their conversation; the two men are resting from their pursuit of the French architect. "Joker" and "pack" find ready referents – the architect walks on stilts and boasts a funny hat and trick suspenders; the Haitians run as a pack and will eventually "bay" him (p. 206). Where the deck is allusively stacked so black, the Spanish "joker" can only be a dark, wild, and Jacobinical card.

Even without the evidence of "shadow," "Spaniard," "black-jack," and "joker," Grandfather must know. We are told that Sutpen goes to Compson's law office in 1864 in order to engage a legally trained ear (p. 225). Listen to the client as he phrases his grounds for setting aside a first wife:

> I accepted them [planter and daughter] at their own valuation while insisting on my own part upon explaining fully about myself and my progenitors: yet they deliberately withheld from me the one fact which I have reason to know they were aware would have caused me to decline the entire matter, otherwise they would not have withheld it from me – a fact which I did not learn until after my son was born. [p. 212]

Juridical training is barely necessary to find the withheld fact; logic and syntactical proximity link "progenitor" to "baby," and since Sutpen has been white about his antecedents, Eulalia must have kept hers dark. Ergo, since the baby is the evidence, the fact is out –

Sutpen's son had a black "progenitor." Quentin has his grandfather almost announce as much:

> He chose the name himself, Grandfather believed, just as he named them all – the Charles Goods and the Clytemnestras and Henry and Judith and all of them – [p. 214]

Although at no point does the General overtly indicate that he knows that Bon is Sutpen's son, Quentin credits him with a telling mistranslation of the name. Just *how* telling depends on one's readiness to play anagrams. The plantation owner from whose door Sutpen was turned is unnamed; however, in 1835, Grandfather hears Sutpen speak of Pettibone almost in the same breath as he speaks of turning from the door. Sutpen's father beats one of Pettibone's slaves and runs (p. 187). Sutpen is sent around the back (probably) by another of Pettibone's blacks and runs (p. 188). Each runs from an encrypted recognition of interdependency. Sutpen runs into a plantocracy whose founder may, for him, be Pettibone. However, on joining his putative maker, Sutpen is brought down and belittled by the very "goods" that were always a substantial part of his founder's name. Indeed, if one takes the "bon" out of Sutpen's titular source, one is left with little, or, more correctly, with "small" in veiled form ("petite").[79] Haiti, "Spaniard," a tissue of cryptic verbal clues, an economic pun ... the evidence mounts, but it remains tacit.

Second witness: Mr. Compson. Evidence: a conspiracy of silence between father and son (my supposition being that if the father knows, and offers his son the taciturnities, the son must also know). But "conspiracy" was ever an elusive charge; moreover, as the witnesses grow more distant in time from the Haitian question, with its capacity to blacken, we cannot automatically assume that they share Sutpen, Rosa, and the General's sense of that place. Back to the evidence. Mr. Compson almost gives the game away during his first use of Bon's name; within the same page, while summarizing Sutpen's meteoric success, he notes:

> there were some among his fellow citizens who believed even yet that there was a nigger in the woodpile somewhere. [p. 56]

The subsemantics of the terms accompanying this revelation play catch-as-catch-can with "nigger," as Mr. Compson piles on the evidence. To the sentence that contains the epithet, and to the paragraph that contains his first reference to "Bon" by name, Mr. Compson adds that certain citizens believed that "the plantation was just a blind" to Sutpen's "actual dark avocation" (p. 56) (cotton speculation), while others held that "the wild niggers which he had brought there" could "conjure" high yields from the soil. The blacks in question are Haitian. Haiti was noted as a haunt of voodoo. "Conjure" means not simply to "magic" or "summon" but "to swear together; combine by oath; confederate." With whom are the Haitian conjurors to combine, if not with the "dark" master whose plantation serves only to obscure that which calls him away from it, or his "avocation" as one who actually confederates with "niggers"? The manner of his confederation is at once miscegenous ("Bon" is close enough to the "woodpile" to proffer a toehold) and, given talk of bale price and yield, a labor pact. On both counts, the covert combination smacks of interdependency, as black passes into white and vice versa. Of course, I have looked for a toe to catch, seeing through the woodpile where others might see only trees, but I am systematically encouraged to do so by a dominant strand in Mr. Compson's lexicon.

Many are the "shade[s]," "shadow[s] and "shadowy[s]" that "pass" the reader who pursues Mr. Compson's Bon. His vocabulary of "shadow" has its more occasional modifiers; Bon is a "black-guard" (p. 71) who appears in Mississippi "phoenix-like," as though from ash (p. 58), and whose legal studies at the university involved "digging into Blackstone and Coke" as Henry "aped" his clothing (p. 81). Prior to the end of the war, and having written Judith many letters that are "jackanape antics," he writes to her in "*stove polish*" (p. 102), or blacking, a letter that darkens Mr. Compson's hand as he passes it to his son – "the hand looking almost as dark as a Negro's against his linen leg" (p. 71). My list is selective, but even in fuller form its contents would cunningly avoid making a prima facie case, because many of its items invite a particular form of duplicitous inflection. Mr. Compson is much given to the thespian mode; he is liable to appeal to Greek tragedy (p. 21) or to decry Fate as a stage manager playing fast and loose with the scenery (p. 5). Spoken through a theatrical idiom, Sutpen's various activities amount, for Mr. Compson, to an incomplete script – hence his famous insistence, "they dont explain and we are not supposed to know" (p. 80). But ignorance, here, comes carefully care of theater – or, more particularly, of Act V, Scene V of *Macbeth*, admitted to provenance via Mr. Compson's earlier performance in *The Sound and the Fury*. If Sutpen et al. are "poor players," then they amount to "nothing," which is exactly (if only partially) the kind of burial a planter's heir would devoutly wish upon a Bon known to be black. Articulated through theatricality, the lexicon of "shadow" translates those to whom it refers into tricks of lighting ("candle"), wardrobe ("aped"), and makeup (blacking). However, a thespian shading may

only disguise (as transience) the ethnic "shadow" whose perma-
nence it cannot efface.

Rather than vanishing into the ramifications of the *Macbeth/Ab-
salom, Absalom!* intertext, let me try *Hamlet*, or Justice Jim Hamblett
into whose court an indictment is brought against Charles Etienne
Saint-Valery Bon, for disturbing the peace of a black congregation
at prayers. Hamblett's name contains the case in miniature; the justice tries Etienne as "white" (p. 16), but even as he pronounces the
word, he recognizes what he is and "let[s]" him be "Ham['s]" son.
Of course, the Dane's name demands another emphasis, casting Bon
as Old Hamlet to his haunted child. My point is that, as with "Hamblett" so with "shadow" (out of *Macbeth*), Mr. Compson's "dark"
vocabulary might signify rather too well, were it not liable to a dra-
maturgic emphasis, whereby it signifies "nothing."

As Mr. Compson's terms for Bon, along with their repressed semantic rumblings, build into a network, so the influence of their
occluded double articulation extends, drawing obsolescent meanings
from etymologies, activating intertexts and triggering puns in a semantic uprising that threatens to let the "nigger" go freely through
the surface meanings of Mr. Compson's story. Release never quite
happens, but one or two sightings should serve to suggest the semantic strain under which Mr. Compson labors as he struggles to
bury Bon.

Take "durance," Mr. Compson's synonym for the "probation"
that he proposes in explanation of the four-year gap between
Henry's visit to Bon's morganatic wife and his decision to kill Bon
for that marriage. Repetition of "durance" (pp. 73, 94 twice) draws
attention to a word which, because it appears to be little more than
a synonym, might otherwise appear redundant – "that abeyance,
that durance" (p. 94), "the probation, the durance" (p. 94). However, as a probationary term applied to Bon's access to an octoroon,
"durance" resonates with the echo of a common African American
pun. Freedmen and postbellum blacks would not apply "during" to
slavery times, preferring to say "endurin' slavery."[80] The residual
black play releases a matching archaic usage, from "durance"; instead of meaning mere "duration," "durance" becomes "forced
confinement, imprisonment" endured. So Mr. Compson's temporal
term turns penal, indicating his latent fear of Bon's sexuality, a fear
rooted in the unconfessed intimation that Bon is black. "Durance"
adds a punitive guarantee to "probation," clandestinely seeking to
do as masters did, and to police slave sexuality in ways that would
deny the slave's access to marital and family connection. Bon is not
on "probation"; he is "in durance" for four years, during which

time he may not approach Judith. "Durance" must be punitive, perhaps because Mr. Compson senses that with the duration of the "durance" over, Bon dead and Henry gone, Sutpen's estate will "fall into abeyance," there being no person remaining "in whom freehold, dignity of title may be invested." Of course, Mr. Compson cannot say as much, because to do so would be to acknowledge not only that Bon is Sutpen's black son but that such a son might also have been heir to "white" property.

Or, take "saccharinity," whose ungainliness persuades an attention that is rewarding. But first the context: Mr. Compson, speaking of Bon's second visit to the Hundred (1860), notes that he is a "shadowy character" and reiterates, "Yes, shadowy," before offering an exegesis that stresses "artifice" via a theatrical inflection of the colorant:

> Yes, shadowy: a myth, a phantom: something which they engendered and created whole themselves; some effluvium of Sutpen blood and character, as though as a man he did not exist at all. [p. 82]

Despite censorship via cumulative synonym, "shadowy" remains pressured by ethnicity through its links to *engender* and "effluvium." As a triangulation, these terms may be heard trying to say something that their syntax forbids. Angled toward "engendered," "effluvium" – or *outflow* or *issuance* – receives seminal force, displacing Henry, Judith, and Ellen from the plural pronoun ("they") and placing Thomas Sutpen there instead (*he*). *Their* grip on the pronoun is slight; "they" nominates a subject unspecified within the particular sentence, a subject available only to the reader prepared to work back through the paragraph. However, within a syntactical unit (the sentence) granted leeway by the genealogical emphasis, "they" can be made to yield to *he* (or Sutpen), since it is *he* who *engenders* or *begets* (male usage) Bon – though, in congress with Eulalia, that which his blood *bears* or *conceives* (female usage) is markedly an "effluvium," or *a subtle and invisible emanation* that strikes him as a *noisesom or noxious exhalation*. Bon, as Sutpen's "shadowy . . . effluvium," cannot be allowed to exist. Consequently, the singular pronoun does not subvert the plural form but remains veiled within it ("*they*"). The veil, however, is thin; within two sentences, Mr. Compson compounds a duplicitous pronoun with a term whose etymology betrays Bon's ethnic plot in the Garden. We are told that over two days Bon and Judith achieve "love" and not "mere romance," which "would have perished, died of sheer saccharinity and opportunity" (p. 83). Saccharine is a "sugar substitute," "white in color, and remarkable for its sweetness." Webster adds a comparison with sugar cane, observing that saccharine may be between 300 and 500 times sweeter than cane sugar, "depending on the purity of the product." He concludes with a note concerning manufacture "from the tortuene of coal tar." Here we have it; Sutpen does not take sugar in his coffee (because of Haiti), but in his house and garden his Haitian son sweetens the life of his daughter by achieving a "pure whiteness" despite derivation from "coal tar." The "tar" in "saccharine" may be etymologically deep, but it sticks to Mr. Compson's usage, removing "shadowy" from the subset of "artifice" by putting the "black" back into it.

The he in t*hey*, the tar (baby) in saccharinity, and the endurance in durance exemplify what I earlier called terms in hiding or words marked by what they don't quite say. Such words subvert the superficial meaning of Mr. Compson's version, offering comprehension where he declared incomprehension ("we are not supposed to know"). I have space only for one more piece of evidence, but hope that incrementally my examples indicate that Mr. Compson is only *supposed* "not . . . to know" who Bon is.

Concluding evidence: while on a quail shoot, Mr. Compson and Quentin shelter from the rain under the cedars that mark the Sutpen burial lot. Gravestones are read. Mr. Compson tells the story of Bon's son by his octoroon mistress, Charles Etienne St. Valery Bon, who during his childhood at the Hundred is attended by Clytie, playing "Spanish duenna" to his "Spanish virgin" (p. 162). Mr. Compson's choice of chaperone may have been prompted by his fondness for Beardsley (encouraged by Etienne's Symbolist nomenclature – Valery); he earlier set Bon's funeral among the cedars as "a garden scene by . . . Wilde" (p. 157), a scene in which a duenna, dressed in black, and attendant upon a boy "whom Beardsley might not only have dressed but drawn" (p. 157), would not have been out of place. However, it is at least as likely that Etienne owes his decadent pedigree to Mr. Compson's sustained depiction of Bon as a man delighting in mauve postures, among which the dressing gown is mighty (p. 76). In which case, "duenna" and "virgin," applied to Etienne, recall a paternity textually gendered out of the Symbolist movement. However, the reiteration of "Spanish" renders Symbolist decoration transparent to the issue of descent. Etienne's grandmother was nominally a Spaniard; it follows that her grandson retains a Spanish strain, merits a Spanish attendant, and boasts a Spanish virginity. However, each Iberian incidence, save nominally the first, sets a white mask on a known black face. By inference, the association of "Spanish" and "black" infects, or derives from, the initial usage in Haiti, allowing "black" to be glimpsed through its antonym ("Spaniard") as applied to Eulalia's mother. It follows that the "nigger" in Mr. Compson's "woodpile" identifiably derives from Haiti.

Identified as Sutpen's son, the "shadow" will necessarily run through Mr. Compson's understanding of the father, troubling surface articulation. I offer as an evidential subset examples of Sutpen, who, according to this witness, is a white with a tendency not only to turn black but, more specifically, to turn into black labor. From the first, Mr. Compson's Sutpen is a man in a mask, "a short reddish beard which resembled a disguise" (p. 24), behind which, as his father will have told him, lurks "a secret mind" (p. 28). But Rosa plucks at the beard when she notifies Quentin that it alone distinguishes Sutpen from the Negroes with whom he works (p. 28). So adumbrated, the beard is a "disguise," covering a "secret" whose content is that without it the master cannot be distinguished from the slave. Quentin may or may not have conveyed Rosa's observation to his father. Nonetheless, Mr. Compson can identify a disguised slave when he sees one – witness his curious remark while describing Sutpen's arrest, by Jefferson committee, for an unspecified "felony" (involving, according to Ackers, steamboat furnishings [p. 34]). Here is the relevant detail: "they arrested him. . . . when he reached the courthouse, Sutpen had a larger following than if he actually had been the runaway slave" (p. 36). Because no runaways have been mentioned, one might have expected the indefinite article ("a" runaway slave); the comparison might then have passed. Coupled with "actually," "the" marks a degree of emphasis sufficient to encourage the speculation that Sutpen may "actually" *be* "the" generic black absentee to whom he is only and oddly likened. Casual comparison or positive identification . . . ? The phrasing, at the very least, allows Mr. Compson a divided intentionality, so that Sutpen's slave status may remain partially *un*available to him.

But it should be remembered that Mr. Compson transmits Sutpen I to his son and that, consequently, we might expect him to know that in the Sutpen story masks and faces have an awkward habit of changing color and switching places. Since he, Mr. Compson, received the tropic "balloon" face of interdependency (from his own father), we should be ready for a degree of self-consciousness on his part in any subsequent use of that trope:

> The flesh came upon him suddenly, as though what the negroes and Wash Jones too called the fine figure of a man had reached and held its peak after the foundation had given away

and something between the shape of him that people knew
and the uncompromising skeleton of what he actually was had
gone fluid and, earthbound, had been snubbed up and re-
strained, balloonlike, unstable and lifeless, by the envelope
which it had betrayed. [pp. 63–4]

Sutpen fattens in 1867. Mr. Compson is specific as to the date[81]: that
is to say, only after his slaves have quit the house does his "skeleton"
or "foundation" liquify and assume the form of a flaccid balloon.
Care of Sutpen I, the contents of any balloon in this text are ethnically mixed. Ergo – take the black breath away, and the master's
structure and body fail. Rosa will liken the Hundred to a "skeleton"
(p. 109), whose enunciation may be white or may be black. Mr.
Compson suffers from the same ethnic doubletalk in the matter of
labor on "foundation[s]." His use of "skeleton" carries its own architectural synonym ("foundation"), which, within four pages, he
has glossed as a site of divided ownership

as though his [Sutpen's] presence alone compelled that house
to accept and retain human life; as though houses actually possess a sentience, a personality and character acquired not from
the people who breathe or have breathed in them so much as
rather inherent in the wood and brick or begotten upon the
wood and brick by the man or men who conceived and built
them – [p. 67]

Again, the passage is date-specific, alluding to the house in 1864,
after two announced departures – Ellen's death (1862) and the "desertion" of "Sutpen's negroes" "to follow the Yankee troops"
(1864). Superficially, it is Sutpen's "presence" within the Hundred
that "compelled" Ellen's continuing life and the residency of the
slaves. However, the compelling "sentience" of the house is located
in several sources; dismissing the residents (those who breathed
there), Mr. Compson cites the materials (brick and wood), only to
move to the "man" who "conceived" the place, before settling on
the "men" who "built" it. I have tidied up his transitions to produce an ethnic plot whereby the "sentience" of the Hundred shifts
from white ownership to black labor. However, my preferred narrative is blocked by an asymmetrical use of "and" after "or," in "the
man *or* men" (so that "the man *or* men" is followed by "who conceived *and* built"); which "and" possibly posits a singular "man" as
both designer and the builder of the house. Since we know that
Sutpen's slaves did not "conceive" his house, we can safely resolve
any irresolution, over the matter of conception, in favor of the

"man" Sutpen. However, earlier, Mr. Compson had gone further, attributing the entire plantation to "little else but . . . [Sutpen's] bare hands" (p. 39). Nonetheless, a ghostly "or," maintained by symmetry within the final conjunction and held there in no small part by Mr. Compson's continuing uncertainty over the site of "sentience" (residents, materials, owner, and labor all being mooted in the same sentence), continues to trouble his attribution of a source to the "sentience" of the house. Latently, at least, "or . . . and" proposes "either . . . or," rather than "and . . . or" – which is to say, the form of the phrase is contentious rather than conjunctive (*"either* white thought *or* black work" built it). Inflection must depend upon who inflects, but if the inflector routes the architectural dispute back through the "foundations," via the "skeleton," to the "balloon" from which the "design" sprang (Sutpen I), there is every reason to suppose that Mr. Compson, like his father before him and Sutpen and Rosa before that, must live within a double articulation which requires that the "sentience" of Sutpen and his Hundred be *both* a dominant expression of white mastery *and* a subordinate yet resistant expression of black labor. In Mr. Compson's case, it seems that an encrypted knowledge of Bon's identity accompanies, and derives from, an equally encrypted sense of Sutpen as an extension of the bound.

With the departure of this witness, I shall risk a few premature remarks by way of summary. My case for the ubiquity of Bon, as a partially known entity, rests on a peculiar form of evidence, produced through a laborious work of "designification."[82] I have read each testimony, whether of eyewitness or bearer of hearsay, to discover within its words quite other and subordinated words, out of whose repression the offered testimony has materialized in its dominance. License to designify is twofold. First, the *bulk* of the testimony (too many signs from too few sightings of the subject [Bon]). Second, the *strangeness* of those signs, excessive in quality as in quantity, and characteristic of a genus, "double articulation," whose subsets are many. I offer examples of subsets drawn from evidence already in place: anagram (Hamblett), rhythm ("or . . . and"; Quentin's "*I don't . . .*" times seven), disguised pun (Bon, Pettibone), magical play of letters (Eulalia[r], "t*hey*"), syntactical leeway (resulting in pronounal shiftiness). Each is cryptic and suggests a secret whose persistence "arrest[s]" thought,[83] causing the semantic processes of testimony and reception to buckle, becoming for a moment "configuration[s] pregnant with tensions."[84] To speak my Benjaminian borrowings more fully – the tendency of testifiers to testify in cryptograms, whose temporal form is "monad[ic],"[85] stems from their need to substantiate a past whose properties have made them what they are, while simultaneously recognizing that those "goods" derive from the "lifework"[86] of a master class dedicated to the contradictory denial of its own substance (Bon as Sutpen). Possessed of an unbearable knowledge, the Compsons, like grandfather like grandson, and like Sutpen and Rosa before them (though perhaps with less intensity), live in two times at once – the time of testimony, and the time of a traumatic founding event (whose die is Sutpen I). Consequently, each of the moments to which they allude is potentially "monad[ic]," constituted as a double-optic through which one set of events postfigures another. Likewise, each of their meanings is potentially a tense configuration, or "loophole,"[87] through which the alternative consciousness of labor may be felt. For example, I have already sketched how Sutpen's moment at the door in 1820 contains and rewrites the Haitian revolution, and how that recomposition composes Rosa's 1848 as 1791. Mr. Compson, cast through Sutpen's die, also has his revolution – brief and inexplicable (because underexplained), it too reaches deviously back to Haiti. According to Mr. Compson, Henry objects to Bon as a brother-in-law because of his previous morganatic marriage. On which grounds, Mr. Compson's plot must go to New Orleans, where Bon duly confronts Henry with the octoroon wife, in a manner patterned on the boy at the door. This is another threshold in black and white, except that there are two thresholds; at the first, as the "barrier" dissolves, Henry witnesses "the supreme apotheosis of chattelry" (p. 89), a row of morganatic wives. But, thanks to Bon, admission is automatic and relatively trauma-free, though significantly it leads to a second and more substantial barrier, guarding the dueling ground, adjacent to the place of wives, presumably to accommodate disputes arising from miscegenous issues:

> now would come the instant for which Bon had builded: – a wall, unscalable, a gate ponderously locked, the sober and thoughtful country youth just waiting, looking, not yet asking why? or what? the gate of solid beams in place of the lacelike iron grilling and they passing on, Bon knocking at a small adjacent doorway from which a swarthy man resembling a creature out of an old woodcut of the French Revolution erupts, concerned, even a little aghast, looking first at the daylight and then at Henry and speaking to Bon in French which Henry does not understand and Bon's teeth glinting for an instant before he answers in French: "With him? An American? He is a guest; I would have to let him choose weapons and I decline

to fight with axes. No, no; not that. Just the key." Just the key;
and now, the solid gates closed behind them instead of before,
no sight or evidence above the high thick walls of the low city
and scarce any sound of it, the labyrinthine mass of oleander
and jasmine, lantana and mimosa walling yet another the strip
of bare earth combed and curried with powdered shell, raked
and immaculate and only the most recent of the brown stains
showing now [pp. 89–90]

I quote at length to establish that the second door, with its twofold
wall (first of brick, then of foliage) and its reiterated "key," is that
for which Mr. Compson's Bon has "builded." At *this* door Henry
will play the Sutpen part, but with differences. Gone are the "monkey dressed . . . nigger" and the "performing tiger"; in their place
stands a nominally white gatekeeper. His language marks him as a
Creole, or French-speaking citizen of Louisiana. But the signs are
contradictory, as a "swarthy" "creature" of the dark, who blinks
"aghast" in sunlight, his mother tongue is forked and capable of
double origin. The revolutionary posture may be French, but so was
that of Toussaint L'Ouverture;[88] moreover, "swarthy," passing by
way of "woodcut" toward Mr. Compson's infamous "woodpile" (p.
56), darkens to yield a barely hidden Haitian, speaking the language
of revolution at a gate. To the objection that my markers are ambivalent merely because they are Gothic, I would counter that Mr.
Compson's preferred source text is likely to be Poe and that the
woodcut in question would then, almost inevitably, be an illustration
for "Murders in the Rue Morgue," a Parisian story featuring a notably "swarthy" Ourang-Outang, given to eruptions, and itself, arguably, a coded harbinger of black revolt.[89] Ergo, the Gothic twist
produces yet another "nigger," dressed as a "monkey," and at a
door. Whichever way the latencies are turned, once noted, they re-
capitulate a primary trauma. In this version, the white on the threshold gains entry, but only after having listened to two concealed
Haitians discuss whether or not violence will be necessary.

If pushed, Mr. Compson's scenario will yield a white-negro Sutpen
(Bon as structural core of the peculiar institution and its owners)
telling a white "monkey . . . nigger" that the duel (or labor uprising)
may be postponed, at least while the white master (Henry) observes
the site of violence. It should be remembered that the duel, though
barely proposed, is merely deferred. Mr. Compson undertakes his
account of events in New Orleans in 1860 precisely to explain why
Henry kills Bon at the gates to the Hundred five years later.[90] Or,
reading for the first event (1791) in the third (1865), as in the

second (1860), why a master should choose to suppress a black uprising when that suppression will be the deferred death of him. My argument nominates labor, rather than miscegenation, as the "key" to the projected duel – a preference justified both by the sustained presence of Haiti in the subtext and by Mr. Compson's setting. Although Mr. Compson makes morganatic miscegenation superficially central, his architectural sense (a cityscape proposing to represent the interior of Bon's consciousness) designs miscegenation simply as the first in a set of double doors (the "lace" in front of the "solid beams") through which one must pass in order to reach the solid and stained grounds of labor resistance and its violent control.

Mr. Compson's "1791" lacks the phenomenological anxiety of Rosa's "1848" or of Sutpen's "Haiti" in western Virginia for a combination of reasons. First, the discovery of the black face in the white is more occluded. Second, and perhaps more important, the passage of black into white, via labor, is partially displaced into the disturbing, though not finally debilitating, issue of sexual pathology. But, at this point, I merely stress that Mr. Compson *has* his "1791," and that because he knows Bon for Haitian "goods," and knows Haiti as a synonym for "revolution," it follows that his temporal sense is monadically liable to require that he live in two times at once, where the first, because of its excessive character, seeks the second "to release its traumatic force."[91] In this instance, although that force is moderated, it remains structurally present and ever ready to summon the speaker to a primal scene (Sutpen I), thereby involving him in a "rendez-vous . . . with a real" that does not finally and sufficiently elude him.[92] Of course, the "real" "work" of black labor is liable to rise up within the "life-work" of the master class most emphatically at times of revolution. Hence, *Absalom, Absalom!*, as the story of Sutpen's "design," grounds that "design" in Haiti and comes into textual existence during a successful labor revolution.

IV

My remarks, intended only in summary, have gone on too long. I had best return to my third and final witness – Quentin Compson – and to the evidence for his knowledge of Bon (prior to meeting Henry in 1910). Evidence: boredom, consequent upon perceived conspiracy of silence. From first to last, Quentin is bored "sullen" (pp. 147, 177, 206). Summoned by Miss Coldfield to hear her peroration, he listens because he *has* to listen (p. 4), having heard his grandfather's version and his father's addenda several times. Indeed, at times, most notably in chapters five and seven, he evacuates himself, to become a ventriloquial site through which ur-Sutpens pass on their way to Shreve in the Harvard study. Which study frames what is said to imply that most of it, bar minimal omniscient voice-over plus Shreve's largely late contributions, passes through Quentin's mouth in a tone "reposed" (p. 147), "flat" (p. 206), and "dead" (p. 208). Small wonder that he insists, *"Yes, I have had to listen too long"* (p. 157), and reiterates, *"Yes, I have heard too much"* (p. 168), and bemoans *"having to hear it all over again because he* [Shreve] *sounds just like father"* (p. 171). Since Shreve returns the rebuke, "Dont say it's just me that sounds like your old man" (p. 215), only to have Quentin affirm and extend patrivocality, *"Yes, we are both Father* [p. 210] . . . *so apparently not only a man never outlives his father but not even his friends and acquaintances do"* (p. 222), it is only a slight exaggeration to say that for much of the novel, and certainly until chapter eight, Quentin listens to the same story, told in all but the same voice – a recipe for terminal boredom. Moreover, he listens and tells in deathly circumstances. Miss Coldfield's room is like a hot "tomb" (p. 6) and she a dry "ghost" in it (p. 4), while the Harvard study is deathly cold, it being "zero outside" (p. 176), the air "tomblike" (p. 240), and Shreve having a habit of leaving a window open (p. 176). Under these conditions, Quentin becomes an early genre-victim; although "too young to deserve . . . to be a ghost," he *has* "to be one" because those around him will keep "telling him about old ghost-times" (p. 4). Or, more properly, about the one old ghost, in variants that Quentin seems impelled to repeat. Yet he remains passively patient. Aside from an occasional outburst, along the lines of "Why me?" over Miss Coldfield's invitation (p. 7), or "Why Canadian bad manners?" in the matter of addressing a lady (p. 301), Quentin persists, in reiterated sullenness, reiterating the one about Sutpen, in a "curious repressed calm voice" (p. 177), "curiously dead" (p. 208). But why?

Before answering, and as a part of that answer, let me assume what I have yet to prove – that Quentin knows who Bon is, prior to his visit to the Hundred – in the hope that what follows will warrant my assumption. I am prompted to fast footwork by the self-delighting general logic that, because Quentin has *"heard too much"* from previous witnesses, and because it is my case that their testimonies express occluded knowledge as to Bon, then Quentin's "repressed . . . voice" shares the repressed knowledge of his informants. But let that go. . . . In the matter of his boredom, I shall deploy a terminology of which I do not approve. Appeals to "other," in the name of "difference," skirt a double risk. First, they may abstract from the margins the experience of living on them, thereby victimizing the

victims again, but this time with theory. Second, they may preclude
the possibility of telling one "other" from another, thereby rendering differences the same. Either way, "other" proves an opportun-
ist's term. But I shall use it, not least because I'm tired of splitting
semantic subknots and could do with a good verbal diagram. So, to
the opportunism (with the rider that "other," in what follows, be
considered as historically particular, arising from precise though extended labor circumstances). In his discussion of "disaster," Maurice
Blanchot argues for an order of experience that is so "other" to its
survivor that his or her sense of self is dislocated, resulting in a form
of death survived. Among Blanchot's terms are those I have been
using with reference to Quentin's boredom, "passive" and "patient," to which he adds "insomnia," "inattention," and being held
"hostage" – each a possible reaction to a catastrophic intrusion of
alterity. From Hegel to Blanchot is but a short step, and both offer
annotations on slavery's foundational trauma (or Sutpen I). Blanchot plots how a subject, say Sutpen at the door, may respond to
the proximity of a traumatic disaster that threatens the notional integrity of that subject's position[93]:

> In the relation of the self (the same) to the Other, the Other
> is distant, he is the stranger but if I reverse this relation, the
> Other relates to me as if I were the Other, and this causes me
> to take leave of my identity. Pressing until he crushes me, by
> the pressure of the very near, from the privilege of the first
> person. When thus I am wrestled from myself, there remains a
> passivity bereft of self. . . . There remains the unsubjected, or
> the patient.[94]

Blanchot glosses himself with Levinas:

> The hostage . . . is the irreplaceable one who is not in his own
> place. It is through the other that I am the same, through the
> other that I am myself: it is through the other who has always
> withdrawn from myself. The other, if he calls upon me, calls
> upon someone who is not I.[95]

Either comment might serve as schematic introit to Sutpen's
panic as a strange "balloon" face causes him to "take leave of himself" and, "through the other," to enter contradictory subject positions whereby he is "not I," contradictory both in terms of class
and race. But alterity in western Virginia results in panic mastered.
Sutpen's decision to go to Haiti constitutes him as a plantocratic
subject by means of a sustained *and* faulty repression of the laboring
other. On June 2, 1910, Quentin's pursuit of an alternative other,

in the joint form of a "dark" Italian girl[96] and a darker Deacon, though less traumatic, proves more disastrous because, in *The Sound and the Fury*, or at least in Quentin's section of it, the "stranger" remains dominant within the pursuant self. Or, to lodge Blanchot within Joel Williamson's sense of southern racial interdependency, having released the sister from the incestuously defended "bubble" or "vase" of her culturally manufactured virginity, via an encounter with a working-class "sister" in all her foreignness or "difference," and having recognized in Deacon not simply the poverty of the white image of the Negro but also the impoverishment of his own "white" reality, with the emergence through it of an other who does not comply, Quentin "withdraws" from "the privilege of the first person" and enters what looks initially, at least in 1929, like death. But Quentin does not entirely die; witness his resurrection in 1936.

More is involved here than an author's decision to reuse a character. In an earlier chapter, I suggested that first-, second-, and third-time readers may not experience Quentin's death day as particularly deathly because there's so much else going on en route to the river. I now add that for Quentin, too, death is less than fatal since it involves release, and, more particularly, the release of those bound within a singular form of the self, a form constituted by their binding. Because, on June 10, 1910, Quentin lets the other, as a "different" sister and a "different" black occupy him, he comes to recognize "stranger[s]" as intimates, and his prior self as a disposable "stranger." Deacon and the Italian girl release him from himself, insofar as their class of self had been kept in place by a linked set of racial and sexual pathologies, whose limits they proceed to transgress (by departing them). Under pressure from the other, he carries himself outside his culturally preferred identity, becoming the revisionist historian of those very structures of feeling that had allowed him to exist. His death is not, therefore, experienced as death but as relief, release, and even, ludicrously, as resurrection – the eyes rising out of the shadowed water, in which black and sister combine as a darkened mirror, *through* and not into which Quentin jumps.[97] Hence, survival of the suicide, at least for Faulkner, to whom Quentin is too knowing to leave dead.

But he who comes back into *Absalom, Absalom!* resuscitated by a dark and foreign couple comes back with a difference and for different purposes. He enters a transformed context. A lengthened genealogy and a broader historical range ensure that his concerns shift. Because Sutpen's story is unavoidably about the building and preservation of a great house, its key narrator can scarcely indulge his preoccupation with particular sexual forms (virginity, incest, and miscegenation) without relation to the property structures that, arguably, they exist to defend – particularly since Sutpen's two stories, and their necessary if occluded relation, serve to keep issues of labor (Sutpen I) loosely tied to issues of sexuality (Sutpen II). Quentin is at least positioned to trace how a system's labor fears may be displaced into sexual fears or annealed through culturally preferred forms of desire. Redisposed through labor, Quentin's sites of embodied desire might read as follows: first, female virginity – iconic color line; second, brother/sister incest – that which preserves the line by ensuring that dark others stand on the far side of it; third, miscegenation – covert retention of the expelled body of labor in a form that ensures both the troubled potency and the untroubled property of the owning male.

Whether or not Quentin erogenizes the zone of bound work is finally less important than the recognition that, thanks to *The Sound and the Fury*'s relation to *Absalom, Absalom!*, Faulkner is in a position to do so. However, to speak schematically, having let the other preoccupy and dispossess a key character, the decision to revive that character (seven years dead) in order to explore the roots of an intervening labor revolution must involve the recognition that the owner who reads his body through the body of the worker puts his entitlement to the embodied "privilege[s] of the first person," both sexual and proprietorial, at mortal risk. If I am right and Quentin narrates the bulk of *Absalom, Absalom!* exactly *because* he already knows that to release the dark other is to deviate and die, then he knows enough to appreciate how and why his co-narrators stay alive. Hence sullenness and boredom, since, from the perspective of June 10, 1910, not only has he heard it all before, but he knows it for what it is – a systematic structure of denial by means of which the members of a class dedicated to, and deriving from, a peculiar regime of accumulation preserve an integrity through which he has already passed, by means of a story that he knows to be a tissue of repressions. Perhaps he is just plain tired of deception.

All of which puts a rather different slant on the resurrection. Faulkner does not resurrect Quentin in a full sense; he cannot do so, because many of his readers know the character to be dead. Rather, he recalls a character who is dead and acknowledged to be a "ghost" (p. 4) so that he may live a life marked for death, during which he struggles to articulate a sense not only that *he* has outlived his own death but that his class is similarly engaged in patching together an archaic longevity in the teeth of their own social demise. This is all very well, but Quentin manifestly fails again, in that what he eventually gets said – that Bon is Sutpen's black son – is simply what he (and they) already knew, and as such it is barely testimony to a social revolution. In effect, he releases Bon the miscegenated miscegenator (he who will "*sleep with your sister*" [p. 286]) but retains Bon as "goods" or the "nigger sweat" at the foundation of white property. He releases one dark other, specifically in order to retain an other. It follows that the miscegenation revelation (p. 285) is merely the last and most successful veil cast over the primal trauma of labor (Sutpen I).

As so often, I find myself far ahead of any substantiated case and must backtrack to discover grounds on which to stand. At the start of this detour, I proposed that Quentin's bored silence, interspersed with ventriloquial talk, demonstrates his knowledge both of who Bon is and of a conspiracy to silence that knowledge among his co-narrators. My evidence has been speculative and needs substantiation. Yet I am loath to extend the lexicon of "shadow" in order to establish that yet another witness is fond of a set of words at cross-purposes with itself, and that he, like his informants, uses many "shade[s]" (p. 253) of "*shadow*" (p. 254), from "niggard" (p. 105) to "pass" (p. 129), specifically because they are words that lie and in lying enable him to resist the meanings that they raise. By now, any readers still with me, and still caring, can do that one for themselves. Instead, and in evidence, I offer a point in the testimony when Quentin blocks Shreve's access to who Bon is. Shreve reappraises Bon's visit to the Hundred over the Christmas of 1859; specifically, and in Bon's voice, he worries over why Sutpen gives no paternal sign to his estranged son:

> ["]*My God, I am young, young, and I didn't even know it; they didn't even tell me, that I was young,* feeling that same despair and shame like when you have to watch your father fail in physical courage, thinking *It should have been me that failed; me, I, not he who stemmed from that blood which we both bear before it could have become corrupt and tainted by whatever it was in mother's that he could not brook.* – Wait," Shreve cried, though Quentin had not spoken: it had been merely some quality, some gathering of Quentin's still laxed and hunched figure which presaged speech, because Shreve said Wait. Wait. Before Quentin could have begun to speak. "Because he [Bon] hadn't even looked at her [Judith]" [p. 257]

The interchange is peculiar, not least because Quentin interrupts without interrupting, causing Shreve to change the subject and to miss his own point. The point is crucial and all but made that Eulalia is black. Something in Quentin distracts Shreve from the very thing he is looking for, an explanation of Sutpen's indifference. Synonyms for passive, "lax" and "hunched," are not exactly cast off, but momentarily Quentin's body "gathers." In Blanchot's terms, the Haitian other is about to come home to roost. Of course Quentin has known, in some sense, of Eulalia's status at the very least since meeting Clytie and Henry in 1909, but he has said nothing; which is to say that he joins his co-narrators as co-keepers of a dark secret. Quentin's body "gathers" because the Jacobinical truth appears about to emerge, at which point he will join Henry, becoming what he effectively is already, a corpse in all but name – a revenant finally deprived of his structural heart. But Shreve postpones revelation, perhaps because he genuinely misses his own point. However, it is as likely that, in response to Quentin's physical reaction (a precursor of his final rigidity [p. 298]), and recognizing how troubled Quentin is by things Haitian, Shreve backs off. Yet he returns to the material "taint," in the same words, twice within ten pages. Moreover, on both occasions he accentuates his formulation as particularly significant, first by having Bon say it "loud and fast" (p. 263) and then by saying it himself in mimicry of Quentin's initial "interruption":

> yet he [Bon] had stemmed from the blood after whatever it was his mother had been or done had tainted or corrupted it.
> – Nearer and nearer, [to the Hundred] until suspense and puzzlement and haste and all seemed blended into one [pp. 264–5]

". –", a full-stop extended into an awkward pause by way of a barely grammatical dash, is evidentially difficult. The marks make some sort of space, but what happened there or who articulates it is more complex. Plainly Shreve must know – tainted blood in triplicate and out of Haiti, even to a Canadian, must be "black." But, equally plainly, he is not saying. Instead he tries to make Quentin say by giving his minimal hiatus (". –") back to him. Hesitantly, I suggest that Shreve struggles to keep his friend alive. Knowledge alone will not bring forgiveness; only by knowledge confessed may absolution be achieved. Shreve's name holds at its root the verb "to shrive," "to hear confession," "to impose penance," "to administer absolution." Eventually, partial confession will be exacted in the form of the famous dramatization of the meetings between Sutpen and Henry, and Henry and Bon during the retreat through Carolina in 1864.

But where does the explication of a pause take me in the matter of Quentin's prior knowledge of Bon? Faced with ". –," Brooks would probably reiterate that Quentin has known since meeting

Henry in 1909, but that simply makes the pause both knowing and culpable, while ignoring Shreve's distress over Quentin's impacted understanding. Kartiganer might counter that Quentin doesn't fully know for another twenty-five pages, or until Shreve annotates Clytie's look of terror:

> "and she didn't tell you in the actual words because even in the terror she kept the secret; nevertheless she told you, or at least all of a sudden you knew –"
> He ceased again (p. 280)

"–" signals Shreve's need to shrive – and it works; the pause prompts immediate confession, albeit incomplete ("They were both in Carolina and the time was forty-six years ago" [p. 280]). However, Kartiganer's account, in its desire to relieve Quentin of the hypocrisy of withheld information, quite unintentionally reduces him to troubled foolishness; Shreve's triple return to tainted blood, accompanied by his triple refusal to read that blood right, is unmistakably a demand that Quentin tell the truth – a truth he has long known – and tell it himself, presumably to release him from whatever it is that gives him such pause (". –"), and deadens him before Shreve's eyes. Because, for Kartiganer, Bon's blackness results from a "momentous leap from the theme of incest to that of miscegenation," an "imaginative" leap, made late, exclusive to Harvard, and into "the fiction we believe,"[98] that blackness is no more than one among several "blackbirds,"[99] and as such it has no point of reference beyond the anguish of its two narrators. Bon is no longer "goods"; he is just a good, if painful, idea stretched over an "original meaninglessness."[100]

Epistemological voids were ever thin on material conditions, and in a critical tradition much given to them, Sundquist offers the fullest material account of ". –", or of the historical circumstances underpinning what Quentin represses. But even he mistakes a distorted symptom for the trauma itself and so sites the trauma's primal scene in the place of interethnic sexuality rather than that of interdependent labor. Sundquist argues that *Absalom, Absalom!* turns on a family crisis:

> ... which appears in the admixture of blood and identity when incest is involved with, and ultimately paired with, miscegenation ... a crisis of blood in which sons are not sons and brothers are not brothers, and in which the distinctions between them that must be maintained, however fantastically, are also the ones that keep the lost dream [of familial and regional

integrity] in place long after it has collapsed. . . . It is exactly
the nature of the crisis that leads the South into the Civil War
. . . that it grows out of a 'monstrous' system in which, at the
simplest level, slaves were and were not human beings, and in
which, at a more significant level for our purposes, sexual violence could issue in a state of simultaneous differentiation
and non differentiation between father and son or brother and
brother.[101]

Affirming the sexual orientation of his purposes, Sundquist goes on
to insist that *Absalom, Absalom!* "has virtually nothing to say about . . .
slavery as a labor system."[102] He errs because Quentin leads Shreve
into error when they finally explicate ". – " by way of Bon's statement
to Henry, on the retreat across Carolina, "*So it's the miscegenation, not
the incest, which you cant bear*" (p. 285). In the last instance, neither
incest nor miscegenation, either of themselves or together, is as central to the case as Sutpen I. Consequently, confession brings no relief, and Quentin ends the novel as he began in a pattern of evasive
vocal repetition, paralyzed rather than freed by the fullness of what
he knows. Or, to state it less epistemologically, the novel ends with
a false confession, made in a Harvard study paid for by the sale of
plantation-based lands. As the beneficiary of the "goods" of a dying
class, Quentin is not disposed to dispossess himself of these goods
by pursuing their (and his own) materialization within a regime of
bound labor. So, he does what his progenitors did, all the way back
down the class line – where labor stood (Sutpen I) he makes miscegenation stand (Sutpen II), the better to veil an unspeakable
trauma within its more bearable displacement.

For all his illuminations, Sundquist is fooled perhaps because in
1936 Faulkner needs almost to fool himself. His reasons are complex, involving literary recognition of a historical conjunction. The
years of the first Agricultural Adjustment Program (1933–8) and of
the STFU (1934–7) are years of labor revolution in the South, during which two regimes of accumulation clash, the one archaic and
"bound," the other "free" and emergent. By 1938 the collapse of
tenancy, diaspora, and the release of the "bound" black into "free"
wage labor (or "free" migratory destitution) marked, if not the end
of regional labor constraint, then its redundancy as a typifying form
of work. The "bound" black worker could no longer be said to
contain "the laws of future development" of both those who enforced and those who lived under the laws of constraint. Between
October and December of 1934, and while working on *The Dark
House*, Faulkner wrote *Pylon*. Immediately after finishing *Absalom, Ab-*

salom!, and between September 1937 and June 1938, he completed *The Wild Palms*, writing the novel on his return home from eighteen months in Hollywood contracted to Twentieth Century–Fox.[103] *Pylon* and *The Wild Palms* are readings of modernity undertaken during the last days of a long and pre-modern system of labor. In effect, while the owners' counterrevolution collapsed, Faulkner went to southern California to read up on commodity spectacle and to learn what the revolution was for. He returns convinced that Hollywood is "no longer in Hollywood but is stippled by a billion feet of burning colored gas across the face of the American earth."[104] It follows that *The Wild Palms*, his Hollywood novel, is set prevalently in Louisiana and Mississippi, and more particularly in a New Orleans gaol and in Parchman prison, from which the narrative voices of its two counterpointed novellas emerge to proclaim that the wages of free-wage labor are absolute and extended constraint. If the relationship between *The Sound and the Fury* and *Absalom, Absalom!* begs questions about the end of one realm of necessity (bound labor), the relationship between *Absalom, Absalom!* and *The Wild Palms* suggests that the realm of freedom (wage labor), offered to induce the unbinding of labor, involves an alternative form of enslavement – not to wages but to the commodity perceived as a "prison," and so, in Adorno's terse summation, as "an image of the bourgeois world of labor taken to its logical conclusions."[105]

On June 2, 1910, Quentin releases the dark other and finds death in the form of a partially open question; his decision "not . . . to be me any more"[106] might kill him, or by way of passage through foreign bodies and dark faces – the traces of an "other" history – might grant access to an alternative past that could have been but was not. Walter Benjamin speaks of an "oppressed past,"[107] denied by the praxis of those who oppress it, but one that nevertheless might yet become possible, under a different and supportive set of social relations. On the day of his death, Quentin gathers objects stranded at the limits of his own experience . . . expressions of immigrant Italian faces (pp. 77, 78, 79, 84); a shift among Deacon's vernaculars (p. 61); an uncensored response by his own body (p. 93); plain speech from a sister (pp. 91–100). . . . These traces initiate an archive to a history that might have been. Each is an instance of parapraxis, or an action to the side of an action from which it deviates; in deviating, it has been lost. But memory on June 2, 1910, grants to such remainders and structural irritants the power to undo the narrative that had previously ensured their repression. Released, the "stranded objects"[108] become parts not simply of other bodies but of other praxis, involving Quentin in an alternative realization of his

own past, through which his "lifework" is undone by the freeing of
the "work" that it conscripted and denied – the release prevalently
of the sister but also of the immigrant and the black. Arguably,
Quentin glimpses a lost avenue of praxis, another way of existing, in
quite another relation to sisters and blacks – a way so shocking to
that self, composed within a pattern of sexual pathology which constitutes his class apprenticeship in *The Sound and the Fury*, that for a
time he has to die.

Plainly, I am re-reading Quentin's section through my understanding of the preoccupations of *Absalom, Absalom!*, which involves
reading his suicide for signs of resurrection. I feel justified because,
during the years of Faulkner's work on the later novel, a labor revolution generalized the structure of feeling that lies close to the
heart of Quentin's revisionist day. That is to say, as owners found it
in their interest to break the share contract that bound black tenants
to the land and to the land's owner, so they dispossessed themselves
of the dark other whose denied presence, under chattel and debt
slavery alike, had founded and given form to the selfhood of their
class. Dispossessed tenants went North or into southern cities, in
either case entering the realm of wage and commodity. Dispossessed
planters – dispossessed of themselves but not necessarily of their
lands – transformed those lands, farming their fields like factories,
or risked incorporation into the nearest successful unit of production. Under pressure throughout the thirties, planters "altered their
mode of production fundamentally."[109] The impulse to change, a
revolution from without, completing a long revolution, was the federal program (1933–8).[110] Kirby refers to a "shocking modernization"[111] in which pre-modern paternalism, laced with capitalist
exploitation, was ousted by the impersonal rule of the international
labor market, backed by the federal government in its capacity as
off-season welfare source.[112] Federal support for the cash nexus completed the work undertaken by the Freedmans Bureau in the 1860s
and in conclusively "freeing" the "bound" finally deprived planters
of their status as labor lords. Whereupon they ceased their resistance
to a waged system and conclusively entered the "partial relations"[113]
of commodity.

Whereas, in 1929, loss of the dark other and attendant self-loss
looked like a potential path through death to regeneration; the same
process, culturally generalized and seen from the perspective of the
revolution's end in California circa 1935, looks plain deathly. So
Quentin is set to die again, but this time utterly. Letting Bon go and
departing the identity founded upon him looks merely self-
destructive in the absence of emergent social forms that might ben-

efit from the wasted social praxis. There is no point in Quentin's
extending his parapraxic archive because, for Faulkner, its "stranded
objects," trailing traces of liberatory narrative, have gone to California to die. In his Californian fictions Faulkner will encounter no sign
of "other" history or potential for an alternative past. Instead, he
will discover in the lives, words, faces, and bodies that he creates
evidence of a collective failure of memory among people who, in
submitting themselves to the free market, become human commodities, designed to protest that they have no past.

Quentin's second death is, in a sense, Californian, because Faulkner writes the last two chapters of *Absalom, Absalom!* under contract
to Twentieth Century–Fox.[114] Quentin's account of his last visit to
the Hundred (1909) leaves him "rigid," on his back, "breathing
hard but slow" and quoting the punchline from Poe's "The Raven"
– a poem whose titular bird is Death's harbinger (pp. 298–9). Quentin knows that he is all but dead because in Henry, also prostrate,
"hands crossed on the breast as if he were already a corpse" (p.
298), he sees a version of himself.[115] Henry, having effectively been
dead a long time (since 1865), comes alive, but only *"To die. Yes."*
(p. 298). Similarly, Quentin (in 1936), having been dead a shorter
time (since 1929), comes alive again (albeit retrospectively in 1910)
"To die – ?" (p. 298). Quentin's question is answered by his structural resemblance to the living corpse. In killing Bon, Henry murders that which makes him what he is and therefore kills himself.
Quentin's confession, abetted by Shreve, is false; by casting Bon into
a cliché as the "nigger" who will sleep with his own sister, Quentin
turns a labor trauma into a family crisis; and by veiling Sutpen I in
Sutpen II he buries Bon's revolutionary praxis, repressing it to reconstruct a form of class life that, by 1936, is a dead remnant. Yet
again I find myself back with revolutionary-praxis-denied and with
the founding atrophy of a class – perhaps because it is my case that
Absalom, Absalom!, as a study of the first and last days of the plantocracy, is grounded precisely in cryptogramic denial, a denial which,
faced with California, Faulkner all but compounds.

All but . . . but not quite, since from the first Faulkner consistently
lets his first-, second-, third-time readers . . . innocently bewildered
or exasperated numb . . . suspect, via the persistence of undercoded
subtexts, a mute hermeneutic in which layer after layer leads down
to labor. Witness whatever it is that Quentin "could not pass" at the
close of chapter five. Listening to Miss Rosa wind up her long account of Sutpen with an objection to his death (*"you're not dead"*),
Quentin has stopped listening because "there was also something
which he too could not pass" (p. 139). For Sutpen's death he sub-

stitutes Bon's or, more particularly, the scene inside Judith's bedroom, into which Henry bursts to announce his murder of Bon. The
scene is violent and erotic; Judith, "the white girl" "in her underthings," catches up her wedding dress, a "creamy mass" of satin and
lace, to cover herself as her brother, all "bayonet-trimmed hair" and
"pistol" to "flank," crashes through the door. Their exchange is
verbal but might as well be sexual:

> the two of them, brother and sister, curiously alike as if the
> difference in sex had merely sharpened the common blood to
> a terrific, an almost unbearable, similarity, speaking to one an-
> other in short brief staccato sentences like slaps, as if they stood
> breast to breast striking one another in turn, neither making
> any attempt to guard against the blows:
> *Now you cant marry him.*
> *Why cant I marry him?*
> *Because he's dead.*
> *Dead?*
> *Yes. I killed him.*
> He (Quentin) couldn't pass that. [pp. 139–40]

The first-time reader has only the page to go on, since she knows
next-to-nothing of Bon, save that he is Henry's older student friend
whom few have seen but several have loved. Mr. Compson has pos-
ited two relevant plot possibilities: that Henry, not Bon, courted Judith, doing so in Bon's name (p. 85); and that Bon may or may not
have an octoroon wife by way of morganatic marriage. Incest and
miscegenation have, therefore, been mooted, with an emphasis on
the former, since, as yet, miscegenation is localized and lives in New
Orleans. Certainly Judith and Henry might be mistaken for an incestuous couple, though meeting in a verbal violence that incest
alone will not explain. Their coupling is sadomasochistic, with the
added twist that dominator and supplicant are interchangeable,
since neither party exclusively gives or receives blows. Jessica Benjamin, addressing fantasies of erotic domination, suggests that "the
desire for submission represents a peculiar transposition of the desire for recognition."[116] Remember that in this, Quentin's first instance of the fantasy, both parties may play submissive at least some
of the time. Benjamin argues that the masochist sees in the masterful
other the power for which his or her self longs; by submitting to
him or her, the masochist gains that power vicariously and achieves
a kind of selfhood. In so doing, the masochist's sacrifice "actually
creates the master's power, [producing] his [or her] coherent self,
in which the masochist can take refuge."[117] This position makes it

plain that the masochist's pleasure cannot be understood as enjoyment of pain ("sharp," "unbearable," slaps"); rather, the pain of violation substitutes physical pain for the greater psychic pain of lost recognition, thereby avoiding the absolute pain attendant on a failure of that recognition. At least, through pain, the masochist feels that he or she is being reached and is therefore safe from self-loss, because he or she continues to be "subject" to a power that recognizes the submissive's self. Or, aphoristically put, "masochism is the desire for self discovery in the space provided by the other."[118] Sadists, à la Benjamin, pursue a linked desire for an other who will grant recognition, though here the quest is for the other as a limit case, in whose recognized and erotically sustained desires they will be granted the image of their own desired mastery. Note that Benjamin insists that domination, for the "good sadist,"[119] involves an intuition as to the other's desires (and as to the other's difference), since the dominator who dominates too much, allowing the submissive no independent consciousness, inevitably creates a deadened thing, or an inert other, who cannot grant the sadist's coherent self through recognition. Plainly, for Benjamin, self and other within the sadomasochistic couple are caught up within each other's hearts and anchored there by a redemptive and essentially metaphoric violence. Theirs is not an oppositional pairing but a mutually and necessarily interdependent meeting.

Which excursus may cast some light on what Judith and Henry are doing in Quentin's mind, and in the mind of the first-time reader. "Incest," as a caption, takes that reader only to "sameness" in that under it "like" bloods meet. But here they meet, and, in the recent and dramatic absence of an "other," each acts like a sadist lost for an adequate and mutual submissive *and* like a masochist lost for an adequate and "good" dominator. Bon is the missing person whom Judith and Henry metaphorically break into one another to find and without whom their marks of "difference" or selfhood fail. His absence renders their "similarity" "unbearable" because it signals the collapse of that other who is responsible for the selfhood of these selves. As a result, both will forgo a portion of their entitlement, wounding their "common bloods." Henry absents himself from the inheritance to which Judith, by remaining unmarried, refuses extension. "Sutpen," their generic self, fails. Bon is plainly the key to all this; but the notional first-time reader, in possession of neither the traumatic interdependencies of labor (Sutpen I) nor of those involved in miscegenation (Sutpen II), can have little sense of why this should be so. However, there are clues, triggered by a parenthesis and a pun.

In "He (Quentin) couldn't pass that," an under-identified third-person, following an italicized passage of dialogue that has scant nomination, can be forgiven for leaning toward ellipsis in the teeth of parenthetical correction. So, by providing a referent for "he," the bracket promotes the very pronounal shift that it seeks to avoid. If not "(Quentin)," why not "(Bon)," since Bon cannot "pass" his own passing? Or even "(Henry)," so soon to "pass" from the frame of events? Semantic slippage works on the center from each end as "pass" is prompted to pun by the elusiveness of both its subject and object. "That" joins "he" on the skids, being a directional imperative nominating an object which is missing until the reader finds it. "That" is simply indexical; it points ... but to what? "Pass," anchored by a seeping bracket, loosened by an untraced object, shudders with polyvalency – not least because, short on secure syntactical relations, it proves long on prepositional terms of relation. "To pass by," or "to get beyond a particular place and time." Or, again, "to pass by" as in "to ignore, passing by on the other side." "To pass away," as in "to die." (Quentin stopped listening to Rosa's story and turned to the unpassable scene in Judith's bedroom, exactly where Rosa issued an exclamatory inquiry, in triplicate, over whether or not Sutpen was "*Dead*" [p. 139]. Moreover, his own scenario is accompanied by the "faint shot" [p. 139] that leaves Judith and Henry twinned as little more than revenants.[120]) "To pass away," as a euphemism for death, generates another prepositional and euphemistic option, "to pass over"; the phrase might be dismissible as just one euphemism too far, were it not for Shreve's famous insistence that he and Quentin "overpass" to love (p. 253). I hesitate to induct "passover" back through "overpass" into the verb "to pass" as used here, since in *Exodus* (Chapter 12) the blood spilled on sideposts and lintel protects the Hebrew first-born from visitation by the angel of death, whereas here blood spilled at the gate *is* that of the first-born and is blood whose spillage brings down the house of Sutpen – even as its hypothetical equivalent, in distinguishing the houses of the Israelites from those of the Egyptians, marks the deliverance of those households into independent nationhood. But, even as I hesitate, and as my hypothetical first-time reader plays across the prepositional variables, a case for the inclusion of "pass over" is made. The gunshot at the gate that "(Quentin)" cannot in some sense "pass" (over) is tied by Faulkner's title to another Old Testament event of murderous founding. Amnon, David's first-born and presumably his successor, is killed by Absalom, the next heir, for violating his half-sister Tamar. So far, the intertext casts Henry as Absalom since both are protectors of a sister's honor. But Absalom, as heir apparent, has himself declared king and is eventually killed against his father's express instructions. Henry now doubles as one Joab, though in his case he acts with the tacit approval of the head of his household in killing Bon, who, though not quite head-locked by a branch, is not to be allowed to pass by *"the shadow"* of one (p. 106).[121] Title to "Absalom" passes from Henry to Bon . . . but should not stop there. Many are the readings read off from *Absalom, Absalom!* by means of a template taken from *The Book of Samuel*, but none that I know of indicates that the narrative of the relevant chapters traces how a way is prepared for the succession of Solomon. The deaths of Amnon and Absalom (David's sons) are stages in a genealogical purge, preparing a path for the predicted ascent of Solomon, who is not a son of David but who will build Yahweh's house, the Temple at Jerusalem. David's famous cry, "Oh my son Absalom, my son, my son Absalom! Would God I had died for thee,"[122] a cry that Faulkner's title takes up to the point of excla-mation but that Sutpen conspicuously does not voice, is, in its larger context, an incident on the way to the housing of Yahweh and the consolidation of the Children of Israel.

As so often with *Absalom, Absalom!*, picking a word can reveal a hoard – "pass," "overpass," "passover," "Absalom," II Samuel, chapters 10 to 20 . . . by way of which horde, I return to "passover" (recovered from "pass"), recognized now as one of a sequence of linked foundations, running from the exodus to the Temple, by which the blood on the Passover threshold leads, indirectly, to a house for the Arc of the Covenant. *If* Quentin cannot "pass" the blood at the gate to the Hundred, it may be because that blood, prompted by biblical antecedents and an exasperating intertext, con-tains the first and last of the Dark House of Thomas Sutpen, even as its Old Testament equivalent contained the first and last of the House of David (though not of the House of Israel).

All of which may be nonsense. In every sense, biblical exegesis of an underarticulated pun, depending on a missing preposition, pushes credibility. But my substantial point remains only that, in the simplest of sentences – ("He (Quentin) couldn't pass that") – a level of semantic diversity provokes a resistance to meaning, as a result of which the simple sentence cannot simply settle. So that were neither end of "pass" to warrant a preposition, "pass," as a verb, would still beg two puns: one on ethnic passing – a deviant variant of that lex-icon of "shadow" already much used by Quentin in the opening five chapters; and a second on physical emission, or passing material from the body, which, particularly in the form of vomiting, is among the novel's more persistent metaphoric frames.[123] Masked crossing

of the color line becomes relevant once it is recognized that "He,"
as a pronoun containing traces of a triangular nomination, slips both
Henry and Bon into Quentin's bracketed subject position; since Bon,
even at first reading, has crossed the racial divide in morganatic
marriage, Quentin too may darken by association. Perhaps "he" cannot "pass" *that* (as in "emission") from his person, because "that"
twice induces blocked transmission. As at the close of chapter five,
so at the close of chapter four, Quentin stops listening in order to
reprise the extended moment which he seems unable to "pass" at
the close of either chapter. That the moment is a hiatus may be
gathered from its irruption across two voices (Mr. Compson's in
chapter four, Miss Rosa's in chapter five) and from its positioning
as the violent conclusion to two chapters. In its earlier manifestation,
Quentin runs the scene of Henry and Bon's return from war up to
Henry's threat made at the gate, but only to stop short. He does so,
even as his father tells him the same story, though Faulkner's device
of blocking the father's voice with the son's makes it absolutely possible that both tellers don't tell of the shot itself. If so, both are
unable to "pass" ("emit") by passing on ("transferring") the moment of death. Faulkner deploys dashes to ensure a joint silence as
to the gunshot itself. Mr. Compson notes:

> the one [Bon] calm and undeviating, perhaps unresisting even,
> the fatalist to the last; the other [Henry] remorseless with im-
> placable and unalterable grief and despair –" (It seemed to
> Quentin that he could actually see them, facing one another
> at the gate [p. 105]. . . . the two faces calm, the voices not even
> raised: *Dont you pass the shadow of this post, this branch, Charles*;
> and *I am going to pass it, Henry*) "– and then Wash Jones sitting
> that saddleless mule before Miss Rosa's gate, shouting [p. 106]

Whether or not Mr. Compson can reconstruct the killing, Quentin
plainly cannot because, at the close of chapter six, he restarts the
story from behind Judith's door with the sound of Henry's running
on the stairs "almost a continuation of the faint shot" (p. 139). But
what he literally leaves out, allowing it to be displaced by the entirety
of Rosa's narrative (chapter five), returns via vocal and textual in-
terference. At the close of chapter four, Wash Jones shouts Henry's
crime as the shooting of a "French feller," translated by death into
"beef" ("Kilt him dead as a beef"[p. 106]): a version that, in the
context of "pass," partakes of devious illumination as Melville, Cable, and a poor white tenant interlocute within a pun. I may at this
point overstep the reach of the confusedly plural projections of my
first-time reader, though by how much depends on how far such a

reader is prepared to ride the valencies of "*pass*" . . . which should be pretty far, given that "*pass*," acting on "*shadow*," calls two famous literary echoes into that word. In Melville's "Benito Cereno" (1855), Captain Delano, troubled by Cereno's inability to recover from the experience of a slave revolt on his ship the *San Dominick* (code name, Haiti), rebukes him:

> ' . . . you are saved: what has cast such a shadow upon you?'
> 'The Negro.'
> There was silence, while the moody man sat, slowly and unconsciously gathering his mantle about him, as if it were a pall.[124]

A shadow falls to linked effect in George Washington Cable's *The Grandissimes* (1879):

> "We forget that we ourselves are too *close* to see distinctly, and so continue, a spectacle to civilization, sitting in a horrible darkness, my-de'-seh!" He frowned.
> "The Shadow of the Etheopian," said the grave apothecary.
> M. Grandissime's quick gesture implied that Frowenfeld had said the very word.
> "Ah! my-de'-seh, when I try sometimes to stand outside and look at it, I am *ama-aze* at the length, the blackness of that shadow" (He was so deep in earnest that he took no care of his English.) "It is the *Nemesis* w'ich, instead of coming afteh, glides along by the side of the mortal, political, social mistake! It blanches my-de'-seh, ow whole civilization! It drhags us a centrhy behind the rhes' of the world! It rhetahds and poisons everhy industrhy we got! – mos' of all our-h immense agrhicultu'e! It brheeds a thousan' cuses that nevva leave home but just flutter-h up an' rhoost, my-de'seh, an ow *heads*; and we nevva know it! Yes, sometimes some of us know it."
> He changed the subject.[125]

I quote at length not just to take pleasure from Cable's remarkable novel but to indicate how for M. Grandissime, as for Quentin, "the shadow of the Etheopian" falls virtually invisibly on all things ("blanches," "pass"), dislocating meanings through labyrinthine distortion ("*ama-aze*," "passover"), and evading all but whispered articulation (Frowenfeld puts "shadow" into the mouth of the French creole who, at the chapter's close, repeats the phrase but in a "lowered" voice). On entry into such an intertext, Wash Jones's "beef" resonates. Jones turns Bon into dead "stock," or a quantity of meat. If even a trace of the Etheopian's Jacobinical "shadow"

touches the victim, then Jones's shout in the street has got it right –
"Bon," French for "good[s]," *is* a quantity of white stock. Arguably,
Quentin violently expels this potential recognition, leaving Faulkner
to set it in code, care of Mr. Comson, outside the bracket, even while
Quentin refuses to countenance the shot itself. Yet the self-censoring
parenthesis contains evidence enough to suggest that Jones's inad-
vertent point is taken. What Quentin "actually see[s]" inside his
parenthesis is a park, extending from the gate, "in shaggy desolation
. . . like the unshaven face of a man just waking from ether, up to a
huge house where a young girl waited in a wedding dress" (p. 105).
That house is "a skeleton giving of itself in slow driblets of furniture
and carpet, linen and silver" in the southern cause (p. 105). Park
and house combine anatomically to suggest "amputation," particularly since the contents of the Hundred go to help "die torn and
anguished men" – that is, wounded Confederate troops among
whom by far the most common surgical operation was the amputation of a limb.[126] At the gate itself, Henry and Bon face each other
in a statuesque tableau:

> . . . faces gaunt and weathered as if cast by some Spartan and
> even niggard hand from bronze . . . [p. 105]

In "Barn Burning" (1938), a "niggard blaze," plus Conrad, adds
up almost to a "nigger" with or in fire; here, "niggard," plus Melville, plus Conrad, plus Jones, adds up to a "nigger" amputee (or
amputated) – particularly since Bon's face, via "weathered" (a term
as often applied to architectural as to human profiles), is linked
through the house's "scaling desolation" (p. 105) to the park's "unshaven face . . . waking from ether." With the metonymic displace-
ments in place, one is forced toward the question, "To what do all
the bits add up?" If Bon's and Henry's faces are at one with the
"face" of the estate, and that face is the face of an amputee, who
or what has been cut off? Nothing . . . since Quentin will not allow
the shot to sound. But, filling in as directed by Jones et al., the
missing matter is Bon or a quantity of "nigger" meat, whose removal
leaves the heir all but dead, since he has cut from his own body (and
estate) the substance that made him. If this is so, neither Quentin,
nor Mr. Compson, nor any member of their class can "pass" beyond,
over, or around it; nor can they pass it on in acknowledged form,
because it is the traumatic moment at which their class achieved its
masterful and ruined body.

Quentin's moment joins Sutpen's "1791" (in western Virginia),
Rosa's 1848 (at the doors to Jefferson's church), and Mr. Compson's
undated Jacquerie (at the gate of the New Orleans dueling ground).

Each is a palimpsestual tableau in which time stands layered (and impassable), rupturing the continuity of past and present in order to expose, in partially denied forms, those essential lines of economic force that impel bodies toward structurally rigid and rigorously traumatic forms of social relations.[127] For the keepers of the tableau to say as much would be to betray their class by casting the black out from the collective white body that bound labor sustains. Instead, each reaches for his or her version of the veil. Quentin goes for incest, veiling the explosive shot so that he may slip away from all but its echoes. Quentin's task, as it was for Sutpen and Rosa before him, is to create a preservative repression within which Bon may both die (or be denied) in the cause of white mastery *and* be revived (or acknowledged) in a similar cause. His solution is Judith's bedroom. Yet even as he obstructs what he *really* cannot "pass," by means of an incest that he can and has passed, his materials implicitly reveal the unabsorbed trauma of Bon's death. For example, the wedding dress is caught up and decorated in a manner guaranteed to distract, but it covers "underthings" that, being made of "flour sacking" and "window curtains," are at odds with the erotics of "satin" and "lace" – "things" that because they are marked by labor, both in field and house, mark the body of the mistress as transparent to the work which adorns it. A similar transparency attends Judith's and Henry's words; minimal, percussive, interrogative, and italicized, they stand as the chronological precursor of Quentin's words with Henry (1909). Both dialogues turn on deaths questioned and asserted (*"Dead? / Yes. I killed him."* [pp. 139–40]; *"To die? / Yes. To die."* [p. 298]). The echo marks the second conversation as a continuation of the first and prompts the recognition that the first death contains those that follow, because, for those who converse, separation from Bon must feel structurally like death (by amputation).

V

For Quentin to prove self-obstructive in a matter so central indicates that much of his revisionist work with Shreve in their Harvard study needs reconsideration. The critical tradition has garnered their achievements largely from chapters eight and nine under some variant of the generic title "creative history." The contents are impressive, featuring Eulalia's lawyer (pp. 240–53); switched bodies on the field of Shiloh (p. 275); "overpassing" to love (p. 253); and the dramatized scene on the retreat through Carolina (pp. 280–6). I shall gloss what happens to these items if they are considered not as

imaginative constructions born of the "ceaseless play of signification"[128] nor as "a marvellous process of fictional creation"[129] organized by a "need for narrative" coherence[130] but as evidence of a
pervasive repression, to be interpreted through an evaluation of
their resistance to a meaning (or traumatic situation), which they
obscurely retain at a lower level as their determining ground.

First: the lawyer, nominally of Shreve's making, but into whose
creation Quentin puts considerable energy. The plot requires some
sort of continuity between Sutpen's two families, if only at the level
of information. The lawyer is the link. In nascent form he services
Mr. Compson's morganatic hypothesis as a tacit source for Sutpen's
knowledge of New Orleans. Developed, he ups the ante on the incest
option, as Shreve and Quentin have him ship Bon to Oxford and
calculate blackmail profits. However, the narrativist premise requires
only Shreve's authorship and cannot explain why Quentin should
commit himself to a distracting device. Which is exactly the point –
the lawyer is a quintessential bourgeois; coming into existence as a
financial "check" (p. 240), he treats people as clients, and clients
as property (Eulalia is a rich acreage [p. 241], and Bon a "race
horse" to be tethered in New Orleans [p. 242] before being sent to
stud in Jefferson [p. 249]). Quentin claims authorship ("Both thinking as one" [p. 243]) because the lawyer allows him to indulge the
idiom of contract and speculation, within which bigamy and incest
are economic ploys, and "secrecy" is merely sound business sense
("the secret drawer in the secret safe and the secret paper in it" [p.
241]). By imagining a lawyer, Quentin can go on holiday to the
bourgeoisie, where he may briefly forget the mire of a dependency
culture. By chapter eight he needs the break, having just spent chapters six and seven recounting to Shreve his father's account of his
grandfather's account of Sutpen. By functioning as a transmission
point for a tissue of retentive denials, Quentin deepens his complic-
ity in the archaic consciousness of his class and is notably "sullen"
about it. Reference to his "dead" or "flat" or "bemused" tone dramatically increases as he repositions the primary veil (Sutpen II) over
the primary trauma (Sutpen I) (pp. 177, 197, 206, 208 . . .). After
which he may, perhaps, be forgiven his trip away from the residual
"secrets" of dependency to the emergent implications of autonomy.

The body switch on the field at Shiloh requires less explanation.
Shreve innovates; where Mr. Compson had it that Bon was wounded
and carried to safety by Henry, Shreve pulls a swap, with which Quentin seems to comply in that the narrator signals joint authorship via
a quick allusion to vocal elision ("First, two of them, then four" [p.
275]). The innovative point lies latent in its lateness. Shiloh is fought

less than ten pages prior to Shreve's reading of Rosa's face at the door to the Hundred in 1909. Arguably, therefore, Shreve already knows that Bon is black[131] and may already be trying to edge Quentin toward speaking his dependency on the bound. His image of the slave carrying the master from the battlefield is an early version of "I [and] . . . you will also have sprung from the loins of African kings" (p. 302). Both images subordinate the white body to the black.

All of which fine tuning to recover a real and labor trauma, retained within and beneath what is most commonly reprised as some version of "fictionalist creativity," comes up short when confronted with Shreve's imperative, that they "overpass to love" (p. 253), which is inescapably fictive. Whether described as narrativist historiography or lyric afflatus, "overpassing," and its resultant scene in Carolina, looks like an invention dreamed up by Quentin and Shreve in a moment of rare amity. For Faulknerians the passages from which I am about to quote require no quotation, having become paradigmatic of the "fictionalist" or "narrativist" premises through which *Absalom, Absalom!* is prevalently read. Because Quentin and Shreve achieve "some happy marriage of speaking and hearing," they "exist in" the "shade[s]" whom they "create" (p. 253), among which "shadows . . . of . . . shades" (p. 243) they "overpass to love," a state of absolute credulity whereby "paradox and inconsistency" will be held to be neither "fault nor false" (p. 253). Which is another way of saying "anything goes" as Quentin goes into Henry, Shreve goes into Bon, and Quentin goes into Shreve, "the two the four the two facing one another" (p. 276), and as Harvard goes into Carolina, all to get Bon to say that he will go into Judith (p. 285) . . . so that finally the whole thing can add up to a sexual cliché involving "*nigger*[s]" and "*sister*[s]":

> all that had gone before just so much that had to be overpassed and none else present to overpass it but them, as someone always has to rake the leaves up before you can have the bonfire. [p. 253]

Leaving aside the prevalence of the troubled lexicon of "shadow," passing on the various subtexts of "pass," ignoring the labyrinthine latencies of "overpass" as biblical intertext, much that remains demands the collapse of credence. I list items of which I shall not speak, to indicate the presence of a number of "enigmatic signifiers"[132] functioning to exhaust readers by prompting unspecific anxiety. "Shadow," "pass," "overpass" have no easily available referents and yet through self-division seem to refer copiously, creating a sheen of verbal substitutions that invite, exclude, and disguise a historical and political trauma lurking as their own barely traceable source of inscription. "Shadow," "pass," and "overpass" promote the expectation that direct speech will lie and that the twisting tongue is the truth teller. Shreve and Quentin may achieve straight talk, but their "happy marriage," in a novel whose marriages run from bad to fatal, inspires little confidence. Doubts increase with the suggestion that in order to "overpass to love" they have "rake[d]" "leaves" for a "bonfire." In a paragraph littered with "enigmatic signifiers," whose key word "overpass" inculcates division and reversal among signifiers, "bonfire" cannot escape intact. To separate the syllables is to witness the extinction of a central character, extinguished among the very "leaves" that gave him life. Whether or not this syllabic conjunction is an un"happy" mistake, it remains the inferential case (for the overnarrator[133] and for the characters) that any narrative coherence based on "love" rests at a lower layer on a suspicion of lynching. Only by keeping Bon down, socially and semantically, and by confessing his presence in a tolerably clichéd form, can these narrators retain him at the core of the story – in Quentin's case, encrypting him as the structural essence of nontenable class and subject positions.

Yet Quentin insists repeatedly that their story stands or falls to the degree that it is about "love" between sisters and brothers and fathers and sons (pp. 258, 263). I cannot better Moreland's overview of what Quentin and Shreve do as they undo first Bon's apparent duplicity toward Henry (in the unspoken matter of his father's identity) and then his ineligibility to marry Henry's sister (Judith, they suppose, will not mind incest). Between them they project Bon as a guiltless lover and a guileless loved one, transferring any vindictiveness he might have felt toward a deserting father onto the deserted mother. Their Eulalia is a study in animosity and sole fount of the impulse to vengeance:

> so Quentin and Shreve tell this 'faery tale' in an attempt to sublimate Bon from an external threat to the Sutpen family into a harmless, all-reconciling seeker after his father and source of meaning in Sutpen.[134]

But for the facts, their tale might end in heroic reconciliation, with Henry granting Bon's incest, Sutpen recognizing and accepting Bon, and Bon trading in the incest for recognition. Instead, as Moreland has it, Bon speaks a cliché to render Henry's borrowed racial and paternal violence overt and retains a picture of the octoroon upon his person so that his corpse will endorse the propriety of his exclusion from the hierarchy.

All of which is neat and good, as far as it goes. But Moreland's very considerable insights may be taken further if they are approached as a stencil through which a still more basic story may be glimpsed. First the stencils and the loopholes must be aligned. Since Quentin co-creates the innocently promiscuous Bon and does so knowing that he is Sutpen's black son, and since he is also the oral archivist who retains, in Sutpen I and II, an incipient sense of the buried truth of white dependency on black labor, it may be surmised that through a particular articulation of Bon's sexuality he seeks to manage the underarticulated sphere of labor. By laying Bon's miscegenated and miscegenating body (first unconfessed and then belatedly confessed) over the body of Bon as a slave, into which goods the master (all unconfessed) must pass and be constrained, Quentin can represent the trauma of labor dependency in ways that render it partially available and thereby retain it as the essential component of white mastery. I would stress that what is involved here is not the mutual articulation of two spheres of domination, the sexual and the economic, but the orientation of one (the sexual) to serve by veiling the other (the economic). But the proof of the loopholes is the image they enable.

Consider exactly who enters Bon's body according to the various fantasies stored by Quentin; but consider the penetration bifocally, with one eye to the sex and the other to the economy. Mr. Compson speaks of "the pure and perfect incest" in which:

> the brother realizing that the sister's virginity must be destroyed in order to have existed at all, taking that virginity in the person of the brother-in-law, the man whom he would be if he could become, metamorphose into, the lover, the husband; by whom he would be despoiled, choose for despoiler, if he could become, metamorphose into, the sister, the mistress, the bride. Perhaps that is what went on, not in Henry's mind but in his soul. [p. 77]

Judith is as redundant as "metamorphose" is polite. What Mr. Compson describes is an autoerotic fantasy in which Henry becomes Bon in order to enter himself as Judith, care of Bon's body. Given that Mr. Compson is aware, however covertly, that Bon is black, and given that he is a child of the Radical era, he fantasizes about a conjunction of bodies in which white potency is achieved through a black mask, but only to violate those twinned icons of white honor, the hymen and the sister. Rudely put, black meets white inside a sister, but what is extraordinary is that the sister is irrelevant. Mr. Compson designs a fantasy that ought to send a Radical master narrative into spasm, as terms chosen to keep ethnic entities absolutely separate are brought into absolute conjunction. Nothing happens because the fantasist's attention is elsewhere as he works his way through sexual cliché and toward labor fact. So that when Mr. Compson reruns the scene, he starts by dismissing Judith:

> it was not Judith who was the object of Bon's love or of Henry's solicitude. She was just the blank shape, the empty vessel in which each of them strove to preserve, not the illusion of himself nor his illusion of the other but what each conceived the other to believe him to be – the man and the youth, seducer and seduced, who had known one another, seduced and had been seduced, victimized in turn each by the other, conqueror vanquished by his own strength, vanquished conquering by his own weakness, before Judith came into their joint lives even by so much as girlname. And who knows? there was the War now; who knows but what the fatality and the fatality's victims did not both think, hope, that the War would settle the matter, leave free one of the two irreconciliables [p. 95]

More is at issue here than the troubling fact that in Faulkner's work, all too often, women are silenced and objectified "in the theatre of male desire."[135] Certainly, Judith is first objectified as a hymeneal "vessel" and then reduced to an optional excuse so that men may meet in Mr. Compson's head without women. But male interpenetration occurs in a form that renders gender itself an option, as seduction becomes an optic through which quite another power play may be traced. With the fading of Judith as a point of internal mediation, desire itself fades as each male lover becomes himself incrementally by passing through the other. So, for example, Henry may see himself only from the other's imagined subject position, while Bon is similarly engaged. By such means the male lovers meet and "know" each other, but "known" ceases to be carnal and becomes cognitive as a prelude to signifying relations of power. With a geometry for the subject's trajectory of self-discovery laid down, Mr. Compson introduces two metaphors through which the formal pattern may be read – seduction and conquest – metaphors that tend to elide insofar as each intimates bondage; although because Bon is covertly black, the sadomasochistic scenario leaves a semantic residue whereby victimizer and victim shift toward alternative sites of mastery. Consequently, "conqueror," within a framework set by "seducer" and "black," retains options on "sadist" and "master," even as "conquered" contains the masochist and the bound man. Although it is clear that Bon and Henry switch subject positions across all available sites, it is equally clear that to the victim go the spoils, since within Mr. Compson's logic the "conqueror" is defeated by his own "strength," whereas the "vanquished" wins through his own "weakness." By removing the white mask from Bon, one can resolve the narrator's preference for subordination in terms of the twin sites of sex and labor. Just as the sadist who destroys the submissive, from whom he seeks recognition, defeats himself, so the master who assumes complete control over the bound man's identity and will negates his own mastery by negating he who might otherwise have affirmed it.

Mr. Compson's fantasy could have been made in western Virginia, though the deathly decision of the boy Sutpen to repress his own recognition of the interdependency of master and slave could not encompass Mr. Compson's sense that the bound submissive, by recognizing the sadist's mastery, actually creates his masterful power as a coherent and sheltering subject position within which the submissive may find himself. Nor, of course, can Mr. Compson dwell too long on the debilitating thought that masters might be what slaves make. Instead, he allows his metaphor of conquest to find a literal referent (the War), thereby expelling his awkward victims from bed and workplace to die for real on a singular site of battle. Yet, to return for a moment to the heart of Mr. Compson's fantasy, it is clear that his evasion (indeed the whole idea of the Civil War as "probation") cannot work, since once seen the untellable contradiction that lodges the bound firmly in the heart of those who bind cannot be dislodged. Masters cannot be "free" of slaves, since those masters who assert mastery by excluding the slave from the center of their consciousness die, almost as certainly as do those who acknowledge his presence there. It follows that, be he "conqueror" or conquered, Henry must carry Bon from the scene at Shiloh because his life depends on it, and that Bon (be he victim or victimizer) does the same and for the same mute structural reason. Each stands "irreconcilabl[y]" at the core of the other, needing the other to survive and to grant him recognition, if he is to recognize himself.

Unexplored, here, is a site of mutual recognition, in which each acts on the other, affecting the other and being acknowledged for it. The boy Sutpen glimpsed as much in western Virginia in "that expression on a balloon face" (p. 190), within which master and slave are mutually sustaining and needs must, by the logic of the metaphor, breathe one another's breath, each exhaling the other to give shape to the features which front an institution that is simultaneously "white" *and* "nigger sweat." But affirmation through the other foregrounds dependency, setting limits on the master's authority. Because Sutpen, representative of his class, seeks to experience mastery as absolute, that dependency, once glimpsed, will be denied – although denial must retain remnants of the denied, keeping bits of the black back, encrypted in the white, to function as the traumatic source of the master's mastery. Hence, the slipping interlock of Mr. Compson's metaphors almost permits the master and the slave to be caught in flagrante, interpenetrant, and interdependent within the cognitively coupled bodies of his male lovers. By such means, at least in this fantasy, gender functions as a stencil through which lines of economic force may be traced.

An impacted appreciation that Bon is black is central to the working of Mr. Compson's erotic speech. Apprenticed to the Radical era, a period aprey to "a social-psychological-sexual order"[136] in which black male sexuality was perceived as a threat, Mr. Compson is bound to police Bon's body. He does so via sustained feminization: Bon retains dominance but in a "Frenchified cloak," "a flowered . . . gown," and "almost feminine garments" (p. 76), so although Henry approaches him most typically as a supplicant, a youth "aping" an older man's style, declaring his love, and requesting that his friend refrain from entering his sister, the "beast's" penetrative capacity is reduced by a clutter of gowns. Quentin reworks Sutpen toward the close of the era of racial rage; inheriting a weakened pathology, along with his father's sense of Bon's dress sense, he develops Bon's femininity to other ends. Yet what Quentin and Shreve do for the love of Bon remains grounded in Mr. Compson's fantasy life. From his father Quentin takes Bon's erotic aura; from his father he takes the notion that Bon loves Henry, not Judith; and from his father, and conclusively, he takes the imperative that he discover a preservative repression, by means of which he may draw Bon into his body as a residue whose presence he must deny. In effect, his conversation with Shreve over a single night (chapters seven to nine) is orientated to finding a form of words or narrative twist that will allow Henry to shoot Bon without being abandoned by him, because, separated from Bon, he will die. I find myself, once again, close to the nub of a structural instability upon which a culture of dependency turns; the master must internalize the slave (and deny it); the sadist must provide shelter for the submissive (and deny it); the white must be black (and deny it) . . . from which sequence of generative contradictions the various stories that make up *Absalom, Absalom!* arise, and to which versions of the labor trauma they variously return.

The conversation on that night, like so much of the novel, is monadic and requires a bifocal reading: that is to say, with an eye to the simultaneous temporal sites lodged in every setting and an ear to the several levels at work within each articulation. Duplicity attends the homoerotic atmosphere gracing the talk in "the rosy orifice above the iron quad" (p. 176). Shreve, all pink flesh (p. 176), deep-breathing deferred (p. 235), and "cherubic burliness" (p. 259), has a preference for vocalizing the outsider Bon. Quentin, of the delicate bones (p. 259), haunted by his glimpse of Henry and sensing that he is his inheritor, prefers to speak Henry's lines. Their "marriage" of voices (p. 253) is framed as erotic:

> There was something curious in the way they looked at one another, curious and quiet and profoundly intent, not at all as two young men might look at each other but almost as a youth and a very young girl might out of virginity itself – a sort of hushed and naked searching [p. 240]

Quentin plays virginal girl to Shreve's virginal youth, but their courtship is conducted through the mask of their preferred roles, so that Bon courts Henry in Harvard and the "orifice" doubles as a "tomb." Quentin insists that they find a story that will allow Bon to act out of pure love for Henry (thinly disguised as Judith) (pp. 258, 263). The demand is considerable since, as Moreland points out, it involves removing the pathology from both incest and (eventually) miscegenation, while disabusing Bon of almost any motive whatever, so that Henry and Judith may receive him in equal innocence, saying, "*We belong to you; do as you will with us*" "every time [they] breathed over [their] vocal chords" (p. 262). Note the duplicities; Henry (Quentin) lays himself open to congress (homoerotic) with a brother but does so in the guise of his sister (incest); the lover is black (miscegenation), and the proposal is also proprietorial ("*belong*"), proposing partnership between the master (Henry) and a male, loving and non-Jacobinical slave. Deep down among the latencies lies a labor trauma recomposed as an acceptable passage of the slave into the master's body, presaging a just exchange of goods based on an acknowledged presence of the slave's labor within the master's substance. Bon, with the "goods" all but removed from his name, becomes simply "good" (with an inclination to "bonheur"). None of which is articulated, or known to Shreve, though all of it is present, layered in a preservative repression for Quentin, "every time he breathed over his vocal chords" (p. 262).

To recompose labor trauma and release it as a sigh of anticipated and utopian passion may explain why Quentin goes on looking for

Bon as motiveless amity. Such a figure might prevent Henry's slow suicide. But the facts are against it. Henry kills Bon, failing to read the mutual recognition encrypted in Quentin's fictional sigh. Faced with Bon, a slave at the gate and wearing the fullness of his social relations on his face, relations through which Henry has manifestly lived, Henry renders Bon socially and actually dead; he makes him less than the dead thing that his peculiar regime of accumulation requires him to be. In killing the source of mastery, the master dies. These are the facts. But in spite of them Quentin achieves a compromise that allows him to confess the wrong blackness (miscegenation) and retain the right one (labor), keeping back the "goods" that materially matter most to him – knowledge of the trauma whose effacing structures him as a class subject. In so doing he aligns himself with a line of narrators whose words have told the truth, mainly, by lying. Having failed to create Bon as Amity, Quentin uses the plot lines established by that trope to lay false trails, culminating in the Carolina playlet and its punchline. Once Shreve has pried from him the belated confession that Bon is black (p. 283), Quentin immediately deploys that blackness, allied to an acknowledged promiscuity, as a stalking horse. Incest is declared to have been a detour, so that miscegenation can be inserted as the main plot, rendering Sutpen's labor trauma redundant. And Shreve buys it; by the close of the Carolina scene he is animatedly discussing the niceties of Bon's sexual etiquette in allowing himself to die with a picture of the octoroon about his person. The point *is* a nice one, readable either as Bon's endorsement of Henry's ethnic cleansing or as Bon's refusal to follow Sutpen in denying his ethnically ineligible past.[137] But neither is to the point, and both allow Quentin to go to bed with his secret intact.

Chapter eight closes with Shreve confident that they have finished the story, and that one thing after another – thanks to miscegenation confessed – has become one thing because of another. However, Quentin's reaction in chapter nine suggests otherwise; retaining his secret, he takes to his bed, only to recall his trip to the Hundred and his encounter with Henry. Whereupon, lying "still and rigid" in "the dead moment before dawn" (p. 298), he experiences paralysis accompanied by sweating and panting. The symptoms of 1910 repeat those of 1909, attendant upon his return from the Hundred. Then he had breathed "fast and hard of the dark dead furnace-breath of air," his eyes "straining into the darkness" (p. 297). In Harvard "the darkness seems to breathe" for him, and to ensure his very circulation, "forced by the weight of the darkness, the blood surged and ran warmer" (p. 288). His symptoms so interanimate "darkness" and bodily functions that he appears metaphorically penetrated by blackness. The metaphor suggests how close he is to death. The room *is* "tomblike," and in it Quentin "peacefully" assures Shreve that he too does not understand Rosa Coldfield, even as he "taste[s] the dust" of "Mississippi September night" (p. 290). Once he is in bed, at "peace" and with an inkling of dust in his mouth, his body assumes the posture of the revenant of 1909 – Henry, "transparent eyelids on the pillow . . . hands crossed on the breast as if he were already a corpse" (p. 298). However, the fatal analogy breaks down. Henry dies lengthily between 1865 and 1909 because he shot his better half. But Quentin keeps that half back by retaining the labor truth of Bon as the master's "good" and "goods," encrypted in the miscegenation misnomer. Because, in the course of getting to the one about the "*nigger*" and the "*sister*" (p. 286), he monadically and almost unreadably tells the one about the bound man who is the internal and external substance of the master's mastery; he (unlike Henry) has welcomed his better half. Effectively, because Quentin's memory work encodes the labor truth about Bon, it resurrects him as a "stranded" structural fact, fulfilling the seemingly impossible imperative, issued by the primal scene upon which his class rests, to recognize *and* deny that the "lifework" of the master depends upon the "work" of the bound man.

On the bed and sick to death, Quentin bears only a passing resemblance to Henry. He too is a living "ghost" (p. 4), but he has functioned to encrypt and not to expel the black "goods." As the secret container of the body of black labor, Quentin's symptoms become readable. While various sources of blackness meet metonymically in, on, or about his person, Quentin quotes not just from "The Raven" but from the very words of the bird, which raven interferes with Jim Bond to loosen a crow from his name.[138] With two dark birds already perched, care of Poe, in the all-pervading "darkness" of the Harvard "tomb," Quentin and Henry's shared recumbency induces a further Poe text, triggering yet more ravens. In "Ligeia" the body of "the fair-haired, the blue-eyed Lady Rowena"[139] provides a delusional conduit through which the dead, dark-eyed, and raven-haired Ligeia returns. "Huge masses" of her "long and dishevelled hair . . . *blacker than the raven wings of the midnight*"[140] burst from the cerements binding Rowena. No such release occurs through the medium of Quentin's corpselike body, though Quentin does say (albeit indirectly) that he has a crow caught in his head when he admits to Shreve that he continues to hear Jim Bond "at night sometimes" (p. 302). So, by way of subsemantics and via an intertext, Quentin, likened both to a ghost and to a young and virginal girl (p. 240), appears possessed of a dark and secret sharer whose body he is unable to give up, "pass," or emit.

I argued earlier that, during his concluding denial of hatred for the South, his mind is fixed on a single term, "Bon" – not as a person but as an associative path through a collection of words, leading back to Sutpen's act of naming. Sutpen's choice of name derives from and represses a prior event (the turning away from the planter's door). By calling the slave who "comes" from his own white body "goods," Sutpen disclaims his earlier version of the master's mastery emerging from the body of black labor. Quentin and Shreve's Carolina play compounds Sutpen's disclaimer. But Quentin disclaims (and retains) only after long attention to a tradition of lying has made him that lie's acolyte. In his case, repressed knowledge of the lie lies closer to the surface that his version of the lie provides – threatening to break through, Ligeia-like, revealing that even the white grandson of the master class is a black in white face who owes his bodily "goods" to the body of a bound man. Quentin's final version buries Bon alive again, but only just.

5

FORGET JERUSALEM, GO TO HOLLYWOOD – "TO DIE. YES. TO DIE?"

(A CODA TO ABSALOM, ABSALOM!)

BY RICHARD GODDEN AND PAMELA KNIGHTS

─────────

I

At the close of "Wild Palms" (1939), Harry Wilbourne, like Quentin before him, survives to be a crypt, but in this case both the construction of the tomb and the identity of its occupant are explicit. Imprisoned for the botched abortion that led to the death of his mistress, Charlotte Rittenmeyer, Harry rejects suicide in the form of a cyanide capsule proffered by the offended husband in favor of fifty years hard labor in Parchman prison, during which time he will turn his body into a mausoleum containing the memory of Charlotte:

> so there was just memory, forever and inescapable, so long as there was flesh to titillate. . . . But after all memory could live in the old wheezing entrails: and now it did stand to his hand, incontrovertible and plain, serene, the palm clashing and murmuring dry and wild and faint in the night.[1]

To come upon this, having read *Absalom, Absalom!* and recognizing that Quentin and Harry share analogous functions as "vault," is to be shocked by the explicitness of the later text. Faced with Quentin's paralyzed "rigidity," and sensing deletions, I searched among mutilated signs in order to locate an encrypted secret that remains finally unspeakable, at least for its bearer. In contradistinction, Harry not only declares that he has introduced a loved body into his own body for safekeeping, but he proves it. That is to say, "thinking of,

Sections of this chapter are drawn directly from a jointly written essay, "The Wild Palms: Faulkner's Hollywood Novel (A Frankfurt School Reading)," *Essays in Poetics*, Vol.10, No.1 (1985), pp. 1–49. Pamela Knights (née Rhodes) has kindly given me permission to incorporate that material into my current re-reading. What follows would not have been possible without her work.

remembering, the body, the broad thighs and the hands that liked bitching" (p. 324), he achieves an erection ("it would . . . even stand still to his hand" [p. 316], "it would stand to his hand . . . and now it did stand to his hand" [p. 324]).

Harry's onanism may not be entirely overt, but "it" in close proximity to "palm" barely conceals the masturbator's "hand." Nor is it meant to; Faulkner appears to have dropped the verbal encryptment that attended Quentin's encrypted recognition that he owes his body, as potency and property, to the work of black bodies – a recognition brutally summarized by Shreve's joke about springing "from the loins of African kings."² Instead, Harry's penis is presented as a barely concealed key to Charlotte's crypt; the logic of the puns on "palm" seems to run – she is not dead, being in him; as one who lives in another she is a revenant, and his prick proves it.

The structural continuity between the end of *Absalom, Absalom!* and the close of "Wild Palms" is striking. Both passages share bodies as vaults, enclosing revenants who induce male rigidity, seminal hints, and overtones of suicide. But the differences are equally apparent: Quentin's body contains an unconfessed black male, whereas Harry's contains a confessed white female. How, then, to explain what amounts to a conjunction of form and a disparity of content? Faced with Harry's and Charlotte's "ambivalent sexualities,"³ much of the more recent scholarship addresses the instability of gender terms characterizing the relationship. Lists are drawn up under the generic heading "cross dressing"⁴ to establish that Harry and Charlotte constitute an "androgynous couple."⁵ Charlotte wears the trousers or, more particularly and at her first appearance, the "man's pants" (p. 6); and Harry, at least metaphorically, the skirts: in Chicago, he will do the cooking and cleaning while Charlotte goes to work. Evidence of gender switching is cumulative, running from Charlotte's introduction as "Charley" (p. 38) through her hard hands (p. 40), to her final refusal of the imperative of her uterus; and from Harry's willingness to drop his internship, two months short of completion (thereby denying himself the qualification that would certify him male in the professional marketplace), through his writing stories for confession magazines from the perspective of a sixteen-year-old unmarried mother (p. 123), to his discourse on the loss of virginity (pp. 136–40). Moreover, the centrality of sexual swapping is underlined among the minor characters. For example, the doctor and the doctor's wife, who rent out their beachhouse on the Mississippi coast, mirror their tenants; he wears a "night shirt" (p. 3) and has "thick soft woman's hands" (p. 4), and he speaks with an increasingly "shrill" voice (p. 200), while she is childless (p. 4), carries the marks of rigidity ("implacable" and "Iron-color[ed]" [p. 15]), and is liable to take command. The couple in situ at the Utah mine similarly alert us to Harry and Charlotte's shifty genders; they wear identical clothes and are called Billie and Buck.

My list of mobile gender marks is culled from extant lists and is far from complete. Its items, seen from the perspective of Charlotte's death, add up to what looks like an unshakeable case: "she" who would be "he" shall die for her ambition. Or as Diane Roberts puts it, Charlotte is assaulted by a narrative determined to silence her because, as that "intolerable incongruity . . . [a] woman who tries to break free of motherhood, domesticity, sexual submission, even the womb itself . . . [she] must be punished.[6] Recent Faulkner criticism seems to be in accordance with this point: Duvall speaks of her as "co-opted by patriarchal categories";[7] Gail Mortimer addresses Harry's oedipally driven and rebarbative fear of Charlotte's fertility;[8] Minrose Gwin speculates as to whether the poisoning of Charlotte's womb represents the repossession of female desire within a phallic model of thought.[9] Despite a variety of inflections, it remains the case in each of these examples that a man with a knife becomes a man (despite earlier ambivalence) because he uses that knife on the womb of a woman, in order to remind that woman that her womb should not be contradicted. Or to allow Roberts her powerful sum- mation, "Wild Palms" is "perhaps Faulkner's most profound ex- pression of men's desperate need to 'penetrate' and contain the female body."[10]

All of which seems very much to the point and yet to miss some- thing of that point – explicitly, the function of Harry as crypt and Charlotte as revenant, a function that is emphasized by a typological line running from Quentin (1936) to Harry (1939) by way of their intertext, *Pylon* (1935),[11] whose key character, the unnamed Re- porter, conducts a losing battle with gravity throughout the text. The Reporter is repeatedly and almost only presented as a corpse – his own perambulating vault.[12] No reason is given for his state, and none is surmisable, beyond a need to play Prufrock and a debilitating mother, but neither symptom amounts to a cause. Instead, he op- erates as a link, a self-containing corpse joining two characters whose lives depend upon the more and less obscure corpses they carry. Without the genealogy in place, it is easy to miss both the structural origins of Harry's relation to Charlotte's body, and his continuing dependency upon and subordination to her life after death.

As in their lives, so in their deaths – hers actual, his institutional – *she* is the master, since his body depends upon hers, to which it is bound, and which it contains and exemplifies. Charlotte's most iconic bodypart is her hands, hands that "like bitching and making things" (p. 88). "Bitching" is a synonym for sexual activity, and Harry's gloss on the act of masturbation with which *her* story closes is evidence that *her* hands continue to "make" Harry a man. Arguably, his preference for "it," as a pronoun with which to refer to what is nominally his own erection, suggests that any laurel for that handiwork should go to more than one set of palms. "It" is not "my" and projects some version of the word "phallus" only as a spectral synonym. Neither coyness nor the censor quite catches the workings of "it," which functions as a possessive in a state of partial dispossession. The word "it," rather than the phrase "my phallus," "stands" because Harry is watching an engorgement that he knows is not solely his own. I am reminded of Pettibone, seen by the boy Sutpen as contained in the "balloon face" of the "monkey nigger"[13]: since the slave's face gives form to the master's breath, that breath, face, and mastery are hardly self-sustaining. For "balloon face" read "it," or Harry's erection.

But, yet again, I run ahead of myself. Let me return to my claim that Harry's onanism is a quasi-spectral manifestation, embodying Charlotte's life after death. I realize that I am on shaky ground here, since I could all too easily be construed as saying that it is all right to kill a woman if you subsequently idealize her. I know that, at a literal level, Harry is using his memory of the body of Charlotte to give himself pleasure. But, for a time at least, I am concerned with levels other than the literal, levels growing out of my sense that the end of "Wild Palms" needs to be read as a coda to the end of *Absalom, Absalom!*

Gender-based readings of "Wild Palms" tend to establish Charlotte and Harry as a sadomasochistic couple. Charlotte dominates, and Harry is submissive. Her hands are the clue to Charlotte's authority; at their first encounter, "she took his hand and drew his finger-tips along the base of her other palm" (p. 40). Harry is taught the contours of "the broad, blunt, strong" hand, a hand whose chosen activity, "bitching," crosses "making sex" with "breakage" ("I have bitched it for you" [p. 47]), to relocate the verb "to bitch" within the lexicon of the dominatrix whose claim to archetypal female cruelty resides in her name, "The Bitch" or "Bitch Goddess." Her lesson is sustained. In the New Orleans hotel room, site of their first and failed liaison, Charlotte strikes Harry in what initially looks like a display of frustrated grief: "She beat her clenched fists on his chest" (p. 46); however, she will go on to insist that "love and suffering are the same thing" (p. 48) . . . and to "double" her fists, "wrench free," and "strike again" (p. 46). Adept at handling "chisel" and "maul," and with her "fist . . . beating on his knee," she commands Harry to book a "drawing room" on the train from New Orleans to Chicago so that she can use sex with him to "cut" and "pluck out" her marriage to Rittenmeyer (p. 59). In Chicago, the hand that she slides "in[to] his hair" (p. 81) is always liable to "shake" (p. 82), "grasp" (p. 83), and "hurt," with a "savage[ry]" that only looks like "obliviousness," since Harry notes that "she knew she was hurting" (p. 83). Further instances could be cited but would serve only to reiterate that for Charlotte, sex is synonymous with a conscious cruelty whose weaponry most typically involves the hand, the fist, the palm, the jabbing elbow – and all of them "hard." Yet it would surely be wrong to suggest, as does François Pitavy, that at times, and most particularly on the train to Chicago, she almost rapes him,[14] since Charlotte's sadism elicits a complementary masochism from her partner.

There is, however, a glitch to my index of predilection; for an overt sadist, Charlotte exhibits a covert masochistic bent. Two instances must make my case. Entrained and crossing Lake Pontchartrain, Charlotte observes that she would prefer to die in water:

Not in the hot air, above the hot ground, to wait hours for your blood to get cool enough to let you sleep and even weeks for your hair to stop growing. The water, the cool, to cool you quick so you can sleep, to wash out of your brain and out of your eyes and out of your blood all you ever saw and thought and felt and wanted and denied [p. 58].

Her preference might pass as a striking instance of some perverse travel game, along the lines of "Who would you most like to meet?" recast as "Name your burial place of choice," were it not that the reader encounters the choice in the second "Wild Palms" section. Consequently, she can refer it back only to the image of Charlotte at the close of the first section, about to hemorrhage for a second time and cursing her partner with six "bloodies" and two "damns" (pp. 20–2). By curse count, at least, the bloody flood, when it comes, will prove fatal. Yet Charlotte was introduced to Harry, by Flint at Rat's party in the Quarter, as a joke abortionist – "Watch him. He's got a pad of blank checks in his pocket and a scalpel in his sleeve" (p. 37). It would therefore seem that at some level she has always known him as the man with the knife who might end up using it, to release in her a burning version of the evacuation that she playfully desires.

Purging is a significant strand in Charlotte's fantasy life. My sec-

ond instance of her latent masochism involves her explanation to
Harry of why she neglected to use birth control during the weeks
between the departure of Buck and Billie from the Utah mine and
the arrival of Buck's letter confirming the termination of Billie's
pregnancy and the consequent success of Harry's first attempt at an
abortion. Charlotte's douche bag having frozen and burst in the
interim, she simply stopped taking precautions on the grounds that
passion is its own precaution:

> I remember somebody telling me once, I was young then, that
> when people loved, hard, really loved each other, they didn't
> have children, the seed got burned up in the love, the passion
> [p. 205].

Her method involves an internal narrative of masochistic intensity;
sperm meets egg in a conjunction of such violence that immolation
results. Note that although her epithet, "hard," is applied to both
parties, "burning" termination occurs within the female body. For
a second time Charlotte's fantasy life causes her tacitly to invite violence into and on her person – an invitation elicited by Buck's terse
testimonial to Harry's skill with a scalpel. Of course, Charlotte wants
the abortion because neither she nor Harry can afford children
(theirs is a Depression story). But it remains the case that she took
a mock abortionist as a lover and fell pregnant to him, by some sort
of choice, only after she had seen him at work. Ergo: Charlotte is a
sadist whose closet masochism will be satisfied (as she has always
known it would be) when Harry the masochist is finally persuaded
to switch roles and play sadist.

Anne Goodwyn Jones offers me a neat escape from my conun-
drum, a way that, although I do not intend to take it, merits consideration in that it demonstrates the benefits and limitations of a
primarily "gendered" response to this text. Jones argues that "Wild
Palms," and indeed *If I Forget Thee, Jerusalem* as a whole, should be
read as a male romance – that is, as a story typical of a popular
romance genre, featuring a love plot with a weak hero, physical tor-
ture, and a sad ending but written out of male fear, by a man for
men, in order to "warn men away from the dangers it articulates."[15]
Those dangers are female and are particularly associated with the
sexual woman as engulfment. Jones, citing the work of Theweleit on
the male fantasies of the Freikorpsmen, notes that the man – be he
the *Tall* Convict, struggling with a flood that mingles the Mississippi
with the broken waters of his pregnant charge, or Harry, scalpel to
womb, or phallus in hand – "defends himself with a kind of sus-

tained erection of his whole body"[16] against the flowing female. By this account, both men make it through the fluxive feminine to a safe male enclave whose very name, Parchman prison, indicates that dryness will attend the rest of their days. The reading is attractive and complements those who, like Roberts, wish to argue for Faulkner's narrative as punitive to the female, or even (and perhaps more subtly) as working toward an account of gender dichotomy as a finally disabling "artifact of patriarchal culture."[17]

Whether one emphasizes the punished woman or the crippled man, one does so by polarizing gender positions that, at the close of "Wild Palms," are manifestly interdependent. Charlotte *is* dead, and Harry *is* in prison, but Harry's capacity to sustain an erection is anything but a defense against the female. Spectrally speaking, although his body holds hers (as a reverent tomb), her body (hand) holds his (phallus) during the masturbatory act. He will presumably "flood" because his body is as much her handiwork as his own. An adequate reading of Harry's final and titular masturbation must account for the continuing interdependency of the lovers even after her death and his incarceration. It should also explain the variety of relations of mutual empowerment and disempowerment and do so in ways that gender switching (as a prelude to gender separation) may illuminate but not finally encompass.

The power shifts within the couple's codependency are several and striking. Charlotte is the sadist in "pants," Harry the masochist with an "apron." She is dominatrix, he is submissive. Yet she becomes what she appears, at some level, to want most to be – pregnant and cut – because she compels he whom she has enslaved to play master. As a result of which, the submissive – doubly rebound as a vault in a cell – services himself by serving the memory of her authority. Because Charlotte and Harry are so centrally a sadomasochistic couple, some further elaboration of that structure of feeling seems necessary.

What does Harry as a submissive get? Jessica Benjamin observes that "the desire for submission represents a peculiar transposition of the desire for recognition."[18] The sadistic "other" has the power for which the masochistic "self" longs; by submitting, the masochist gains that power, albeit vicariously, through the sadist's recognition. Therefore,

> the masochist's sacrifice actually creates the master's power, produces his coherent self, in which the masochist can take refuge. Thus in losing [his] own self, [he] is gaining access, however circumscribed, to a more powerful one.[19]

By these means, domination is "anchored in the hearts"[20] of those who, in submitting to it, create it. Read through Benjamin, Harry runs away to a somewhat tacky romance narrative provided by Charlotte and discovers himself as something quite other than the non-entity he was before his "*amour-faux.*" His erotic obedience to "what [she] ha[s] read in books . . . that love and suffering are the same thing" (p. 48), which "thing" they pursue "across the face of the American earth" (p. 209), releases him from his previous role as an anonymity. Waking on his twenty-seventh birthday (the day on which he will meet Charlotte), he "seemed to see," although "without volition," his twenty-seven "empty years" (p. 34). His summation of his own vacancy occurs when he is prone in a complementary space: he lies on a "steel army cot" in the "barracks-like" room where interns who have "no private means" (p. 33) are required to live. In this recumbency, he casts himself as funerary art, floating on a stream of life that is barely his own toward a death for which he has been prepared from the first:

> he waked and looked down his body toward his foreshortened feet and it seemed to him that he saw the twenty-seven irrevocable years diminished and foreshortened beyond them in turn, as if his life were to lie passively on his back as though he floated effortless . . . upon an unreturning stream. [pp. 33–4]

To borrow a notion from the historians of slavery, Harry is the next best thing to socially dead.[21] Faulkner has just provided a biographical summation, so summary as to evacuate the life it purports to describe. Harry Wilbourne is an "orphan" whose father died when he was two; no mention is made of the mother, save to say that she was "the second wife" of his father's old age. Even his sisters are "half sisters" (p. 31). Like a slave, he carries a paternal name that negates him, insofar as he is "born" solely to do its owner's will. The pun on the name is complex; a "bourne" is a "terminal point of destination," most famously exemplified, care of Hamlet, as that "bourne from which no traveller returns."[22] By implication, the name of the father encodes a will that posits both birth and death. Or, to adopt Orlando Patterson's account of naming within the peculiar institution, Wilbourne is the paternal name productive of "natal death."[23] Certainly, by following his father's will to the letter, Harry has almost ceased to exist. The last paragraph of that will reads as follows:

To my son, Henry Wilbourne, and realizing that conditions as well as the intrinsic value of money have changed and therefore he cannot be expected to obtain his degree in Surgery and Medicine for the same outlay of money which obtained in my day, I hereby bequeath and set aside the sum of two thousand dollars, to be used for the furthering and completing of his college course and the acquiring of his degree and license to practise in Surgery and Medicine, believing that the aforesaid sum will be amply sufficient for that purpose. [pp. 31–2]

The document is dated "two days after Harry's birth" (p. 32) and ensures that from the tenderest age, its beneficiary has been stamped and certified as an investment for a sliding class. With money built into every tissue, it is small wonder that he grows up able to taste only cash, not food (p. 104), and that even his ethics change into capital and start accruing interest; after his initial refusal to perform an abortion on Buck's wife, he finds that his stock as a doctor increases and his price goes up (p. 191). Since money can be anything – "cigarettes," "stamps," "a girl" (p. 32) – it is simultaneously an anonymous and transparent medium. Harry, its subject, has spent his life transforming himself into a cash flow problem:

> he waged a constant battle as ruthless as any in a Wall Street skyscraper as he balanced his dwindling bank account against the turned pages of his text books. [p. 32]

As a result, on the morning of his twenty-seventh birthday, he is little more than an absence built by the poverty of his dead father. Existing only in the mind of a half-sister, with whom he communicates by "money-order" (p. 32), he is all but empty – which is tantamount to saying that, as one who garners scant recognition, he will make a good masochist, since he is primed to find in another that "self" that he has all but lost.

Harry needs Charlotte because, on the day of their encounter, he has woken to a state of separation that feels like death. Fearing abandonment (or "total" loss), he desires her power as a refuge within which his "self" may reappear. Charlotte's "will" is the "bourne," "spring," or "intermittent stream of water" by means of which Harry will be reborn aged twenty-seven.[24] And Charlotte is, above all, willing. At their first meeting, her "stare" drowns his "volition and will" (p. 39). She takes his wrist in a "grasp simple, ruthless . . . firm" (p. 39) and representative of a protective power that will not relax its grip even posthumously. Charlotte's gestures are most typically emphatic. Fond of expletives, her speech inclines to the imperative, and as she instructs, her hands are usually working; they variously "strike," "crumple," "beat," "flip," "bitch" . . . and always in the expectation that what they touch will prove malleable, to a touch that is final:

> "That's what I make: something you can touch, pick up, something with weight in your hand that you can look at the behind side of, that displaces air and displaces water and when you drop it, it's your foot that breaks and not the shape." [p. 41]

What Charlotte makes is an extension of a hand that brings things to heel; the skin of her lower finger joints is "toughened like the heel of a foot" (p. 41). Indeed, her directional imperative "that's," in "That's what I make," takes as its object both her hand, which she has offered for Harry's scrutiny, and an implied, but absent, artifact. Hand and artifact elide in an imperative, because Charlotte has a limited sense of there being much difference between her grasp and whatever it takes. Consequently, what she makes not only hardens her hand but also does as she does . . . it "displaces" and "breaks." As with her art, so with her life; people and things exist only insofar as they come to her hand, since for Charlotte, "the world is all me"[25] and has long been so. As a child, denied the marital right to her eldest brother, whom she "liked best," she married the man closest to him ("he and Rat roomed together in school" [p. 40]). But her husband exists only to be "displaced," along with her two daughters . . . and all, one might say, "for love" (though it might be more accurate to say "all for sadism's sake").

Charlotte dominates because she does not expect to be contradicted by word, person, or thing. She may well be cognitively aware of the difference between her "self" and that which lies beyond it, but her behavior suggests that any such awareness does not limit her desire to control what she encounters. Such desire has its risks, in that the sadist's fantasy of omnipotence, by discovering no limit to its power (no "otherness"), courts the fear of dissolution. To negate the "other" absolutely is to be oceanically alone. Charlotte's relation to the waters in which she fantasizes her own death is revealing:

> I love water. . . . That's where to die. . . . The water, the cool, to cool you quick so you can sleep, to wash out of your brain and out of your eyes and out of your blood all you ever saw and thought and felt and wanted and denied. [p. 58]

"The water, the cool, to cool" – a noun is tacitly followed by an apt adjective that remains implicit ("cool") but that operates briefly as a noun ("the cool") before turning into a verb ("to cool"). The transition ensures that agency belongs not to the water itself but to one of its qualities ("coolness"). Consequently, water is no longer an independent object but depends for its essence upon the subject, or she who takes the measure of its coolness. Which coolness, in washing "out of" brain, eyes, and blood, is for a moment a product of those body parts from which it wells. The conclusion of the sentence, by supplying objects to be "washed" away (sights, thoughts, feelings), restores purgation to the water. But if water, specifically the water of Pontchartrain, is now what "washes," it does so through a verb "to cool" that belongs at least as much to the body (subject) as to the element (object). It follows that when Charlotte is most at a loss for her "self" and is exploring the limits of the erasure of limits, she recoups what she has lost by partially insisting that what drowns her issues from her. Faulkner splits agency in a verb ("to cool") and stretches the reach of a repeated prepositional phrase ("out of") to create a lengthy antonym (turning on "out of" understood as "up from"), which devices distort the meaning of their host sentence, implying the persistence of Charlotte's mastery. Even as she is negated by an "other" (water), she claims that which negates her as the agent of her own will. Once again, the world is all Charlotte.

And Charlotte floods. In the first section she bleeds; in the last section she bleeds. Her bleeding takes on the dimensions of a flood because it is tied, via association, to the broken waters of the countrywoman's womb, and so to the Mississippi flood of 1927. Just as the water in "Old Man" erases boundaries – levees, state lines, city limits, federal roads[26] – so Charlotte's liquidities of womb and eye submerge available limits. Hers is a "feral eye" (p. 11) according to the doctor. Harry affirms that her eyes are "like a cat's" while he is "drowning" in their " yellow stare" (p. 39). The submersive capacities of Charlotte's feline eyes are liable to flood once one hears the "strong purring power" of the Mississippi as it toys with the convict's skiff, "in a series of touches light, tentative, and cat-like" (p. 150). Charlotte's streams are a critical commonplace, but generally they are deployed to affirm a tacitly anatomical determinism that, whether radical or conservative, tends to tie desire to symbolic body parts (to vagina [blood] or phallus [scalpel]). So, for Roberts, because Charlotte bleeds she is woman as Irigarayan "excess,"[27] whereas for Faulkner, according to Porter and Jones respectively, because Charlotte bleeds she is woman as the inescapable task of the womb, or as the threat of maternal engulfment.[28] My point is that her blood should be understood not as a finally reductive symbolic marker but as part of a pattern of desire that Faulkner explores as relational, as a shifting power play between lovers caught up by sadomasochistic dependency.

Charlotte "grasp[s]" Harry and insists on the absoluteness of their love, not because she has read too many romances or because she is an idealist, although both of these may well be true, but because as a sadist she needs to discover the thing that she cannot dissolve – a "love," in the form of Harry, which will provide a limit or "other," guaranteeing that there *is* something beyond her own imperiously drowning body and gaze. Harry is her submissive of choice because he is more "other" than the others with whom she surrounds herself. Penurious, without aesthetic knowledge and in a borrowed suit, he is someone from another class who will require of her that she recognize his "difference" and acknowledge his independence.

There is scant evidence of such acknowledgment. Indeed, Charlotte seems convinced that the edifice of their love, or her love for an "other" who is submissive but un-negated, will fail. On only the second morning in their Chicago hotel, she demands:

> Listen: it's got to be all honeymoon, always. . . . They say love dies between two people. That's wrong. It doesn't die. It just leaves you, goes away, if you are not good enough, worthy enough. It doesn't die; you're the one that dies. It's like the ocean: if you're no good, if you begin to make a bad smell in it, it just spews you up somewhere to die. [p. 83]

Her central simile combines her own imperious impulse (her love must be oceanic) with a fear of the dissolution such feelings court. Since the phrase "bad smell" is the germ of one of her figures, which figure is male, it is clear that the "you" who rots and is "spew[ed] up" is Harry, presumably destroyed in no small part by the "solvent" of Charlotte's tidal sadism. Elsewhere, her "unwinking yellow stare" is likened to "a liquid chemical precipitant" capable of "dissolv[ing]" "dross" (p. 87). When the Bad Smell materializes as the last of the *papier-mâché* effigies it is predictably diminutive ("not three inches tall"), "shapeless," and "disorganized" (p. 95). Charlotte creates the figure to warn both Harry and herself, since should the masochist's love fail, the sadist, at a loss for the recognition of the submissive enclosed within her protective flood, must die too. However, since Charlotte is conducting the lesson, she concludes by granting herself the better death:

You die anyway, but I had rather drown in the ocean than be urped up onto a strip of dead beach and be dried away by the sun into a little foul smear with no name to it [p. 83]

The "smear" or "urp" is Harry, who, should he betray the love of a good sadist, will be restored to the anonymity that characterized his life prior to his rebirth within Charlotte. By the logic of her own extended simile, Charlotte is finally a bad sadist. Masterful and self-deluding, she is content to indulge her conviction that the world is all her and so, at the last, is compelled to "urp" the bound source of her own recognition out of her oceanic body. It follows that Charlotte's hemorrhage is structurally determined by the particular form of her own desire. She looks for a man with "a scalpel up his sleeve" (p. 37) because at some level she knows that her compulsion to experience something "other" than things and persons as extensions of her own will may fail, leaving her no option but to ingest the reality of that "otherness," expelling it as "dross," "urp," "smell," or "smear." The scalpel is her guarantee that, at the last, she can adopt that ultimate otherness – the position of the submissive – receiving, through the cut, hard evidence of an other's agency, and release from her own deluded dominance. Prone and requesting the blade, Charlotte renders herself emblematic of the will-less and the bound: "What was it you told me nigger women say? Ride me down, Harry" (p. 221).

II

By now it may be tiresomely apparent that I am addressing Harry and Charlotte's sadomasochistic love because I see in their desire evidence of another and buried structure of feeling. Harry and Charlotte reconfigure the master–slave relationship, but in conciliatory form. What was in *Absalom, Absalom!* an untenable trauma becomes by the close of "Wild Palms" an absolute amity. To recognize Harry's masturbation as a revision of Quentin's concluding rigidity, it is simply necessary to read the submissive as the slave and dominatrix as the master – at which point Harry's phallus becomes utopia, or at least the site of a utopian moment. Whereas Quentin's body (the master) contains the body of Bon (the slave) as its unbearable and unacknowledged substance, Harry's body, and more particularly his phallus, openly contains the master and is the product of the master and the slave's mutual labor. In this manifestation, the bound man dedicates his life of bondage to preserving the memory of the master, to whom his body will give pleasurable substance. He has, after

all, recognized that his master, Charlotte, is "a better man than I
am [p. 133] . . . *and a better gentleman . . . a better everything than I will
ever be*" (p. 207). Charlotte is, of course, the master transformed:
s/he is feminized, dead, and the creator of *openly* perverse children,
though perhaps her marionettes (p. 91) are only superficially more
damaged than Sutpen's progeny. She is mastery reduced to the scale
of 1939, a master for post–federal funding days, when mastery is on
the wane as the members of the owning class finally transform themselves from labor lords to wage payers. Furthermore, and to compound her reduction, she is the master as a dead woman, killed by
the slave's hand. Even here, the hidden structure works to reconcile
its encoded participants; the bound man rose against his lord on
lordly instruction and subsequently, and of his own volition, returns
to bondage. Prison gives spatial form to his statement to McCord
that, "there is something in me she is not mistress to but mother"
(p. 141); this master is not only a "better man" than this slave, she
is mother to him; an image that fulfills paternalism's wildest dream
by allowing the slave to be not merely childlike, but to be the child
of his master's womb, which womb is a prison deeply to be desired.
If Harry can be transcoded as out-samboing Sambo, he nonetheless
manifestly retains a phallus. But that which "stand[s] to his hand"
and brings the slave as child and the slave as "black beast rapist"
into unlikely conjunction is also held by the master as mistress. Sel-
dom can there have been such an amorous meeting of opposites.
Whereas the sexuality of the male Compsons depended upon shadowy and debilitating suspicions about black potency, Harry's erection
contains the slave's phallus in accepted and unthreatening form.

Once again I find myself ensnared in the logic of barely uttered
plots and being led through a text by hints that I can only just dis-
cern. What is more, in this instance, the whispers form stories that
these particular characters do not even feel they need to deny, since
they have no grounds for containing them. A taint of nonsense at-
taches to my account of Harry's final grief, because that account is
based on the claim that Harry plays host to a corpse about which he
knows nothing, and that as a result genders shift and ethnicities drift,
allowing Harry's crypt to encrypt the intolerable interdependencies
of the master and the slave in a form that edges them toward the
tolerable.

At its bluntest, my case is that Harry, at levels below his own conscious motivation, grieves for that which he does not know lives
within him. He is occupied by a residual trauma he would not recognize. But how might this be? The psychiatrists Nicolas Abraham
and Maria Torok speak of encountering instances of "transgenera-

tional haunting";[29] their patients appear "oppressed not by [their] own unconscious but by someone else's"[30] and are subject to "phobias that come from elsewhere."[31] Because they "unwittingly" receive "a secret which was someone else's psychic burden,"[32] it is extremely difficult for them, or for those who seek to help them, to "read" their symptoms. The haunted, having been left the unfinished social traumas from other persons' lives, are essentially "custodians"[33] preserving the unsaid and the unsayable of another:

> The silence, gap or secret in the speech of someone else "speaks," in the manner of a ventriloquist, through the words and acts of the subject.[34]

Abraham and Torok are primarily concerned with traumas generated by, and transmitted through, family histories, though they do emphasize that the phantom (or unspeakable drama) *can* be generated outside the family. Presumably, wherever there are founding facts that cannot be assimilated into psychic or social life, there the untold, the unsayable, and the secret are liable to make "phantoms" and to build "preservative tombs"[35] among those who receive the social and psychic consequences of that generative silence. Indeed, I have contended throughout this study that the unassimilable trauma which forces a major strand of Faulkner's work into being occurs within a particular regime of accumulation and through relations of dependency that inform or extend far beyond the family as such. However, if "Wild Palms" is read as part of that strand, along with *The Sound and the Fury* and *Absalom, Absalom!*, and if, as a consequence, Harry and Quentin are read as recipients of the same "founding silence,"[36] located in an omission in the speech and the behavior of someone else (of Sutpen as carrier of the primal scene from which the planter class takes its form), then one is still left with the problem of the transmission.

How is the recipient to receive that of which he appears to know nothing? The question is more easily answered in relation to Quentin, for whom exposure to the oral tradition of his class has involved an increasing recognition that "doing Sutpen in different voices" involves strategies of omission so shared as to draw eventual attention to a founding suppression. The verbal behaviors of father, grandfather, and Miss Rosa transfer the specter of the unthinkable about which they all strive not to think. Harry lacks any such lineage, and yet he remains Quentin's descendant, and the inheritor of Quentin's vault. Faulkner's two-year commitment to the verbal habits of an owning class, and to the generative secret they encode, extends, though in weakened form, to Harry, ensuring that he too is the unwitting recipient of the encrypting aesthetic of *Absalom, Absalom!* Harry completes a Faulknerian lineage.

Note, for example, that although *If I Forget Thee, Jerusalem* is not set in Yoknapatawpha, its title, taken from verse 5 of Psalm 137, stems nominally from the mouth of David[37] and therefore shares a titular source with *Absalom, Absalom!* (David's cry for his murdered son). The tangent is worth pursuing. *Absalom, Absalom!* offers two candidates for the filial role, Henry and Bon; but Bon as the claimant who was forgotten and must be denied has the stronger case. A referent for *Jerusalem* is more awkward: several candidates have been mooted, ranging from Helen Baird[38] to "love itself,"[39] but a reading of the Psalm as a whole suggests a significant parallel between the circumstance of the novel's creation and the condition of the Jews who are called upon to remember. *If I Forget Thee, Jerusalem* was started in Hollywood,[40] but was substantially completed between September 1937 and June 1938, that is over the period immediately following a one-and-a-half-year stint working for Twentieth Century–Fox.[41] Faulkner's scriptwriting contract had been his lengthiest to date, and he had made only intermittent visits back to Mississippi. Psalm 137 addresses those held in Babylonian captivity by masters who "required of [them] a song . . . one of the songs of Zion" (verse 3). They, however, protest their inability to "sing the Lords's song in a strange land" (verse 4). An astute homonym forms, whereby Jerusalem liaises with Mississippi and Hollywood goes to Babylon. Throughout August 1936 Faulkner worked on a script for *The Last Slaver* (later *Slave Ship*) while reading the galleys of *Absalom, Absalom!*; later, he attempted to sell the novel to the movies[42] – conjunctions that may well have exacerbated his sense of being required to "sing" about the South while held captive elsewhere.

If *Jerusalem* is read as "home," and Babylon is cast as southern California, the unfinished hypothesis on which Faulkner's chosen title turns is completed. Verse 5 reads in full, "If I forget thee, Oh Jerusalem, let my right hand forget *her cunning.*" Faulkner probably expected his readers to complete the verse, but making good the omission results in an intertextual hermeneutic of distracting complexity; in effect, what was silent generates sufficient talk between texts to sketch the outline of a secret history from which they both arise. A "right hand" sans "cunning" adds up to a writer who cannot write; verse six compounds his difficulty by "cleav[ing]" his "tongue to the roof of [his] mouth." But much more is involved than Faulkner's sense that a contract with popular culture may impair his authorial capacity. According to a letter to Robert Haas in July 1938, the title Faulkner wanted and could not get "invented itself as a title for the chapter in which Charlotte died and where Wilbourne said, 'Between grief and nothing I will take grief.' "[43] Faulkner seems to be tying the "right hand" to the "wild palm" and to the "cunning" onanism whereby a captive Harry ensures that he will not forget Charlotte. Charlotte, as we have seen, is the body of the labor lord recast, and it is a short though tidy step, by way of the title, from her mastery to her "Lordship," and so to her status as the embodiment of a southern Jerusalem. Moreover, verse 5 specifies that the commemorative hand in question is *"her"* hand: the female pronoun confirms that Harry's phallus is spectral evidence of the co-presence of Charlotte's "bitching" and masterful revenant. Consequently she takes a hand in the singing of *"her"* own song, so that the master and the bound man may become one in a single body (feminized, in order that the body of the bound man who contained the Lord may, in turn, be contained by the Lord's body).

The manual dexterity of the titular moment is compounded, once it is recognized that this unheard "song" about s/he who is Jerusalem, or the South, cast as a utopian site in which master and slave are reconciled, is entirely unsingable – particularly between September 1937 and June 1938, these being the last days of that long revolution which was to turn masters into employers. Faulkner's writing hand, recently released from Babylonian captivity, finds that Hollywood is no longer in Hollywood but "stippled by a billion feet of burning colored gas across the face of the American earth" (p. 209). In which case the distinctions between Jerusalem and Babylon, and between Hollywood and the South, collapse, releasing the recognition that "the Lord's song" is redundant.

Prompted by Faulkner's anger over Hass's decision to change his original title,[44] I have pursued a titular tangent for too long. Nonetheless, together, and in code, the titles *Absalom, Absalom!* and *If I Forget Thee, Jerusalem* reveal Faulkner's writing as ensnared within the increasingly archaic task of finding a form – historical or utopian – for what he takes to be a secret drama generating the lord's essence, and with it the existence of the southern labor lords as a class.

In "Wild Palms," that form is utopian; its gnomic imperative is to turn trauma into pleasure, thereby rewriting a large part of *Absalom, Absalom!* Consider again the boy Sutpen at the plantation house door; he is a poor white who becomes a planter in order to deny that the master necessarily emerges and achieves mastery through the body (or "balloon face") of a "monkey nigger." Consider Sutpen's class inheritors as they revise the body of the black "Bon" through a range of narratives all of which, at their deepest level, are driven by the need to suppress his ethnicity while acknowledging and retaining his black body within the body of the lord, where it may act as a systemic guarantee of the master's mastery. Now consider Harry, spectrally inhabited by Charlotte at the close of "Wild Palms." Harry and Charlotte are a sadomasochistic couple *because*, at a structurally deep level, their roles as master and slave recast labor dependency as mutual, sexual coupling. Reversing the prevalent hermeneutic of *Absalom, Absalom!* that ran through erotics to labor, they offer a tacit eroticization of labor – and do so in order that the sadist's seduction of the masochist may act as an optic through which the master's liaison with the slave shall be seen as producing a sigh of utopian passion. I should add that, since neither Harry nor Charlotte could give a kiss for a master or a slave, one can only assume that at some level Faulkner's own needs are being met. It might be fairly objected that such satisfaction is hardly likely to satisfy when it comes in code. To those who want their lovers to struggle only against the market imperatives of 1939[45] and who wish to see no evidence of an earlier economic paradigm, I can suggest only that the force of Faulkner's utopian subtext commands protean alterations in order to achieve its amities. So, the master must have a womb into which the slave can go, first as a Jacobin and then as lover and child. So, the slave must whiten, retaining only a hint of coloration, derived from his position on the paradigm, otherwise his erection might summon the "black beast" of radical pathology – a presence that could only dispel *bonheur*. Susan Willis provides a useful gloss on these metamorphic impertinences, in that her definition of "utopian space" stresses its transformative energy:

> Myth creates a Utopian space within which contradictions that have their bases in the real world are transformed into more manageable textual problems. Once inside the mythic space, the text generates a number of features which evoke the resolution of contradiction.[46]

Perhaps the recognition that the uterine master and the white slave are quasi-mythological beasts, lodged in the deep structure of "Wild Palms," makes their presence there more formally acceptable. Neither is any more monstrous than a virgin who conceives, in order that heaven and earth may be drawn into a more manageable relation.[47] Nonetheless, I remain slightly aghast at what my tracing of the *Absalom, Absalom!*/"Wild Palms" intertext has revealed. Nor am I convinced that my appeal to formalism does anything more than obscure three questions that continue to worry my conviction that Faulkner is using one text to remember and revise another. Why does the trauma of 1936 become the *bonheur* of 1939? Why keep that revision a secret? And, does Faulkner intend any of this?

To take my last question first and evasively . . . I have no sense that Faulkner *knew* that the year of Harry's birth (1910) is also the year of Quentin's death; and that because Harry can "stand," by way of Charlotte or Charley's masterful body, Quentin can rise again from the Charles River (reborn in 1910, care of 1936 and 1939). That the conjunction of dates and names feels like happenstance does not reduce my conviction that such chances happen because the primal scene of *Absalom, Absalom!* exerts an overdetermining influence on its successor.[48] None of which takes one any closer to the matter of "intent."

Perhaps I can accommodate that issue by considering what makes Faulkner revive Quentin for a third time. Harry is arguably more than Quentin's inheritor; as the "curator" of the primal scene, he is Quentin come yet again in much but name. In a very real sense, Harry completes Quentin's career; dead in 1929; resurrected but left for dead in 1936; revived in 1939, and bound over to play host to a pleasurable version of what traumatized him in the first place. His character spans a decade because in him Faulkner finds his first and best historian of the owning class, and more particularly of the racialized identity of the master and his recipients.[49] Quentin's inability to stay dead is evidence of the persistence of the paradigmatic moment of class formation that is Quentin's subject. Quentin finds his thesis in *The Sound and the Fury*, and it appears to kill him. The historian takes leave of himself, and of the regional pathology through which he has become himself, because he learns that a "foreign" sister and a "dark" servant live beyond the reach of that pathology. Since he owns himself because of his previous misrecognition of them, the onset of their new histories destroys the cultural "pre-narratives" through which he has plotted himself. On June 2, 1910, viewed from the perspective of 1929, a nascent historian died, leaving the history of class sketched but unwritten.

Between 1934 and 1936, as Faulkner wrote *Absalom, Absalom!*, the meaning of that death changed so drastically that Faulkner had to rescind it. Quentin had died largely because he released the "dark" and "foreign" bodies that had sustained him. During the 1920s, one million African Americans quit the South in a continuation of that diaspora initiated by the recruitment policies of northern rail road companies (1915–18). Cheryl Lester argues that Quentin died in 1910, rather than in any year after 1915, in order to predate a migration of which Faulkner was necessarily aware.[50] The date may deny the exodus, but the cause of death implies it. And although the outmigration slowed during the '30s, as depression hit northern labor markets, the New Deal–induced agricultural revolution of the mid-30s did as much as if not more than the diaspora to separate the owner from the owned. I have already described how, between 1933 and 1938, a "Second Civil War" (Wiener), bringing with it a "Second Reconstruction" (Grubb), finally disassembled a regionally distinctive "plantation mode of production" (Mandle). After this, blacks no longer had to leave the South to leave a "tradition of dependence" (Johnson) and its labor lord; indeed, thanks to New Deal programs, these lords were most typically likely to evict them, plow their crops under, and take the federal subsidy. Structurally speaking, during the mid-'30s, federal legislation and its consequences ensured that in the houses and the fields the bound removed themselves or were expelled from the bodies of those who had variously bound them since the inception of slavery in the South.

Cast in the revolutionary light of 1936, Quentin's death looks like the death of a class – and who better to say as much than Quentin? Except that, in order to say it, his death and its typicality will have to be denied. By reviving him to explore the origins of a regime of accumulation during its last days, Faulkner catches himself in a curious double bind. The dead narrator who expelled the bound black (bound in the toils of a sexual pathology) must live again to take him back (Bon as laboring body will be retained), since only with the "exquisite corpse"[51] restored to the master's body can the longevity of that body as a social type be explained.

However, by 1939 the planter is dead and the bound man has either gone or is on wages. On the face of it, Faulkner has no reason to bring Quentin back in any form, least of all utopian. A furtive refiguration occurs because, in California, Faulkner learns where wages go. Exiled in the heartland of commodity, he recognizes what awaits the South stripped of its peculiar but distinguishing regime of accumulation. Quentin is revived as a sexual slave who openly loves the body of his lord, reversing the *Absalom, Absalom!* pattern in which those of the lord's party covertly "love" (and contain) the body of the slave. Revival and reversal take place in an intertext that Faulkner, quite literally, creates as he addresses modernity. In effect, while he writes about what will be, he simultaneously and against his own grain composes a secret script about what was, which is displaced into the quasi-invisibility of the intertext. Secrecy is essential since the pleasurable fantasy released by the intertext is triply shameful; it abuses the body of the woman upon whom it is written; it neutralizes the Jacobinical intent of the slave, and it misrecognizes what Quentin saw in 1929. I can explain the intertext only as a partially intended product of cultural panic. Faced with what in southern terms is the corrosive energy of a free-market economy, dissolving those forms of dependency to which he, both as a class subject and as a writer, has been indebted, Faulkner reacts by recollecting a poisonous past as it never was, and by using that "hidden" memory to sustain him through the analysis of a poisonous future.

To read "Wild Palms" as a coda to *Absalom, Absalom!*, shadowed by the intertext that it forms with its predecessor, is to sense within it the co-presence of two regimes of accumulation, one residual, the other emergent. Loosely periodized as "pre-modern" and "modern," and as divided by the first Agricultural Adjustment Program (1933–8), these regimes might be schematized as follows:

Plantation mode of production	Market capitalism
Share-tenant agreement	Wage labor contract
Bound laborer	Free employee
Dependency	Autonomy
Total relations	Partial relations
Yoknapatawpha	Hollywood

More important than either the terms or the dates, about which there might be dispute, is the effect of this co-presence on the text. I am not talking about a divided thematics but about the capacity of implied and antithetical sets of social relations to require a semantic split in the reception of key textual elements. So, for example, a New Orleans prison cell, read as pre-modern, is a means to constraint within which the bound sustain and preserve the lord's body. The same cell, modernized, becomes a vault of a different sort – the closed room into which the consumer of commodities must pass. Likewise, on the one hand the abortion looks like the master's submissive accommodation of the slave (both as will and body), while on the other, and particularly preceded by the suggestion "We've done this lots of ways but not with knives, have we" (p. 221), it resembles the ultimate refinement in the sexual consumer's search for stimuli.

III

In order to keep the referents "split," I had best turn from my preoccupation with the intertextual and archaic latencies of "Wild Palms" to explore the narrative as an overt analysis of the emergent commodity form. Consider the cell again; as a pre-modern item it is the site of a "preservative repression"[52] in which the unfinished business of a defunct regime is concluded "happily." What Harry does in it is semanticized by his role as the "curator" of an indispensable object – the psychic and social trauma from which a particular class arose. His words and actions allow Faulkner to release a grief that cannot be expressed, for the loss of a system that is not worthy of that grief. Perhaps "loss" exaggerates the demise; when Harry famously affirms, "*Yes, . . . between grief and nothing I will take grief*" (p. 324), *he* dedicates himself to the preservation of Charlotte. At the same time, the pre-modern Faulkner acknowledges, without acknowledging, a loss that is not a loss, because the device of the cell allows him to retain the traumatic scene of the master's recognition of dependency upon the bound man, with its structure, feelings, and images recast as *bonheur*.

However, the cell can be read in quite another way and as an accessory to quite another plot, implying modern times and modern places. In December 1935, Faulkner arrived in southern California to take up his new contract as a screenwriter. Horace McCoy's *They Shoot Horses, Don't They?* was published in the same year. Faulkner's biographers make no reference to McCoy,[53] but it seems possible that he and Faulkner could have met through Nathanael West, with whom Faulkner now renewed an earlier acquaintance. West was then working with Republic, where, according to Tom Dardis, McCoy was probably the best-known writer on the payroll. Both McCoy and West frequented Stanley Rose's bookstore, and West introduced Faulkner there.[54] Even given Faulkner's own reticence about literature, and discounting actual conversations and acquaintance, Faulkner may well have heard of McCoy, and as Rose was well known for his enthusiastic promotion of the writers who were regulars at his shop, it seems likely that McCoy's recent novel could have been much in evidence, at least during Faulkner's visits early in 1936. Faulkner had a 1935 paperback copy of the novel in his library,[55] and it seems not unreasonable to assume that he bought and read it in California in the year before he wrote *If I Forget Thee, Jerusalem.*

The literary-historical niceties matter because McCoy's novel typifies an emerging genre, dealing with Hollywood, in which some version of a locked room containing an ineffectual voice stands as the *locus classicus* for the cry of the little man raised against the market's invasion of every aspect of his life. If Faulkner had read in the genre, he would have encountered several versions of voices traveling in circles and heard from within institutions, whose speakers find their words co-opted by publicity and authority as soon as they try for the exits. Harry's voice is one among several, insofar as it comes from a cell and works best when "he could say it to himself" (p. 6). Moreover, although Faulkner appears to be writing in the third person, the authorial sleight-of-hand that produces a first-person "manuscript" and simultaneously shows the closed room from which it emerges supplies him with a penal acoustic echoing that of contemporaries who engage with the problem of mass culture. Only on the penultimate page of *The Postman Always Rings Twice* (1934) does James M. Cain finally let Frank let us know:

> So I'm in the death house, now, writing the last of this, so Father McConnell can look it over and show me the places where maybe it ought to be fixed up a little for punctuation and all that.[56]

Fitzgerald's room was notional; he planned that we should find Celia's voice in a sanatorium (*The Last Tycoon* [1941]). West's sudden dislocation of the final chapter of *The Day of the Locust* (1939) is a more complex trick; he offers a potentially liberating moment in the form of a riot on a premiere night, but the crowd remains effectively silent, permitted to "roar" only when the publicity mechanism requires. The artist is equally subservient. Tod Hackett's record of the event, a canvas entitled "the Burning of Los Angeles," is less artwork than film poster. Not surprisingly, the painter's voice is finally heard imitating a police siren.[57]

With the exception of *The Postman Always Rings Twice*, these novels were published after Faulkner had finished *If I Forget Thee, Jerusalem*; in choosing them, I wish merely to indicate the modernity of Harry's housing. However, it is likely that Faulkner found in *They Shoot Horses, Don't They?* not only a paradigm for the species but also a source text for "Wild Palms."

Much to Horace McCoy's annoyance, since he had completed a draft in 1933, his first novel, *They Shoot Horses, Don't They?* (1935), was generally taken to be a derivation from James M. Cain's *The Postman Always Rings Twice*. Certainly Cain's death-house line typifies the genre's sudden revelation that voice and manuscript are locked within a punitive institution. Frank's story is a "confession" in its crudest form, and in its attempt finally to implicate the reader it performs like much pulp, by absorbing its public through empathy. As Joyce Carol Oates writes,

> Frank, begging the reader to pray for him and Cora, is the very voice of mass man. There is no doubt but that brutality brutalizes, and sentimentality is but one form of brutality.[58]

Given its reputation, Faulkner might well have read *Postman*, but McCoy's is the more complex and analytical novel, and even if McCoy did not use Cain, there is enough in the way he pursued and organized the "Hollywood" lines of thought to suggest that Faulkner may have used McCoy, to focus his own ideas on the "prison" of a commodity-based society.

From the beginning of *They Shoot Horses*, man overtly stands condemned: "The prisoner will stand"[59] acts almost as an epigraph to a novel dominated by a judge's voice. McCoy contains the narrator's story within the trial, letting us hear his narrative only within the interrupting cadences of the death sentence. Moreover, it soon becomes clear that the juxtaposition is not simply contrasting the trial with "freedom" and "innocence," but that McCoy intercuts two forms of prison, to argue that the one is the logical conclusion of the other. In McCoy's Dance Marathon, Faulkner would have read a perfect representation of the prison of commodity exchange, where every aspect of life is exploited as novelty for the "customers" (p. 35). The image of the dance focuses the use of mass culture as a mediating agent of domination; the floor is presented as an arena; "a marathon dance is like a bull-fight" (p. 35), a commercialized ritual. On it, McCoy drew in miniature the features Faulkner would apply to his lovers, with the Derby event, especially, summing up both the rootlessness and mobility of the characters, and the structure of free enterprise of which they are a symptom. Robert and his partner Gloria are both drawn to Hollywood by the magazines, read in Gloria's case during her hospital convalescence after the suicide bid (p. 19). Detective magazines led to the arrest of Mario (p. 56), and the fifty-year sentence he gets becomes "the best break we ever had" (p. 58), anticipating Robert's own reabsorption when his hanging becomes publicity, guaranteeing customers more excitement at future contests.

If death serves the profit motive, so too does conception. In looking at the way the culture industry has used up all real experience, Faulkner might have been struck by Gloria's final statements. As she asks Robert to kill her she speaks of her own refusal of reproduction. It took him a few sentences, Robert tells us, before "it dawned on" him what she was talking about. Then she asked, "Suppose I get caught?" He goes on:

> "You're not just thinking of that, are you?" I asked.
> "Yes, I am. Always before this time I was able to take care of myself. Suppose I do have a kid?" she said. "You know what it'll grow up to be, don't you. Just like us."

"She's right," I said to myself; "she's exactly right. It'll grow up to be just like us."

"I don't want that," she said. "Anyway, I'm finished. I think it's a lousy world and I'm finished" [p. 122].

Faulkner's couple also agonize about the benefits of abortion as opposed to the problems of parenthood. For Charlotte, children "hurt too much." It takes Harry, like Robert, a while to follow what she is saying:

Then he understood, knew what she meant. . . . He was about to say, "But this will be ours," when he realised that this was it, this was exactly it. [p. 217]

Faulkner, like McCoy, gives the aggression and force of dissent to the female. The women's protest finds theoretical expression in Lukács' question:

How far is commodity exchange together with its structural consequences able to influence the total outer and inner life of society?[60]

The relevance of a question from a Hungarian Marxist to a disgruntled southerner, exiled in Hollywood, may seem tenuous – but even as Faulkner wrote his Hollywood tale, a group of anxious Jewish philosophers, soon to be exiled from Germany, were considering the problem of commodity: their work would find its final and focused form in Hollywood, where Adorno and Horkheimer were writing during the '40s. The Frankfurt School were the first thinkers to take seriously the need to analyze mass culture from a radical perspective. Faulkner, perhaps promoted by McCoy, shares something of this perspective.[61] "Wild Palms" might be read as Faulkner's answer to Lukács, as he displays the condition of a world where a man appears just as an instrument of passage for the circle of commodities.

Basic to my orientation of the novel toward modernity is Faulkner's transformation of society into a prison and of each half of the novel into an escape story. Like Horace McCoy, Faulkner allows his escapees to seek an exit from commodity and to quest for a form of authentic experience. The sphere of freedom is a notional realm beyond the market, but escape proves difficult. McCoy has a particularly suggestive paragraph in *They Shoot Horses* when Robert first meets Gloria and offers her the movies or the park:

I was glad she wanted to go to the park. It was always nice there. It was a fine place to sit. It was very small, only one block square, but it was very dark and filled with dense shrubbery.

All around it palm trees grew up, fifty, sixty feet tall, suddenly
tufted at the top. Once you entered the park you had the il-
lusion of security. I often imagined they were sentries wearing
grotesque helmets: my own private sentries, standing guard
over my own private island [p. 17].

Robert's needs for self-enclosure and the safe retreat find their echoes throughout "Wild Palms," in the locations Faulkner gives Harry
for his dreaming, sealed finally by the use of the New Orleanean cell
– doubling as a private island shadowed by the significantly Californian presence of a palm tree. The Hollywood memorabilia remind
us of how, in an overmarketed world, the park and the cell *are* movies, since Hollywood has sold its "stipple" far beyond itself (p. 209).
Faulkner's specific references to California, dotted like a rash, are
merely the superficial signs that the whole southern metabolism has
been invaded by the dominant commodity form.

Others have read Harry and Charlotte's story as symptomatic of
what Faulkner called "the Kotex Age"[62] in an aphoristic periodiza-
tion that correctly identifies the consumer as "she"; *Printers Ink*
makes the same point in 1929: "The proper study of mankind is
man . . . but the proper study of the markets is *woman*."[63] Faulkner,
in line with market studies of "Mrs. Consumer,"[64] tacitly announces
a product for every orifice, a profit from every flow, and a body
whose inner and outer surfaces, considered from "the viewpoint of
exchange,"[65] are little more than an extension of the commodities
they carry. Harry and Charlotte's bodies can be critically anatomized
as embodied commodities; I shall gloss a general case, with an eye
to those elements that retain a troubling capacity for double articulation, or a way of speaking that summons the pre-modern into the
subtext of the modern, thereby creating an unannounced standoff
between two readings and between the antithetical social relations
that they carry into the interpretive impasse.

First and foremost, according to the Hollywood scenario, Harry
and Charlotte are lovers who run away. Each runs from a dominant
institution – Harry from the medical profession, Charlotte from a
middle-class marriage. Their bodies are their route to freedom, by
way of an intensity that is to release them from the social ties that
they associate with "time," "money" and "respectability." In effect,
they object to the commercial imperative of the bourgeois marketplace. Prior to Charlotte, Harry was an item of merchandise, priced
by his father and dispatched into a professional economy whose costs
eviscerated him. Prior to Harry, Charlotte (at her best) was an artist
whose art was determined by commodity exchange, insofar as she

felt compelled to "beat" (p. 41) an art market designed to promote "culinary"[66] forms existing only to ease circulation. As she tells Harry – at their first encounter – what she proposes to make are anti-commodities because they will be nonconsumable:

> Not just something to tickle your taste buds for a second and then swallowed and maybe not even sticking to your entrails but just evacuated whole and flushed away into the damned old sewer [p. 41]

We later learn that these artifacts have not been made. But since Charlotte talks about Harry (p. 47) in the same way as she does about her preferred materials, choosing him as her "clay" (p. 84), it is clear that their love, like her art, is to function as the antithesis of commodity.

The social worlds they seek to leave are pervaded by what Wolfgang Haug calls "the viewpoint of exchange," in which persons and things are considered mainly as means to money. Haug argues that for the seller an object's use is a "transitory phase" or "lure" existing to facilitate exchange. For this to happen, the use of objects or persons must be subordinated to their appearance, so that their function as part of the real needs of another is secondary to their capacity to carry a "promise" that will ensure purchase. Use, therefore, takes on a "double reality," with the emphasis on its second term, since "use," taken to market, dwindles or inflates to "appearance" or "impression" of use:

> The commodity's aesthetic promise of use-value thus becomes an instrument in accumulating money.... Sensuality in this context thus becomes the vehicle of an economic function.[67]

Or as Fredric Jameson puts it:

> Little by little, in the commercial age, matter as such has ceased to exist, and has given place to commodities, which are intellectual forms, or the forms of intellectualized satisfactions: this is to say that in the commodity age, need as a purely material and physical impulse (as something "natural") has given way to a structure of artificial stimuli, artificial longings, such as it is no longer possible to separate true from false, the primary from the luxury satisfaction in them.[68]

In "Wild Palms" Faulkner introduces a couple who are in danger of losing touch with "matter" and "use," whose "needs" have atrophied, and who consider themselves items of exchange in a market that, at least from the perspective of his monastic dormitory and her stable marriage, appears to control them. Harry's is the more developed case, though Charlotte fears and rages against his symptoms, insisting that they must not allow "natural" impulse to evaporate or spontaneity to turn into habit. Appeals to "natural impulse," "genuine experience," "real needs," or indeed to the notion of "authenticity" itself, are liable to be viewed suspiciously when deployed in relation to a novel preoccupied with commodity culture, particularly by a critical community often eager to advance beyond Adorno's sense of receding concreteness and toward Baudrillard's confident assumption that, in a globalized commodity age, nothing is anything more than a moment in the circulation of commercial signs. I have argued elsewhere that Baudrillard too readily forgets that commercial entities, though ubiquitous and protean, remain made things, and because they are manufactured under particular conditions (and continue to wear those conditions and their consequences about them, though often in disguised forms), they are not quite as immaterial as he might claim. Faulkner's two-year immersion in the consciousness of the southern owning class, as it passes through a long-deferred labor revolution, and his subsequent pursuit of the possibility of "free" labor (in "Old Man"), ensures that for him, labor remains a "primary" site of subject formation, one whose "authenticity" commodification may suppress but not erase.[69]

When "genuine" experience appears to be lost, one of the problems we have in identifying it again is, as Jameson says, that "a degraded culture intervenes between us and our projects."[70] A good part of the criticism has devoted itself, quite justifiably, to itemizing the novel's extensive bibliography, but the function of the intertextual here is not primarily literary.[71] Instead, literary allusions clutter the story with what amounts to the chewed-over bits of those cultural objects that the characters need in order to define themselves but that simultaneously get in their way, preventing any achievement of "real" feeling. At the lake, McCord's "ninth-rate Teasdale" (p. 100) articulates Harry's behavior; he cannot experience sensation until he has struck it off his reading. His activity when Charlotte is dying turns up a varied library. First, he needs voices to tell him what is happening; the wind's "whisper" turns out to be the "sound " of the lamp that begins to "rustle and murmur" on Charlotte's flesh (p. 281). They speak in Elizabethan imagery as Harry tries and fails to realize his own "cuckolding" and "horning" by death (p. 284). Then, a few minutes later, he snatches at Owen Wister, characteristically at a scene of a woman as an object, feted and dying, "the

whore in the pink ball dress" (p. 287), "remembering and forgetting it in the same instant since it would not help him."

Nor is Charlotte exempt from degradation by literary artifice,
though the intertextual range of her language is less immediately
apparent. Indeed, linguistically, she seems to seek the pre-verbal,
trying to validate her language through gesture and being given to
monosyllables, to the terse and to imperatives that she iterates with
thrusts from a "hard and painful elbow" (p. 116). However, her
"short brutal sentences like out of a primer" (p. 205) do not return
her to the sources of verbal productivity; instead they sound secondhand, touched by the sheen of commodity and well used already by
Hemingway and hard-boiled films. Moved to intensity, Charlotte will
speak to Harry "as if he were a child just learning English" (p. 218),
but her "primer-bald" lessons (p. 123) lead not to authenticity but
to the pulps. From such language, Harry will compose his romantic
fables, addressing his own fantasies in a cheapened idiom for the
likes of Mrs. Waldrip (whose own writing was "primer-like too" [p.
339]) and supplying more cultural litter (ur-text, Charlotte) to prevent genuine feeling.

The "genuine," for the lovers, is premised on motion. In fending
off the market, Harry and Charlotte put their trust in prepositions –
they travel outside, behind, beyond it – but their journeys remain
claustrophobic. Movement goes in circles, ends in cul-de-sacs, and
even appears to advance not at all, being a mere sensation of motion,
induced by a trick of the landscape:

> The train gathered itself . . . departure came back car by car
> and passed under his feet [p. 141] . . . the scaling palm trunks
> began to flee past. [p. 227]

When the fugitives manage to reach new territory, they have always
been there before. The stone "canyons" of Chicago (p. 119) and
Utah (p. 180) were clearly designed by the same architect. Even
Harry's final arrival in the cell has been prefigured by the insistent
typology of all the rooms he has lived in on the way. By showing how
his couple confuse mobility with freedom, Faulkner demonstrates an
infinite regress that allows no exit and no future; his is a precise
representation of the prison of liberal utopianism that elects flight
from the bourgeois relations rather than their transformation. He
frames the lake sequence with the Chicago ones, takes the characters
there and brings them back on urban money, and shows how knowledge of the "primitive" is possible only through its bond with the
"civilized." Harry, for instance, can feel the "still, dawn-breathing

liquid" only through his memory of "the temperature of the synthetic ice water in hotel rooms" (p. 100). The choice to go to the cold mountains seems essentially the same as the impulse to hide at the lake, though "money" prompts one and "respectability" the other; both appear to offer a way back to "nature."

Geographically, both Utah and Wisconsin pose as journeys to the neck of the womb – the road ends at the lake, the mine is at the end of the rail line – by the lake, Harry will achieve a "foetus like state" (p. 110); at the mine, Charlotte will conceive. However, Faulkner's evidence indicates that there are no untouched places. The lake cabins stand in second-growth spruce, expressing the land's history, worked over, left, bought by entrepreneurs from the city (Doc Gillespie, McCord, Bradley), and shaped into a wilderness to be rented to summer visitors like the Doctor's Gulf Coast shacks. The presence of the mine, obviously, refuses to allow the "pristine" to behave like a blank sheet. The snow is "scarred and blemished," the canyon a "gutter," and even the "unassailable" peaks (p. 180), to which Charlotte apologizes for importing her mouth-dirt, prove capable of expressing consumer fantasy, promising instant treasure out of their skies:

> "One of them big airplanes fell somewhere back in yonder just before Christmas. . . . There's a reward for it. I guess I wont stop." [p. 204]

The market is not to be escaped via the pre-technological if transportation is paid for by waged work whose forms seem selected to establish the compliance of the travelers with the very system they seek to transcend. In Chicago, Harry's lack of certification ensures that the only medical work available to him involves "making routine tests for syphilis . . . in a charity hospital in the negro tenement district" (p. 85). His task has several economic ramifications; Wassermanns check one circulatory system for evidence of the passage of sexual favors, for marginal profits, through another. Both the place of work and the standardization of the routine suggest that Harry is employed to check the health, and police the pleasure, of one portion of a depression-swollen reserve army of labor, maintained, presumably, to hold down the wage levels among white workers elsewhere in the city. With a background in doctoring the labor market, Harry is clearly qualified to work at Callaghan Mines. The job description, straight from the boss's mouth, is "to protect the mine, the company" (p. 128), with an emphasis on the punning pronoun. Harry goes to Utah, not to minister to the damaged body of immigrant labor – a task so redundant that Faulkner does not bother to describe it – but to represent the probity of capital to the stockholders and to the workforce. A company receipt indicating that a doctor was paid to go to a plant may be offered in evidence of an owner's intent to maintain that plant, on which evidence financiers may invest in an unseen mine. As Buck, Callaghan's manager, puts it, having ascertained who paid the fare (p. 183), "he's got to keep his mine looking like it's running. . . . So he can keep on selling the stock" (p. 189). The doctor's presence also operates as a promissory note issued to labor, indicating that an employer, concerned for the health of his workers and interested in maintaining their labor power, is likely to pay for that labor, at some later date. Again, the manager interprets the boss's symbolic logic; he notes that after three months without a payroll, the miners will "probably think . . . you brought it and that Saturday night they'll all get thousands of dollars apiece" (p. 189).

Harry carries the owner's false promises even *after* he has seen and recognized something of capital's fictive purpose.[72] He gets behind the "opaque glass door," to meet Callaghan:

> a red-faced cold-eyed man of about fifty, with a highwayman's head and the body of a two-hundred-and-twenty-pound college fullback gone to fat, in a suit of expensive tweed which nevertheless looked on him as if he had taken it from a fire sale at the point of a pistol . . . [pp. 127–8]

From behind a conspicuously empty desk, carrying only a telephone and a game of Canfield, the robber puts Harry in his place in the structure of domination, telling him that he will be employed to prevent Callaghan Mines from being sued for industrial injury by "wop pick-and-shovel men and bohunk powder-monkeys and chink ore-trammers" (p. 128). Note the lyric ease with which Callaghan compounds workers with their tasks, while uttering a string of epithets that onomatopoeically echo the machine processes into which the bodies have been cast ("wop . . . bo . . . hunk . . . chink"). Yet, Callaghan's threat is not his espousal of Fordist principles (efficiency and standardization) but the emptiness of his office; he is an abrasive front man for a system as extensive as General Telephones and as self-reflexive as solitaire. From the "viewpoint of exchange," the office offers the "appearance of use"; Callaghan's mine is an "impression," his ore a "lure," and his doctor a "promise." Having seen the office and knowing something of the real nature of the work, Harry takes the job – content, it would seem, to doctor fictitious dollars. However, Faulkner reserves his most cutting joke for the last task on Harry's employment roster. By turning a doctor into a W.P.A. crossing guard, Faulkner stamps him firmly as one who molests the bodies of those whom he is nominally hired to serve (p. 220). He who, in Utah, offered placebos to the exploited now leads their children safely across the road into the very institution that will initiate their socialization as victims. And just in case we miss the point, Charlotte tells him why he has taken the job – "So you can rape little girls in parks on Saturday afternoons" – a particularly vicious comment, given Harry's predilection for public benches.

Nor is Charlotte exempt from recognizing and servicing "the viewpoint of exchange." Despite her declared aesthetic commitment to nonconsumable objects, while in Chicago she produces two sets of figures that go straight to market. The first collection is taken by a leading department store for sale and for window display (p. 87); the second – a number of marionettes – is made to be photographed "for magazine covers and advertisements" (p. 90). A gradation is evident, from anti-commodities heavy enough to break feet, via window dressing made from *papier-mâché*, to photographs, or paper images derived from puppets (constructed from wire, paper, and paint) that are themselves derived from literary works (Quixote, Falstaff, Cyrano, Roxanne).[73] The marks of Charlotte's hand are gradually erased from her labor; the marionettes no longer represent her conceptions – as puppets they require the hands of another to work properly, and a photographer must intervene to realize their full purpose. Adorno's phrase "receding concreteness"[74] springs once again to mind as Charlotte remakes herself as a promotional artist whose goal is "capitalist realm,"[75] or the production of objects whose sole purpose is sale in a world where everything is priced. In her Chicago apartment, converted first into a "studio" and then into a "club," where art is made in front of an "audience" (p. 88), she commits herself to images that will induce an economic spectacle and whose surfaces dissolve the surfaces of their originals (retained as a waning "impression" of literary use), to redesign the source figure by way of a "second skin,"[76] geared for display and preparing the way for purchase.[77]

Charlotte has a talent for commodity aesthetics. On their return to Chicago from the lake, the first store to take Charlotte's figures employs her to "dress" windows and showcases (p. 119). Historians of American sales techniques stress that stores were "schools for . . . the culture of buying,"[78] which "pictured the desirable" by "eliminating the store"[79] in the cause of a "theatrification of shopping"[80] (the phrase is as ugly as the purpose). Caught up in the spectacle, customers learned to be "double-bodied," that is to desire the perfect "second skin" of a particular "look" that might give them back to themselves remade. Faulkner likens Charlotte's work to that of "surgeons and nurses," struggling in an operating theater "for some obscure and anonymous life" (p. 120). Presumably, their surgical task, undertaken among "jointless figures" and "organless bodies," and by means of "brocade," "sequins," and "rhinestones," is to produce that Frankensteinean body, surrounded by "chromium glass" (p. 120)[81] in whose look customers will see themselves quasi-surgically remodeled by what they can buy.

Shop windows and showcases feature a particular kind of object:

> There, in the market place and in shop windows, things stand still. They are under the spell of one activity alone; to change owners. They stand there waiting to be sold. While they are there for exchange they are not there for use. A commodity, marked out at a definite price, for instance, is looked upon as being frozen to absolute immutability during the time which its price remains unaltered. And its spell does not only bind the doings of man. Even nature herself is supposed to abstain from any ravages in the body of this commodity and to hold her breath, as it were, for this social business of man.[82]

Things behind plate glass – Charlotte's things – are positioned to hide the means that brought them there. Much must be forgotten if "nature" is to appear to "hold her breath." Industry, labor, distribution, the social processes that "breathed life" into the commodity and that necessarily vary according to material costs, technical innovation and workplace conflict, are designedly absent. Charlotte is hired (and kept on after the Christmas rush) to design that absence. In 1938, looking back on the development of advertising, *Printers Ink*, the advertisers' journal, observed:

> The first advertising told the name of the product. In the second stage the specifications of the product were outlined. Then came emphasis upon the use of the product. With each step the advertisement moved further away from the factory viewpoint and edged itself closer into the mental processes of the consumer.[83]

Working nights, so that darkness may obscure the designing of the design, Charlotte labors – as does Harry in Charity Hospital, at the mine and on the school crossing – to control the body of labor by advancing "the viewpoint of exchange," within whose optic labor vanishes from those objects labor made; which objects, recast in the "spell" of commodity aesthetics, propose to window shopper and showcase browser that their labors, like their bodies, are things best forgotten and remade in the image of commodities, designed to realize a price.

To step back for a moment; just as eviction and diaspora may finally inform Quentin's retentive account of Bon, so an agricultural revolution, in the last instance, determines Faulkner's choice of what Harry and Charlotte shall do in Chicago. Both work in the field of labor control; Harry at the production end, ensuring passivity among "pre," "under," and "un" employed workers; Charlotte at the ex-change end, designing desire. Their work is not just an index of what awaits those who go North for autonomy at a price but is also a measure of what awaits the labor lord, at a loss for the labor that made his body, and turning to price and commodity for a revised sense of his status as a modern subject.

Charlotte works on the new body, rendering "sensuality . . . the vehicle of an economic function" (Haug), work that has conse-quences for her own body. As Harry waits for her at the store, he watches her "vanish" into the "obscure and anonymous life" being produced there by her co-workers. I have already described that "life" as an embodied "look" designed to "dis" and "re" embody the window shopper. Not surprisingly, Harry has some difficulty sep-arating the designer from the design. Charlotte may "vanish," but she does not "disappear"; instead, he sees her as "entering or leav-ing a window" (p. 120), that space in which the "anonymous life" of Mrs. Consumer is recomposed. Charlotte's own body is necessarily modified by what she does and the place in which she does it. Pri-vately, her palms are "wild," like "bitching," and take Harry in a desperate attempt to rediscover matter and induce feeling in nerves deadened by the artificial stimuli of commodities. But publicly, and in the workplace, those hands organize promotional spectacles; in-deed, the very hysteria of the affair indicates that, like Nathanael West's inert crowds, Harry and Charlotte need extremities to "make taut their slack minds and bodies,"[84] because reification has restruc-tured the tissue itself.

Charlotte's flesh is remade as a commercial "promise of use"; consequently she often refers to herself as a "whore," finding it difficult to escape her sense of her own commodification. Faulkner compounds this by having her first appear for the reader through the leer of the real estate agent (p. 6), and his assessment of her ratable value is confirmed in the gaze of most of the other men she meets. More important than Coffer's annexation of her as a por-nographic image is Faulkner's suggestion that Charlotte needs an audience, and more specifically the gaze of a sexualized market, in order to achieve an adequate sense of herself.[85] McCord, Bradley,

Buck and Billie, and even an unseen but ever-potential detective are pressed into service. But the main spectator is Francis, the respectable husband seen always in terms of his suit; Charlotte tells him before she goes to her hotel assignation, needs him to hand her over to Harry on the honeymoon journey, and reports back to him at the end. He is even tacitly present as a necessary third party as the lovers finally achieve intimacy in the drawing room of a Pullman car:

> "Lock the door," she said. He set the bags down and locked the door. He had never been in a drawing room before and he fumbled at the lock for an appreciable time. When he turned she had removed her dress: it lay in a wadded circle about her feet and she stood in the scant feminine underwear of 1937, her hands over her face. Then she removed her hands and he knew it was neither shame nor modesty, he had not expected that, and he saw it was not tears. Then she stepped out of the dress and came and began to unknot his tie, pushing aside his own suddenly clumsy fingers. [p. 60]

The passage, which concludes the second section of "Wild Palms," turns on the implied question "What is 'it'?" "It" is initially a "wadded dress," a garment that, in a pornographic scenario, is not something that has been worn, but a prop introduced to place "beneath" or to scatter "close" in a simulation of "abandon"; "it" is an old erotic contrivance. I introduce the making of a pornographic image because Charlotte's gesture appears to require it, rendering the proffered glosses on "it" – "shame," "modesty," "tears" (each quite properly negated) – inappropriate and indeed archaic in their immaterial stress on moral absolutes. Nor is "it" anything as universal as "lust" since "it" seems to inhere in the look Charlotte achieves by combining a covered face and "scant . . . underwear." In a single gesture, aware that her husband is still on the train and that her lover will turn from the door to see her, she sees and reproduces herself as he (a generic and male sexual shopper) would like to see her, and in a frisson close to autoeroticism she is excited by what she has made of herself. Faulkner dates the underwear precisely to indicate that by reproducing herself as a commercial style Charlotte renders her sexual surfaces as temporary as the cut, color, and sheen of that style. The commercial erotics of the moment are structured around an implied and male audience made up of Harry, Rat, the author, the reader (designedly male for the occasion), and the presence of those constitutive male gazes within Charlotte's inner eye.

Because "it" is an inescapably commodified sensuality, "it" must also be climactic without delivering a climax, since the produce that "satisfies" commands limited sales. Consequently, Faulkner stops the scene in order to douse arousal. He cuts significantly from one mode of transport to another; from a Pullman car bound for Chicago, containing locked bodies in a locked compartment, to a truck en route to a flood, containing convicts "shackled by the ankles to a single chain which . . . was riveted by both ends to the steel body of the truck." The convicts are "packed like matches in an upright box" or "like the pencil-shaped ranks of cordite in a shell" (p. 61). Faulkner's point is as emphatic as it is salacious; the convicts are erect and potentially inflamed ("matches," "cordite"); they are, by the logic of at least one simile, a product of writing ("pencil . . . like"); they are bound labor destined for unwaged work on the levees, and their position is structurally analogous ("counterpoint[ed]"[86] point by point) to the transported bodies whose climax they have displaced. So, working back through the argument proposed by the analogy, Harry and Charlotte are prisoners, "shackled" to an "explosive" desire, "written" into them by way of a commercial genre – which desire poses as a utopian escape but is in fact as much a market item as the "picks" and "shovels" that clutter the feet of the standing convicts. Where love is a conclusively market value it is perhaps inevitable that Faulkner should end the journey, undertaken on its behalf, exactly where he does – in a prison cell.

All of which extended gloss on the commercial foundations of "Wild Palms," read as a Hollywood fiction, takes me once again to the twin characteristic of abortion and masturbation. Whether by road or by rail, Harry and Charlotte are in motion to achieve these points.

Within the shadowy and pre-modern narrative formed between *Absalom, Absalom!* and "Wild Palms," Harry's penetration of Charlotte's womb with a scalpel is a Jacobinical insurgency invited by the master. The bound man enters the master's body, but no struggle to the death ensues. Each survives in modified form for and through the other. The master may *seem* dead, and the bound man *is* re-enslaved, but recast in the intertext as revenant and curator each releases the other from the need to be absolute and independent (that need which traumatized Sutpen and drove Henry to slow suicide). Instead, each survives for and through the other in fantastical mutual recognition. Charlotte takes leave of herself by her slave's hand: dislocated through the other, she finds herself in the other's subordinate position (a "nigger" woman [p. 221]) and dies, but is recovered in modified mastery by the slave's hand and within his bound body. Where previously a slave's manual labor deferred to a master's pleasure and stood as evidence of a slave's potentially in-dependent will, here and by Harry's hand, that work makes an erec-tion in which, unlike Sutpen's Hundred, the wills and pleasures of master and slave are conjoined in loving dependency.

However, according to the Hollywood narrative, the couple's re-lated climaxes add up to a very different story. Charlotte counters the fertility of her own womb as a final expression of her more gen-eral refusal of marriage, gender categories, and commodities. With impeccable logic, she uses Harry's sex to cut herself free from the institutions that bind her, and then his scalpel to remove herself from all social categories. When Harry sees her dead (p. 306), he envisions a return to a "profound and primal level." The instant is "arrested for the moment for him to return and look at," and what he thinks he sees is the recovery of origin, with the image of the body collapsing "as undammed water collapses" echoing the release of the levee, as social containment washes away. By the time Char-lotte is on the stretcher, there is "no especial shape beneath the sheet now at all," and "no weight either" (p. 306). The papery image recurs as Harry, in prison, recalls her body, "the shape of it under the drawn sheet, flat and small" (p. 315). Released from her commodification, restored to a blank sheet, it could be argued that, at the last, Charlotte achieves purification.

But to see it this way is to see it only as Harry sees it, and there is much to suggest, in contradistinction, that Charlotte's abortion (like Mrs. Babbitt's appendicitis) expresses the sickness of the con-sumer and the logic of the market. Faulkner's gynecology is distinctly individual, but his surgical choices are quite deliberate. Charlotte aspires to make her sterile womb the last shelter from all forms of reproduction, but the market abhors the vacuum, and "to let the air in" (p. 192) is to allow a takeover. For Faulkner the womb be-comes a *"safe"* (p. 297). Harry pursues that analogy, casting the abortionist as a cracksman and the embryo as more of the "cheap money with which the world was now glutted" (p. 299). To extend his figure, if children are cash, the family is now solely an economic unit molding little consumers; the novel offers many samples, among them Harry, the doctor, and the young Rittenmeyers. Consequently, in his "bungling," Harry is directly involved in capital. He insists to the official that the instruments were "clean" (p. 297), but they were given him by Callaghan in Chicago, of whom McCord warned, "that guy is poison" (p. 131). Predictably they give Charlotte toxe-mia as Faulkner literalizes the pervasive infection. We need only think back to the Wassermann tests (p. 85) in Chicago to realize that in the pathology of commodity, all circulation is contaminated.

Moreover, Charlotte enters the abortion by offering herself as a sexual commodity; she who had thought Billie Buckner "a perfect whore's name" (p. 179), finding herself in the same position as Harry's first client, casts herself as a whore who won't "buck" if "ridden" ("Ride me down, Harry" [p. 221]), prefacing her assurance with the observation that, "We've done this lots of ways but not with knives, have we?" (p. 221). That her joke should be echoed by Harry's arresting officer suggests how easily the operation may be read as the ultimate refinement in the couple's search for new stimuli, as they try to avoid the tired "preprandial . . . relieving of the ten years' married" (p. 129). Where slackened muscles can be tautened only with a knife, sexuality does not overthrow the structures of domination but introverts them to achieve a kind of satiety as victim.[87]

In which case Harry, as a man holding the shaky knife, bears little resemblance to what more traditional scholarship has made of him. I see no sign of Brooks' "innocent," or of Reid Broughton's "humane" respondent "to pity and terror." Certainly Harry suffers, meditates upon a "drawn sheet" and a grave, and eventually sets himself up as a piece of memorial sculpture (p. 315), but in doing so he does not become a monument to "endurance," "authenticity," and "the grandeur of the human spirit."[88] Rather, as he muses, one of the significant difficulties of "Wild Palms" begins to resolve itself – the problem of where the voice is coming from. The narrative is in the third person, but apart from the doctor's passages, it approximates to Harry's consciousness. Furthermore, there are fairly frequent anticipatory moments implying that the story is complete and is being reconsidered from a particular location:

> Then for the first of the two times in their lives he saw her cry [p. 50].

> Later he was to recall . . . [p. 60]

> He approached the bed (it was now that Wilbourne seemed to remember him putting the pistol into the bag) . . . [pp. 293–4]

These have the care for exactitude of someone going over the episodes, trying to fix the detail and get the story right. Faulkner's debt to the solipsistic and imprisoned narratives of *The Postman Always Rings Twice* and *They Shoot Horses, Don't They?* helps situate "Wild Palms" as a retrospective narrative, issuing from a prison cell, an idea finding support in "Old Man," which has a similar form and is also told from the penitentiary. "Old Man," however, is an oral tale, with the short convict being used, as Faulkner said,[89] to draw out the performance, whereas Harry is his own best audience. We know he has a propensity for mental home movies. He sits in the park playing out the domestic scene of the Rittenmeyer parting – for a screen, "he watched against his eyelids" (p. 221). Harry's use of projection grants him habitual and artificial satisfactions.

The habit of screening his own life is so pervasive that he represents Charlotte's eventual death by way of the language of cinematic simulation; she dies in a "theatre" illuminated by "Kliegs" (lamps used in making movies); he knows that she is dead when the Kliegs are turned down; the nurse switches off a fan (which cools a projection lamp), and when Harry leaves the theater he reacts like a customer walking from a darkened auditorium into daylight that "leave[s] him blinking steadily and painfully at his dry granulated lids" (p. 307).[90] I am reminded of an observation by Adorno:

> The pronouncement . . . that memories are the only possessions which no-one can take from us, belongs in the storehouse of impotently sentimental consolations that the subject, resignedly withdrawing into inwardness, would like to believe the very fulfilment that he has given up. In setting up his own archives, the subject seizes his own stock of experience as property, so making it something wholly external to himself.[91]

Harry ingests his past, as another commodity for his own consumption, turning his narrative not into archives but into a hybridization of two popular forms – the movie and the pulp novel – projected onto and written over the body of Charlotte. Joseph Moldenhauer sees Harry's pulp-writing as masochistic self-indulgence and "exhibitionist self-degradation."[92] His observation catches the way the activity both arouses and frustrates (pp. 121–3). Given the paradigm of Harry's writing for romance magazines in Chicago, the entire "Wild Palms" narrative might join "At sixteen I was an unwed mother" (p. 123) as simply the last in a line of "confession[s]" and "sexual gumdrop[s]" (p. 123) bought with "emotional currency" explicitly to "titillate" (p. 136). In which case, and with its source genres established, Harry's retrospective narrative is written to arouse its writer who, with pen and phallus in hand, can hardly stand as a "noble Martyr," an esteemed "artist figure," or as a "tragic" hero.[93] To make him any or all of these is to accede to consolations issued by those in authority, that a maimed life is better than nothing. As Adorno and Horkheimer write in *Dialectic of Enlightenment*:

The pathos of composure justifies the world which makes it necessary. . . . Tragedy . . . comforts all with the thought that a tough, genuine human fate is still possible.[94]

This, their recipe for the whole of mass culture, from the idiotic women's serial to the top production, could well fit Harry's last manuscript, for which a synopsis might run, "Brief spell of happiness, paid for by woman's death. Unhappy ending, used to affirm indestructibility of life." The culture industry would undoubtedly approve of "Wild Palms" so read.

IV

If *If I Forget Thee, Jerusalem* were simply Faulkner's Hollywood novel, the cell, the abortion, the masturbation, and the pervasive intertextuality could all be read as symptoms of a modern malaise associated with commodity production as a "cultural dominant."[95] Yet each acts as a split referent; so, to recoup, the cell is both the locus of a utopian vault, and "an image of the bourgeois world of labor taken to its logical conclusion";[96] the abortion is both a slave revolt absorbed, and a fetishist's gratification, while the onanism, read backward, signals euphoric interdependency among binders and bound, and read forward, constitutes a critique of market autonomy as autoeroticism. Similarly, the intertext that forms between "Wild Palms" and *Absalom, Absalom!* articulates the lovers within archaic structures of feeling, even as that which develops between "Wild Palms" and *They Shoot Horses* (et al.) situates them in innovative patterns of consumption. Yet the prevalence of split referents, with their implication of a divided author and a fissured recipient, is not of itself the problem; such referents have, after all, been crucial to my reading of both *The Sound and the Fury* and *Absalom, Absalom!* It is just that, in each of these earlier instances, the semantic options generated within the divided sign existed in a traceable relation of "impertinence," "distortion," "tension," or "antipathy." In *The Sound and the Fury*, Quentin's "master narrative,"[97] grounded on a received sexual pathology, encounters in the stories of a black servant and an immigrant "sister," marginalized counter-narratives whose effects traceably modify his section. The tension between what he can and cannot easily tell destabilizes the semantics of certain key words ("shadow," "sister," "father," "temporary" . . .), releasing options that eventually seize the meaning of his day, so that Quentin starts June 2, 1910, intending to die for one set of reasons, and ends it dying for quite another. The important point here is that the valencies within the key words, like the repressive and the repressed narratives, exist in traceable tension. Similarly in *Absalom, Absalom!* despite the systematic encryptment of the unspeakable within the spoken, the pressure of Sutpen's founding social trauma in western Virginia continues to fold the inadmissible back into those versions that would seek to occlude it. We may have to stretch if we are to reach from one end of "Bon" or "overpass" or "durance" to the other, but – care of the boy turned from the door – the novel contains a map whereby the reach may be undertaken, ensuring that the antipodean options within single words, like the more estranged versions of the Sutpen story, can eventually be tied to a generative primal scene of labor trauma.

No such ties exist in "Wild Palms." My divided readings of key elements of the text – which I have characterized as pre-modern (recessive) and modern (emergent) – do not interfere with each other; rather, they exist in distant tandem. The reason for this may finally be, once again, a consequence of the First Agricultural Adjustment Program, or better, of the long revolution it effectively concluded. With dependency gone as a typifying feature of southern labor relations, and with the effects of the diaspora structurally acknowledged, owner and owned were at long last "free" of each other. It may, therefore, simply be that Faulkner could no longer in good conscience see southern labor and southern owners as codependents (though in bad conscience he might still fantasize their amorous dependency). In *If I Forget Thee, Jerusalem*, with the implications of Hollywood, wage labor, and mass consumption absorbed and recognized as on their way South,[98] the classes are firmly separated.

Indeed, the demarcation between the two sections of the novel establishes a clear class division. To "Old Man" goes labor, and to "Wild Palms" goes its management, or at least Charlotte's management of desire, and Harry's maintenance, if not of labor power, then of capital's capacity to bargain with that power. When Harry encounters a labor force in a non-professional capacity in the store, his response is revealing; he graces Charlotte and the creators of commodity aesthetics with the metaphors of his profession – they are "surgeons" and "nurses" (p. 120); the cleaners are "another species" who "crawl . . . on their knees," cannot raise their eyes above the ground, and vanish lavatorially via an "orifice" into a "subterranean region" under the commodity outlet (pp. 120–1).[99] Harry's recognition that while he and Charlotte work in Chicago they are little more than a renewable quantity of labor power (p. 127) does not, as far as he is concerned, place him in the laboring class. Instead it prompts his insistence on his own professional and Charlotte's managerial status. That status is underlined, when, at the mine, and confronted with imminent revolt by the labor force, Charlotte's political cartooning, although it clarified the miners' exploited condition, serves to disperse their resistance at the cost to the owners of a few tins of beans and some shirts (p. 202). The couple service capital and, unlike most workers, work only to go on semipermanent, though admittedly down-market, erotic vacations.

The sectioning of *If I Forget Thee* firmly separates the classes because, by 1939, Faulkner's understanding of labor has been transformed. In effect, the New Deal's agricultural programs have evacuated the labor scene lying at the generative core of *Absalom, Absalom!* by separating owner from owned. Under the pre-modern labor relations or "plantation mode of production" (Mandle), characterized by constraint and dependency, the products of labor were always potentially Jacobinical, being the place where wills met and were experienced as meeting. Under modern labor relations in a "free" market, both the things made and the work itself are perceived through the veil of "price." Workers, their "equality" and "autonomy" validated by the fact that they hold property in themselves, or in their bodies as instruments of labor (their labor power), bring that property to market, where they contract with employers, who are similarly "equal" and "autonomous" because of their status as property holders (though in their case the property is either capital, or the means of production, or both). The contract between employer and employee is an unconstrained agreement as to the value of the worker's labor power . . . or so the story of the bourgeois labor contract goes. A contract to work for a wage is mediated by "impersonal," "indifferent," and "abstract" market conditions in ways that were less observably true of share agreements, where the "long pay" ensured an absence of money, and the need to be "known" and to have "a reputation for deference" both localized and personalized labor arrangements.[100] My point is not to idealize a peculiar, violent, and archaic system but to emphasize that subjects formed within that regime of accumulation are constrained to differ from those who have to find their "pre-narratives"[101] in a bourgeois market, where "price" keeps parties abstracted and apart. With the parties separated, and higher wages finally available for consumer goods,[102] and with the veil of dependency torn, independent classes are recognized as distinct bodies with distinctive interests (in the South as in the North).

So finally, in *If I Forget Thee*, the story of labor is a separate story, because a lengthy labor revolution has withdrawn labor from its phenomenological centrality to the experience of ownership. Labor is now at liberty to experience itself, for itself, through the activity of work – which is essentially the story of the Tall Convict. Never again will labor be so intimate an irritant in the being and becoming of the owner – which is essentially why "Old Man" exists apart from, and in "counterpoint" to, "Wild Palms." I shall eventually return to the class issues lying behind Faulkner's choice of narrative "counterpoint," but first I would like to sketch a case for "Old Man" as a relatively independent proletarian narrative.

Taken alone and as addressing modernity, Harry's sealed and onanistic chamber typifies the closed and rigid thought forms of commodity production, presenting themselves as immoveable and eternal, a pretension that "Old Man" seems at pains to deny. Marx suggests that:

> all the mystery of the world of commodities, all the sorcery, all the fetishistic charm which enwraps as with a fog the labor products of a system of commodity production is instantly dispelled when we turn to consider other methods of production.[103]

It is a recommendation that Jameson appears to have in mind when describing the Surrealist opposition to the amnesia of the commercial age:

> Surrealism presents itself . . . as a reaction against the intellectualised. . . . The Surrealist image is a convulsive effort to split open the commodity forms of the objective universe by striking them against each other with immense force.[104]

Striking against the inert blocks of "Wild Palms," "Old Man" attempts through a violent intensity – stylistic, thematic, and comic – to smash open the forms of reification. In its subject matter, Faulkner is testing the hypothesis framed here by Lukács as an absolute, that "Only the consciousness of the proletariat can point to the way that leads out of the impasse of capitalism."[105] Taking the Tall Convict as his sample, Faulkner submits him to a process that examines this claim. The convict's role as representative for the proletariat was noted by one of the earliest reviewers, Edwin Berry Burgum, writing in *New Masses* in 1939.[106] His reading is perhaps over-optimistic, since Faulkner goes to some pains to point out that the bourgeois and the proletariat share the same "objective" reality, where reification touches every sphere of life. Hence the sustained parallels between the Tall Convict and Harry. In their own terms, they share similar environments, being more or less of an age, arrested adolescents, of limited experience, institutionalized and influenced by their particular reading. Faulkner's placing of Harry's father as doctor to a country community is an especially deft touch, enabling him to give his two subjects similar memories of origin; the Convict is obviously closer, but even Harry has in him the dim residue of the hill farm, which afflicts his perception with the edge of loss, when experience is at its most painful. Charlotte's stretcher is carried by an "[un]matched team" (p. 295); the retreat to an intern's routine is "*like niggers*" drawing up the "*quilt when they go to bed*" (p. 51). The crucial difference between the two men lies in their divergent understanding (or lack of it) of their respective class distinctions.

The alchemical point to which Faulkner tries to take the Tall Convict is the precipitation of class consciousness. The Convict is caught in a hierarchy of mystification resembling that outlined by Lukács:

> And if the proletariat finds the economic inhumanity to which it is subjected easier to understand than the political, and the political easier than the cultural, then all these separations point to the extent of the still unconquerable power of capitalist forms of life in the proletariat itself.[107]

In the penitentiary, musing in a "kind of enraged impotence" (p. 24) on the "incorporeal names" (p. 23) of the hardboiled writers whom he blames for initiating his attempts to rob a train, and so for his subsequent imprisonment, the Tall Convict has much to understand. Faulkner takes him through the flood, in a process of undoing, to bring him to culture's very edge, the critical chance for the first economic insight that would allow him to escape domination and to invent himself as a free man, liberated by unconstrained labor.

The penitentiary serves as the platform for defining the shape of departure. It is a model of a closed world that poses as an absolute, gracing itself with generic distinction, "the Farm" (p. 30). Faulkner overlays it with a ghost of another total form of production; "it is a cotton plantation" (p. 23), with its inmates seen as slaves, the chains of society being quite literal ones, "ankle to ankle" (p. 28). However, although they are bound to the cotton they tend, they are neither chattels nor croppers; their labor has lost *any* meaning, as "refusal" or "share" or "price," and as mere activity signals a degree of alienation emblematic of capital's dehumanization of those who work its lower strata:

the land they farmed and the substance they produced from it belonged neither to them who worked it nor those who forced them at guns' point to do so, that as far as either – convicts or guards – were concerned, it could have been pebbles they put into the ground and *papier-mâché* cotton and corn-sprouts which they thinned. [p. 30]

In choosing the Tall Convict, Faulkner gives himself the challenge of trying to set free one of the most passive prisoners, whose resilience is physical, not political, and who is securely locked into an estranged consciousness. It is all these barriers the flood tries to break down.

The multiple derangements (and the humor) of "Old Man" seem in part to be an extreme effort to carry out a cleansing abrasion on the body and senses of the Tall Convict. The often synaesthetic purgation expresses Faulkner's realization that the coefficient of commodity fetishism and of man's dissociation from his own labor is a flattening of perception itself. Harry's color-blindness is a symptom of his debilitation as a consumer accompanying the way he views the world as a two-dimensional spectacle. The external forms of his environment – the glare, the neon, and the glitter – all collude with the market and conspire to help him forget materiality. In contemplating the phenomenon, Adorno writes:

> The "equivalent form" mars all perceptions: what is no longer irradiated by the light of its own self-determination as "joy in doing," pales to the eye. . . . Disenchantment with the contemplated world is the sensorium's reaction to its objective role as a "commodity world." Only when purified of appropriation would things be colorful and beautiful at once.[108]

Faulkner mobilizes the flood in order to direct its force at the forces of appropriation. Against the flood he arrays a heavy population of every kind of authority. The convicts are characterized by their submission, their "clashing" shackles are "mute" (p. 67); and objects have primacy, as they do in "Wild Palms," with even the train apparently running "under its own power" (p. 68). Since the convicts are there to life-save and to resuscitate drowning property, it seems to be an unlikely spot for any radical alteration. Indeed, Faulkner keeps urbanizing the landscape in terms unavailable to the convicts, turning tree trunks into "decorative shrubs on barbered lawns" (p. 63), and the roar of the current into a "subway train passing far beneath the street" (p. 62). He gives the guards no trouble in ad-

justing to the new cartography. Directions to the cotton house are
as easy as pointing the way to the Post Office:

> "Follow them telephone poles until you come to a filling sta-
> tion. You can tell it, the roof is still above the water." [p. 75]

Once the Tall Convict is out on the water, all the helpful urban
similes and authoritative demarcations vanish. To be outside reification almost defies description, assaulting consciousness "like the
notion of a rifle bullet the width of a cotton field" (p. 145). The
reader undergoes the active physiotherapy of facing "something
which the intelligence, reason, simply refuse[s] to harbor" (p. 145).
At the peak of the Mississippi's histrionic decision to flow backward,
"waiting his chance to scream" (p. 157), the Convict too has his
perceptions rehabilitated. The darkness acquires tactile powers, be-
having energetically to stretch and tauten his slack muscles, and in
battling with it, he begins "wrenching almost physically at his eyes
as if they were two of those suction-tipped rubber arrows shot from
the toy gun of a child" (p. 164). The startling comparison turns
eyesight almost inside out, in a retinal engagement with matter, making the Convict anything now but a passive spectator, receiving only
the manufactured images of a One Dimensional World. With the
taking apart of perception, all logical categories vanish too. If to end
reification it is necessary first to be seen to dissolve facts into process,
as Lukács prescribes, then "Old Man's" ludic parentheses take the
injunction to the extreme, as the entire objective world, Harry's
parks included, "leaped and played about him like fish" (p. 161).

Given the general unhealthiness of flesh in the novel, it is essential that Faulkner batter and wring the Tall Convict into feeling. He
suffers multiple lacerations, itches, burns, and blisters, as matter that
has been forgotten rises up and hits him on the back of the head
to remind him – by making his nose bleed. Faulkner's precise motivation for the Convict's hemophilia is elusive. In part perhaps it is
another form of purging. Like the Chicago slums, and Harry and
Charlotte, the Tall Convict has his own brand of poisoned circulation, which the flood is intent on flushing out of him. With such
strenuous therapy, the body does indeed appear to gain access to a
new kind of life. Reading that "he seemed to hear the roar of his
own saliva" (p. 232), it is almost possible to believe again in "primary needs." Perhaps after all, Lukács and Hegel are right in arguing that "It is easier to bring movement into a sensuous existence
than into fixed ideas";[109] at least it certainly seems so when the Convict, having seen a deer only on a Christmas card, is restored through
instinct into swimming as it did (p. 234).

While still reconditioning his subject, Faulkner deposits him on an Indian mound, the earliest specimen he can offer of land known to man through its uses. Here the Convict begins to be conscious of himself as economic man. Faulkner gives him all at once the activities though which man comes into being. Critics have noted how the Tall Convict races through a condensed evolutionary history;[110] as he does so, his hands are restored to their material. The mound is essential as a training place for "infant" man, teaching him midwifery, hunting, tool making, and cooking, but Faulkner does not let him linger there too long. With the Convict primed and practiced, Faulkner at last brings him to the swamp.

Like the mound, the swamp lies on society's very periphery, not outside or before it. Harry and Charlotte's lake, posing as a juvenile, exhibited one form of the land in its senility, its productivity long since over, turned now into a service area for the city. The Cajun's wilderness is the other extreme; a fully functioning economic system in the first stages of its working into which the Tall Convict makes his entry. Faulkner saves this moment until he has told us that he was "in partnership now with his host" (p. 255), hunting on halvers. Here "halvers" are not "shares." Whereas the tenant often lacked access to the owners' books and was required to take his crop to the owner's facility to be weighed and ginned by another,[111] the Convict at all times keeps his hands on the objects of his labor. The skins are divided in front of him and to the satisfaction of both parties. In matters of work, "truth" can be learned from a close observation of phenomena. The Convict is sure that, "*even if he cant tell me how I reckon I can watch him and find out*" (p. 257). Newly energized as he is, his gaze works actively, "going here and there constantly" (p. 257), teaching him that he must make his own world through his perception of it, possessing it by description: "*What? What? I not only dont know what I am looking for, I dont even know where to look for it*" (p. 257). The two sentences that follow are crucial ones.

First Faulkner makes the reader participate in the Convict's activity, through a syntactic strenuosity, extreme even for "Old Man":

> Then he felt the motion of the pirogue as the Cajan moved and then the tense gobbl*ing* hiss*ing* actually, hot rapid and repressed, against his neck and ear, and glanc*ing* downward saw project*ing* between his own arm and body from behind the Cajan's hand hold*ing* the knife, and glar*ing* up again saw the flat thick spit of mud . . . [p. 257]. (italics added for emphasis)

Faulkner demands a sequence of decisions, forcing the reader to assign the designated words to their status as substantive, qualifier, and verbal participle, and so to sort out the ownership of the limbs, the Convict meanwhile being similarly preoccupied. Then, having galvanized perception, Faulkner takes both sets of eyeballs, Convict's and ours, to the alligator. It is the most exciting moment in the novel. The "mud" turns to "log," then "still immobile" seems to "leap suddenly against his retinae" (p. 258) – and at this instant, it is as if the reified "spectacle," already badly bruised, bursts open, as Adorno said, "irradiated by the light of its own self-determination." The alligator takes form in "three – no, four – dimensions," and the fourth it turns out is "pure and intense speculation" (p. 258). The phrase explodes with meanings perceptual, judgmental, and economic, purging them of appropriation. The Convict gathers his whole self together, concentrating all his experience on the logistics of the task, in what amounts to the crucial chance for transition. That he kills the animal, surface to surface, using a knife, is essential to make this the moment of phenomenological impact with matter and the ultimate abrasion of the husk of commodity, the instant of interchange between man and nature that makes life. There is a quick here that allows complete knowledge, and apparently the "speculation" pays off, bringing the convict the full value of his own labor, the plenteous moment: "Tout l'argent sous le ciel de Dieu!" (p. 259), admitting him to the oral history of the swamp, as a victor celebrated by the Cajan. Not surprisingly, Faulkner turns him into the "*matador*" surrounded by his "*aficionados*" (p. 263), using Hemingway as index to the intensity of experience, as he was to its debasement.[112] In "Wild Palms," Faulkner had been intent upon dramatizing man's loss of expressive labor and of reciprocity with worked things. In the swamp, the Convict rejects the gun to become the stylist who insists upon a material engagement with his objects, learning from his relationship with them a sense of his own alterability. The rigid fact, "*Will have to get on back*" (p. 261), suddenly stops and looks at itself as the Convict sees, in the light issuing from "the rich strange desert which surrounded him," how the "last seven years had sunk like so many trivial pebbles into a pool" (p. 261). The swamp prompts him to recover an earlier simile used at "The Farm," where he and the other prisoners sensed as an "instinctive perception" that "it could have been pebbles they put in the ground" (p. 30). Now, and in a place of unalienated labor, he can fully articulate a distinction between "toil" and "work" (p. 264). The Tall Convict is poised on the edge of seeing himself as subject not object, controlling his own market, with the meaning of his work returned to memory: "*I had forgot how good it is to work*" (p. 264). With the worked hide pegged out like a "mahogany board table," and himself a member of a "corporation" (p. 261), the relations are all on the surface for the Convict to understand and act upon. Even his sweat is now measurable, so that he can make the choice between investing his efforts in one tedious night carving the paddle or in a few energetic minutes carving up an alligator. Having seen himself as economic man, he is in a position to move on through the hierarchy.

Yet Faulkner turns him back at the threshold. From the start we know that the sojourn at the swamp is just a nine-day wonder (pp. 252, 264); we suspect that the percentage will never acquire a denomination (p. 261) and that plenitude will stay in a foreign language, so that it does not really need the mordant, "Damn your hides" (p. 272) to tell us that the skins will never enter the market. The work finally has little more status than the "hunkies' " pleasure in dynamiting rock for the money that will never arrive (p. 198) – and we are led to increasingly pessimistic conclusions – conclusions that are dangerously reminiscent of the position of the more eccentric Agrarians. (John Crowe Ransom in 1933 requested that fertilizers should be highly taxed so that subsistence farmers might better enjoy the delights of their subsistence.[13])

Faulkner's point is not to advocate work for work's sake but to situate subject formation within the experience of labor, prior to situating labor within its appropriation by the market, by way of the juxtaposition of the two stories. Faulkner develops sustained parallels between the crucial swamp chapter and formative moments in "Wild Palms." An argument by homology emerges. The previous section of "Wild Palms" was the end of a movement begun at the party in the French Quarter, where Harry's perception was jolted for a moment by the pictures which "impacted" upon him, making "the very eyeballs seem to start violently back in consternation" (p. 37). Moreover, Harry is cast as "a yokel" who, having seen "a drawing of a dinosaur," "was looking at the monster itself" (p. 38), at which point Charlotte materializes behind him to personify new possibilities. The terms are the same as the "alligator" passage – a dislocation of vision, a glimpse of a different reality, and the introduction of a means of exit. But the process ends in Harry's action with the knife in chapter seven. By starting the next chapter of "Old Man" (chapter eight) with "When the woman asked him if he had a knife" (p. 229), Faulkner clearly intends to encourage the after-image. The knowledge of the abortion lingers when we see the birth of the child, swaddled at once in the private's tunic, marked from the start by the institutions it will grow up to occupy; but worse, and more horribly, the abortion mediates our reading of the "birth" of the Tall Convict.

The natal moment is represented as rupturing his reified vision, but the means both to transition and to transition's negation surface simultaneously and are telescoped into the killing of the alligator. Just as Charlotte turned the operation into a parodic sexual penetration, so, too, "straddling" the "thrashing" beast (pp. 258–9), the Convict engages in a grotesque variant in the bid for "true" carnal knowledge. In allowing the Convict the knife, Faulkner awakens echoes of the abortion, showing the Convict "probing for the life and finding it, the hot fierce gush" (p. 259). In so doing, Faulkner, like Charlotte, identifies the moment of coming to life (conception/birth) with the moment of its ruin. (Charlotte needed the immolation of the seed and the termination of the embryo to prevent her "fall" into commodity exchange.) It is a moment Faulkner carries out here to show that the very instant of the origins of labor is shadowed by its consequences at the extreme end of the market. With its "temperature close to blood heat" (p. 262) and its miniature gestatory cycle (everything happens in nines), the swamp has itself been seen as a womb.[114] In aborting the Convict, Faulkner is making it grimly clear that new social dynamics will not arise spontaneously in the power of the proletariat to see "from the center" (Lukács). The swamp for all its energies remains as Lukács' "mire of immediacy,"[115] from which man cannot extricate himself.

For a time, the Convict is oblivious; delighting in his own singleness, he is content to ignore even the evacuation of the swamp since it affirms that singleness. Temporarily released from prison and no longer the direct guardian of the female charge, he is the self-employed paddler of his own pirogue. But the solitude quite suddenly reverses itself. What was positive is negative – in a passage of some difficulty:

> he departed too with his knotted rope and mace . . . as though not only not content with refusing to quit the place he had been warned against, he must establish and affirm the irrevocable finality of his refusal by penetrating even further and deeper into it. And then and without warning the high fierce drowsing of his solitude gathered itself and struck at him . . . it was his very solitude, his desolation which was now his alone and in full since he had elected to remain; the sudden cessation of the paddle, the skiff shooting on for a moment yet while he thought *What? What?* Then, *No. No. No,* as the silence and solitude and emptiness roared down upon him in a jeering bellow: and now reversed, the skiff spun violently on its heel, he the betrayed driving furiously back toward the platform

where he knew it was already too late, that citadel where the
very crux and dear breath of his life – the being allowed to
work and earn money, that right and privilege which he believed he had earned to himself unaided . . . was being threat-
ened, driving the home-made paddle in grim fury, coming in
sight of the platform at last and seeing the motor launch lying
alongside it with no surprise at all but actually with a kind of
pleasure as though at a visible justification of his outrage and
fear, the privilege of saying *I told you so* to his own affronting
. . . [pp. 269–70].

What has flowed in with the motor launch are the workings of the
Mississippi, the authority's efforts to control those workings, and
even perhaps the bureaucratic process that elects to flood Cajan territory rather than a New Orleans suburb. It is all this and more that
the Convict's solitude has silenced. Despite this, Faulkner's assertion
that his character "could not have told this if he had tried" (p. 269),
the consciousness is not solely Faulkner's. The Convict's negative
bolt from the blue is the moment of dialectical reversal that characterizes the historical imagination. The Convict sees with his mind's
eye a motor boat standing where once there was a vacancy and the
odd "sauric protagonist" (p. 270). What matters here is less the
content than the structure of the image, which allows him to recognize what his isolation is through a simultaneous awareness of
what it is not.[116] For a moment he is no longer a comfortable prisoner of the swamp's immediacy; his singleness is ruptured by the
laws of its future development.

The negative cry is long and threefold because it contains the
pain of self-dissolution. The launch is "no surprise"; it does not
intrude because it has always been potentially present in the mind
of the Convict. Its arrival is a visible materialization of that suppressed specter – the money form. The Convict must have thought
he was in a "citadel" of his own making, but even the gratifications
of innocent labor pleased him only because he playfully "com-
puted" (p. 269) them against what the market would give him on
the final day of reckoning. It is a reckoning that he hardly thinks
about – he hardly needs to since he is doing it all the time. When
he declines the Cajan's paddle (p. 269) he sets up elaborate equiv-
alences, translating an evening, a sapling, a quantity of alligator skin,
and some of his own sweat into "something" sufficiently "embracing
and abstractional" (p. 268) to include volume, number, time, and
energy. Money fits the bill. Though alligator hides are a primitive
money form, their computer understands their rewards and is plainly

at home in the system of exchange that measures Cajan swamps against civic suburbs, and sends a launch.

If the "citadel" has always been insubstantial, the "crux" is equally delusive. The Convict persuades himself that he can experience directly and labor immediately, and as a result he at last feels truly potent. In "penetrating even further and deeper," he closes his ears to the voices of the market in himself and so enters a place that, for all its labors, gives his self-knowledge a holiday. A voice makes itself heard – "*No. No. No*"; the shock of self-consciousness negates his potency and "he strove dreamily with a weightless oar, with muscles without strength or resiliency" (p. 270). What he triply refuses is the choice to return to "the silence and solitude and emptiness," the pre-verbal and pre-social. Instead, his acceptance of the penitentiary is the compromise of a half-life. Like the modern Harry, he is caught inescapably in the fact of his reified consciousness. Telling his story in prison, he tells a thrice-enclosed tale; enclosed by Faulkner's telling it for him, by what he does not tell, and by the jail setting. His audience desires only a verbal peep show delivered by the man who has lived the censored pages of the "impossible pulp-printed fables" (p. 149). Despite the Convict's momentary recognition of release through the phenomenology of independent labor, "Old Man" leaves the oral tale of the proletariat as confined and impotent as the bourgeois reverie of "Wild Palms."

But, to return briefly to the structure of the Convict's negative definition: such dialectical reversal is typical of the novel's contrapuntal form, in that the threefold cry, like the alternating pattern, requires a capacity to read one circumstance in the light of another that appears at best marginal to it. Similarly, the altercation with an alligator draws Charlotte's abortion into its interpretative purview, even as sexual transport in a Pullman bound for Chicago summons the transportation of prisoners from Parchman to a levee, so that the "belated streaming" (p. 61), which attends both, may be understood in each instance as a false release. Read from the perspective of *both* scenes, "streaming" operates as a pun linking the lovers' deferred orgasm to the Convict's experience on the swollen Mississippi – a "stream" that is "belated" because much of its activity is related seven weeks after the events, from a "bunk in the barracks" (p. 159).

There is, however, a distinction to be drawn here: "*No. No. No*" belongs in some sense to the character, whereas the homologies provoked by the counterpoint result from Faulkner's stimulation of his readers' imaginative agilities. Because the two stories that together make up *If I Forget Thee* rigidly divide along class lines,[117] readers are most typically asked to bring together that which the novelist has set apart; reunion affects a social totality that Faulkner's chosen structure is at pains to declare invalid. Intellectually, as part of the exercise of reading, we may posit evidence of a social whole and in so doing condemn both class parties to some form of containment by commodity (saying "no" alike to sexual utopianism and to redemptive labor). Experientially, those parties have limited access to forms of life and thought that might enable *them* to totalize, and so to overwhelm themselves by questioning their imprisonment. They, for the most part, are denied the dialectical habit of mind toward which readers are structurally nudged; and so they are unable to turn themselves around and, by reaching toward a history larger than their own immediate history, to become what they are not – free. For a moment, in his skiff on the swamp, the Convict can see what he is (an independent worker) by the light of what he is not but will soon be (a bureaucratic subject); his dialectical instance denies him what he has chosen to become; consequently his free work is merely an epiphanic moment occurring at an archaic site within a system that is about to undertake its evacuation.

The Convict's moment is as rare as it is brief. For the most part, any dialectical subtleties remain latent in the novel's structure. Their latency is, I believe, a function of Faulkner's recognition that by 1939 there is no way back across the divide made by the revolution of the '30s to an integrated account of the interdependency of worker and owner. So, his fictional class representatives of labor (now all but white) and master (now all but managerial) remain apart, and in semi-ignorance of each other. The uncomfortable perception that white was black, having haunted Faulkner to a greater and lesser degree during the '30s, eases as the social conditions for its formation are dramatically transformed. The revenant and the curator, with their joint implication that the black is a functioning part of the white body, are revised and relegated to a substructural echo; and with their demotion, *If I Forget Thee* comes apart, lacking the founding and traumatic torsion that locked the narratives of *Absalom, Absalom!* together.

As at the start, so at the close, I find myself with a book in bits. For me the sections of *The Sound and the Fury* cannot be put together again because the temporal and social trajectories tacit in the interior voices of the Compson brothers are at such odds. Each has a version of the novel's key words, "sister" and "father," whose several valencies leave Faulkner in fine ventriloquial voice, but in experiential tatters – tatters primarily induced by Quentin's debilitating insights. What, for Quentin, is essentially a long day's journey into his own and his class's sexual pathology becomes in *Absalom, Absalom!* a matter of labor. The emphasis recurs in *If I Forget Thee*, which conflates a dystopic account of wage labor, a utopian vision of bound labor and a proletarian epiphany. Faulkner's dystopia ("Wild Palms") addresses what he fears the modern South will become; his utopia (the *Absalom, Absalom!*/"Wild Palms" intertext) posits what the antebellum South never was, and his workers' epiphany ("Old Man") has absolutely no place to go in space or time. The three texts, antithetical in their various ways, fragment because black labor and white owner have come unbound in the New Deal South. Consequently, Faulkner is no longer possessed by the unwanted, shameful, and occluded ethnic reality that distorted *Absalom, Absalom!*, his major novel, into its awkwardly necessary existence.

AFTERWORD

What follows concerns the end and is less a conclusion than an allusion to work undone. I have contended that during the '30s, or more properly between 1929 and 1939, Faulkner uses the Compson material to mount a sustained exploration of how owners owned so much, for so long, by such "peculiar" means, and in the teeth of partial self-knowledge and sustained opposition. Faulkner's recognition that in the South black passes into white by way of a typical and persistent pattern of labor generates a style of speech that adds up to his key class inheritance. However, by deploying that speech to anatomize the labor impasse of the southern owning class, Faulkner risks taking himself, perceptually and stylistically, apart. On which self-defeating grounds it is perhaps understandable that the vocalist most adept at the doubling, division, reflexivity, and extension that characterizes Faulkner's turn to labor in the '30s should die, rise again, almost die, and partially recover (though in debilitated form). Quentin's last manifestation, as Harry, is little more than a figment of an intertext, a figure glimpsed occasionally among the implicit structures of an under-announced relationship between novels. With Quentin falling finally silent, white will never be quite so black again, and, arguably, the voices through which Faulkner returns to issues of labor and mastery will lack the tensile extension, the taut self-splitting, the driven and occlusive virtuosity of the work that has been studied here.

Labor remains central to *The Hamlet* (1940), but in Frenchman's Bend "there was not one Negro landowner," and "strange Negroes would absolutely refuse to pass through it after dark."[1] And while Lucas Beauchamp's sharecropping is a recurrent issue in *Go Down, Moses* (1942), I would want to argue that hunting displaces planting as the novel's central preoccupation, and that, consequently, it is to Sam Fathers, and not to Lucas, that readers turn for insight into how black passes into white and white passes into black. Significantly, in Sam the mixture is less social than mythic, because it involves "blood" rather than economics, and includes in the sum of those "bloods" the Chickasaw "red." Sam Fathers is a vessel in which three ethnicities meet and flow in amity. He is also Ike McCaslin's surrogate father who displaces first the slaveholding grandfather, Luicius Quintus Carothers McCaslin, and then the manumitting male parents, Buck and Buddy. Such genealogical revision leads away from the issue of bound labor and toward a utopian space in which, to repeat Susan Willis's telling words, "contradictions which have their basis in the real world are transformed into more manageable textual problems."[2]

My claims are arguable, and I have begun to argue them elsewhere.[3] But *Fictions of Labor* has been a study of what I take to be a key strain in Faulkner's writing during a decade of radical labor transformation. The relationship between Faulkner's work and the "modernized" patterns of social exchange associated with a regime of accumulation based on "free" rather than "bound" labor, and on "autonomy" rather than "dependency," is quite another matter – and remains work yet to do.

NOTES

<hr style="width:30%">

Introduction

1. Nathaniel Hawthorne, *The American Claimant Manuscripts* (Columbus: Ohio State University Press, 1977), p. 287.
2. Fredric Jameson, *The Political Unconscious: Narrative as a Socially Symbolic Act* (London: Methuen, 1983), p. 102.
3. Jay Mandle, *Not Slave, Not Free: The African American Experience Since the Civil War* (Durham: Duke University Press, 1992).
4. William Faulkner, *Absalom, Absalom!* (New York: Random House, 1990), p. 214.
5. V. Vološinov, "Discourse in Life and Discourse in Poetry: Questions of Sociological Poetics," collected in *Bakhtin School Papers*, ed. Ann Shukman, *Russian Poetics in Translation*, Vol. 10 (1983), p. 10.
6. *Ibid.*, p. 11.
7. *Ibid.*, p. 15.
8. *Idem.*
9. *Idem.*
10. *Ibid.*, p. 16.
11. Faulkner, *Absalom, Absalom!*, pp. 3, 4.
12. William Faulkner, *The Sound and the Fury* (New York: Norton, 1987), p. 53.
13. Nicholas Rand, "Introduction" to Nicolas Abraham and Maria Torok, *The Shell and the Kernel: Renewals of Psychoanalysis* (Chicago: University of Chicago Press, 1994), p. 21.
14. Nicolas Abraham and Maria Torok, *The Wolfman's Magic Word: A Cryptonomy* (Minneapolis: University of Minnesota Press, 1986); see, usefully, Nicholas Rand, "Translator's Introduction: Toward a Cryptonomy of Literature," pp. i–xxii.

1. Quentin Compson: Tyrrhenian Vase or Crucible of Race?

1. William Faulkner, "An Introduction to *The Sound and the Fury*," *Mississippi Quarterly*, 26 (Summer 1973), pp. 410–15. Reprinted in David Min-

ter's edition of the novel (New York: Norton, 1987), p. 222. All references to *The Sound and the Fury* will be to this edition; pagination will be included in the body of the text.

2. *Ibid.*, p. 224.

3. William Faulkner, *Flags in the Dust* (New York: Random House, 1973), p. 153.

4. William Faulkner, "Interview with Jean Stein," collected in Minter (ed.), *The Sound and the Fury*, p. 240.

5. *Ibid.*, p. 240. A quick flick through Faulkner's interviews and seminars will show how obsessionally he held to this story of the novel's origin. See particularly James Meriwether and Michael Millgate (eds.), *Lion in the Garden: Interviews with William Faulkner, 1926–1962* (New York: Random House, 1968), and Frederick Gwynn and Joseph Blotner (eds.), *Faulkner in the University: Class Conferences at the University of Virginia, 1957–1958* (New York: Random House, 1959).

6. Jean-Paul Sartre, "On *The Sound and the Fury*: Time in the Work of Faulkner," collected in Minter (ed.), *The Sound and the Fury*, p. 253.

7. John T. Matthews, *The Play of Faulkner's Language* (Ithaca, N.Y.: Cornell University Press, 1982), p. 74.

8. See André Bleikasten, *The Most Splendid Failure: Faulkner's The Sound and the Fury* (Bloomington: Indiana University Press, 1976), p. 56, and Matthews, *The Play of Faulkner's Language*, pp. 25–7, 70.

9. Faulkner adopts the term in "Appendix. Compson: 1699–1945," collected in Minter's edition of the novel, p. 234.

10. Meriwether and Millgate, *Lion in the Garden*, p. 240.

11. Faulkner, "An Introduction to *The Sound and the Fury*," p. 223.

12. Irena Kaluza, *The Functioning of Sentence Structure in The Stream of Consciousness Technique of William Faulkner's The Sound and the Fury* (Krakow: Nakladem Universytetu Jagiellonskiego, 1967), p. 85.

13. Lois Gordon, "Meaning and Myth in *The Sound and the Fury* and 'The Waste Land,'" collected in Warren French (ed.), *The Twenties* (Deadland, Fla.: Everett Edwards Inc., 1975), p. 272.

14. Bleikasten, *The Most Splendid Failure*, p. 71.

15. Edmond Volpe, *A Reader's Guide to William Faulkner* (London: Thames and Hudson, 1964), p. 90.

16. Matthews, *The Play of Faulkner's Language*, p. 68.

17. Walter Taylor, *Faulkner's Search for a South* (Urbana: University of Illinois Press, 1983), p. 41.

18. Thadious Davis, *Faulkner's Negro: Art and the Southern Context* (Baton Rouge: Louisiana State University Press, 1983), p. 77.

19. Wolfgang Iser, *The Implied Reader* (Baltimore: Johns Hopkins University Press, 1974) p. 140.

20. Wesley Morris and Barbara Alverson Morris, *Reading Faulkner* (Madison: University of Wisconsin Press, 1989), p. 136.

21. Stephen Ross, *Faulkner's Inexhaustible Voice: Speech and Writing in Faulkner* (Athens: University of Georgia Press, 1989), p. 179.

22. Philip Weinstein, *Faulkner's Subject: A Cosmos No One Owns* (Cambridge: Cambridge University Press, 1992), p. 119.

23. Bleikasten, *The Most Splendid Failure*, pp. 71–2.

24. Paul Ricoeur, *Time and Narrative: Volume 1* (Chicago: University of Chicago Press, 1984), p. 75.

25. Mark Poster's account of the emergence of *Oedipus* as *the* bourgeois family narrative catches something of what I mean. Poster, *Critical Theory of the Family* (London: Pluto Press, 1978), p. 23. See also Sebastiano Timpanaro, *The Freudian Slip* (London: New Left Books, 1974), particularly Ch.11, pp. 173–212.

26. See James Meriwether, "The Textual History of *The Sound and the Fury*," collected in J. B. Meriwether (ed.), *The Merrill Studies in The Sound and the Fury* (Columbus: Merill, 1970), pp. 9–13.

27. Volpe, *A Reader's Guide to William Faulkner*, pp. 363–4.

28. Weinstein, *Faulkner's Subject*, p. 119.

29. Orlando Patterson, *Slavery and Social Death: A Comparative Study* (Cambridge, Mass.: Harvard University Press, 1982), p. 8.

30. Faulkner, "An Introduction to The Sound and the Fury," *Southern Review* Version, reprinted in Minter (ed.), p. 219.

31. *Ibid.*

32. *Ibid.*

33. Eric Sundquist proposes incest (sameness) and miscegenation (difference) as antithetical poles in Faulkner's work. Their pairing, in the character of Charles Bon, precipitates (he says) the central crisis both of *Absalom, Absalom!* and of Faulkner's South. While I have reservations about Sundquist's argument, he does isolate a conjunction that is most typically traumatic for Faulkner; that it should not be so here is a measure of how, in thinking about the writing of *The Sound and the Fury*, Faulkner adopts cognitive strategies in line with those of Benjy.

34. William Faulkner, *Flags in the Dust*, p. 180.

35. John T. Irwin, *Doubling and Incest/Repetition and Revenge: A Speculative Reading of Faulkner* (Baltimore: Johns Hopkins University Press, 1975), p. 43.

36. *Ibid.*, p. 37.

37. Neil R. McMillen, *Dark Journey: Black Mississippians in the Age of Jim Crow* (Champaign: University of Illinois Press, 1989), p. 7.

38. Joel Williamson, *The Crucible of Race: Black–White Relations in the American South Since Emancipation* (New York: Oxford University Press, 1984), p. 322. Williamson's work has been formative for my argument.

39. *Ibid.*, p. 318.

40. W. J. Cash, *The Mind of the South* (London: Thames & Hudson, 1971), p. 89.

41. Eric Sundquist, *Faulkner: The House Divided* (Baltimore: Johns Hopkins University Press, 1983), p. 26.

42. Richard Lichtman, *The Production of Desire: The Integration of Psychoanalysis into Marxist Theory* (New York: The Free Press, 1982), pp. 250–4.

43. A few phrases should serve to convey the virulence of the bad press. Quentin's section has been characterized as "a chaos of broken images" (Bleikasten, *The Most Splendid Failure*, p. 136) set among "deranged musings" (John T. Matthews, *The Sound and the Fury: Faulkner and the Lost Cause* [Boston: Twayne, 1991], p. 15) and "vapid philosophizing" (Sundquist, *Faulkner*, p. 15). Few put more than "minimal faith" in what Quentin says (Donald Kartiganer, *The Fragile Thread* [Amherst: University of Massachussetts Press, 1979], p. 8) since his is the "clinical case" (Irving Howe, *William Faulkner: A Critical Study* [New York: Random House, 1952], p. 167) of someone who has clearly "gone insane" (Irwin, *Repetition and Revenge*, p. 35) – if not mad, "emotionally infantile" (Davis, *Faulkner's Negro*, p. 77), or variously guilty of "myopic intellection" (Arthur Kinney, *Faulkner's Narrative Poetics: Style As Vision* [Amherst: University of Massachusetts Press, 1978], p. 147), "willful decadence" (Kartiganer, *The Fragile Thread*, p. 13), "repetitive obsessions . . . death wish . . . [and] aesthetic escapism" (Morris and Morris, *Reading Faulkner*, p. 121), or simply of having "no 'world' except himself" (Richard King, *A Southern Renaissance* [Oxford: Oxford University Press, 1980], p. 115). Philip Weinstein offers an aptly dismissive summary: "Quentin is a memory box, a porous container of others' throw-away discourse. Unable to consolidate what he has absorbed, unable to shape his own thoughts into the coherence of a temporal project, he is a figure in motley" (Weinstein, *Faulkner's Subject*, p. 85).

44. Jean-Paul Sartre, "On *The Sound and the Fury*," collected in Minter (ed.), p. 255.

45. Irwin, *Repetition and Revenge*, p. 38.

46. Kinney, *Faulkner's Narrative Poetics*, p. 147.

47. King, *A Southern Renaissance*, p. 115.

48. Paul Ricoeur, "The Metaphoric Process as Cognition, Imagination and Feeling," collected in Sheldon Sacks (ed.), *On Metaphor* (Chicago: University of Chicago Press, 1979), p. 144. See also Ricoeur, *The Rule of Metaphor* (London: Routledge & Kegan Paul, 1978), particularly study 1, pp. 9–43.

49. Olga Vickery, "*The Sound and the Fury*: A Study in Perspective," *PMLA*, 64 (December 1954), pp. 1017–37, collected in Minter (ed.), *The Sound and the Fury*, p. 301.

50. Myra Jehlen, *Class and Character in Faulkner's South* (New York: Columbia University Press, 1976), p. 43.

51. Sartre, "On *The Sound and the Fury*," p. 253.

52. Bleikasten, *The Most Splendid Failure*, p. 131.

53. Gwynn and Blotner (eds.), *Faulkner in the University*, pp. 262–3.

54. Davis, *Faulkner's Negro*, pp. 92–3.

55. Definitions drawn from *The Random House Dictionary of the English Language* (Unabridged) (New York: Random House, 1966), and from *Webster's Third New International Dictionary* (Springfield, Mass.: Merriam-Webster, 1961).

56. Matthews, *The Sound and the Fury: Faulkner and the Lost Cause*, p. 102. See also his important essay "The Rhetoric of Containment in Faulkner," collected in Lothar Hönighausen (ed.), *Faulkner's Discourse* (Tubingen: Max Niemeyer Verlag, 1989), pp. 55–67.

57. Kelly Miller, "Roosevelt and the Negro," collected in his *Radicals and Conservatives* (New York: Schocken Books, 1968), p. 319.

58. John Hope Franklin, *From Slavery to Freedom* (New York: Knopf, 1980), p. 316.

59. Matthews, *The Sound and the Fury: Faulkner and the Lost Cause*, p. 103.

60. "Quentin has a very self-conscious sense of how life should be, which derives most of its force from notions of gentility and *noblesse oblige* traditionally attached, in the South, to the plantation aristocracy. . . . [He] has constructed [an] idealized version of things . . . that has himself as a gentleman at its center, and the purity of white womanhood (and of one white woman in particular) as its emblem and apotheosis" (Richard Gray, *Writing the South: Ideas of An American Region* [Cambridge: Cambridge University Press, 1986], p. 212). I would exempt Matthews, for whom the smell of the "foreign" or "black" coin in the girl's hand does not remind Quentin of female impurity, but of "the economic aspiration of the newly enfrachised" (*The Sound and the Fury: Faulkner and the Lost Cause*, p. 103).

61. Kinney, *Faulkner's Narrative Poetics*, p. 147.

62. Gray, *Writing the South*, p. 211.

63. Sundquist, *Faulkner: The House Divided*, p. 12.

64. I stress that the branch transcript is for the most part without shadows and their attendant racial pathology. Incest and its founding term "virginity" do not prompt the co-presence of miscegenation. Gone are the "bluegums," the "blackguards," and the "blackouts." Where "shadow" does occur (four times in the space of less than a page), the term is focused on Dalton Ames and is used to mythologize a rival's potency. Indeed, Quentin self-consciously withdraws from the shade, "the blur of her face leaning down from his high shadow I drew back" (p. 94).

65. Lord Acton, quoted by E. H. Carr in his *What Is History?* (Harmondsworth: Penguin, 1967), p. 44.

66. Williamson, *The Crucible of Race*, p. 499.

67. *Ibid.*, p. 498.

68. *Ibid.*, p. 499.

69. What I have said about Benjy credits him with a temporal paradigm and a consciousness capable of organizing his experience around that paradigm; this is at odds with prevalent critical accounts. Kinney is exceptional in recognizing the "assimilative" force of "Benjy's narrative consciousness" (*Faulkner's Narrative Poetics*, pp. 141–2). See also Richard Godden, "William Faulkner and Benjy Compson: The Voices that Keep Silence," *Essays in Poetics*, Vol. 4, No. 1 (1979), pp. 1–19, and Matthews, *The Sound and the Fury: Faulkner and the Lost Cause*, pp. 35–44.

70. V. N. Vološinov, *Marxism and the Philosophy of Language* (New York: Seminar Press, 1973), p. 199.
71. C. Vann Woodward, *Origins of the New South* (Baton Rouge: Louisiana State University Press, 1971), p. 154.
72. William Faulkner, "Appendix. Compson: 1699–1945," collected in Minter (ed.), *The Sound and the Fury*, p. 233.
73. Paul Goodman, *Speaking and Language* (New York: Random House, 1971), p. 171.
74. Frank Kermode, *The Classic* (London: Faber, 1975), p. 62.
75. Gwynn and Blotner (eds.), *Faulkner in the University*, p. 1.
76. Bleikasten, *The Most Splendid Failure*, p. 184.
77. Maurice Coindreau, "Preface to *The Sound and the Fury*," *Mississippi Quarterly*, Vol. 19 (Summer 1966), pp. 107–15.
78. Many readings make the appeal; see, particularly, Carvel Collins, "Faulkner and Mississippi," *University of Mississippi Studies in English*, Vol. 15 (1978), pp. 139–59.
79. James Snead, *Figures of Division* (New York: Methuen, 1986), pp. 35–9.
80. Vickery, "*The Sound and the Fury*: A Study of Perspective," pp. 308–11.

2. Absalom, Absalom!, Haiti, and Labor History:
Reading Unreadable Revolutions

1. Eugene Genovese, *From Rebellion to Revolution* (Baton Rouge: Louisiana State University Press, 1979), p. 85.
2. *Idem.*
3. Dirk Kuyk Jr. is unusual in that, although he recognizes the misdating, he removes it from the provenance of history; in his version Haiti becomes the "wild, alien space" where the "quester" of "romance" faces "adventures and tests" with "valour" before "he wins the maiden and gains riches." See Kuyk, *Sutpen's Design: Interpreting Absalom, Absalom!* (Charlottesville: University Press of Virginia, 1990), p. 85. See also Robert Dale Parker, *Absalom, Absalom!: The Questioning of Fictions* (Boston: Twayne, 1991); Parker points to the anachronism but concludes that what emerges in *Absalom, Absalom!* is not a historical Haiti "so much as a projection of American anxieties, indicating a guilty fear that white Americans have done things horrible enough to provoke so frightfully violent and – to most Americans – incomprehensibly foreign a revenge [i.e., the revolt]. And it also indicates an opposite fantasy that whites have done nothing horrible enough to provoke a response they cannot still put down with one bold strong white man" (pp. 107–8). In a recent essay Ramón Saldívar recognizes that Sutpen's experiences in Haiti occur after the Revolution but does nothing with his recognition. He is, however, intriguing on the contrast between the racial polarities of the slaveowning South and a Haitian social world "where one might indeed elect to identify, or act, as if race were not a constitutive category." Saldívar, "Looking for a Master Plan: Faulkner, Paredes, and the Colo-

nial and Postcolonial Subject," collected in Philip M. Weinstein (ed.), *The Cambridge Companion to William Faulkner* (Cambridge: Cambridge University Press, 1995), pp. 92–120.

4. Sylvia Frey, *Water from the Rock: Black Resistance in a Revolutionary Age* (Princeton, N.J.: Princeton University Press, 1991), p. 231.

5. See Eugene Genovese, *From Rebellion to Revolution*, p. 95; William Freehling, *Prelude to Civil War: The Nullification Controversy in South Carolina, 1816–36* (New York: Harper & Row, 1969), pp. 58–60; and Stephen Oates, *The Fires of Jubilee: Nat Turner's Fierce Rebellion* (New York: Mentor Books, 1973), pp. 12, 17.

6. Herbert Gutman, *The Black Family in Slavery and Freedom, 1750–1925* (Oxford: Blackwell, 1976), p. 24.

7. C. Vann Woodward (ed.), *Mary Chesnut's Civil War* (New Haven, Conn.: Yale University Press, 1981), p. 834.

8. Rod Prince, *Haiti: Family Business* (London: Latin American Bureau, 1985), p. 11.

9. William Faulkner, *Absalom, Absalom!* (New York: Random House, 1990), p. 202. Subsequent pagination will refer to this edition and will be included in the text.

10. C.L.R. James, *History of Negro Revolt* (London: Race Today Publications, 1985), p. 9. Neither Prince nor James cites sources for these figures. But the main point of reference in discussions of this subject is usually Philip Curtin, *The Atlantic Slave Trade: A Census* (Madison: University of Wisconsin Press, 1969). There have, however, been recent criticisms of Curtin; see especially J. E. Inkikori, "Measuring the Atlantic Slave Trade," *Journal of African History*, Vol. XVII, No. 2 (1976), and the discussion in Vol. XVII, No. 4 (1976). Alasdair Pettinger enabled me to trace these materials.

11. C.L.R. James, *The Black Jacobins* (London: Allison and Busby, 1982), pp. 85–6.

12. See William Faulkner, "Appendix. Compson: 1699–1945," in *The Sound and the Fury* (New York: Norton, 1987), p. 227.

13. Sylvia Frey, *Water from the Rock*, p. 235.

14. Joel Williamson, *The Crucible of Race: Black–White Relations in the American South Since Emancipation* (New York: Oxford University Press, 1984), p. 31.

15. Eugene Genovese, *Roll Jordan Roll: The World the Slaves Made* (New York: Random House, 1972), p. 91.

16. Sylvia Frey, *Water from the Rock*, p. 232.

17. Eugene Genovese, *From Rebellion to Revolution*, p. 95. Alfred Hunt makes it quite clear that the South did not forget Haiti: "southern slave owners and their sympathizers used St. Domingue and the Haitian Revolution as one of the cornerstones of their argument against all critics of their 'peculiar institution.' From the earliest reports of the events . . . in 1791 until the last days of the Confederacy in the spring of 1865, they offered their own self-serving historical interpretation of the Haitian Revolution

as bona fide evidence of the dangers of a humanist ideology in a slave society. These attitudes, expressed in every decade of the antebellum period, were found not only in private letters, official correspondence and newspapers but also among the more influential proslavery spokesmen. It was a lesson they never forgot" (Hunt, *Haiti's Influence on Antebellum America: Slumbering Volcano in the Caribbean* [Baton Rouge: Louisiana State University Press, 1988], pp. 145–6).

18. William Faulkner, "Appendix. Compson: 1699–1945," p. 227.

19. See Vernon Lane Wharton, *The Negro in Mississippi: 1865–1890* (New York: Harper & Row, 1965), pp. 11–13, and William Freehling, *Prelude to Civil War: The Nullification Controversy in South Carolina, 1816–1836*, pp. 11, 363–7.

20. Significantly, when Mary Chesnut recorded her fear of "a new San Domingo" on July 4, 1865, she added a further overheard remark, in qualification: "A Jacquerie not a French Revolution" (*Mary Chesnut's Civil War*, p. 834). "Jacquerie" derives from "Jack-the-man" and refers to a spontaneous peasant protest. Presumably, the soldiers who draw the distinction (whether Union or Confederate is not noted) are unwilling to credit even ex-slaves with the political acumen of the Jacobins, preferring to see them as an unstable peasantry.

21. James Snead, "The 'Joint' of Racism: Withholding the Black in *Absalom, Absalom!*", collected in Harold Bloom (ed.), *Modern Critical Interpretations: William Faulkner's Absalom, Absalom!* (New York: Chelsea House, 1987), p. 132.

22. *Ibid.*, p. 133. Snead's essay is important in that he reads the issue of withheld meaning in terms of a more general "censorship and effacement of the black within the southern social narrative" (p. 135). However, "censorship" and a consequent "return of the repressed" are not traced to specific and changing institutional issues. For all his insights, Snead can finally answer the question as to why meanings are withheld only by appealing to a generic "racial antagonism."

23. G.W.F. Hegel, *The Phenomenology of Mind*, Vol. 1., translated by J. B. Baillie (New York: Macmillan, 1910), p. 184.

24. *Ibid.*, p. 176.

25. *Ibid.*, p. 182.

26. *Ibid.*, p. 186.

27. *Ibid.*, p. 187.

28. *Ibid.*, p. 186.

29. *Ibid.*, p. 173.

30. *Ibid.*, p. 175.

31. *Ibid.*, p. 176.

32. *Ibid.*, p. 179.

33. *Ibid.*, p. 176.

34. On the various forms of tacit resistance see Eugene Genovese, *Roll Jordan Roll*, pp. 599–621.

35. Hegel, *The Phenomenology of Mind*, Vol. 1, p. 186.

36. Quoted in Eric Foner, *Reconstruction: America's Unfinished Revolution: 1863–1877* (New York: Harper & Row, 1988) p. 103.

37. Caddy climbs the tree in 1898 (the year of Damuddy's death). No word in Benjy's section antedates 1898; in 1897 Benjy was quite literally a blank. The tree and the stain prompt his earliest encounter with signs and therefore signal his fall into language and consciousness. Sutpen's lapse is less sudden; he and his family "fell . . . by gravity" from mountain to Tidewater plain (p. 180), but the boy's fall into social consciousness occurs on being told "to go around to the back" – at which point "he just had to think" (p. 188). Like Benjy, he has words with himself for the first time, but in a voice divided against itself along class lines.

38. Hegel, *The Phenomenology of Mind*, Vol. 1, p. 176.

39. Kuyk offers useful commentary: "In chapter 7 . . . the third-person narrator, while remaining ever-present, recedes so that Quentin seems to carry most of the weight of the narrative. The bulk of his information comes from General Compson, who learned much of it from Sutpen himself. Through General Compson, Quentin can quote Sutpen directly." Kuyk adds that by receding, the narrator lets Quentin's account stand and therefore "authenticates" it. See Kuyk, *Sutpen's Design*, p. 38.

40. See Genovese, *Roll Jordan Roll*, p. 432.

41. It must be remembered that Sutpen recalls his Virginian childhood in 1835, four years after Nat Turner's revolt, a rising that prompted the Virginia slavery debate (1831–2), the last significant debate over slavery in the antebellum South. Contention was sectional, articulating three decades of dispute between prevalently nonslaveholding western counties (self-sufficient, household production) and eastern slaveholding counties (plantation production). The holding of property in slaves (and its attendant political influence) had long been contentious in Virginia. Benjamin Leigh's contribution to the Virginian Convention of 1829–30 epitomizes the lengthy dispute; Leigh insisted that the slaveholding east must resist "to the bitter end [any] transfer of power" to the nonslaveholding west. "In every civilized country under the sun there must be some who labor for their daily bread"; westerners who "tend the herds and dig the soil" could never have adequate "political intelligence" to participate in government. Leigh equated western "daylaborers" with Tidewater slaves in terms of their "place in the political economy"; consequently, he reiterated that slaveholding planters should never submit to the "grinding tyranny" of the "peasantry of the West." Quoted by Alison Goodyear Freehling, *Drift Toward Dissolution: The Virginia Slavery Debate of 1831–1832* (Baton Rouge: Louisiana State University Press, 1982), p. 58. See also her chapter 3, "A Temporary Patchwork of a Constitution," pp. 36–81.

42. Joseph Blotner (ed.), *Selected Letters of William Faulkner* (New York: Vintage, 1978), pp. 78–9.

43. Jean-Paul Sarte, *Critique of Dialectical Reason*, Vol. 1 (London: Verso, 1982), p. 323. See also pp. 178–9.
44. *Ibid.*, p. 328.
45. *Ibid.*, p. 332.
46. Various guides to dating are available, often expanding upon and suggesting errors in Faulkner's Chronology and Genealogy; see Cleanth Brooks, *William Faulkner: The Yoknapatawpha Country* (New Haven, Conn.: Yale University Press, 1963), pp. 424–6; Edmond Volpe, *A Reader's Guide to William Faulkner* (New York: Farrar, Straus & Giroux, 1965), pp. 387–92, and Kuyk, *Sutpen's Design*, pp. 46–60.
47. The issue has recently prompted considerable, and regionally specific, historical debate. See particularly John C. Inscoe, *Mountain Masters, Slavery and the Sectional Crisis in Western North Carolina* (Knoxville: University of Tennessee Press, 1989), ch. 2, "Mountain Community and Commerce," pp. 25–58; Lacy K. Ford Jr., *Origins of Southern Radicalism: The South Carolina Upcountry, 1800–1860* (New York: Oxford University Press, 1988), pp. 44–95; and James Oakes, *Slavery and Freedom: An Interpretation of the Old South* (New York: Knopf, 1990), pp. 113–36.
48. It is worth considering the whole quotation, ". . . where a certain few men not only had the power of life and death and barter and sale over others, they had living human men to perform the endless repetitive personal offices such as pouring the very whiskey from the jug and putting the glass into his hand or pulling off his boots for him to go to bed that all men have had to do for themselves since time began and would have to do until they died and which no man ever has or ever will like to do but which no man that he knew had ever anymore thought of evading than he had thought of evading the effort of chewing and swallowing and breathing." [pp. 179–80]
49. Given his labor trauma, it is understandable that Sutpen adopts continence as a shield against mingling and co-present bodies.
50. See W. J. Cash, *The Mind of the South* (London: Thames and Hudson, 1971), p. 86; Richard Gray, *Writing the South: Ideas of an American Region* (Cambridge: Cambridge University Press, 1989), p. 189; and Joel Williamson, *The Crucible of Race*, pp. 303–8.
51. See James Oakes, *Slavery and Freedom*, p. 135.
52. Quoted by Stephen Hahn, *The Roots of Southern Populism: Yeomen Farmers and the Transformation of the Georgia Upcountry, 1850–1890* (New York: Oxford University Press, 1983), p. 133.
53. Kuyk, *Sutpen's Design*, pp. 20, 22.
54. Carolyn Porter, *Seeing and Being: The Plight of the Participant Observer in Emerson, James, Adams and Faulkner* (Middletown, Conn.: Wesleyan University Press, 1981), p. 222.
55. Cleanth Brooks, *William Faulkner: Toward Yoknapatawpha and Beyond* (New Haven, Conn.: Yale University Press, 1979), p. 299.
56. *Ibid.*, pp. 296, 294, 299.
57. Eugene Genovese notes that the pre-bourgeois spirit of the planters

meant that they "could not accept the idea that the cash nexus offered a permissible basis for human relations." Brooks quotes him, p. 294. I have modified Brooks's use of the Genovese quotation.

58. Porter, *Seeing and Being*, p. 222.

59. Brooks, *William Faulkner: Toward Yoknapatawpha and Beyond* (New Haven, Conn.: Yale University Press, 1979), p. 299.

60. Porter, *Seeing and Being*, p. 236.

61. Kuyk, *Sutpen's Design*, p. 21.

62. Brooks, *William Faulkner: Toward Yoknapatawpha and Beyond*, p. 295.

63. Porter, *Seeing and Being*, p. 234.

64. *Idem.*

65. *Ibid.*, pp. 234–5.

66. Quentin's observation is strange since, at least nominally, General Compson knows neither that Bon is Sutpen's son nor that he is black. Quentin may be exaggerating his grandfather's point, or he may be hinting at his own suspicion that the General had worked out Sutpen's paternal secrets.

67. Orlando Patterson, *Slavery and Social Death: A Comparative Study* (Cambridge, Mass.: Harvard University Press, 1982), p. 8.

68. Edgar Allan Poe, *Selected Writings* (Harmondsworth: Penguin, 1974), p. 80.

69. C. Vann Woodward, *The Strange Career of Jim Crow* (New York: Oxford University Press, 1959), p. xvi.

70. Pallas/Minerva lends herself to the bird motif, being much associated with both cock and owl. However, I am aware that in establishing this particular associative pattern, I risk straining my reader's patience. I offer in mitigation Nicolas Abraham and Maria Torok's psychoanalytic claim that trauma and its repression can so distort the signs through which it is represented that a "cryptonomy" forms – that is, a grouping of words that obstructs comprehension but that can operate as guides when properly read. See Nicolas Abraham and Maria Torok, *The Wolf Man's Magic Word: A Cryptonomy* (Minneapolis: University of Minnesota Press, 1986).

71. I am borrowing a point from Peter Brooks, "Incredible Narration: *Absalom, Absalom!*", collected in Harold Bloom (ed.), *Modern Critical Interpretations* (New York: Chelsea House, 1987), pp. 105–37. Brooks argues that the novel posits a relationship between its own plot and southern history but omits the narrative that might allow these two terms to cohere significantly. As a result, *Absalom, Absalom!* is "perilously close to a narrative without a motive" (p. 110). While disagreeing, I find his sense that plot particulars are informed by apparently untraceable historical pressures, which they express but do not represent, extremely helpful.

72. Nicholas Rand glosses Abraham and Torok's "cryptonomy" as follows: "Cryptonomy (coined from the Greek prefix crypto for 'hiding' and an analogy with rhetorical terms such as metonymy) is a verbal procedure leading to the creation of a text (in the Wolf Man's case, understood as co-extensive with life) whose sole purpose is to hide words that are

hypothesized as having to remain beyond reach. . . . Divested of metaphorical reach and the power to institute or depose an extralinguistic
event or action, cryptonyms create a collection of words, a verbarium,
with no apparent aim to carry any kind of knowledge of conviction."
However, such repression wears its marks on its own face, indicating the
lost knowledge that it dissembles. Rand adds, "Carrying out repression
on the word implies that cryptonomy inhibits the process of definition
of meaning by concealing a segment of the associative path that normally
allows one to move freely from one element to another in a verbal
chain." See Nicholas Rand, "Translator's Introduction: Toward a Cryptonomy of Literature," in Abraham and Torok, *The Wolf Man's Magic
Word*, pp. lviii and lix. Derrida's essay in the same volume, "Forward:
Fors: The Anguished Words of Nicolas Abraham and Maria Torok," enhanced my understanding of the significant opacity of "cryptonomy."

73. Elizabeth Fox-Genovese and Eugene Genovese, *Fruits of Merchant Capital:
Slavery and Bourgeois Capital in the Rise and Expansion of Capitalism* (New
York: Oxford University Press, 1983), p. 5.

74. James Oakes, *Slavery and Freedom*, p. 45. But the Genoveses would add
that "the market did not directly impinge upon their [the planters']
system of production or upon their relation with their labor force"
(*Fruits of Merchant Capital*, p. 94).

75. Mark Tushnet, *The American Law of Slavery: Considerations of Humanity and
Interest* (Princeton, N.J.: Princeton University Press, 1981), p. 232.

76. Johann Fichte, *The Science of Rights* (Philadelphia: J. B. Lippincott & Co.,
1869), quoted by Evgeny Pashukanis, *Law and Marxism* (London: Ink
Links Ltd., 1978), p. 114. My discussion of contract is heavily informed
by Pashukanis's chapter "Commodity and Subject," pp. 109–33.

77. Pashukanis, *Law and Marxism*, p. 121.

78. Tushnet, *The American Law and Slavery*, p. 33.

79. *Ibid.*, p. 6.

80. *Idem.*

81. Oakes, *Slavery and Freedom*, p. 48.

82. Fox-Genovese and Genovese, *Fruits of Merchant Capital*, p. 131.

83. *Idem.*

84. Genovese, *Roll Jordan Roll*, p. 91.

85. Quoted by Tushnet, *The American Law of Slavery*, p. 60.

86. The assumption that the facts cannot be known has ghosted readings of
the novel from the first, though the influence of poststructural ideas
about language has intensified epistemological uncertainty over the past
two decades. For an early and perceptive example of the know-little-or-at-
least-less stance, see Olga Vickery, for whom "the relation of the reader to
the center . . . points out the essential ambiguity of fact and the multiplicity of 'subjective' truths to which it can give rise" (*The Novels of William
Faulkner* [Baton Rouge: Louisiana State University Press, 1959], p. 102).
See also Michael Millgate, *The Achievement of William Faulkner* (London:
Constable, 1966), p. 153. Later and more emphatically, Hugh Ruppers-

burg insists, "the novel suggests that the search for truth is irrelevant. . . . Correlations between truth and historical reality simply do not exist" (*Voice and Eye in Faulkner's Fiction* [Athens: University of Georgia Press, 1983], p. 130). Once the "truth" about Sutpen becomes so "multiple" as to be "irrelevant," Sutpen himself vanishes, becoming he about whom nothing can be known; see Estella Schoenberg, *Old Tales and Talking: Quentin Compson in William Faulkner's Absalom, Absalom! and Related Works* (Jackson: University Press of Mississippi, 1977). For Derridean versions of Sutpen's recession from "fact" to "absence" see particularly Stephen Ross, "The Evocation of Voice in *Absalom, Absalom!*," *Essays in Literature*, 8, Fall 1981, pp. 135–49, and John Matthews, *The Play of Faulkner's Language* (Ithaca, N.Y.: Cornell University Press, 1982), pp. 115–61.

87. Contemporary observers agree that after emancipation, miscegenation between white men and black women was much reduced. "Freedom" blocked white access to the quarters, while segregation functioned to separate black and white lives. See Joel Williamson, *The Crucible of Race*, particularly chapter 7.

88. Elizabeth Fox-Genovese draws a distinction between "home" (or the separate and feminine sphere developing in the antebellum, bourgeois North) and "household" – a term that refers to a unit of domestic production in which people (some willingly and some under compulsion) pool income and resources. Where the northern "home" narrows social relations into an essentially private, feminized, and familial space (oedipal), the southern "household" necessarily links private to public and locates familial relations within production relations (anti-oedipal). "Within households, personal ties cross class-lines. Slave-holders and slaves participated in a shared imaginative universe that could shimmer with mutual affection or . . . shatter in mutual antagonism." See Elizabeth Fox-Genovese, *Within the Plantation Household: Black and White Women in the Old South* (Chapel Hill: University of North Carolina Press, 1988), pp. 27, 37–99.

3. Absalom, Absalom! and Rosa Coldfield: Or, "What Is in the Dark House?"

1. William Faulkner, *Absalom, Absalom!: The Corrected Text* (New York: Random House, 1986), p. 115. Subsequent pagination will refer to this edition, and will be included in the text.

2. John T. Matthews, *The Play of Faulkner's Language* (Ithaca, N.Y.: Cornell University Press, 1982), p. 152.

3. Eric J. Sundquist, *Faulkner: The House Divided* (Baltimore: Johns Hopkins University Press, 1983), p. 114.

4. James Oakes, *Slavery & Freedom: An Interpretation of the Old South* (New York: Knopf, 1990), p. 4.

5. William Faulkner, "Barn Burning," collected in his *Dr. Martino and Other Stories* (London: Chatto & Windus, 1965), p. 18.

6. "A Dark House" or "Dark House" was a working title for *Absalom, Absalom!*, indicating perhaps that from the start Faulkner was preoccupied not simply with "the more or less violent breakup of a household family from 1860 to about 1910" (as he put it) but with the family's propertied embodiment. See Joseph Blotner, *Faulkner: A Biography* (Vol. 1) (New York: Random House, 1974), p. 830.

7. Clytie as "*sphinx*" (lion bodied) and "*Cerberus*" (dog bodied) (p. 112) joins the motley zoo of significant guardians at thresholds (along with "*monkey nigger*" and "*tiger*"). These blacks are bestialized because the covert knowledge of white dependency that they protect is too dangerous to leave underpoliced.

8. Toni Morrison bases her deployment of the bit as an instrument of slave constraint (*Beloved* [1987]) on antebellum drawings detailing its use in the peculiar institution. "Bit" necessitates "bridle." Josephine Anderson, an ex-slave interviewed during the 1930s by members of the Federal Writers' Project, may be describing a dream, but her emphasis on the "bit" and "bridle" intimates the trauma of that "*curb*" as it was used by slaveholders: "You ain' never been rid by a witch? Well, you mighty lucky. Dey come in de night, ginnerly soon after you drop off to sleep. Dey put a bridle on your head an' a bit in your mouth an' a saddle on your back. Den dey take off deir skin an' hang it upon de wall. Den dey git on you, an' some nights dey like to ride you to death. You try to holler but you kain't, counta dey ride you back home an' into your bed" (collected in *Bullwhip Days: The Slaves Remember*, ed. James Mellon [New York: Weidenfeld and Nicholson, 1988], pp. 89–90). In Allen Tate's *The Fathers* (1938), Lucy Buchan dreams of Brother George, "charging down the course, his lance perfectly balanced . . . astride . . . the man Yellow Jim whose face was as white as his master's" (*The Fathers* [Chicago: Swallow Press, 1974], p. 227).

9. Erik Olin Wright, Andrew Levine, and Elliott Sober, *Reconstructing Marxism* (London: Verso, 1992), p. 25.

10. Rosa's distinction is usefully glossed by Elizabeth Fox-Genovese's separation of the southern "household" from the northern "home." She argues that the antebellum household cannot be read through the bourgeois optic. Even as the North was transforming the household, as locus of domestic production, into the home or "female sphere," the South was reinforcing the centrality of plantation and farm households. "Within households," Fox-Genovese comments, "personal ties cross class lines. Slaveholders and slaves participated in a shared imaginative universe that could shimmer with mutual affection or . . . shatter in mutual antagonism" (Elizabeth Fox-Genovese, *Within the Plantation Household: Black and White Women in the Old South* [Chapel Hill: University of North Carolina Press, 1988] p. 27; see also chapter 1, pp. 37–99). The logic of northern development engaged the woman with the market (as a consumer); the development of southern slave society did not. "To be a 'middle-class' employer of free labor or of no labor at all was one

thing. To be a 'middle class' owner of human flesh was – materially, ideologically, psychologically – quite another" (*ibid.*, p. 41). Rosa's return to the memory of childhood in a merchant's "house" is a proto-bourgeois appeal to the notion that things and persons have a price and that as such they enjoy autonomous and independent value (one from another).

11. Sundquist, *The House Divided*, p. 113.

12. Not less traceable but not untraceable. Prior to Rosa's cry, Clytie's face is a split referent referring both to Sutpen's paternity and to Haitian maternity. With the word "*sister*" Rosa writes out, or brackets, the Haitian feature, but traces of revolution remain. Witness how the obstructive sororal term directs us to "Bon," a name that if distorted into a pun on "goods" continues to reflect the trauma it was coined to suppress.

13. Alfred Hunt, *Haiti's Influence on Antebellum America: Slumbering Volcano in the Caribbean* (Baton Rouge: Louisiana State University Press, 1988), p. 146.

14. Rosa's access to what General Compson knew can fairly be assumed in that first the General and then his son act in a legal capacity for the Coldfield estate. Plainly Mr. Compson believes that Rosa has sorted out the clues; he notes that even as Ellen tells Rosa about the Bon/Judith liaison (1859), speaking of Bon "as if he were three inanimate objects in one" (p. 59) (a gown, a piece of furniture, and an etiquette primer), Rosa "got the picture from the first word, perhaps from the name, Charles Bon" (p. 59). Mr. Compson's tacit point seems to be that, at sixteen, Rosa appreciates Sutpen's pun. (I shall later argue that she deploys a version of that pun herself.) If Rosa reads back from the play on "goods" to her father's exacting appreciation of a black body as a quantity of labor time (Mr. Coldfield requires his two manumitted slaves to work off the cost of their own manumission [p. 66]); and if, to this, she adds her unspoken knowledge of the Haitian source – then Rosa has the whole story.

15. Elizabeth Fox-Genovese and Eugene D. Genovese, *Fruits of Merchant Capital: Slavery and Bourgeois Property in the Rise and Expansion of Capitalism* (Oxford: Oxford University Press, 1983), p. 5.

16. Rosemary Coleman, "Family Ties: Generating Narratives in *Absalom, Absalom!*," *Mississippi Quarterly*, Vol. 43, Part 3 (1988), p. 429.

17. Patrick O'Donnell, "Sub Rosa: Voice, Body & History in *Absalom, Absalom!*," *College Literature*, Vol. 16, Part I (1989), pp. 32–3.

18. Minrose C. Gwin, *The Feminine and Faulkner: Reading (Beyond) Sexual Difference* (Knoxville: University of Tennessee Press, 1990), p. 79.

19. René Girard argues that desire cannot come into being without the mediating presence of a third party. By insisting that another attends any loving couple, he offers diagnostic access to Rosa's passionately triangular love: "Jealousy and envy imply a third presence: object, subject, and a third person to whom the jealousy or envy is directed.

These two 'vices' are therefore triangular; however we never recognize a model in the person who arouses jealousy because we always take the jealous person's attitude toward the problem of jealousy. Like all victims of internal mediation, the jealous person easily convinces *herself* that *her* desire is spontaneous, in other words, that it is deeply rooted in the object and in this object alone. As a result *she* always maintains that *her* desire preceded the intervention of the mediator. *She* would have us see him as an intruder, a bore, a *terzo incomodo* who interrupts a delightful tête-à-tête. Jealousy is thus reduced to the irritation we all experience when one of our desires is accidentally thwarted. But true jealousy is infinitely more profound and complex; it always contains an element of fascination with the insolent rival" (*Deceit, Desire and the Novel* [London: Johns Hopkins University Press, 1965], p. 12). To facilitate application of the quotation to chapter five of *Absalom, Absalom!*, I have feminized and italicized some of Girard's pronouns.

Rosa denies "*jealousy*," but with the same breath she denies "*spying*" (p. 119). If one sets her denial aside, Rosa's desire either addresses Bon and is mediated by Judith or addresses Judith and is mediated by Bon. In each case, read through Girard, Rosa's fascination must address Judith, and, I would add, must pass into Judith, either through Bon or in order to reach him. Ergo, Judith is possessed by Rosa.

20. Coleman, "Family Ties: Generating Narratives in *Absalom, Absalom!*," p. 423.
21. Matthews, *The Play of Faulkner's Language*, p. 124.
22. See Edmund Leach, "Genesis as Myth," collected in his *Genesis as Myth and Other Essays* (London: Cape, 1969), pp. 7–23.
23. Coleman first alerted me to Rosa's claim that Bon is her father. See "Family Ties: Generating Narratives in *Absalom, Absalom!*," p. 429.
24. I am playing with Paul Goodman's powerful aphorism "A style of speech is an hypothesis about how the world is" in his *Speaking and Language: Defense of Poetry* (London: Wildwood House, 1973), p. 171.
25. Walter Benjamin, "Theses on the Philosophy of History," in his *Illuminations* (Glasgow: Fontana/Collins, 1977), p. 257.
26. *Ibid.*, p. 257.
27. *Ibid.*, p. 263.
28. *Ibid.*, p. 264.
29. *Ibid.*, p. 265.
30. *Idem.*
31. Benjamin deploys Marx in order exactly to reverse his emphasis. In "The Eighteenth Brumaire of Louis Bonaparte," Marx notes, "The tradition of the dead generations weighs like a nightmare on the minds of the living. And, just when they appear to be engaged in the revolutionary transformation of themselves and their material surroundings, in the creation of something which does not yet exist, precisely in such epochs of revolutionary crisis they timidly conjure up the

spirits of the past to help them; they borrow their names, slogans and costumes, so as to stage the new world-historical scene in this venerable disguise and borrowed language. Luther put on the mask of the apostle Paul; the Revolution of 1789–1814 draped itself alternately as the Roman Republic and the Roman Empire . . ." collected in *Surveys from Exile*, ed. and introd. David Fernbach (Harmondsworth: Penguin Books, 1973), pp. 146–7.

32. Benjamin, "Theses on the Philosophy of History," p. 263.

33. Walter Benjamin, "Eduard Fuchs, Collector and Historian," quoted by Rolf Tiedemann, "Historical Materialism or Political Messianism? An Interpretation of the Theses 'On the Concept of History,' " trans. Barton Byg, Jeremy Gaines, and Doris L. Jones, in Gary Smith (ed.), *Benjamin: Philosophy, Aesthetics, History* (Chicago: University of Chicago Press, 1989), p. 181. I prefer this phrasing to that offered by Edmund Jephcott and Kingsley Shorter in their translation of the Eduard Fuchs essay in *One-Way Street and Other Writings* (London: New Left Books, 1979), p. 360.

34. Benjamin, "Eduard Fuchs, Collector and Historian," quoted by Tiedemann, p. 181. Tiedemann's essay is vital to my argument here.

35. Quoted by Tiedemann, "Historical Materialism or Political Messianism?," p. 181.

36. *Ibid.*, p. 182.

37. Benjamin, "Theses on the Philosophy of History," p. 265.

38. Quoted by Tiedemann, "Historical Materialism or Political Messianism?," p. 182.

39. Benjamin, "Theses on the Philosophy of History," p. 259.

40. *Ibid.*, p. 264.

41. *Ibid.*, p. 265.

42. A closer look at the manner in which each experiences temporal dislocation underlines the match between Faulkner and Benjamin's notion of "cessation of happening." Each character is "arrest[ed]" by his or her temporal crisis. Sutpen, turned from the door, has no memory of turning; he simply finds himself on the way to the fallen oak (p. 188). Rosa's "glimpse" deploys Keats to catch a "tornado"; the racing Sutpen carriage (all "replica" and "miniature") is cast as a frieze, around a moment whose violence it simply cannot contain. The image "struggle[s]" to escape but "cannot fade" since Rosa will carry it to her "grave" (p. 16).

43. Benjamin, "Eduard Fuchs," in *One-Way Street and Other Writings*, p. 353.

44. Benjamin, "Theses on the Philosophy of History," p. 259.

45. James Oakes, *Slavery and Freedom: An Interpretation of the Old South*, p. 85.

46. John Forrester, *The Seductions of Psychoanalysis: Freud, Lacan and Derrida* (Cambridge: Cambridge University Press, 1990), p. 141.

47. Jacques Lacan, quoted by Forrester, *The Seductions of Psychoanalysis*, p. 213.

48. Sigmund Freud, "From the History of an Infantile Neurosis," collected

in *The Standard Edition of the Complete Psychological Works of Sigmund Freud*, Vol. 17 (London: Hogarth, 1955), p. 45, note 1.

49. Jean-François Lyotard, *Heidegger and "the jews"* (Minneapolis: University of Minnesota Press, 1990), pp. 16–17.

50. Jacques Lacan, *Écrits* (London: Tavistock, 1977), p. 48.

51. Peter Nicholls, "The Belated Post-Modern: History, Phantoms and Toni Morrison," *Borderlines*, I (1994), p. 197. Section II of this essay would not have been possible without Peter Nicholls' work. The patience of his conversation and the pertinence of his reading suggestions underpin the entire argument, particularly in its relation to the temporal implications of the moment of psychoanalysis.

52. Peter Nicholls, *ibid.*, p. 7.

53. Jean Laplanche, *New Foundations for Psychoanalysis* (Oxford: Basil Blackwell, 1989), p. 118.

54. Jacques Derrida, *Memoirs for Paul de Man* (New York: Columbia University Press, 1989), p. 58.

55. Jacques Derrida, *Dissemination* (Chicago: University of Chicago Press, 1981), p. 210.

56. Benjamin, "Theses on the Philosophy of History," p. 262.

57. *Ibid.*, p. 262.

58. It may seem odd to speak of victors, at least in Rosa's case, since the South loses the Civil War. But Radical Reconstruction did not redistribute plantation land, and the plantation system essentially remained in place (though deploying a modified order of labor) until the 1930s. More of this later.

59. Philip M. Weinstein, "Marginalia: Faulkner's Black Lives," collected in Doreen Fowler and Ann J. Abadie (eds.), *Faulkner and Race* (Jackson: University Press of Mississippi, 1987), p. 181.

60. I take the notion of textual "whispering" from Frank Kermode, who in the "Prologue" to his *Essays on Fiction, 1971–82* (London: Routledge & Kegan Paul, 1983) speaks of "occult, non referential patterns" (p. 13) that form a "surplus of sense" (p. 22) or "hermeneutical increment" (p. 25) requiring of readers a "third ear" (p. 30) whereby they locate "displaced" and secondary elaboration[s]" (p. 30). See also "Recognition and Deception," pp. 92–113, in the same collection.

61. Karl Marx, "Economic and Philosophical Manuscripts" (1844), collected in *Early Writings*, ed. Lucio Colletti (Harmondsworth: Penguin Books, 1977), p. 318.

62. Max Black, "Metaphor" in his *Models and Metaphors* (Ithaca, N.Y.: Cornell University Press, 1962), pp. 25–47.

63. The phrase derives from Paul Ricoeur's notion of "split reference." See Ricoeur, "The Metaphoric Process of Cognition, Imagination and Feeling," collected in Sheldon Sacks (ed.), *On Metaphor* (Chicago: University of Chicago Press, 1979), pp. 152–3.

64. Raymond Williams, *The Long Revolution* (Harmondsworth: Penguin Books, 1965), pp. 64–5.

65. Paul Ricoeur speaks of "semantic impertinence" occurring within meta-phor: "metaphoric meaning does not merely consist of semantic clash but of new predicative meaning which emerges from the collapse of the literal meaning, that is, from the collapse of the meaning which obtains if we rely only on the common or usual lexical value of our words." See "The Metaphoric Process of Cognition, Imagination and Feeling," p. 144.

66. Effectively, in Act IV, Rosa keeps the Hundred by retaining Bon at its systemic core. It is therefore significant that, having detailed the funeral, she immediately (though briefly) loses her voice (pp. 123–4). Until she restores the house by reviving Bon, she talks quite literally as though she were someone else, addressing the issue of why she stayed in 1865 first from the perspective of Quentin (*"You will say . . ."* [p. 124]), and then from within the context of the town (*"neighbours . . .* [who] *thought not only as I thought but as my forbears thought"* [p. 123]). Rosa talks like Rosa, that is to say, one whose structure of feeling is articulated around a particular social trauma, only when evidence of that trauma (in this in-stance, Bon) is available in a form that is both buried and yet alive.

67. Rosa also speaks of him as *"diffused (not attenuated to thinness but enlarged, magnified, encompassing as though in a prolonged and unbroken instant of tre-mendous effort embracing and holding intact that ten-mile square . . ."* (p. 131). Sutpen's symptoms, as diagnosed by Rosa, resemble those of Roderick Usher (though in active form). Usher, whose name "in the minds of the peasantry" "seemed to include . . . both the family and the family mansion," complains of the influence of his house upon his person, "an influence which some peculiarities in the mere form and substance of his family mansion, had, by dint of long sufferance, . . . obtained over his spirit – an effect which the *physique* of the grey walls and turrets, and of the dim tarn into which they all looked down, had, at length, brought about upon the *morale* of his existence." See "The Fall of the House of Usher," collected in *Edgar Allan Poe: Selected Writings* (ed. David Galloway) (Harmondsworth: Penguin Books, 1974), pp. 140–4.

68. Jay R. Mandle, *Not Slave, Not Free: The African American Experience Since the Civil War* (Durham, N.C.: Duke University Press, 1992), p. 21.

69. Charles S. Johnson, *Shadow of the Plantation* (Chicago: University of Chi-cago Press, 1966), p. 16.

70. John T. Irwin, "The Dead Father in Faulkner," collected in Robert Davis (ed.), *The Fictional Father: Lacanian Readings of the Text* (Amherst: Univer-sity of Massachussetts Press, 1981), p. 154. See also, in the same collec-tion, André Bleikasten, "Fathers in Faulkner," pp. 115–46.

71. Gwin, *The Feminine and Faulkner,* p. 71.

72. Jessica Benjamin, *The Bonds of Love: Psychoanalysis, Feminism and the Problem of Domination* (New York: Pantheon, 1988), p. 39.

73. Rosa has Sutpen syntactically echo Mulciber's staggered fall from *Para-dise Lost,* Book I, lines 740–6, thereby enhancing her deceptive demon-izing of him.

4. The Persistence of Thomas Sutpen: Absalom, Absalom!, Time, and Labor Discipline

1. Eric Foner, *Reconstruction: America's Unfinished Revolution: 1863–1877* (New York: Harper & Row, 1988).
2. The phrase is Jonathon Wiener's, "Class Structure and Economic Development in the American South, 1865–1955," *American Historical Review*, vol. 84, No. 4 (1979), pp. 970–1006.
3. Mark Tushnet, *The American Law of Slavery: Considerations of Humanity and Interest* (Princeton, N.J.: Princeton University Press, 1981), p. 33.
4. Charles S. Johnson, Edwin R. Embree, and W. W. Alexander, *The Collapse of Cotton Tenancy: Summary of Field Studies and Statistical Surveys, 1933–35* (Freeport, N.Y.: Books for Libraries Press, 1972), p. 22. Originally published 1935.
5. Quoted by Jack Temple Kirby, *Rural Worlds Lost: The American South, 1920–1960* (Baton Rouge: Louisiana State University Press, 1987), p. 239.
6. Tushnet, *The American Law of Slavery*, p. 6.
7. "The first stage in the consolidation of plantations was the wholesale eviction of tenants of all classes, especially sharecroppers. This process was protracted, but it seems to have been underway all over the South by 1934, the first full crop year following the creation of the AAA." Jack Temple Kirby, *Rural Worlds Lost*, p. 64.
8. Gilbert Fite cites Jonathon Daniels, who observes (in 1941) that thousands had been "set free from tenancy, which means they are free to squat in idleness, to stand on small-town street corners, to hope only for occasional day labor – free to starve but for the intervention of relief." Quoted by Gilbert Fite, *Cotton Fields No More: Southern Agriculture, 1965–1980* (Lexington: University Press of Kentucky, 1984), p. 210.
9. Donald H. Grubbs, *Cry from the Cotton: The Southern Tenant Farmers' Union and the New Deal* (Chapel Hill: University of North Carolina Press, 1971), p. 125.
10. Quoted by Stuart Kidd, "The Cultural Politics of Farm Mechanization: Farm, Security Administration Photographs of the Southern Landscape, 1935–1943," unpublished paper, delivered at the Southern Studies Forum: On Southern Landscape (1993).
11. *Ibid.*
12. Jonathan Wiener, "Class Structure and Economic Development in the American South, 1865–1955," pp. 970–1006.
13. Grubbs, *Cry from the Cotton*, p. 135.
14. Gavin Wright, *Old South: New South: Revolutions in the Southern Economy Since the Civil War* (New York: Basic Books, 1986), particularly Chs. 3 and 4, pp. 51–123.
15. Foner estimates that at the war's end, for the South as a whole the real value of property (discounting that represented by slaves) stood 30 percent lower than its prewar figure. "Southern planters emerged from the

Civil War in a state of shock. Their class had been devastated – physically, economically, psychologically. The loss of the planters' slaves and life savings (to the extent that they had invested in Confederate Bonds) wiped out the inheritance of generations." Foner, *Reconstruction*, p. 129.

16. See Mandle, *Not Slave, Not Free: The African American Experience Since the Civil War* (Durham, N.C.: Duke University Press, 1992), particularly Ch. 3, pp. 33–43.

17. Norman Thomas, in a letter to Senator Robert F. Wagner, quoted in Vera Rony, "The Organization of Black and White Farm Workers in the South," collected by Thomas R. Frazier (ed.), *The Underside of American History: Other Readings, Vol. II: Since 1865* (New York: Harcourt and Brace, 1971), p. 165.

18. Johnson, Embree, and Alexander, *The Collapse of Cotton Tenancy*, p. 11.

19. Charles S. Johnson, *Shadow of the Plantation* (Chicago: University of Chicago Press, 1966), p. 4. Originally published 1934.

20. Hoffsommer, in his study "The AAA and the Cropper," based on interviews undertaken in 1934, and quoted by Johnson (et al.), *The Collapse of Cotton Tenancy*, p. 58.

21. Mandle, *Not Slave, Not Free*, p. 89.

22. *Ibid.*, p. 90.

23. Pete Daniel, *The Shadow of Slavery: Peonage in the South (1901–1969)* (London: University of Illinois Press, 1972), particularly Chs. 8 and 9.

24. I understand "typically" via Engels on "realism" (as mediated through Raymond Williams): "Engels defined 'realism' as 'typical characters in typical situations,' which would pass in a quite ordinary sense, but which in this case has behind it the body of Marxist thinking. . . . For the 'typical,' Soviet theorists tell us, must not be confused with that which is frequently encountered; the truly typical is based on 'comprehension of the laws and perspectives of future social development.' " Raymond Williams, *The Long Revolution* (London: Chatto, 1961), p. 276.

25. Harold D. Woodman, "The Reconstruction of the Cotton Plantation in the New South," collected in Thavolia Glymph and John Kushman (eds.), *Essays on the Postbellum Economy* (Arlington: Texas A & M University Press, 1985), p. 100.

26. Foner, *Reconstruction*, p. 170.

27. *Ibid.*, p. 156.

28. *Ibid.*

29. See Wright, *Old South: New South*, particularly Ch. 4, "Plantation, Farm and Farm Labor in the South," pp. 81–123.

30. Vera Rony, "The Organization of Black and White Farm Workers in the South," collected in Thomas R. Frazier (ed.), *The Underside of American History*, p. 159.

31. Wiener, "Class Structure and Economic Development in the American South, 1865–1955," p. 992.

32. Foner, *Reconstruction*, p. 596.

33. Mandle, *Not Slave, Not Free*, p. 23.

34. *Ibid.*, p. 67.
35. This distinction is borrowed from Stuart Ewen, *Captains of Consciousness: Advertising and the Social Roots of the Consumer* (New York: McGraw-Hill, 1976).
36. For a correlation between the international cotton price and the pattern of spurt and lapse in the southern economy, see Wright, *Old South: New South*, pp. 51–60.
37. Wiener, "Class Structure and Economic Development in the American South, 1865–1955," p. 992.
38. Harold Woodman, "Sequel to Slavery: The New History Views the Post Bellum South," *Journal of Southern History*, vol. 43, no. 4 (Nov. 1977), p. 554.
39. Gerald Jaynes, quoted by Mandle, *Not Slave, Not Free*, p. 21.
40. Jacqueline Jones, "The Political Economy of Sharecropping Families: Blacks and Poor Whites in the Rural South, 1865–1915," collected in Carol Bleser (ed.), *In Joy and Sorrow: Women, Family and Marriage in the Victorian South* (New York: Oxford University Press, 1991), p. 200.
41. Johnson, *Shadow of the Plantation*, p. 127.
42. Tenant immobility was, in part, imposed by the cropper's need to demonstrate creditworthiness to the planter. This required that he cultivate "a reputation for deference"; but because such reputations did not travel far, the cropper had to stay "known" by staying local. Ronald Davis notes that "the average black family moved from place to place, from landlord to landlord, and even from supplier to supplier without even leaving the neighbourhood" (Davis, *Good and Faithful Labor* [Westport, Conn.: Greenwood Press, 1982], p. 179). See also Mandle, *Not Slave, Not Free*, p. 22.
43. Johnson, *Shadow of the Plantation*, p. 104.
44. Foner, *Reconstruction*, p. 604.
45. Wiener, "Class Structure and Economic Development in the American South, 1865–1955," p. 992.
46. Daniel, *The Shadow of Slavery*, p. 11.
47. Woodman, "The Reconstruction of the Cotton Plantation in the New South," collected in Glymph and Kushman (eds.), *Essays on the Postbellum Southern Economy*, p. 97.
48. Barbara Jeanne Fields, "The Advent of Capitalist Agriculture: The New South in a Bourgeois World," collected in Glymph and Kushman (eds.), *Essays on the Postbellum Southern Economy*, p. 84.
49. Jones, "The Political Economy of Sharecropping Families," collected in Carol Bleser (ed.), *In Joy and Sorrow*, p. 200.
50. *Idem.*
51. *Ibid.*, p. 208.
52. Harold Woodman, "How New Was the New South?," *Agricultural History*, vol. 58, Oct. 1984, p. 542.
53. See George B. Tindall, *The Emergence of the New South 1913–1945* (Baton Rouge: Louisiana State University Press, 1967), p. 410.
54. William Faulkner, *Collected Stories of William Faulkner* (New York: Random

House, 1977), p. 9. Subsequent pagination will refer to this edition and will be included in the text.

55. I am reminded of Faulkner's terse summary of *Absalom, Absalom!*, "Roughly the theme is a man who outraged the land, and the land then turned and destroyed the man's family." *Selected Letters of William Faulkner* (ed.) Joseph Blotner (New York: Random House, 1978), pp. 78–9.

56. Hegel, *The Phenomenology of Mind*, Vol. I, p. 187.

57. See Joel Williamson, *The Crucible of Race: Black, White Relations in the American South Since Emancipation* (New York: Oxford University Press, 1984), particularly Ch. 6.

58. Kirby cites a figure of 51 to 52 percent as the black proportion of the population in the plantation districts of Mississippi in 1920. See *Rural Worlds Lost*, Ch. 7.

59. I have done scant justice to the political scope of the story. Ab is first at odds with Harris over a tenant's right to leave a hog unfenced. DeSpain writes into his contract that he must pen the shoat. Faulkner alludes to late-nineteenth-century stock law disputes, whereby tenants struggled to preserve unfenced stock, fenced crops, and common grazing as part of a wider resistance to planter attempts to control labor's relation to its crops, and to circumscribe labor mobility. See Stephen Hahn, *The Roots of Southern Populism: Yeoman Farmers and the Transformation of the Georgia Upcountry, 1850–1890* (New York: Oxford University Press, 1983), particularly pp. 239–68.

60. Colonel Sartoris Snopes appears only in "Barn Burning"; arguably, his name is blotted from the canon because an emphatic severance of its dependent parts mirrors the singularity of southern labor's political circumstances at the close of the 1930s.

61. See Neil R. McMillen, *Dark Journey: Black Mississippians in the Age of Jim Crow* (Champaign: University of Illinois Press, 1989), particularly pp. 257–81.

62. Joseph Conrad, *The Nigger of the Narcissus* (New York: Norton, 1979), p. 1.

63. Billie Holiday first recorded "Strange Fruit" in 1939 for a small label – Commodore – with no southern outlets. The song was later recorded on larger labels during the mid- and late '40s. Lillian Smith's novel *Strange Fruit* (1944) is said to have been inspired by the song. Mary Ellison did the work of detection.

64. V. N. Vološinov, *Marxism and the Philosophy of Language* (New York: Seminar Press, 1973), p. 92.

65. Kirby, *Rural Worlds Lost*, p. 140.

66. Faulkner's biographers are not overly concerned with issues of class. Fredrick Karl draws a distinction between Murry Falkner's "frontier establishments" and Maud Falkner's "genteel joinerism" (*William Faulkner: American Writer* [New York: Widenfeld and Nicolson, 1989], p. 79). More usefully, Joel Williamson details the Falkners' declining position within the Oxford middle class (during William's adolescence) by mea-

suring them against the ascendent Oldhams. Williamson traces the implications of Murry's transition from livery stable career to hardware business and pursues young William's fondness for his paternal grandfather, the banker and local businessman John Falkner (*William Faulkner and Southern History* [New York: Oxford University Press, 1993], pp. 165–74). He notes of the great-grandfather William C. Falkner, "contrary to popular myth, [he] was never a great slaveholding planter. Indeed, he was not a planter at all and never held more than several adult slaves. He had a substantial amount of money to invest in the 1850s, but obviously he chose not to do so in plantations and slaves. . . . He was a town dweller and a town lawyer and businessman who took advantage of such opportunities as came his way and grew to affluence without the benefit of slaves and a plantation.

"Indeed, over the generations, the most ambitious Faulkner men seemed to operate in this mode" (p. 36). Arguably William C. Falkner (great-grandfather), John Falkner (grandfather), and Murry Falkner (father) all prospered, to a greater or lesser degree, by servicing rather than joining the planter class. See also Joseph Blotner, *Faulkner: A Biography*, Vol. 1 (New York: Random House, 1974), pp. 149–52, 186–7.

67. William Faulkner, *Absalom, Absalom!* (New York: Random House, 1990), p. 233. Subsequent pagination will refer to this edition and will be included in the text.

68. For Faulkner's exploration of common use rights in land as opposed to enclosure, see the Mink Snopes/Houston dispute in *The Hamlet* (1940). See also Hahn, *The Roots of Southern Populism*, pp. 239–68.

69. Faulkner, *Collected Stories*, p. 538.

70. Engels, quoted by Williams, *The Long Revolution*, p. 276.

71. Nineteen-thirty-six is also the year of the infamous bruising of Miss Blagden's bottom, a misguided act of planter aggression against a union sympathizer that "more than any other single event . . . made the nation demand action on behalf of sharecroppers." Grubbs, *Cry from the Cotton*, p. 113.

72. Jessica Benjamin, *The Bonds of Love: Psychoanalysis, Feminism and the Problem of Domination* (New York: Pantheon, 1988), p. 39.

73. Williamson, *The Crucible of Race*, p. 499.

74. Cleanth Brooks, *William Faulkner: The Yoknapatawpha Country* (New Haven, Conn.: Yale University Press, 1963), pp. 424–42. For a direct genre descendant, see Dirk Kuyk's "The Fabula of *Absalom, Absalom!*," in his *Sutpen's Design: Interpreting Faulkner's Absalom, Absalom!* (Charlottesville: University Press of Virginia, 1990), pp. 46–60.

75. Gary Stonum, *Faulkner's Career: An Internal Literary History* (Ithaca, N.Y.: Cornell University Press, 1979), p. 145.

76. Donald Kartiganer, *The Fragile Thread: The Meaning of Form in Faulkner's Novels* (Amherst: University of Massachusetts Press, 1979), p. 99.

77. Bernard Radloff, "Dialogue and Insight: The Priority of the Heritage in

Absalom, Absalom!," Mississippi Quarterly, Vol. 42, Part 3, 1989, p. 266. Radloff summarizes the detective work so far undertaken.

78. "There is no direct evidence in the novel that Rosa ever knows Bon is a 'Negro,' but then there is no direct evidence that Quentin does either, as his peculiar testimony is assumed to be conclusive, at least to the extent that nearly all readers of the novel take it for granted." Sundquist, *Faulkner: The House Divided*, p. 112.

79. The eye for anagram is not mine but John Matthews', who pointed out the Pettibone play during a generous and extended response to my *Absalom, Absalom!* materials.

80. See Eugene Genovese, *Roll Jordan Roll: The World the Slaves Made* (New York: Random House, 1976), p. 437.

81. Fuller quotation yields the date: "He had filled out physically from what he had been not only when he first rode into Jefferson that Sunday in '33, but from what he had been when he and Ellen married. He was not portly yet, though he was now getting on toward fifty-five. The fat, the stomach, came later. It came upon him suddenly, all at once, in the year after whatever it was happened to his engagement to Miss Rosa" (p. 63).

82. The idea of "designification" comes from David Marriot's "L.A.N.G.U.A.G.E. Writing: Fetishism and Disavowal," a paper given at the conference "Writing at the Limits: The Poetics and Politics of Recent American Poetries," University of Southampton, May 1994.

83. Benjamin, *Illuminations*, p. 264.

84. *Ibid.*, p. 265.

85. *Idem.*

86. *Idem.*

87. For "the word with a loophole," see Mikhail Bakhtin, *Problems of Dostoevsky's Poetics* (New York: Ardis, 1973), p. 195.

88. For Toussaint L'Ouverture's conscious debt to French Revolutionary ideas and practices, see C.L.R. James, *The Black Jacobins* (London: Allison and Busby, 1982).

89. See Richard Godden, "Edgar Allan Poe and the Detection of Riot," *Literature and History*, Vol. 8, No. 2, Autumn 1982, pp. 206–31.

90. Mr. Compson comes up with a duel barely proposed in New Orleans in 1860, and deferred for a probationary period, during which Bon will set aside his octoroon wife in order to gain legitimated access to Judith. In the absence of the repudiation, or so Mr. Compson's story goes, Henry kills Bon in 1865, and the duel is completed.

91. Peter Nicholls, "The Belated Postmodern: History, Phantoms, and Toni Morrison," *Borderlines*, Vol. 1, No. 3 (March 1994), p. 197.

92. Lacan, quoted by Forrester, *The Seductions of Psychoanalysis*, p. 213. It may be noticed that I have turned Freud and Lacan on their heads to achieve this form of words.

93. I am aware that I beg a whole set of theoretical problems with my appeal to an integral subject. Philip Weinstein's *Faulkner's Subject: A Cosmos No*

One Owns (Cambridge: Cambridge University Press, 1992) makes a sustained case for the prevalence of "splintered . . . subjectivity" in Faulkner's work (p. 2). His case rests on Derridean linguistic assumptions lodged within an essentially Lacanian model of the subject. Consequently, he is unwilling to ground subject division in material circumstances beyond either discourse (pp. 6–9) or psychoanalytic "ordeal" (p. 82). I could not agree more as to the divided nature of the Faulknerian subject. I could not agree less as to the source of division. Here is Weinstein on Sutpen: "Sutpen becomes available for representation as a dijin, an explorer, a gambler, an Agamemnon, a Faust: any role imaginable so long as it may be mythic, larger than life, transcending the confines of class, time and region" (p. 138).

94. Maurice Blanchot, *The Writing of Disaster* (Lincoln: University of Nebraska Press, 1986), p. 18.

95. Emmanuel Levinas, quoted by Blanchot, *idem.*

96. I am using the epithet "dark" in summation of my argument that the Italian girl takes over from Deacon as Quentin's "shadow" in *The Sound and the Fury.*

97. My somewhat gnomic utterance conflates various references to mirrors, water, shadows on water, and eyes rising through water, which run through the Quentin section of the novel.

98. Kartiganer, *The Fragile Thread*, pp. 101–2.

99. While talking at the University of Virginia, Faulkner linked the different accounts of Sutpen given in *Absalom, Absalom!* to Wallace Stevens' poem "Thirteen Ways of Looking at a Blackbird," his point being that each version has its illuminations and that together they form a relativistic sequence. His comment has been grist to a scholastic mill that predominantly reads the novel as an exercise in narrativist historiography. See *Faulkner in the University*, eds. Frederick Gwynn and Joseph Blotner (New York: Random House, 1959), pp. 273–5.

100. Kartiganer, *The Fragile Thread*, p. 106.

101. Sundquist, *Faulkner: The House Divided*, pp. 124–5.

102. *Ibid.*, p. 130.

103. The first page of the surviving holograph manuscript is dated September 13, 1937. See William Faulkner, *Helen: A Courtship and Mississippi Poems* (Oxford, Miss., and New Orleans: Yoknapatawpha Press and Tulane University, 1981), introduction by Carvel Collins, pp. 88–9.

104. William Faulkner, *The Wild Palms* (New York: Random House, 1939), p. 209.

105. Theodor Adorno, quoted by Pamela Rhodes and Richard Godden, "*The Wild Palms:* Faulkner's Hollywood Novel," *Amerikastudien*, Vol. 28, No. 4 (1983), p. 1.

106. Williamson, *The Crucible of Race*, p. 499.

107. See sections VI–VII of Benjamin's "Theses on Philosophy of History," in his *Illuminations*, pp. 258–9.

108. Eric Santner, *Stranded Objects: Mourning, Memory and Film in Postwar Ger-*

many (Ithaca, N.Y.: Cornell University Press, 1990). Santner's discussion of the problems involved in "recollecting a cultural identity out of the stranded objects of a poisoned past" (p. 146) was particularly helpful, as was his notion of "an archive of symptoms and parapraxes" as a potential source for a lost legacy of social forms (pp. 152–3).

109. Kirby, *Rural Worlds Lost*, p. 51.
110. My dates are those of the first Agricultural Adjustment Program (inaugurated by the first Agricultural Adjustment Act [1933] and closed by the second [1938]). Although federal programs – their emphasis much changed by war – continued to have considerable effect on southern agriculture, the shock of their impact was felt most fully during their initial years. For details, see Murray R. Benedict, *Farm Policies of the United States, 1930–1950: A Study of Their Origins and Development* (New York: The Twentieth Century Fund, 1953), pp. 276–430.
111. Kirby, *Rural Worlds Lost*, p.133.
112. *Ibid.*, p. 338.
113. Tushnet, *The American Law of Slavery*, p. 6.
114. See Joseph Blotner, *Faulkner: A Biography* (Vol. 2) (New York: Random House, 1974), pp. 920–7.
115. By having Quentin remember his encounter with Henry from his own bed (indeed from two beds, one in Harvard and the other in Jefferson), Faulkner encourages readers to confuse those beds with the bed in the Hundred. As he recalls his entry into Henry's room, Quentin, prostrate in the combined darknesses of 1909 and 1910, wonders, " 'I have been asleep' it was all the same, there was no difference" (p. 298). On entry, punctuation permits an elision of bodies, and the repeated "waking or sleeping it was the same" positively requires a shared insomnia: "waking or sleeping he walked down that upper hall between the scaling walls and beneath the cracked ceiling, toward the faint light which fell outward from the last door and paused there, saying 'No. No' and then 'Only I must. I have to' and went in, entered the bare stale room whose shutters were closed too, where a second lamp burned dimly on a crude table; waking or sleeping it was the same: the bed, the yellow sheets and pillow, the wasted yellow face with closed, almost transparent eyelids on the pillow, the wasted hands crossed on the breast as if he were already a corpse; waking or sleeping it was the same and would be the same forever as long as he lived" (p. 298). To whom does the final use of the personal pronoun refer?
116. Benjamin, *The Bonds of Love*, p. 56.
117. *Ibid.*, p. 61.
118. *Ibid.*, p. 72.
119. *Ibid.*, p. 64.
120. In many senses Judith's life starts *after* Bon's death, in terms of its range of achievement. I mean revenant status to apply only to her genealogical function.

121. The relevant passage is explicit, *"Dont you pass the shadow of this post, this branch, Charles;* and *I am going to pass it, Henry"* (p. 106).

122. II *Samuel,* Ch. 18, v. 33.

123. See Richard Moreland, *Faulkner and Modernism: Rereading and Rewriting* (Madison: University of Wisconsin Press, 1990), pp. 23–78.

124. Herman Melville, "Benito Cereno," collected in his *Billy Budd and Other Tales* (New York: Signet, 1961), p. 222.

125. George Washington Cable, *The Grandissimes* (Athens: University of Georgia Press, 1988), pp. 155–6.

126. In Mississippi, with one-third of the white men of military age killed or crippled, one-fifth of the state's revenue in 1866 was spent on artificial limbs for war amputees. See L. Connelly and B. L. Bellows, *God and General Longstreet: The Lost Cause and the Southern Mind* (Baton Rouge: Louisiana State University Press, 1982), p. 8.

127. This sentence derives from John Matthews' commentary on these materials at manuscript stage.

128. David Krause, "Reading Bon's Letter and Faulkner's *Absalom, Absalom!"* (*PMLA* 99, 1984), p. 238.

129. Judith Wittenberg, *Faulkner: The Transfiguration of Biography* (Lincoln: University of Nebraska Press, 1979), p. 154.

130. Arthur Kinney, *Faulkner's Narrative Poetics: Style as Vision* (Amherst: University of Massachusettss Press, 1978), p. 202.

131. He knows, some ten pages before Shreve's redisposition of the bodies, "Shreve and Quentin" hypothesize a meeting between Bon, Henry, and Eulalia in New Orleans; the parenthetical terms in which Eulalia is described are ethnically marked, as though realizing the implication of the conjoined clues "Haiti" and "Spaniard": "– four of them who sat in that drawing room of baroque and fusty magnificence which Shreve had invented and which was probably true enough, while the Haiti-born daughter of the French sugar planter and the woman who Sutpen's first father-in-law had told him was a Spaniard (the slightly dowdy woman with untidy gray-streaked raven hair coarse as a horse's tail, with parchment-colored skin and implacable pouched black eyes which alone showed no age because they showed no forgetting, whom Shreve and Quentin had likewise invented and which was likewise probably true enough)" (p. 268). I offer this example to indicate that Shreve's earlier preoccupation (in triplicate) with *"whatever it was in . . .* [Eulalias's] *blood that he* [Sutpen] *could not brook. –* " (p. 257) has come to fruition prior both to Shiloh and to Rosa's face at the door of the Hundred.

132. Jean Laplanche, *New Foundations for Psychoanalysis* (Oxford: Blackwell, 1989), p. 126.

133. Recent critical work "monumentalizes" the voice of the over-narrator. Weinstein argues that Faulkner's voice in *Absalom, Absalom!* "signs on" to the lost cause at the very moment when "the Southern agrarian myth – more than ever insolvent, more than ever in demand – required defenders." He concludes, "It is satisfying to claim that *Absalom, Absa-*

lom! rehearses antebellum dreams in order to image their revision and to re-enact their collapse. It is more disturbing to suggest that it re-enacts their collapse as the necessary condition for legitimising their passionate rehearsal" (Weinstein, *Faulkner's Subject*, pp. 140–2). However, Stephen Ross points out that the failure of Sutpen's design is also the failure of his (and perhaps of the over-narrator's) linguistic monumentality. Consequently, "evocative as it is, [the] oratorical voice also creates the conditions for [its own] interrogation," and so for the interrogation of that "pressure within the discourse itself to coalesce into a spatial and temporal form that confronts the reader as a *monument* to be contemplated, accepted and appreciated, rather than as a document to be interpreted" (Stephen Ross, *Faulkner's Inexhaustible Voice: Speech and Writing in Faulkner* (Athens: University of Georgia, 1989), pp. 208, 226–9). I am of Ross's oratorical interrogation party and seek only to extend his argument about a prevalent poetics by grounding it in historically generative conditions.

134. Richard Moreland, *Faulkner and Modernism*, p. 114.
135. John T. Matthews, "Shortened Stories: Faulkner and the Market," collected in *Faulkner and the Short Story*, (eds.) E. Harrington and A. A. Abadie (Jackson, Miss.: University Press of Mississippi, 1992), p. 29.
136. Williamson, *The Crucible of Race*, p. 318.
137. See Moreland, *Faulkner and Modernism*, chapter six. Moreland's entire discussion of *Absalom, Absalom!* is among the most persuasive I have read.
138. "Crow" emerges from "Jim Bond" by way of "bond," "constraint," and "Jim Crow." My discussion of this play in *"Absalom, Absalom!*, Haitian and Labor History" provides a fuller account.
139. Edgar Allan Poe, *Selected Writing*, (ed.) David Galloway (Harmondsworth: Penguin Books, 1978), p. 125.
140. *Ibid.*, p. 126.

5. *Forget Jerusalem, Go to Hollywood* – "To Die. Yes. To Die?" (*A Coda to* Absalom, Absalom!)

1. William Faulkner, *The Wild Palms* (New York: Random House, 1939), pp. 323, 324. All references will be to this edition; pagination will be included in the body of the text.
2. William Faulkner, *Absalom, Absalom!* (New York: Random House, 1990), p. 302.
3. Diane Roberts, *Faulkner and Southern Womanhood* (Athens: University of Georgia Press, 1994), p. 208.
4. *Idem.*
5. John N. Duvall, *Faulkner's Marginal Couple: Invisible, Outlaw, and Unspeakable Communities* (Austin: University of Texas Press, 1990), p. 55.
6. Roberts, *Faulkner and Southern Womanhood*, p. 205.
7. Duvall, *Faulkner's Marginal Couple*, p. 51.

8. Gail Mortimer, "The Ironies of Transcendental Love in *The Wild Palms*," *The Faulkner Journal*, Vol.1, No. 2 (Spring 1986), pp. 30-42.

9. Minrose C. Gwin, *The Feminine and Faulkner: Reading (Beyond) Sexual Difference* (Knoxville: University of Tennessee Press, 1990), pp. 148-52.

10. Roberts, *Faulkner and Southern Womanhood*, p. 212.

11. Faulkner began writing *Absalom, Absalom!* early in 1934. In February of that year he flew to New Orleans for the dedication of the Shushan Airport, which provided him with material for *Pylon*. *Pylon* was published in March 1935, while Faulkner was working on *Absalom, Absalom!*, which was completed in January and published in October 1936. The chronology of writing establishes that *Pylon* may be considered as a midpoint between what appear to be two later texts.

12. The Reporter's first appearance is typical, "the two men . . . were now looking at something which had apparently crept from a doctor's cupboard and, in the snatched garments of an etherized patient in a charity ward, escaped into the living world. He [Jiggs] saw a creature which, erect, would be better than six feet tall and which would weigh about ninetyfive pounds, in a suit of no age nor color, as though made of air and doped like an aeroplane wing with the incrusted excretion of all articulate life's contact with the passing earth, which ballooned light and impedimentless about a skeleton frame as though suit and wearer both hung from a flapping clothesline" (William Faulkner, *Pylon* [New York: Random House, 1985], p. 17).

13. Faulkner, *Absalom, Absalom!*, p. 189.

14. François Pitavy, "Forgetting Jerusalem: An Ironical Chart for *The Wild Palms*," collected in Michel Gresset and Noel Polk (eds.), *Intertextuality in Faulkner* (Jackson: University of Mississippi Press, 1985), p. 122.

15. Jones, " 'The Kotex Age': Women, Popular Culture and *The Wild Palms*," collected in Doreen Fowler and Ann Abadie (eds.), *Faulkner and Popular Culture* (Jacksonville: University Press of Mississippi, 1990), p. 156.

16. Anne Goodwyn Jones's perceptive argument suffers from an implicit and ahistorical universalization of male fears and assumptions, though this is a tendency indulged by her theoretical source, Klaus Theweleit, *Male Fantasies, Vol. 1: Women, Floods, Bodies, History* (Minneapolis: University of Minnesota Press, 1988), pp. 283-99. See Jones, " 'The Kotex Age': Women, Popular Culture and *The Wild Palms*," *Faulkner & Popular Culture*, pp. 142-62.

17. Jones, " 'The Kotex Age': Women, Popular Culture and *The Wild Palms*," p. 145. See also Duvall, *Faulkner's Marginal Couple*, p. 55.

18. Jessica Benjamin, *The Bonds of Love: Psychoanalysis, Feminism and the Problem of Domination* (New York: Pantheon, 1988), p. 56.

19. *Ibid.*, p. 61.

20. *Ibid.*, p. 52.

21. James Oakes, *Slavery and Freedom: An Interpretation of the Old South* (New York: Knopf, 1990), p. 4.

22. William Shakespeare, *Hamlet*, Act III, Sc. 1.

23. Orlando Patterson, *Slavery and Social Death: A Comparative Study* (Cambridge, Mass.: Harvard University Press, 1982), p. 8.

24. Those who cast Harry's phallus and scalpel as irrepressible evidence of a resurgent patriarchy ignore the degree to which Harry escapes the dead hand of a poisoned and dying father and is reborn, precisely because Charlotte disabuses him of the need to extend the life of the father by living it again.

25. Benjamin, *The Bonds of Love*, p. 67.

26. Charles Hannon, "Signification, Simulation and Containment in *If I Forget Thee, Jerusalem*," *The Faulkner Journal*, Vol. 7, Nos. 1 & 2 (Fall 1991), p. 139.

27. Gwin, *The Feminine and Faulkner*, p. 132.

28. Roberts, *Faulkner and Southern Womanhood*, p. 207; Jones, " 'The Kotex Age': Women, Popular Culture and *The Wild Palms*," pp. 157–9.

29. Esther Rashkin, "Tools for a New Psychoanalytic Literary Criticism: The Work of Abraham and Torok," *Diacritics* (Winter 1988), p. 37.

30. Nicolas Abraham and Maria Torok, "Notes on the Phantom: A Complement to Freud's Metapsychology," collected in *The Shell and the Kernel*, Vol. 1 (Chicago: University of Chicago Press, 1994), p. 173.

31. Abraham and Torok, "The Story of Fear: The Symptoms of Phobia – the Return of the Repressed or the Return of the Phantom?," in *The Shell and the Kernel*, p. 181.

32. Nicholas T. Rand, "Introduction: Renewals of Psychoanalysis," prefatory to *The Shell and the Kernel*, p. 22.

33. Rashkin, "Tools for a New Psychoanalytic Literary Criticism," p. 40.

34. *Idem.*

35. See particularly Abraham & Torok, "The Illness of Mourning and the Fantasy of the Exquisite Corpse" and "Mourning or Melancholia: Introjection *versus* Incorporation," collected in *The Shell and the Kernel*, pp. 107–38.

36. Rand, "Introduction," p. 21.

37. Modern Biblical scholarship challenges the tradition that addressed the *Psalms* as a whole as the work of David. Nonetheless, the most fruitful period of psalmody is recognized to be that of the Davidic monarchy. John H. Eaton comments, "It is interesting that some modern scholars have thought that the worshipper in many of the Psalms uttered by an individual is a king, and that in addition to the Psalms sung by or for a king at the grand ceremonies . . . there are many arising from particular royal crises – sickness, invasion, conspiracies. . . . In some of these cases it could be that the king was David himself." *The Psalms Come Alive* (London: Mowbray, 1984), pp. 41–2. See also Eaton, *Kingship and the Psalms* (Sheffield: JSOT Press, 1986), pp. 1–26.

38. For a perceptive summation of Faulkner's tangled sexual life just prior to his work on *If I Forget Thee, Jerusalem*, see Richard Gray, *The Life of William Faulkner: A Critical Biography* (Oxford: Blackwell, 1994), pp. 239–42.

39. Pitavy, "Forgetting Jerusalem: An Ironical Chart for *The Wild Palms*," p. 118.
40. Gray, *The Life of William Faulkner*, p. 240.
41. The first page of the surviving holograph manuscript is dated September 13, 1937. See William Faulkner, *Helen: A Courtship and Mississippi Poems* (Oxford, Miss., and New Orleans: Yorknapatawpha Press and Tulane University, 1981), introduction by Carvell Collins, pp. 88–9. Also Joseph Blotner, *Faulkner: A Biography* (Vol. 2) (New York: Random House, 1974), p. 995.
42. Blotner, *Faulkner*, pp. 943–7.
43. William Faulkner, *Selected Letters of William Faulkner*, ed. Joseph Blotner (New York: Random House, 1977), p. 106. When speaking of the novel as a whole, I have used Faulkner's chosen title, *If I Forget Thee, Jerusalem*, in keeping with usage adopted by *William Faulkner: Novels 1936–1940* (New York: Library of America, 1990).
44. See Blotner, *Faulkner: A Biography* (Vol. 2), p. 1002.
45. The manifest anxiety over masculinity exhibited by "Wild Palms" could, without its "shadow" text, be read as typical of a more general and cultural sense of diminished manhood. See Barbara Melosh, *Engendering Culture: Manhood and New Deal Public Art & Theatre* (Washington: Smithsonian Institute, 1991), particularly pp. 15–31, 83–109.
46. Susan Willis, "Aesthetics of the Rural Slum: Contradictions and Dependency in 'The Bear,' " *Social Text*, Vol. 1, No. 2 (Summer 1979), p. 100. Willis's essay remains the exemplary Marxist study of the relationship between a Faulknerian text and its determining historical context.
47. See Edmund Leach, "Virgin Birth," collected in his *Genesis as Myth and Other Essays* (London: Cape, 1969), pp. 85–112.
48. *The Unvanquished* was published in 1938 (written and assembled from 1934 to 1938) and therefore stands between *Absalom, Absalom!* and *If I Forget Thee, Jerusalem*. However, the sustained affinities between Quentin and Harry indicate that *Absalom* and *If I Forget* are the more intimately related texts. Indeed, reacting to a suggestion that *The Sound and the Fury* and *As I Lay Dying* be published in a joint edition, Faulkner objected, proposing instead (to Robert N. Linscott, 13 March 1946), "I would like to see TSAF and THE WILD PALMS section from that book, the part of it about the doctor who performed the abortion on his own sweetheart [together]" (*Selected Letters of William Faulkner*, ed. Blotner, p. 228). For a full account of the parallels between the Quentin section of *The Sound and the Fury* and "Wild Palms," see Gary Harrington, "Distant Mirrors: The Intertextual Relationship of Quentin Compson and Harry Wilbourne," *The Faulkner Journal*, Vol. 1, No. 1 (Fall 1985), pp. 41–5, and his *Faulkner's Fables of Creativity: The Non-Yoknapatawpha Novels* (Athens: University of Georgia Press, 1990), pp. 87–90.
49. Cheryl Lester argues that, "As the perpetrators of racialized injustice . . . white Southerners were reluctant to speak of it. The reluctance to acknowledge their role in encouraging black migration produced a re-

sponse to migration and its roots in Southern racialism characterized by silence, indirection, contradiction and denial. . . . Faulkner's writings consistently illustrate yet also struggle against this culturally constructed denial, in order to articulate a critique of Southern racialism and the construction of racialized subjects." Lester, "Racial Awareness and Arrested Development: *The Sound and the Fury* and the Great Migration (1915–1918)," collected in *The Cambridge Companion to William Faulkner*, ed. Philip M. Weinstein (Cambridge: Cambridge University Press, 1995), pp. 133–4.

50. *Ibid.*, pp. 136, 129–32.

51. I borrow the phrase from one of Abraham and Torok's essays, "The Illness of Mourning and the Fantasy of the Exquisite Corpse," collected in *The Shell and the Kernel*, pp. 107–24.

52. *Ibid.*, p. 102.

53. Richard Gray is the exception, though his reference is to a literary rather than a biographical connection. See Gray, *The Life of William Faulkner*, p. 243.

54. Tom Dardis, *Some Time in the Sun* (London: André Deutsch, 1976), pp. 111, 189. Blotner, *A Biography* (Vol. 2), p. 934, also mentions the bookstore, but not McCoy, whom Dardis places, without comment, in a general list of persons Faulkner may have heard there.

55. Joseph Blotner, *William Faulkner's Library – A Catalogue* (Charlottesville: University Press of Virginia, 1964), p. 41.

56. James M. Cain, *The Postman Always Rings Twice* (Harmondsworth: Penguin, 1954), p. 120.

57. Nathanael West, *The Day of the Locust* (New York: New Directions, 1950), p. 167. For further examples of voices stultified by Hollywood, see Horace McCoy's *I Should Have Stayed Home* (1938), where the motif is used extensively.

58. Joyce Carol Oates, "Man Under Sentence of Death: The Novels of James M. Cain," collected in *Tough Guy Writers of the Thirties*, ed. David Madden (Carbondale: Southern Illinois University Press, 1968), p. 124.

59. Horace McCoy, *They Shoot Horses, Don't They?* (Harmondsworth: Penguin, 1970), p. 5. All references will be to this edition; pagination will be included in the body of the text.

60. Georg Lukács, *History and Class Consciousness* (London: Merlin Press, 1968), p. 84.

61. Faulkner wrote *If I Forget Thee, Jerusalem* between 1937 and 1938. I list some of the more significant pieces of cultural analysis from the Frankfurt School, choosing those that are most nearly the novel's contemporaries. Herbert Marcuse, "The Affirmative Character of Culture" (1937), in *Negations* (London: Penguin, 1968); T. W. Adorno, "On the Fetish-Character in Music and the Regression of Listening" (1938), in *The Essential Frankfurt School Reader*, eds. A. Arato and E. Gebhardt (New York: Urizen Books, 1978); T. W. Adorno, "On Popular Music," *Studies in Philosophy and Social Science*, Vol. 9, No. 1 (1941); T. W. Adorno and

Max Horkheimer, *Dialectic of Enlightenment*, first published in 1947, but collaborated on in Hollywood and New York during the '40s. See also Pamela Rhodes and Richard Godden, "*The Wild Palms*: Faulkner's Hollywood Novel (A Frankfurt School Reading)," *Essays in Poetics*, Vol. 10, No. 1 (1985), pp. 1, 49. More recently, and more optimistically, John Matthews has applied a Frankfurt School perspective to Faulkner's work as a scriptwriter and to his understanding of the relation between high and low culture; see Matthews, "Faulkner and the Culture Industry," collected in *The Cambridge Companion to William Faulkner*, ed. Philip M. Weinstein, pp. 51–74.

62. Faulkner used the phrase in a letter to Morton Goldman (probably June 1936); see *Selected Letters*, ed. Blotner, p. 96. See also Jones, " 'The Kotex Age': Women, Popular Culture and *The Wild Palms*," pp. 142–62; Gray, *The Life of William Faulkner*, pp. 239–53; Hannon, "Signification, Simulation and Containment in *If I Forget Thee, Jerusalem*," pp. 133–50.

63. Quoted by Roland Marchand, *Advertising the American Dream: Making Way for Modernity, 1920–1940* (Los Angeles: University of California Press, 1985), p. 66.

64. I take the term from the title of Christine Frederick's study of advertising, *Selling Mrs. Consumer* (1929).

65. W. F. Haug, *Critique of Commodity Aesthetics: Appearance, Sexuality and Advertising in Capitalist Society* (Oxford: Polity Press, 1986), p. 16.

66. Adorno, "On the Fetish-Character in Music and the Regression of Listening," *The Essential Frankfurt School Reader*, p. 273.

67. Haug, *Critique of Commodity Aesthetics*, p. 17. The terms used in the preceding discussion of Haug's work are all taken from pp. 1–16 of *Critique*.

68. Fredric Jameson, *Marxism and Form* (Princeton, N.J.: Princeton University Press, 1971), p. 96.

69. See Jean Baudrillard, *For a Critique of the Political Economy of the Sign* (St. Louis: Telos, 1981), and Richard Godden, *Fictions of Capital* (Cambridge: Cambridge University Press, 1990), pp. 4–5.

70. Fredric Jameson, *Fables of Aggression* (Berkeley: University of California Press, 1979), p. 73.

71. The most extensive account of intertextuality in the novel is to be found in Thomas L. McHaney, *William Faulkner's The Wild Palms* (Jackson: University Press of Mississippi, 1975). McHaney seeks to stabilize intertextual plurality by appealing to Schopenhauer's systems; he also deploys Jung to fix parodic deferrals. See also Rhodes and Godden, "*The Wild Palms*: Faulkner's Hollywood Novel," pp. 7–8, 34–6; and Gray, *The Life of William Faulkner*, pp. 243–7, for attempts to trace the meaning of the form itself, rather than to find meaning among the textual interstices.

72. Harry can analyze the shape of his general economic situation clearly. His protest that he and Charlotte are "robots" (p. 129) has perhaps lost some of its force, but, as a comparatively new coinage, in 1937 it might have struck the ear more freshly, and his use of the word indicates

that he understands his own ailment. In a letter to Lowenthal, Horkheimer wrote, "The mechanisms which govern man in his leisure time
are absolutely the same [as] those which govern him when he works. . . .
Consumption tends to vanish today, or should I say, eating, drinking,
looking, loving, sleeping become 'consumption,' for consumption already means that man has become a machine outside as well as inside
the workshop" (California, 1942, cited in Martin Jay, *The Dialectical Imagination* [Boston: Little, Brown, 1973], pp. 213–14). Harry, who is no
Critical Theorist, offers a similar analysis. As a robot, his body has become a mere extension of the machine, and the functions of living are
reduced to restoking it with further inputs of energy, which will be converted directly back into labor; as he tells Charlotte, ". . . and when we
eat together its in a crowded restaurant inside a vacant hour they allow
you from the store so you can eat and stay strong so they can get the
value of the money they pay you every Saturday. . . ." (p. 127).

73. My reading of Charlotte's figures relies heavily on Hannon, "Signification, Simulation and Containment in *If I Forget Thee, Jerusalem*," p. 144. I
would add that Charlotte's fall into promotional art serves also to display
Faulkner's own problems as a producer for the market. Indeed, Faulkner
introduces himself into the narrative via his choice of the term "marionettes" for Charlotte's second range of figures. As a young man Faulkner
had written out in meticulous hand six copies of *The Marionettes*, which he
now recasts as puppets "almost as large as small children" (p. 91), already
blasted with syphilis, and being bred for magazine covers.

74. T. W. Adorno, *Minima Moralia: Reflections from Damaged Life* (London:
New Left Books, 1974), p. 235.

75. The phrase belongs to Marchand, *Advertising the American Dream*, p. xviii.

76. Haug, *Critique of Commodity Aesthetics*, p. 50.

77. Guy Debord's notion of the "society of spectacle" is useful here. Debord argues that "the spectacle is *capital* to such a degree of accumulation that it becomes an image." Debord's notion is merely as gnomic
as the history that it compresses; to unpack – "degree of accumulation" refers to corporate capital's growing difficulty over the quick realization of surplus value. Only if a product can be promoted can it be
sold with seemly haste, therefore its image is of its essence. Labor and
price are secondary considerations; like money before it, the capacity
to be imaged (advertised) has become a form of equivalence essential
to sociability. See Debord, *Society of the Spectacle* (Detroit: Black & Red,
1973), subsection 49.

78. Susan Porter Benson, "Palace of Consumption and Machine for Selling:
The American Department Store, 1880–1940," *Radical History Review*,
No. 12 (Fall 1979), p. 203.

79. William R. Leach, "Transformation in a Culture of Consumption:
Women & Department Stores, 1890–1925," *The Journal of American History*, Vol. 71, No. 2 (Sept. 1984), p. 322.

80. Haug, *Critique of Commodity Aesthetics*, p. 69.

81. Advertising images of the period frequently featured mirrors whose presence prompted anxiety, as the consumer (most typically a woman) checked her appearance to measure it against an ideal impression promised via the purchase of a particular product. See Marchand, *Advertising the American Dream*, p. 15, and Stuart Ewen, *Captains of Consciousness: Advertising and the Social Roots of Consumer Culture* (New York: McGraw-Hill, 1976), pp. 92–102.

82. Alfred Sohn-Rethel, *Intellectual and Manual Labor: A Critique of Epistemology* (London: Macmillan, 1978), p. 25.

83. Quoted by Ewen, *Captains of Consciousness*, p. 80.

84. West, *Day of the Locust*, p. 157.

85. Haug argues for a general "sexualization" of commodity: "by taking on sexuality as an assistant, exchange value transforms itself into sexuality" and "the background of sexual enjoyment becomes the commodity's most popular attire." See Haug, *Commodity Aesthetics*, p. 56; see also Ch. 2, pp. 45–87.

86. "To tell the story I wanted to tell, which was the one of the intern and the woman who gave up her family and husband to run off with him. To tell it like that, somehow or another I had to discover counterpoint for it, so I invented the other story, its complete antithesis, to use as counterpoint." William Faulkner, *Lion in the Garden*, eds. James B. Meriwether and Michael Millgate (New York: Random House, 1968), p. 132; see also pp. 54, 247; and *Faulkner in the University*, eds. F. L. Gwynn and L. L. Blotner (New York: Random House, 1959), p. 179.

87. See Zoltán Tar, *The Frankfurt School* (New York: Wiley, 1977), pp. 87–9, for a summary of the thesis.

88. The references are to: Cleanth Brooks, *William Faulkner: Toward Yoknapatawpha and Beyond* (London: Yale, 1978), p. 229; Panthea Reid Broughton, *William Faulkner: The Abstract and the Actual* (Baton Rouge: Louisiana State University Press, 1974), p. 169; and Harrington, *Fables of Creativity*, pp. 83–6.

89. Faulkner, *Faulkner in the University*, p. 179.

90. See Hannon, "Signification, Simulation and Containment in *If I Forget Thee, Jerusalem*," p. 148.

91. Adorno, *Minima Moralia*, p. 166.

92. Joseph Moldenhauer, "Unity of Theme and Structure in *The Wild Palms*," collected in *William Faulkner: Three Decades of Criticism*, eds. F. J. Hoffman and O. L. Vickery (New York: Harcourt Brace, 1963), p. 311.

93. The references are to Brooks, *William Faulkner*, p. 228; Harrington, *Fables of Creativity*, pp. 85, 87; and Broughton, *William Faulkner*, p. 169.

94. Adorno and Horkheimer, *Dialectic of Enlightenment*, pp. 151, 153.

95. Fredric Jameson, "Postmodernism, or 'The Cultural Logic of Late Capitalism,'" *New Left Review*, No. 146 (July–August, 1984), p. 55.

96. Theodor Adorno, quoted by Pamela Rhodes and Richard Godden, "*The Wild Palms*: Faulkner's Hollywood Novel," *Amerikastudien*, Vol. 28, No. 4 (1983), p. 1.

97. Jean-François Lyotord, *The Postmodern Condition: A Report on Knowledge* (Manchester: Manchester University Press, 1979), p. xxiv.

98. For an exploration of Faulkner's early recognition of the harbingers of modernization, see John T. Matthews, *"As I Lay Dying* in the Machine Age," *Boundary 2*, Vol. 19, No. 1 (Spring 1992), pp. 69–94. My point remains that without a structural change at a regional level, capable of generating not only generalized wage labor but also higher wages than had been typical until the late '30s, the presence of consumer items and attitudes in the South is neither typical nor representative.

99. Places of labor are characteristically labeled as orifices, gutters, or chutes that discharge workers; those discharged are "never actually see[n]" (p. 130), or are seen, care of Harry, distorted into "giants" (p. 186), or into untiring machines with "piston-like legs" (p. 199). In dividing itself from its own dirt, the body aspires, like the department store, to be organless, glittering and unchangeable, forbidding awareness of the totality, which would demand alteration.

100. See note 42, Ch. 4.

101. Paul Ricoeur, *Time and Narrative: Volume 1* (Chicago: University of Chicago Press, 1984), p. 75.

102. The existence of the South as a low-wage economy was not finally broken until the 1940s. See Gavin Wright, *Old South, New South* (New York: Basic Books, 1986), particularly pp. 198–238.

103. Karl Marx, *Capital Vol. 1* (London: Dent, 1951), p. 50.

104. Jameson, *Marxism and Form*, p. 96.

105. Lukács, *History and Class Consciousness*, p. 76.

106. Edwin Berry Burgum, *New Masses*, Feb. 7, 1939, pp. 23–4.

107. Lukács, *History and Class Consciousness*, pp. 76–7.

108. Adorno, *Minima Moralia*, p. 227.

109. Cited by Lukács, *History and Class Consciousness*, p. 171.

110. See Olga Vickery, *The Novels of William Faulkner* (Baton Rouge: Louisiana State University Press, 1961), pp. 158–60; and Arthur F. Kinney, *Faulkner's Narrative Poetics* (Amherst: University of Massachusetts Press, 1978), pp. 79–80.

111. See Harold D. Woodman, "Post Civil War Agriculture and the Law," *Agricultural History*, Vol. 53, 1979, pp. 319–37.

112. See, particularly, Edward H. Richardson, "The 'Hemingwaves' in Faulkner's 'Wild Palms,' " *Modern Fiction Studies*, 4 (Winter 1959), pp. 357–60; and McHaney, *William Faulkner's "The Wild Palms,"* pp. 12–13.

113. John Crowe Ransom, "Land!," *Harper's*, 145 (July 1932), p. 222. See also Ransom, "The Aesthetic of Regionalism," *American Review*, Vol. 2 (January 1934), pp. 290–310; and Alexander Karinikas, *Tillers of Myth* (Madison: University of Wisconsin Press, 1966), Ch. 3.

114. See, particularly, John Feaster, "Faulkner's 'Old Man': A Psychoanalytic Approach," *Modern Fiction Studies*, Vol. 13, No. 1 (Spring 1967), pp. 92–3.

115. Lukács, *History and Class Consciousness*, pp. 163–4.

116. At this point I am paraphrasing Jameson, *Marxism and Form*, p. 311, and am more generally indebted to Ch. 5.
117. The division is reinforced by the temporal separation of the sections. McHaney claims that the "physical evidence" in the manuscript shows that Faulkner had originally planned to set both halves in 1927. See McHaney, *William Faulkner's "The Wild Palms,"* p. 38.

Afterword

1. William Faulkner, *The Hamlet* (London: Chatto & Windus, 1979), p. 5.
2. Susan Willis, "Aesthetics of the Rural Slum: Contradictions and Dependency in 'The Bear,' " *Social Text*, Vol. 1, No. 2 (Summer, 1979), p. 100.
3. Richard Godden, *Fictions of Capital* (Cambridge: Cambridge University Press, 1990), pp. 154–61, and "The Authorship of William Faulkner: An Under-Authorized Version," *The Mississippi Quarterly*, Vol. XLII, No. 3 (Summer 1989), pp. 339–46.

BIBLIOGRAPHY OF WORKS CITED

Abraham, Nicolas, and Torok, Maria. *The Wolf Man's Magic Word: A Cryptonomy*. Minneapolis: University of Minnesota Press, 1986.
The Shell and the Kernel, Vol. 1. Chicago: University of Chicago Press, 1994.
Adorno, Theodor. *Minima Moralia: Reflections from Damaged Life*. London: New Left Books, 1974.
"On the Fetish-Character in Music and the Regression of Listening," in Arato, A., and Gebhart, E. (eds.), *The Essential Frankfurt School Reader* (New York: Urizen Books, 1978), pp. 270–99.
Adorno, Theodor, and Horkheimer, Max. *Dialectic of Enlightenment*. London: Verso, 1979.
Arato, A., and Gebhart, E. (eds.). *The Essential Frankfurt School Reader*. New York: Urizen Books, 1978.
Bakhtin, Mikhail. *Problems of Dostoevsky's Poetics*. New York: Ardis, 1973.
Baudrillard, Jean. *For a Critique of the Political Economy of the Sign*. St. Louis: Telos, 1981.
Benedict, Murray R. *Farm Policies of the United States, 1930–1950: A Study of Their Origins and Development*. New York: The Twentieth Century Fund, 1953.
Benjamin, Jessica. *The Bonds of Love: Feminism and the Problems of Domination*. New York: Pantheon, 1988.
Benjamin, Walter. *Illuminations*. Glasgow: Fontana/Collins, 1977.
One-Way Street and Other Writings. London: New Left Books, 1979.
Benson, Susan Porter. "Palace of Consumption and Machine for Selling: The American Department Store, 1880–1940," *Radical History Review*, No. 21 (Fall 1979), pp. 11–30.
Black, Max. *Models and Metaphors*. Ithaca, N.Y.: Cornell University Press, 1962.
Blanchot, Maurice. *The Writings of Disaster*. Lincoln: University of Nebraska Press, 1986.
Bleikasten, André. *The Most Splendid Failure: Faulkner's The Sound and the Fury*. Bloomington: Indiana University Press, 1976.
"Fathers in Faulkner," in Davis, Robert (ed.), *The Fictional Father: Lacanian*

Readings of the Text (Amherst: University of Massachussetts Press, 1981), pp. 115–46.

Bloom, Harold (ed.). *Modern Critical Interpretations: William Faulkner's Absalom, Absalom!* New York: Chelsea House, 1987.

Blotner, Joseph. *Faulkner: A Biography, Vols. 1 and 2.* New York: Random House, 1974.

Blotner, Joseph (ed.). *William Faulkner's Library: A Catalogue.* Charlottesville: University Press of Virginia, 1964.

Selected Letters of William Faulkner. New York: Random House, 1977.

Brooks, Cleanth. *William Faulkner: The Yoknapatawpha County.* New Haven, Conn.: Yale University Press, 1963.

William Faulkner: Toward Yoknapatawpha and Beyond. New Haven, Conn.: Yale University Press, 1979.

Brooks, Peter. "Incredible Narration: *Absalom, Absalom!*," in Bloom, Harold (ed.), *Modern Critical Interpretations: William Faulkner's Absalom, Absalom!* (New York: Chelsea House, 1987), pp. 105–37.

Broughton, Panthea Reid. *William Faulkner: The Abstracts and the Actual.* Baton Rouge: Louisiana State University Press, 1974.

Burgum, Edwin Berry. "Review, *The Wild Palms.*" *New Masses*, 7 February 1939, pp. 23–4.

Cable, George Washington. *The Grandissimes.* Athens: University of Georgia Press, 1988.

Cain, James M. *The Postman Always Rings Twice.* Harmondsworth: Penguin, 1954.

Carr, E. H. *What Is History?* Harmondsworth: Penguin, 1967.

Cash, W. J. *The Mind of the South.* London: Thames and Hudson, 1971.

Coindreau, Maurice. "Preface to *The Sound and the Fury*," *Mississippi Quarterly*, Vol. 19 (Summer 1966), pp. 107–15.

Coleman, Rosemary. "Family Ties: Generating Narratives in *Absalom, Absalom!*," *Mississippi Quarterly*, Vol. 43, Part 1 (1989), pp. 421–31.

Collins, Carvel. "Faulkner and Mississippi," *University of Mississippi Studies in English*, Vol. 15 (1978), pp. 139–59.

Connelly, L., and Bellows, B. L. *God and General Longstreet: The Lost Cause and the Southern Mind.* Baton Rouge: Louisiana State University Press, 1982.

Conrad, Joseph. *The Nigger of the Narcissus.* New York: Norton, 1979.

Curtin, Philip. *The Atlantic Slave Trade: A Census.* Madison: University of Wisconsin Press, 1969.

Daniel, Pete. *The Shadow of Slavery: Peonage in the South (1901–1969).* London: University of Illinois Press, 1972.

Dardis, Tom. *Some Time in the Sun.* London: André Deutsch, 1976.

Davis, Ronald. *Good and Faithful Labor.* Westport, Conn.: Greenwood Press, 1982.

Davis, Thadious. *Faulkner's Negro: Art and the Southern Context.* Baton Rouge: Louisiana State University Press, 1983.

Debord, Guy. *Society of Spectacle.* Detroit: Red and Black, 1973.

Derrida, Jacques. *Dissemination.* Chicago: University of Chicago Press, 1981.

"Forward: *Fors*: The Anguished Words of Nicolas Abraham and Maria Torok," in Abraham, N., and Torok, M. (eds.), *The Wolf Man's Magic Word: A Cryptonomy* (Minneapolis: University of Minnesota Press, 1986), pp. xl–xlviii.

Memoirs for Paul de Man. New York: Columbia University Press, 1989.

Duvall, John N. *Faulkner's Marginal Couple: Invisible, Outlaw, and Unspeakable Communities.* Austin: University of Texas Press, 1990.

Eaton, John H. *The Psalms Come Alive.* London: Mowbray, 1984.

Kingship and the Psalms. Sheffield: JST Press, 1986.

Ewen, Stuart. *Captains of Consciousness: Advertising and the Social Roots of the Consumer.* New York: McGraw-Hill, 1976.

Faulkner, William. *The Wild Palms.* New York: Random House, 1939.

Dr. Martino and Other Stories. London: Chatto and Windus, 1965.

Flags in the Dust. New York: Random House, 1973.

"An Introduction to *The Sound and the Fury*," *Mississippi Quarterly*, 26 (Summer 1973), pp. 410–15.

The Marionettes. Oxford, Miss.: Yoknapatawpha Press, 1975.

Selected Letters. (ed.) Blotner, Joseph. New York: Random House, 1977.

Collected Stories. New York: Random House, 1977.

Helen: A Courtship and Mississippi Poems. Oxford, Miss., and New Orleans: Yoknapatawpha Press and Tulane University, 1981.

Pylon. New York: Random House, 1985.

The Sound and the Fury. New York: Norton, 1987.

Absalom, Absalom! New York: Random House, 1990.

Fields, Barbara Jeanne. "The Advent of Capitalist Agriculture: The New South in a Bourgeois World," in Glymph, Thavolia, and Kushman, John (eds.), *Essay on the Postbellum Economy* (Arlington: Texas A & M University Press, 1985), pp. 73–94.

Fite, Gilbert. *Cotton Fields No More: Southern Agriculture, 1865–1980.* Lexington: University Press of Kentucky, 1984.

Foner, Eric. *Reconstruction: America's Unfinished Revolution: 1863–1877.* New York: Harper & Row, 1988.

Ford, Lacy K., Jr. *Origins of Southern Radicalism: The South Carolina Upcountry, 1800–1860.* New York: Oxford University Press, 1988.

Forrester, John. *The Seduction of Psychoanalysis: Freud, Lacan and Derrida.* Cambridge: Cambridge University Press, 1990.

Fowler, Doreen, and Abadie, Ann J. (eds.). *Faulkner and Popular Culture.* Jackson: University Press of Mississippi, 1990.

Fox-Genovese, Elizabeth. *Within the Plantation Household: Black and White Women in the Old South.* Chapel Hill: University of North Carolina Press, 1988.

Franklin, John Hope. *From Slavery to Freedom.* New York: Knopf, 1980.

Freehling, Alison Goodyear. *Drift Toward Dissolution: The Virginia Slavery Debate of 1831–1836.* Baton Rouge: Louisiana State University Press, 1982.

Freehling, William. *Prelude to Civil War: The Nullification Controversy in South Carolina, 1816–1836.* New York: Harper & Row, 1969.

Freud, Sigmund. *The Standard Edition of the Complete Works of Sigmund Freud,* Vol. *17.* London: Hogarth, 1955.

Frey, Sylvia. *Water from the Rock: Black Resistance in a Revolutionary Age.* Princeton, N.J.: Princeton University Press, 1991.

Genovese, Eugene. *Roll Jordan Roll: The World the Slaves Made.* New York: Random House, 1972.

From Rebellion to Revolution. Baton Rouge: Louisiana State University Press, 1979.

Genovese, Eugene, and Fox-Genovese, Elizabeth. *Fruits of Merchant Capital: Slavery and Bourgeois Capital in the Rise and Expansion of Capitalism.* New York: Oxford University Press, 1983.

Girard, René. *Deceit, Desire and the Novel.* London: Johns Hopkins University Press, 1965.

Godden, Richard. "William Faulkner and Benjy Compson: The Voices That Keep Silence," *Essays in Poetics,* vol. 4, No. 1 (1979), pp. 1–19.

"Edgar Allan Poe and the Detection of Riot," *Literature and History,* Vol. 8, No. 2 (Autumn 1982), pp. 206–31.

Fictions of Capital: The American Novel from James to Mailer. Cambridge: Cambridge University Press, 1990.

Goodman, Paul. *Speaking and Language.* New York: Random House, 1971.

Gordon, Lois. "Meaning and Myth in *The Sound and the Fury,* and 'The Waste Land,'" in French, Warren (ed.), *The Twenties* (Deadland, Fla.: Everett Edwards Inc., 1975).

Gray, Richard. *Writing the South: Ideas of an American Region.* Cambridge: Cambridge University Press, 1986.

The Life of William Faulkner. Oxford: Blackwell, 1994.

Gresset, Michel, and Polk, Noel (eds.). *Intertextuality in Faulkner.* Jackson: University Press of Mississippi, 1985.

Grubbs, Donald H. *Cry from the Cotton: The Southern Tenant Farmers' Union and the New Deal.* Chapel Hill: University of North Carolina Press, 1971.

Gutman, Herbert. *The Black Family in Slavery and Freedom, 1750–1925.* Oxford: Blackwell, 1976.

Gwin, Minrose. *The Feminine and Faulkner: Reading (Beyond) Sexual Difference.* Knoxville: University of Tennessee Press, 1990.

Gwynn, Frederick, and Blotner, Joseph (eds.). *Faulkner in the University: Class Conferences at the University of Virginia, 1957–1958.* New York: Random House, 1959.

Hahn, Stephen. *The Roots of Southern Populism: Yeomen Farmers and the Transformation of the Georgia Upcountry, 1850–1890.* New York: Oxford University Press, 1983.

Hannon, Charles. "Signification, Simulation and Containment in *If I Forget Thee, Jerusalem.*" *The Faulkner Journal,* vol. 7, Nos. 1 & 2 (Fall 1991), pp. 133–50.

Harrington, E., and Abadie, A. A. (eds.). *Faulkner and the Short Story.* Jackson: University Press of Mississippi, 1992.

Harrington, Gary. "Distant Mirrors: The Intertextual Relationship of Quentin Compson and Henry Wilbourne," *The Faulkner Journal*, vol. 1, No. 1 (Fall 1985), pp. 41–5.

Faulkner's Fables of Creativity. Athens: University of Georgia Press, 1990.

Haug, W. F. *Critique of Commodity Aesthetics: Appearance, Sexuality and Advertising in a Capitalist Society*. Oxford: Polity Press, 1986.

Hawthorne, Nathaniel. *The American Claimant Manuscripts*. Columbus: Ohio State University Press, 1977.

Hegel, G. W. F. *The Phenomenology of Mind*. New York: Macmillan, 1910.

Hoffman, F. J., and Vickery, O. L. (eds.). *William Faulkner: Three Decades of Criticism*. New York: Harcourt Brace, 1963.

Hunt, Alfred. *Haiti's Influence on Antebellum America: Slumbering Volcano in the Caribbean*. Baton Rouge: Louisiana State University Press, 1988.

Inkikori, J. E. "Measuring the Atlantic Slave Trade," *Journal of African History*, vol. XVII, No. 2 (1976), and Vol. XVII, No. 4 (1976).

Inscoe, John C. *Mountain Masters, Slavery and the Sectional Crisis in Western North Carolina*. Knoxville: University of Tennessee Press, 1989.

Irwin, John T. *Doubling and Incest/Repetition and Revenge: A Speculative Reading of Faulkner*. Baltimore: Johns Hopkins University Press, 1975.

"The Dead Father in Faulkner," in Davis, Robert (ed.), *The Fictional Father: Lacanian Readings of the Text* (Amherst: University of Massachussetts Press, 1981), pp. 147–68.

Iser, Wolfgang. *The Implied Reader*. London: Johns Hopkins University Press, 1974.

James, C.L.R. *The Black Jacobins*. London: Allison and Busby, 1982.

History of Negro Revolt. London: Race Today Publications, 1985.

Jameson, Fredric. *Marxism and Form*. Princeton, N.J.: Princeton University Press, 1971.

Fables of Aggression. Berkeley: University of California Press, 1979.

The Political Unconscious: Narrative as a Socially Symbolic Act. London: Methuen, 1983.

"Postmodernism, or 'The Cultural Logic of Late Capitalism,' " *New Left Review*, No. 146 (July–August 1984), pp. 53–92.

Jay, Martin. *The Dialectical Imagination*. Boston: Little, Brown, 1973.

Jehlen, Myra. *Class and Character in Faulkner's South*. New York: Columbia University Press, 1976.

Johnson, Charles D., Embree, Edwin R., and Alexander, W. W. *The Collapse of Cotton Tenancy: Summary of Field Studies and Statistical Surveys, 1933–1935*. Freeport, N.Y.: Books for Libraries Press, 1972.

Johnson, Charles S. *Shadow of the Plantation*. Chicago: University of Chicago Press, 1966.

Jones, Anne Goodwyn. " 'The Kotex Age': Women, Popular Culture and *The Wild Palms*," in Fowler, Doreen, and Abadie, Ann J. (eds.), *Faulkner and Popular Culture* (Jackson: University Press of Mississippi, 1990), pp. 142–62.

Jones, Jacqueline. "The Political Economy of Sharecropping Families: Blacks and Poor Whites in the Rural South, 1865–1915," in Bleser, Carol (ed.),

In Joy and Sorrow: Women, Family and Marriage in the Victorian South (New York: Oxford University Press, 1991), pp. 196–214.

Kaluza, Irena. *The Functioning of Sentence Structure in the Stream of Consciousness Technique of William Faulkner's The Sound and the Fury.* Krakow: Nakladem Universytetu Jagiellonskiego, 1967.

Kartiganer, Donald. *The Fragile Thread: The Meaning of Form in Faulkner's Novels.* Amherst: University of Massachussetts Press, 1979.

Kermode, Frank. *The Classic.* London: Faber, 1975.

Essays on Fiction, 1971–1982. London: Routledge & Kegan Paul, 1983.

King, Richard. *A Southern Renaissance.* Oxford: Oxford University Press, 1980.

Kinney, Arthur. *Faulkner's Narrative Poetics: Style as Vision.* Amherst: University of Massachussetts Press, 1978.

Kirby, Jack Temple. *Rural Worlds Lost: The American South, 1920–1960.* Baton Rouge: Louisiana State University Press, 1987.

Krause, David. "Reading Bon's Letter and Faulkner's *Absalom, Absalom!*," *PMLA*, 99 (1984), pp. 225–41.

Kuyk, Dirk, Jr. *Sutpen's Design: Interpreting Absalom, Absalom!* Charlottesville: University Press of Virginia, 1990.

Lacan, Jacques. *Écrits.* London: Tavistock, 1977.

LaPlanche, Jean. *New Foundations for Psychoanalysis.* Oxford: Blackwell, 1989.

Leach, Edmund. *Genesis as Myth and Other Essays.* London: Cape, 1969.

Leach, William R. "Transformation in a Culture of Consumption: Women and Department Stores, 1890–1925," *The Journal of American History*, vol. 71, No. 2 (September 1984), pp. 319–42.

Lester, Cheryl. "Racial Awareness and Arrested Development: *The Sound and the Fury* and the Great Migration (1915–1918)," in Weinstein, P. (ed.), *The Cambridge Companion to William Faulkner* (Cambridge: Cambridge University Press, 1995), pp. 123–45.

Lichtman, Richard. *The Production of Desire: The Integration of Psychoanalysis into Marxist Theory.* New York: Free Press, 1982.

Lukács, Georg. *History and Class Consciousness.* London: Merlin Press, 1988.

Lyotard, Jean-François. *The Postmodern Condition: A Report on Knowledge.* Manchester: Manchester University Press, 1979.

Heidigger and "the jews." Minneapolis: University of Minnesota Press, 1990.

Madden, David (ed.). *Tough Guy Writers of the Thirties.* Carbondale: Southern Illinois University Press, 1968.

Mandle, Jay R. *Not Slave, Not Free: The African American Experience Since the Civil War.* Durham, N.C.: Duke University Press, 1992.

Marchand, Roland. *Advertising the American Dream: Making Way for Modernity, 1920–1940.* Los Angeles: University of California Press, 1985.

Marcuse, Herbert. *Negations.* London: Penguin, 1968.

Marx, Karl. *Capital Vol. 1.* London: Dent, 1951.

Surveys from Exile. Harmondsworth: Penguin, 1973.

Early Writings. Harmondsworth: Penguin, 1977.

Matthews, John T. *The Play of Faulkner's Language.* Ithaca, N.Y.: Cornell University Press, 1982.

"The Rhetoric of Containment in Faulkner," in Honighausen, Lothar (ed.), *Faulkner's Discourse* (Tubingen: Max Niemeyer Verlag, 1989).

The Sound and the Fury: Faulkner and the Lost Cause. Boston: Twayne, 1991.

"Shortened Stories: Faulkner and the Market," in Harrington, E., and Abadie, A. A. (eds.), *Faulkner and the Short Story* (Jackson: University Press of Mississippi, 1992), pp. 3–37.

"*As I Lay Dying* in the Machine Age," *Boundary* 2, Vol. 19, No. 1 (Spring 1992), pp. 69–94.

"Faulkner and the Culture Industry," in Weinstein, Philip M. (ed.), *The Cambridge Companion to William Faulkner* (Cambridge: Cambridge University Press, 1995), pp. 51–74.

McCoy, Horace. *They Shoot Horses, Don't They?* Harmondsworth: Penguin, 1970.

McHaney, Thomas L. *William Faulkner's The Wild Palms.* Jackson: University Press of Mississippi, 1975.

McMillen, Neil R. *Dark Journey: Black Mississippians in the Age of Jim Crow.* Champaign: University of Illinois Press, 1989.

Mellon, James (ed.). *Bullwhip Days: The Slaves Remember.* New York: Weidenfeld and Nicholson, 1988.

Melosh, Barbara. *Engendering Culture: Manhood and New Deal Public Art and Theatre.* Washington, D.C.: Smithsonian Institution, 1991.

Melville, Herman. *Billy Budd and Other Tales.* New York: Signet, 1961.

Meriwether, James. "The Textual History of *The Sound and the Fury*," in his *The Merrill Studies in The Sound and the Fury* (Columbus: Merrill, 1970).

Meriwether, James, and Millgate, Michael (eds.). *Lion in the Garden: Interviews with William Faulkner, 1926–1962.* New York: Random House, 1968.

Miller, Kelly. *Radicals and Conservatives.* New York: Schocken Books, 1968.

Millgate, Michael. *The Achievement of William Faulkner.* London: Constable, 1966.

Minter, David (ed.). *The Sound and the Fury.* New York: Norton, 1987.

Moldenhaur, Joseph. "Unity of Theme and Structure in *The Wild Palms*," in Hoffman, F. J., and Vickery, O. L. (eds.), *William Faulkner: Three Decades of Criticism* (New York: Harcourt Brace, 1963), pp. 305–21.

Moreland, Richard. *Faulkner and Modernism: Rereading and Rewriting.* Madison: University of Wisconsin Press, 1990.

Morris, Wesley, and Morris, Barbara Alverson. *Reading Faulkner.* Madison: University of Wisconsin Press, 1989.

Mortimer, Gail. "The Ironies of Transcendental Love in *The Wild Palms*," *The Faulkner Journal*, Vol. 1, No. 2 (Spring 1986), pp. 30–42.

Nicholls, Peter. "The Belated Post-Modern: History, Phantoms and Toni Morrison," *Borderlines*, Vol. I, No. 3 (1994), pp. 193–220.

Oakes, James. *Slavery and Freedom: An Interpretation of the Old South.* New York: Knopf, 1990.

Oates, Joyce Carol. "Man Under Sentence of Death: The Novels of James M. Cain," in Madden, David (ed.), *Tough Guy Writers of the Thirties* (Carbondale: Southern Illinois University Press, 1968), pp. 110–28.

Oates, Stephen. *The Fires of Jubilee: Nat Turner's Fierce Rebellion*. New York: Mentor Books, 1973.

O'Donnell, Patrick. "Sub Rosa: Voice, Body and History in *Absalom, Absalom!*," *College Literature*, Vol. 16, Part 1 (1989), pp. 28–47.

Parker, Robert Dale. *Absalom, Absalom!: The Questioning of Fictions*. Boston: Twayne, 1991.

Pashukanis, Evgeny. *Law and Marxism*. London: Ink Links Ltd., 1978.

Patterson, Orlando. *Slavery and Social Death: A Comparative Study*. Cambridge, Mass.: Harvard University Press, 1982.

Pitavy, François. "Forgetting Jerusalem: An Ironical Chart for *The Wild Palms*," in Gresset, Michel, and Polk, Noel (eds.), *Intertextuality in Faulkner* (Jackson: University Press of Mississippi, 1985), pp. 114–27.

Poe, Edgar Allan. *Selected Writings*. Harmondsworth: Penguin, 1974.

Porter, Carolyn. *Seeing and Being: The Plight of the Participant Observer in Emerson, James, Adams and Faulkner*. Middletown, Conn.: Wesleyan University Press, 1981.

Poster, Mark. *Critical Theory of the Family*. London: Pluto Press, 1978.

Radloff, Bernard. "Dialogue and Insight: The Priority of the Heritage in *Absalom, Absalom!*," *Mississippi Quarterly*, Vol. 42, Part 3 (1989), pp. 261–72.

Rand, Nicholas T. "Introduction: Renewals of Psychoanalysis," prefatory to Abraham, Nicolas, and Torok, Maria, *The Shell and the Kernel, Vol. 1* (Chicago: University of Chicago Press, 1994), pp. 1–22.

Rand, Nicholas. "Translator's Introduction: Toward a Cryptonomy of Literature," in Abraham, Nicolas, and Torok, Maria, *The Wolf Man's Magic Word: A Cryptonomy* (Minneapolis: University of Minnesota Press, 1986), pp. li–lxxii.

Rashkin, Esther. "Tools for a New Psychoanalytical Literary Criticism: The Work of Abraham, Nicolas, and Torok, Maria," *Diacritics* (Winter 1988), pp. 31–52.

Rhodes, Pamela, and Godden, Richard. "*The Wild Palms*: Faulkner's Hollywood Novel (A Frankfurt School Reading)," *Essays in Poetics*, vol. 10, No. 1 (1985), pp. 1–49.

Richardson, Edward H. " 'The Hemingwaves' in Faulkner's 'Wild Palms,' " *Modern Fiction Studies*, 4 (Winter 1959), pp. 357–60.

Ricoeur, Paul. *The Rule of Metaphor*. London: Routledge & Kegan Paul, 1978. "The Metaphoric Process as Cognition, Imagination and Feeling," in Sacks, Sheldon (ed.), *On Metaphor* (London: University of Chicago Press, 1979).

Time and Narrative: Vol. 1. Chicago: University of Chicago Press, 1984.

Roberts, Diane. *Faulkner and Southern Womanhood*. Athens: University of Georgia Press, 1994.

Rony, Vera. "The Organization of Black and White Farm Workers in the South," in Frazier, Thomas R. (ed.), *The Underside of American History: Other Readings, Vol. II: Since 1865* (New York: Harcourt & Brace, 1971), pp. 153–74.

Ross, Stephen. "The Evocation of Voice in *Absalom, Absalom!*," *Essays in Literature*, 8 (Fall 1981), pp. 135–49.

Faulkner's Inexhaustible Voice: Speech and Writing in Faulkner. Athens: University of Georgia Press, 1989.

Ruppersburg, Hugh. *Voice and Eye in Faulkner's Fiction*. Athens: University of Georgia Press, 1983.

Saldívar, Ramón. "Looking for a Master Plan: Faulkner, Paredes, and the Colonial and Postcolonial Subject," in Weinstein, Philip M. (ed.), *The Cambridge Companion to William Faulkner* (Cambridge: Cambridge University Press, 1995), pp. 92–120.

Santer, Eric. *Stranded Objects: Mourning, Memory and Film in Postwar Germany*. Ithaca, N.Y.: Cornell University Press, 1990.

Sartre, Jean-Paul. *Critique of Dialectical Reason*, Vol. 1. London: Verso, 1982.

"On *The Sound and the Fury*: Time in the Work of Faulkner," in Minter, David (ed.), *The Sound and the Fury* (New York: Norton, 1987), pp. 253–9.

Schoenberg, Estella. *Old Tales and Talking: Quentin Compson in William Faulkner's Absalom, Absalom! and Related Works*. Jackson: University Press of Mississippi, 1977.

Snead, James. *Figures of Division*. New York: Methuen, 1986.

"The Joint of Racism: Withholding the Black in *Absalom, Absalom!*," in Bloom, Harold (ed.), *Modern Critical Interpretations: William Faulkner's Absalom, Absalom!* (New York: Chelsea House, 1987), pp. 129–41.

Sohn-Rethel, Alfred. *Intellectual and Manual Labor: A Critique of Epistemology*. London: Macmillan, 1978.

Stonum, Gary. *Faulkner's Career: An Internal Literary History*. Ithaca, N.Y.: Cornell University Press, 1979.

Sundquist, Eric. *Faulkner: The House Divided*. Baltimore: Johns Hopkins University Press, 1983.

Tar, Zoltán. *The Frankfurt School*. New York: Wiley, 1977.

Tate, Allen. *The Fathers*. Chicago: Swallow Press, 1974.

Taylor, Walter. *Faulkner's Search for a South*. Urbana: University of Illinois Press, 1983.

Theweleit, Klaus. *Male Fantasies, Vol. 1*. Minneapolis: University of Minnesota Press, 1988.

Tiedemann, Rolf. "Historical Materialism or Political Messianism: An Interpretation of the Thesis 'On the Concept of History,' " in Smith, Gary (ed.), *Benjamin: Philosophy, Aesthetics, History* (Chicago: University of Chicago Press, 1989), pp. 175–209.

Timpanaro, Sebastiano. *The Freudian Slip: Psychoanalysis and Textual Criticism*. London: New Left Books, 1974.

Tindall, George B. *The Emergence of the New South, 1913–1945*. Baton Rouge: Louisiana State University Press, 1967.

Tushnet, Mark. *The American Law of Slavery: Considerations of Humanity and Interest*. Princeton, N.J.: Princeton University Press, 1981.

Vickery, Olga. "*The Sound and the Fury*: A Study in Perspective," *PMLA*, 64 (December 1954), pp. 1017–37.
  The Novels of William Faulkner. Baton Rouge: Louisiana State University Press, 1961.
Vološinov, V. N. *Marxism and the Philosophy of Language.* New York: Seminar Press, 1973.
  "Discourse in Life and Discourse in Poetry: Questions of Sociological Poetics," in Shukman, Ann (ed.), *Bakhtin School Papers. Russian Poetics in Translation*, vol. 10 (1983), pp. 5–30.
Volpe, Edmond. *A Reader's Guide to William Faulkner.* London: Thames and Hudson, 1964.
Weinstein, Philip M. "Marginalia: Faulkner's Black Lives," in Abadie, Ann J., and Fowler, Doreen (eds.), *Faulkner and Race* (Jackson: University Press of Mississippi, 1987), pp. 170–91.
  Faulkner's Subject: A Cosmos No One Owns. Cambridge: Cambridge University Press, 1992.
Weinstein, Philip M. (ed.). *The Cambridge Companion to William Faulkner.* Cambridge: Cambridge University Press, 1995.
West, Nathanael. *The Day of the Locust.* New York: New Directions, 1950.
Wharton, Vernon Lane. *The Negro in Mississippi: 1865–1890.* New York: Harper & Row, 1965.
Wiener, Jonathon. "Class Structure and Economic Development in the American South, 1865–1955," *American Historical Review*, vol. 84, No. 4 (1979), pp. 970–1006.
Williams, Raymond. *The Long Revolution.* Harmondsworth: Penguin, 1965.
Williamson, Joel. *The Crucible of Race: Black–White Relations in the American South Since Emancipation.* New York: Oxford University Press, 1984.
  William Faulkner and Southern History. New York: Oxford University Press, 1993.
Willis, Susan. "Aesthetics of the Rural Slum: Contradiction and Dependency in 'The Bear,' " *Social Text*, vol. 1, No. 2 (Summer, 1977), pp. 82–103.
Wittenberg, Judith. *Faulkner: The Transfiguration of Biography.* Lincoln: University of Nebraska Press, 1979.
Woodman, Harold. "Sequel to Slavery: The New History Views the Post Bellum South," *Journal of Southern History*, Vol. 43, No. 4 (November 1977), pp. 523–54.
  "Post Civil War Agriculture and the Law," *Agricultural History*, Vol. 53 (1979), pp. 319–37.
  "How New Was the New South?," *Agricultural History*, Vol. 58, No. 4 (October 1984), pp. 529–45.
  "The Reconstruction of the Cotton Plantation in the New South," in Glymph, Thavalia, and Kushman, John (eds.), *Essays on the Post Bellum Economy* (Arlington: Texas University Press, 1985), pp. 95–119.
Woodward, C. Vann. *The Strange Career of Jim Crow.* New York: Oxford University Press, 1959.

Origins of the New South. Baton Rouge: Louisiana State University Press, 1971.

Woodward, C. Vann (ed.). *Mary Chesnut's Civil War.* New Haven, Conn.: Yale University Press, 1991.

Wright, Erik Olin, Levine, Andrew, and Soler, Elliot. *Reconstructing Marxism.* London: Verso, 1992.

Wright, Gavin. *Old South: New South: Revolutions in the Southern Economy Since the Civil War.* New York: Basic Books, 1986.

INDEX